Real World
LEADERSHIP STRATEGIES
That
WORK

Real World
LEADERSHIP
STRATEGIES
That
WORK

Insight Publishing Company
Sevierville, Tennessee

Real World
LEADERSHIP STRATEGIES
That
WORK

Published by:
Insight Publishing Company
PO Box 4189
Sevierville, TN 37862

Printed in the United States of America

ISBN 1-885640-57-9

Table Of Contents

A Message From The Publisher

Some of my most rewarding experiences in business—or in my personal life, for that matter—have been at meetings, conventions or gatherings, after the formal events have concluded. Inevitably, small groups of ten to fifteen men and women gather together to rehash the happenings of the day and to exchange war stories, recently heard jokes or the latest gossip from their industry. It is in these informal gatherings where some of the best lessons can be learned.

Usually, in informal groups of professionals, there are those who clearly have lived through more battles and learned more lessons than others. These are the men and women who are really getting the job done, and everyone around the room knows it. When they comment on the topic of the moment, they don't just spout the latest hot theory or trend, and they don't ramble on and on without a relevant point. These battle-scarred warriors have lessons to share that everyone senses are just a little more real, more relevant and therefore, worthy of more attention.

These are the kind of people we have recruited for the *Power Learning* series of books. Each title offers contributions from men and women who are making a significant impact on their culture, in their field, and on their colleagues and clients. This edition offers a variety of themes in the area of leadership strategies. It is ripe with "the good stuff," as an old friend of mine used to always say. Inside these pages you'll find ideas, insights, strategies and philosophies that are working with real people, in real companies and under real circumstances.

It is our hope that you keep this book with you until you've dog-eared every chapter and made so many notes in the margins that you have trouble seeing the original words on the pages. There is treasure here. Enjoy digging!

Chapter One

LEADERSHIP IS FOR *EVERYONE!*

Gregory M. Richardson, SPHR, MA-HRD

The Story Begins

This chapter ends where my own journey to understanding the reality of leadership actually began—on the third night of the 1991 Persian Gulf War, after landing safely from a surprisingly violent combat mission, a mission that nearly claimed my trusty F-15 Eagle and, of course, me. You might be tempted to skip ahead and read that vivid recollection now—but don't. Because what precedes that tale are my thoughts on what could be the most valuable commodity that each and every person can contribute to his workplace, his community, his home and indeed, the world.

After twenty years in uniform as an officer of the United States Air Force, I had never truly grasped what it meant to be a leader. But it was that realization, brought about by a conversation with a young sergeant in security police, that changed my view of leadership (and my life), perhaps even more than having just cheated the Grim Reaper. My hope is that what you read in the following pages will prompt a fairly radical shift in your thinking and approach to leadership as well.

I want you to read selfishly and steal something from this chapter that supports a beneficial change in your thoughts, decisions and demonstrations of leadership. You'll get the idea soon enough. In order for this experience to be of greatest utility to you (and that's the key word—"utility"), I am going to make a few requests of you throughout your reading.

REQUEST #1

Set aside your current view of leadership until you finish this chapter.

We use the word "leadership" frequently and easily, but what does it really mean? Over the past ten years, I have been fortunate enough to work with hundreds of work groups and management teams in various fields and with diverse backgrounds, with one primary objective in common: to understand and to capitalize on the essence and value of leadership. Without exception, these groups begin their quests for understanding with repeated reference to the word "leader." And every time I hear the term used, I would cringe inwardly, having previously experienced the learning curve of this particular lesson many times.

Leadership is an evasive concept in our world and among our families and friends. Perhaps like some of you, my wife and I do not have many good friends. Between kids and work, moving and house payments, etc., they just seem to drift away over time; you know the drill. However, we do have two friends in Springfield, Virginia—Ted and Betty Erickson—who have remained with us through thick and thin, regardless of our stages in life or our continents of residence.

In January of 2001, while I was in Washington, D.C. to facilitate a management retreat, Ted and Betty asked me to meet them for dinner at our favorite Chinese restaurant. Ted is an ex-Air Force medical officer who now consults with contractors on how to market services to the federal government. By anyone's standards, Ted would be considered a forward-leaning, anything goes, let's-make-it-happen-now kind of person. Betty, therefore, has a head full of naturally-earned, silver hair and is the quintessential steady worker and patient mom. Her day job is helping coordinate long-range programs for the U.S. Air Force's Directorate of Acquisition at the Pentagon. As you can imagine, Betty has been exposed to a series of high-ranking directors who have come and gone over her thirty-year career in civil service. It was not until that night, waiting for our egg rolls, that I realized Betty had fallen prey to the guardians of the word "leader."

We were discussing the obstacles to becoming a "champion for change" and how many departmental challenges (not to mention those that are prevalent in the Air Force) present themselves as if they were begging, "Please, solve me." Ted made a brief comment that, had I not been listening intently, I might have easily missed. He quipped, "Well, Greg, Betty's not a leader, so what can she do about these kinds of problems?" Before I could express even a hint of dismay, Betty chimed in with, "Ted's right. I'm just a GS-14; I'm not a leader."

In what seemed like suspended time, I wondered how two dear friends had resigned themselves to the notion that such a value-laden identity was not available to Betty. I understood instantly that they, like many others, had unconsciously disassociated the word "leader" from the word (and true meaning of) "leadership." I perceived that the next few minutes would reveal an important destiny for me, and my anxiety level heightened accordingly.

I initiated a rapid barrage of questions that really didn't allow for a response. "Why don't you think that you are a leader? Who there is a leader? What do you mean by a 'leadership role or position'?" I wasn't trying to be rude but, rather, set the stage for a much larger question—one to which I felt Ted and Betty did have the answer. I asked them to think of some people they considered to be leaders. I elaborated on my question as they pondered their response. "Let's pretend that I will pay for an ad in this Sunday's *Washington Post* that will read: Ted and Betty Erickson have witnessed enough leadership characteristics, values and behaviors in the following people to view them as leaders." I then asked how many names would be on their list of nominees for so prestigious a distinction. In other words, I wanted Ted and Betty to consider the qualities that they thought were necessary for one to be viewed as a leader and, in our hypothetical ad, to attach faces and names to those who earned that title the hard way.

Ted held up four fingers, and Betty held up three, adding the qualifier, "Maybe less." I asked them how many people comprised the population from which they chose so few. Their answer, of course, was "hundreds." For now, let's place that ratio, or relatively small statistical percentage, aside and return later to consider what it might mean.

3

In the meantime, I am also asking you to consider those people you have worked alongside, those who have supervised you, those you know in the communities where you have lived—your neighbors, friends and relatives. How many names can you come up with, based strictly on your personal assessment of leadership traits (and not because of anyone's title or position)?

REQUEST #2

Invoke the word "leader" judiciously and only when acknowledging the brand of leadership that makes a difference in your own life.

I asked Ted and Betty to describe one of the people they nominated for their honor roll of leaders. Betty described one person, a master sergeant, whom she believed everyone admired. She said that "Chief Billy" made everyone feel like they mattered, regardless of rank or position. He was always accessible and made the time to listen to folks and help them in any way he could. People just knew that, mixed in with all the rigors of Pentagon craziness and bureaucratic red tape, there was someone who cared about what kind of day they were having. It reminded me of a quote from author Napoleon Hill, who wrote so poignantly, "People don't care how much you know; they want to know how much you care." Betty concluded by saying that Chief Billy knew exactly how to let someone see that even small accomplishments were noticed and appreciated. "People always seemed to have a great day around Chief Billy." "So Betty," I asked, "was Chief Billy a leader in your directorate?" Betty replied, almost casually, "No, he was not one of the leaders."

I must admit that I was not prepared for her answer. Where did I go wrong? I thought we were on a roll. Then it dawned on me that "leader-is-a-position" brainwashing is deeply ingrained in most people. And it would not be undone quite that easily. While there is an all-too-common absence of quality leadership being exhibited, the word "leader" still flourishes.

I decided that shifting focus to Ted's choice might inspire that push over the top and overcome the stereotypical view of leadership, one that is perpetrated by those who have been allowed to steal the title "leader" (as often used in the context of congressional leaders, military leaders, corporate leaders, team leaders, etc.).

"Ted," I probed, "whom did you consider to be leader-like, based on the characteristics and leadership behaviors that you felt were important as well as those demonstrated?" Ted identified a mid-level business development manager named Caroline, who found herself facing a very controlling corporate environment at a time when the company's very survival was in doubt. He remembered with clarity how tenaciously she had fought to sell her creative ideas, regardless of the initial popularity they failed to enjoy. He admired her tolerance for taking risks and her ability to articulate one vision in particular— how to enhance her company's business model by integrating some emerging technologies with its medical expertise. Management admired her, feared her and ultimately fired her before the company's death spiral into Chapter 11 bankruptcy.

"Did you consider her a leader?" I asked Ted. To my surprise, he replied, "You know, I never did consider her a leader until tonight, but now I realize that she may have been one of the very few leaders in a company that was managed out of existence."

"Ted, God will bless you for that conclusion," I responded, to which Betty chimed in and proclaimed (a little too loudly for a restaurant), "I just figured something out; whether or not someone is seen as a leader has absolutely nothing to do with their formal role in the organization! Anyone can be a leader if they demonstrate leadership."

"You got it, Betty. Leadership is in the eye of the beholder, and it can't be legislated by title or position any more than performance can be legislated by a job description." I asked her one confirming question, which was how often she had freely given away the title "leader" to senior officers (and this could apply to corporate officers, or any other as well) based on position and/or rank, rather than leadership qualities. Her response, mixed with a couple of tears, was all too predictable.

REQUEST #3

Accept the following equation: No leadership = No leader, regardless of position, rank or title.

As we were waiting for our entrees, I asked Ted and Betty to write on a napkin a minimum of twenty leadership qualities, skills and values that they believed to be essential in qualifying for the term "leader." They did so quickly, and their lists, which thankfully I saved, have been reproduced in the following pages. As you read the criteria they offered, consider what additional terms you would include. There are many more, some of which I will offer after theirs. But as you will see, a thread of commonality emerges that is critical to understanding leadership as a distinction from other words like "management" and "supervision."

Leadership is...

Ted's List:

Creativity   Mentoring
Caring   Listening
Courage   Flexibility
Understanding   Tolerance
Innovation   Vision
Patience   Responsibility
Ethical
Being Moral
Imagination
Empathy
Risk Tolerance
Respectful
Assertiveness
Encouragement

Betty's List:

Integrity   Initiative
Cooperative   Motivating
High Standards   Passionate
Coaching   Supportive
Team-Focused   Problem Solving
Collaborative   Trustworthy
Inspiring   Committed
Confidential   Reliable
Acknowledging   Results Oriented
Asking vs. Telling

At this point, it was natural to ask Ted and Betty which of these words we shouldn't, couldn't or wouldn't want to demonstrate. In other words, if this was a good illustration of what constituted leadership, then maybe we were one step closer to understanding why Ted and Betty, along with most people, believed that leadership was in shorter supply than we would have liked. More importantly, we may have also been close to understanding that the potential for leadership may exist within each and every person, without regard for position or authority. Perhaps leadership is more a matter of rising to the challenge.

Look at that list again; that's tough stuff. Each of us has very high standards for others to meet, and although we seldom express those standards directly, we are constantly, even subconsciously, determining if others meet our criteria for high quality leadership. Consider how many of your supervisors have earned your respect for the brand of leadership they have exhibited over time. I would imagine that your experience with this exercise might be very similar to those of Ted and Betty; most "leaders" we recognize in our lives are labeled as such because of a position or title rather than personal characteristics.

The Leadership Continuum®

I routinely ask groups what they think the difference is between leadership and management and, naturally, between leader and manager. To further complicate the discussion, I ask for a good definition of leadership and how that differs from their definition of management. To make it even more frustrating, I ask them if you can be an effective manager without being a good leader. By the time this verbal free-for-all (I mean "facilitated discussion") has run its brief course, they agree readily to systematically dissect the operative elements in any given setting, from corporate boardroom to the average kitchen.

I want to introduce you to the Leadership Continuum®, something I developed in 1995 after three years of research and personal study on the subject of leadership (not leaders). What I postulated is that virtually every observable action has its roots in one of the following categories: Work Competencies, Supervision, Management and Leadership.

So why is this important? In order to grow and develop the potential value inherent in leadership, it is essential to isolate it from the muddy waters that can mask its absence or confuse it with another characteristic. Each of these forces plays a critical role in organizational performance, effectiveness, efficiency and profitability. Before I proceed with a synopsis of each category and how it plays out, please do not anticipate that I am going to denigrate management in favor of leadership. Quite the contrary, I am going to try to articulate the case for creating and sustaining the best of both worlds—a balancing act of sorts.

Within minutes of my brief description of this learning concept, a friend and Air Force contemporary, Ford McCormick (Lt. Col., Ret.), created the illustration below to visually portray the continuous and revolving process of how our actions are focused in order to accomplish our missions, objectives and activities, whatever they may be. The premise is that at any given moment, only one of the four main elements is in play for any one person. Now recall the impact you have personally witnessed when someone has not paid attention to the appropriate arm of this windmill. Let me discuss a few key points for each important area of focus.

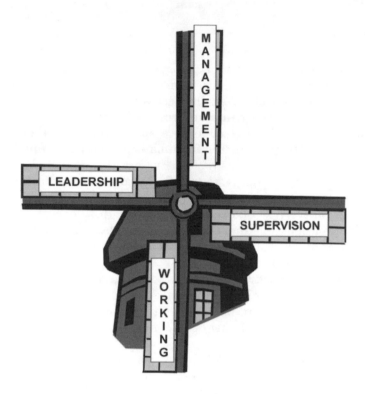

Work Competencies

There isn't a more essential challenge than becoming competent in whatever we do and joining others in the workplace who are competent at their given roles and assigned tasks. If only it were as simple as it sounds! Anyone reading this knows how hard it is to become competent. We go to school, we train, we certify, we get on-the-job "help," and we quietly ask ourselves, "Am I good enough?" My hope is that each reader continuously challenges himself not only to be sufficiently competent but to constantly improve his capabilities. But I would add that this simply reflects the basic requirement that we all be prepared and equipped to do our work. Here are some of the classic and critical factors associated with work competencies:

Education	Capabilities	Skills	Tasks	Procedures
Processes	Mechanics	Productivity	Results	Improvement

Supervision

Doing the work, however, usually involves some degree of help. Supervision is the root of that help. As a concept, supervision is as natural and time-tested as sex, and it probably can be traced clear back to the Garden of Eden. In most situations, one person is accountable for the performance and results of others. This may sound very basic, but how many ineffective supervisors do we encounter? It's not because they are defective humans; it's because supervision is difficult. If it weren't, then who let Eve eat that apple? We make it worse because most, yes most, people in supervisory positions have never received formal training to be competent at that additional line of responsibility. We could probably extend this concept to parenthood. It is very possible that this promotional leap in accountability is the origin of many of the obstacles that prevent us from achieving our stated goals and objectives.

Let's connect Work Competencies to Supervision. What's the relationship between them? You're right on target if you think that it's fairly common for the most competent among us to be promoted to supervisor. Given this tremendous obligation—to be responsible for the decisions, actions and outcomes of people who can be very dissimilar from ourselves—we should not be surprised that we often fail. The elements of supervision seem basic when we take the time to consider what each of us does in daily life as a parent, a colleague or a partner.

Assigning	Scheduling	Training	Guidance	Monitoring
Correcting	Evaluating	Feedback	Counseling	Discipline

How many of those providing the elements of supervision (see block above) have been trained appropriately to understand the diversity in motivational patterns and work styles, the methods available to communicate effectively with others and the process of cultivating a common-goal team? How often do we experience the repercussions of someone in senior management overlooking their obligation to supervise other executives, managers and supervisors below them? The bottom line is that we all deserve, if not need, appropriate and timely supervision that directly supports the effective work competencies that are expected of virtually everyone. Remember the horrific corporate disaster perpetrated by the relatively unsupervised CFO of Enron? His CEO wasn't even embarrassed to admit he spent little time supervising.

Management

People frequently ask, "What's a good definition of management?" My reply has never changed. Management is a series of processes intended to control desired outcomes. The purpose behind management is to position all the necessary elements and resources required to ensure that tomorrow will produce that which was ordained today. I hope you agree that creating a system designed to focus resources, including humans, toward predictable results is an exceptionally important role. The principle elements of management might be summarized as follows:

Organizing	Goals/Objectives	Strategies	Planning	Budgeting
Directing	Resource Allocation	Policies	Measuring	Analysis

It is possible that some of you may find my next couple of sentences hard to embrace, or even callous, but I assure you that is not my intent. What if, en route to demonstrating the best possible brand of people-focused leadership, we pursued management with a more clinical, detached, almost nonhuman approach? In other words, what if we focused on utilizing all the management tools we have available that allow us to assign the right resources to do the right things, in the right way, at the right time? What if we pretended for very brief periods that people were not breathing but primarily instruments of performance and productivity? You would find yourself unemotionally evaluating organizational challenges/goals and positioning a variety of competent resources with the appropriate safeguard in supervision. And then you would analyze the results and make adjustments intended to improve one or more outcomes. See? You didn't really need that MBA from Harvard.

But you know there's more, don't you? People need to perceive themselves as valued and cared for, understood and much, much more. However, I bet you've also seen far too many members of management who have not discovered the essence embodied in that last sentence. And those intrinsic needs of people bring us to...

Leadership

Remember Ted and Betty's lists of attributes a few pages back? Allow me to reiterate only a few just to make a simple but critical point regarding leadership. Every last word that we identify as a descriptor for leadership qualities, values and characteristics will have three things in common, and they will have virtually nothing in common with Work Competencies, Supervision and Management. A cross section of leadership descriptors might be:

Empowering	Accommodating	Encouraging	Trusting	Tolerance
Understanding	Uncontrolling	Accountable	Patience	Respect

Here is what I believe makes leadership such an enigmatic and elusive, yet invaluable ingredient in any situation:

1. Leadership qualities are not visible, like Competencies, Supervision and Management are.
2. Leadership qualities inspire commitment and accomplishment.
3. Leadership qualities can appear or disappear within fractions of a second—they are not permanent.

REQUEST #4

Believe that leadership is the invisible thread with the power to make whole, to weave together as it were, the elements of Competencies, Supervision and Management.

Now let's take an example from a fairly typical work situation (not a workplace, however) that incorporates all of these elements. We'll go into a typical household—the kitchen, to be precise—and see how this concept plays out with the average mom (if there is such a thing). When a homemaker is engaged in the process of cooking, with all the varied action steps that it entails, Work Competencies are being demonstrated. The big point here is that while our selected homemaker is preparing a meal, Work Competencies (following recipes, measuring, cutting, frying, baking, etc.) are the order of the day or the meal will not be prepared acceptably.

Now suppose this homemaker's son finds himself helping (voluntarily or not); we will have all the key ingredients necessary for the next element in the Continuum—Supervision. Our young culinary student is about to be supervised. He will be provided the appropriate instructions, guidance and timing essential to performing the necessary operations connected with the dish or meal. The ability of Mom to supervise the work effectively in the kitchen, just as in the workplace, will be directly proportionate to the outcome—in this case, dinner. Probably all of the components of Supervision will likely be put into play by the time it's ready to eat.

Let's turn to the Management aspects of this example. Consider the amount of planning, organization, budgeting and resource allocation, etc. that is required to produce virtually any tasty meal. Perhaps one of the primary reasons that many homemakers consider themselves underacknowledged is because of the unobserved and unappreciated management obligations that accompany running a household. From analyzing tastes and recent responses to meals to incorporating purchasing strategies that stretch dollars on a frugal budget and still result in healthy meals, the average homemaker has to manage effectively, just like any good CEO.

"So where does all this leadership stuff fit into the equation?" you may be asking. Remember all those admirable qualities we listed? Imagine how that entire experience for our hypothetical son would turn out without all the mother's words of encouragement, patience, inspiration to try and understanding of his competing priorities.

Balancing Management and Leadership

Management is entirely about control, while leadership is the absolute absence of control. Both are essential ingredients to any workplace environment, but they are distinct and should not be intermingled. I would like to share with you the most effective two-option scenario that I have ever developed to distinguish between the person who clings to the management mantra (regardless of his role or title) and the person who demonstrates leadership.

The situation is a senior management meeting (with misguided self-flattery they are commonly called "leadership team meetings") with approximately five corporate executives sitting attentively on either side of a boardroom table. The CEO in Scenario One looks exceedingly gloomy, if not angry, when he says, "Folks, we just had the worst third quarter in five years. I'm not exactly sure what has happened, but we're certainly not going to end the fourth quarter like this." He goes on to issue orders to almost each department head to cut this, change that and refocus any number of resources and processes across the company. He is obviously in command of the situation, undeniably in charge and in total control. He directs that everyone return at the same time next week to discuss their progress and warns with a blank face that, "Missing that meeting should only be preceded by death or quitting."

Our CEO in Scenario Two looks exceedingly gloomy but manages a hint of a smile as he conveys his serious message to his management team. "Folks, I know you are aware that we just completed our worst quarter in five years, give or take a decade. I wish I had all the answers as to how this could have happened, but I only have a few educated hunches and some initial ideas for us to reverse this trend. Here's what I want each of you to do...." He then asks each manager to assemble his key staff and discuss the situation with the focus on identifying obstacles that need to be overcome and generating ideas about how to reduce costs, increase efficiencies and minimize the chances of a fourth quarter recurrence. He requests that each person do whatever is necessary to attend a strategy session one week later, adding, "Please do not die or quit in the meantime; we need your ideas and those of your folks to reverse this trend."

So which executive (manager) is likely to be viewed as a leader? I'm guessing that CEO #2 failed to control anything or anybody. Yet who would have inspired you to solve the dilemma that the company was facing? In our simulated situation, the leadership that was necessary replaced the day-to-day control and management direction that ordinarily may have been appropriate and effective but, in this case, wasn't.

Let's take a brief look at how this concept might look in an illustration. Using the theme of "balancing," imagine the day-to-day challenge of employing the skill sets of both leadership and management, based on your interpretation of each situation and the issues and people involved. The unspoken question is, "Which element would be best suited to address the specifics of what's going on, based on your sense of the situation and desired outcomes?" The basis for your response, and ultimately, the appreciation level of others, should be directly influenced by the situation at hand.

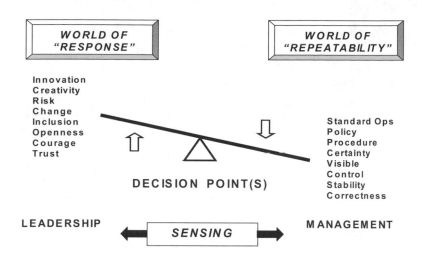

REQUEST #5

Internalize the relationship between situations and the leadership responses that are demonstrated by you and the people around you.

The ABCDs of Great Leadership

I'd like to borrow from the basic building block concept and add the "D" to highlight what I believe to be the four most critical virtues and resources associated with leadership. When closely examining the invisible nature of leadership qualities and characteristics, it's easy to see that transforming behaviors and responding to situations deserving leadership requires considerable personal fortitude and focused effort. My belief is that the four following attributes, if not challenges, make up the absolute core around which all other leadership qualities, skills and behaviors revolve.

Accountability

When was the last time you perceived that someone was demonstrating quality leadership, but they did not exhibit a high degree of accountability for his or her decisions, communication and actions? Probably *never*. The reason lies in the distinction between accountability and responsibility. Without getting too wrapped up in the semantics and Webster's view of language, I'll explain how the distinction is as important as any among the four elements in the Leadership Continuum®

Responsibility is the set of obligations that we attract, based on the expectations of others in various life situations, such as making your bed as a teenager, driving the speed limit or maintaining attendance and image at work. The key here is that someone or something else—our parents, teachers, police, bosses, income, job descriptions—make us responsible for these obligations. And, as we know all too well, it's not uncommon for a person to need some form of encouragement or correction to ensure that the responsibility is met satisfactorily.

Accountability, on the other hand, can be thought of as those behaviors and activities for which a person makes himself responsible. Imagine all the interpersonal struggles that have ensued because someone failed to exercise accountability for his actions and instead waited for someone or something else to make him responsible. Even if you reword that last statement and say, "I'll hold you accountable for this or that," there is no real change; the person has not made himself accountable. Now apply this concept to leadership and I hope you quickly assign considerable importance to the accountability that anyone wishing to demonstrate leadership must exert from within. Never forget the words of Harry S. Truman: "The buck stops here."

Brainpower

If we were to retrace history, I believe you would find that every last innovation and all the solutions to issues or problems were the result of one or more person's use of brainpower. Compare that with a business meeting held to address a major issue, a meeting in which more than one person has just said in a common refrain, "I don't know." I am not referring to the situations we all encounter where we really do not know something and are merely being candid. I am referring to the insidious shutdown of our critical thinking capability caused by any number of factors, from fear of being wrong to the unwillingness to think beyond yesterday's answer.

Now ask yourself if you have ever given anyone credit for a high degree of leadership who did not demonstrate a capability and willingness to think big, to think into tomorrow, to think beyond his current awareness of an issue or opportunity. People who are considered leaders are not only likely to be critical thinkers themselves but they encourage and support others around them to move out of their own thinking comfort zones. If people didn't, what would be the source of all of the next options or answers? And those considered Leaders would certainly not accept the premise that those with the most advanced academic degrees are necessarily the best thinkers. If they did, imagine all the great ideas that might have been prevented.

Commitment

Have you ever seen someone who lacked commitment to the organization, the unit or the cause? Ever think of that person as a leader? I seriously doubt it. In other words, where our commitment lies is usually in close proximity to our passion, our energy, our effort and our dedication to the outcomes. There isn't anyone reading this chapter, including myself, who hasn't lost his or her commitment to something. It didn't make us defective; it meant that our continuous focus on something with which we were once strongly aligned had diminished. In most cases, the reasons are pretty simple: boredom, absence of challenge, little acknowledgment, competing priorities, ineffective use of our talents, etc.

In order for a person to be viewed as leader-like, commitment is job number one, and we all know that it can't be faked. Where a person decides they are committed is usually where you can find them physically and mentally, and, above all, it is where you will see their heart and soul in action.

Discipline

For seven years now, I have supported clients in formulating and achieving their personal goals and objectives though coaching partnerships. Leaving the coaching concept and methodologies aside, my experience has been that 100 percent of the time, the person being coached decides that one of the major challenges to his future success and his past obstacles is exercising the necessary discipline to transform behaviors and accomplish his targeted objectives. Without the discipline to ask before we tell, avoid negative assumptions, encourage instead of correct or delay expedient discussions with the wrong people, our decisions to transform will prove meaningless.

If we review the many words used to describe essential leadership characteristics, I believe you will see that some form of discipline is necessary to demonstrate most of them. Hopefully, you will not take that as a negative comment but rather a pragmatic assessment of the temptations to which we fall prey. Discipline can dissuade us from responding to situations and people in ways that we really didn't intend.

Try this experiment: On your next trip home from work, think of the tasks or activities you may have wanted to accomplish or performed differently. Honestly evaluate the influence that discipline (timing, decision, priorities, etc.) might have had on the outcome(s). I'll bet you see the implications and power of discipline. Then consider how critical it is to leadership.

REQUEST #6

Stop, look and listen. Is one or more of the ABCDs missing? Take on the challenge and address its absence.

The Obstacle Course to Leadership

If only we could attend a seminar, take a college course on leadership or read a couple of self-improvement books and voila—a leader is born! I know a really forward-leaning kind of guy named John Buccarelli, who wrote the biggest damned book on leadership you've ever seen. Not only are you whipped into shape lugging it around but you also quickly acknowledge that leadership is not something you're born with; you have to work awfully hard at earning the brass ring. John's opinion is that most people quit competing for the prize.

If you recall when Ted and Betty Erickson were asked how many people they viewed as leaders, their response was a tiny fraction of the number of people whose paths have crossed theirs. Toward the end of leadership seminars, participants are asked to respond to the following inquiry: "You have all assessed that leadership behaviors and leaders in the workplace are in very short supply. Why do you think that is? Let's find out. Please jot down a minimum of five words or phrases that come to mind when thinking of the anti-leader qualities and behaviors that you deem unacceptable when evaluating someone for his leadership capabilities. In other words, what personal factors have the negative power to prevent leadership from existing?"

I won't create a long list, but a significant number of the characteristics suggested reflect the opposite of the qualities identified for leadership. They are, for example: pessimistic (vs. optimistic), unethical (vs. ethical), close-minded (vs. open-minded), distrustful (vs. trusting), discouraging (vs. encouraging), controlling (vs. empowering), blaming (vs. crediting) and selfish (vs. sharing). Now take another look at the contrasting elements; see how easy it is to give into the negative side? But if you found yourself saying, "No way! It's easier to share than to be selfish" or "It's easier to trust people rather than being disposed to distrust others," I commend you.

Overcoming these temptations and normal human responses to life's situations is not easy, and it's part of our daily struggle to be fair, to be kind, to listen, to be courageous, to be ethical, to envision the future, to encourage others and to be many things that people just as imperfect as we are expect us to be. More importantly, people judge each other by standards that they are hard-pressed to meet themselves. Unfortunately, a mirror isn't usually handy when we are making those judgment calls. I am fully aware of how tough I am being right now, but this world needs and deserves more leadership from everyone, and more falseness and platitudes about so valuable a commodity will not help any of us.

REQUEST #7

Accept the challenge to detect, minimize and overcome the common personal barriers to leadership; everyone is watching, like it or not.

The Beginning at the End

I sincerely hope that you've identified some useful insights and learning points about leadership and the role it plays in both your life and the lives of the people to whom you are exposed. I hope that you act upon those lessons and remember that leadership stripes are earned every day, and they're sewn on by our observers, not ourselves. I have found it interesting to reflect on the variety of places and times we learn lessons that ultimately make a difference to us—those moments that transform us forever.

One of my most important lessons in life began at exactly 28,000 feet, about seventy-five miles west of Baghdad. There I was, minding my own business at 2:30 a.m. on the third night of the Gulf War in January 1991. Even if you have never piloted an airplane, it won't take long to imagine our four F-15 Eagles flying in two perpendicular, twenty-mile-long racetrack patterns with about 1,000 feet of vertical separation between fighters. One pair of Eagles was oriented north-south, and my number two wingman and I were searching in an east-west orientation. As one aircraft finished making its 180-degree turn from north to south, the fighter at the opposing end of the racetrack would make his turn from south to north and so on. The idea was to use the F-15's formidable radar system mounted in the nose of the jet to search and detect anything flying from the treetops to 50,000 feet. We stayed busy.

Our job (or "mission" in our language) was to establish air superiority in advance of an air strike by three B-52s carrying sixty 500-pound bombs apiece, destined for the only facility capable of servicing Iraq's menacing SCUD missiles. Their target, and our location, was the northwest corner of Iraq, near Jordan and Israel. "Establishing air superiority" is a very tasteful way of saying, "You will be very sorry if you venture near us, but your mistake will not be painful for too long."

The F-15 Eagle is armed with all the necessary implements to reach out and touch someone who opposes their presence. On a typical mission, each Eagle is loaded with four radar-guided missiles with an average range of fifteen miles, four heat-seeking missiles with a range of about five miles and 1,000 rounds of twenty millimeter firepower for the six-barrel machine gun. The Gatling gun is meant for close-range, no-alternative "knife fights" and fires its bullet rounds at 6,000 per minute, which equates to about 100 rounds per second! This is reserved for company that definitely wants to mix it up.

We had plenty of company that night, both friend and foe. In addition to our four F-15s and the three B-52s, our strike package included one EF-111 providing electronic signals jamming, two F-4G Wild Weasels with anti-radiation missiles intended to neutralize Iraqi surface-to-air missiles (SAMs) and a couple of special operations aircraft with unique support capabilities. We initiated a few intercepts on suspected bandit aircraft originating in the east, near Baghdad, but no enemy fighters ever pressed within forty miles of our zone of protection. All in all, it was starting to shape up like another routine escort mission.

Despite all our rigorous training, however, nothing had quite prepared me for the rapid transition from an initial warning of an Iraqi SA-3 missile lock-on by my Radar Warning Receiver (like a car's radar detector) to the ear-piercing audio and a rapidly flashing, circled blip on my indicator scope. In plain English, a Russian-made, surface-to-air missile about three feet in diameter and twenty feet long was climbing at roughly twice the speed of sound and had been specifically designated as the Greg Richardson Welcoming Committee.

As I looked over and down the right side of my canopy rail, in the general direction that I had been urgently prompted to search, I realized that I had precious few moments to accomplish the one task that could save my life, and it was associated with my poorest subject in school—geometry. To make matters worse, I was required to demonstrate perfectly timed, nighttime geometry.

Pretend that you are in that cockpit with me, and you'll get the picture quickly. We need to create the most difficult angular equation for our missile to solve. In order to accomplish this, we are going to try to guesstimate the point on its collision course that allows just enough time for us to roll our aircraft almost inverted and then "pull" toward the earth. The idea is to create the maximum angle at the last possible moment. That way, when the missile's proximity fusing reacts to our opposite-direction, high-angle passage, and the warhead detonates, we will have a better chance of being beyond its lethal envelope.

There are only three potential variations on this concept. One: Pull into the missile too early when it's still well below you and has time to adjust its direction, which only results in reaching it sooner. That's considerate of us but not the best solution. Two: Wait too long and only be initiating the angle-generating maneuver when proximity (lethal) detonation occurs. And three: Get lucky and commence the roll and pull somewhere in between. Obviously, option three worked but not without a hitch. As the missile exploded, some of the shrapnel hit one of my two vertical tails and rendered the radar-warning antenna inoperative. At least the next missile launched wouldn't cause as much tension and mess in my cockpit.

By the time I had completed my dive and pullout, I had managed to descend from 28,000 feet to about 9,000 feet, whereupon every nearby, low altitude, antiaircraft battery responded with significant encouragement for me to climb as rapidly as possible back to a theoretically safe altitude. Believe it or not, that max afterburner climb was the first time in the previous forty-five to sixty seconds that I had begun hearing sounds, mostly from my wingman and the AWACS aircraft trying to communicate with me. Every ounce of attention was obviously relegated to my geometry lesson, and it completely overshadowed any other senses.

You may be wondering, or at least I hope you are, how the actual mission went. I am pleased to report that within one minute of my missile defense and recovery to our assigned lookout position, the B-52s turned the industrial and storage complex, which measured about one mile wide by five miles long, into total devastation that appeared as hundreds of vaguely connected fires. Only moments before, at least 150 gun emplacements had been peppering the air relentlessly; now, virtually all were quelled by the attack. That mission was considered extremely successful, and over time, we all saw the results of decapitating the Iraqi SCUD repair and assembly facilities.

During our post-attack air refueling and our return to southeast Saudi Arabia, I found my thoughts leap-frogging from one topic to another, but one pattern of thinking dominated almost everything (except safely leading my wingman home). Without even comprehending the magnitude of my decision, I realized that I wanted the rest of my life to be devoted to something of a different value than military preparedness and service. I was, and am, extremely proud of the preeminent capability that the U.S. military labors tirelessly to maintain almost solely for the purpose of ensuring that freedom is available to everyone around the globe. I simply realized that that chapter of my life was about to end and that it would lead to another important opportunity to contribute something. I certainly had no idea what form it would take.

After landing safely, we completed all the necessary details of ground refueling, weapons accountability, maintenance forms that documented the jets' operational capabilities and intelligence debriefing. Unbeknownst to me, the direction my life would take was about to get a jumpstart. With most of my adrenalin returned to the charging tank, I mindlessly dragged my weary body, now clad in too many layers of clothing and equipment, away from the dispersed aircraft shelters toward the relative safety of our hardened alert area. My cot was my new mission objective. Air raid sirens and SCUD missile attacks were not going to stop this tired puppy from getting a couple hours of sleep. As I returned the salute of a three-striper (sergeant) who was patrolling the high-security zone, I couldn't help but notice that he was crying (that's "choked up" when in uniform). Although tired beyond coherent communication, I could not help but stop and ask with more sincerity than I thought I had, "Sarge, is there anything wrong? Do you have something in your eye?" "No sir, nothing is wrong, and my eye is okay," he answered with a bit of embarrassment. "How was your mission, sir?" he added, in an obvious effort to move us off the original topic.

I asked him if he really wanted to know, or was he just making me feel good by asking. He responded with an affirmation that he was sincerely interested, that he had never really talked to a pilot about an actual mission. I sensed an excitement in him that I had not recognized for a very long time. We're generally on fairly rigid time schedules both before and after missions, even during peacetime training, but something told me that the world—and my cot—could wait and that this young man needed to know what the hell he was risking his life to protect.

Sgt. Jackson and I spoke for about thirty minutes. Actually, he listened while I gave him the most accurate account I could of what we had done that night. He was either a spy (and given the outcome of the war, he must have been a pretty terrible one) or he was one curious person. His desire to understand what went on up there was not satisfied by general descriptions of aircraft capabilities or tactics; he wanted to learn how and why. I tried my best to give him a coherent, nonclassified version of the many facets of air-to-air employment by F-15s and our integration with the air-to-ground campaign. He was the first person to hear of my brief encounter with an SA-3, and the look on Sergeant Jackson's face said "Better you than me."

Sgt. Jackson and I weren't quite ready to part company. I suspected that he knew I would return to the reason I first stopped, and I did. "So, are you going to be all right?" I asked nonchalantly. "Yeah. I mean, yes sir. I think so. Just don't know what gets over me. It's happened a couple times now, and it's not something you just stop— you know, getting teary-eyed." I think he was absolutely stunned when I admitted without any hesitation, "That's happened to me, too." My response may have actually stunned me, too. That was the first time I had allowed myself to really consider that the sudden heart pangs and nagging sense of uncertainty were real and perhaps happening to others. After we laughed about the distinct possibility that it was something "they" had put in the water, we determined that it was the dreaded emotional response to leaving our families and homeland within hours of our units' call to deploy for an unspecified period of time.

Like many service members who were sent to the Gulf, we never had the opportunity to deliver more than a kiss and a wave goodbye to anyone who happened to be awake at 2:00 a.m. back on August 7, 1990. We surmised that the lack of closure and indefinite separation had a greater impact on our psyches than we had imagined. We concurred that we had some company in the ranks of the Macho Tough Guys Club, of which we were proud members. At any rate, thirty minutes soon turned into an hour and a half. It was now 8:30 in the morning (our mission planning/briefing had started about fifteen hours earlier), so I bade Sgt. Jackson goodbye. He turned and said, "Colonel Richardson, thanks for demonstrating true leadership!"

You might think that I would have basked in the light of that compliment, but instead, I found myself confronting his appreciative closing comment. I said, fairly tersely, "Sergeant Jackson, Dave, *that* was not leadership—just my way of trying to help someone I thought needed a few moments with someone else spending part of his life in this sandy paradise without the hula girls and rolling surf. When I am leading a flight of F-15s, that's leadership!"

I fully expected Sgt. Jackson to stand corrected, if not apologize, for his misunderstanding of the term "leadership." On the contrary, he adjusted his bearing a bit, took a long, deep breath and said something that I will never forget: "Colonel Richardson, I believe you know what to do with that fighter in the air, but I can't allow even a superior officer to misunderstand something as valuable as leadership. I believe what you do both on the ground and in the air is almost entirely management. You try to control the outcomes of engagements with routine training against enemy tactics; you said that yourself. You are called flight leaders, and it is true that you are in the lead. But *that* is not the essence of leadership. The leadership I am talking about, Colonel Richardson, is what you just did in the last hour. You shared part of yourself with me, and it means more to me than you'll probably ever know."

I instinctively knew that I could take him on and make some great comeback remarks, but in principal, I agreed with where his emphatic statement was trying to guide me. I decided right then and there, as we shook hands and parted, that I would devote considerable energy and career focus to the nature and the challenge of understanding leadership.

If you happen to have experience as a fighter pilot, please don't throw up your military issue B.S. flag and say, "What a cop-out!" But Sgt. Jackson made a valid point, and when there is an absence of principle, situation and people-based leadership, it is often accompanied by retention and morale issues. All the while, we have never wavered in our capability to decimate virtually any adversary. The reason is that we "manage" to control the necessary resources to ensure that appropriate battlefield outcomes occur. The world marvels at the military's global management; they just insist on calling it leadership.

Epilogue

My strongest held opinion is that demonstrating a valuable brand of leadership for others to appreciate and be influenced by is very challenging. And unfortunately, our stripes are earned every day as people silently judge our words, our decisions and, most of all, our behaviors. I wish leadership could be enhanced by taking a time management course. But it isn't. I wish that by earning the title of CEO, senator, director or general, a person was automatically entitled to demonstrate leadership. But they aren't. I wish that there was a way to prevent people from formulating their own opinions about how they view us. But there isn't. I wish that it were easy to provide the kind of leadership role modeling that matters. But it's not.

I am glad that leadership is totally free, but it certainly is accompanied by a cost. If you aren't already aware, you'll figure out what your costs are. Start with the following phrase and finish it: "More people would see me as a leader, if I _____." Now you have an idea of the cost to you. In other words, each of us has to give up something to get leadership. For some, it will be control and being in charge. For others, it will be giving away some air time, and for others still, it will be to accept a less expedient route to generating results.

In closing, please think about the requests that I have made of you. My most earnest hope is that each reader overcomes the natural tendency to make arbitrary connections between certain positions or titles and the term "leader." I realize how ingrained that relationship can be, but it's essential to first assess the degree of leadership that a person is demonstrating before bestowing the honor of being a "leader." Please take the leadership journey personally and evaluate how you're doing every day. Ask yourself how you could improve, as if you were being studied as a role model. People around us are able and willing to help us; just watch their reactions to you or even dare to ask them. Please remember that people want to know how much you care about them, not how much control you can exercise. And for God's sake, remember that leadership is for *everyone*!

About The Author

Gregory M. Richardson, SPHR, MA-HRD

 Mr. Richardson directs the Human Resource Services Division and is a Partner with Goodman & Company, the largest Virginia-based CPA and business consulting firm. The HR Services Division supports clients with complete HR management and training/development services including specialized recruiting and outplacement programs. The HR Partnership Program™ provides HR services to smaller organizations needing the highest quality HR expertise without the costly overhead of an entire department. Widely recognized for his professional development seminars focused on leadership and for his facilitation of strategic planning meetings and executive retreats, *Leadership is for Everyone* and *Integrating Diverse Workstyles* are two of his most popular workshops. Greg delivers a simple, but powerful message as he works with organizations that are targeting breakthroughs in individual leadership and workplace performance. Messages are delivered through audience participation, focusing on their unique challenges. Participation is the order of the day— soaking up sage advice is *not* on the menu. Mr. Richardson earned two masters degrees, one in Education and Human Resource Development from The George Washington University and the other in Aeronautical Science, and has attained the Senior Professional in Human Resources (SPHR) designation from the Society for Human Resource Management. Greg has been a professional member of the National Speakers Association (NSA) since 1995, and has served on the Board of Directors of the Virginia Speakers Association.

Gregory M. Richardson, SPHR, MA-HRD
Partner, Goodman & Company
701 Town Center Drive
Newport News, VA 23606
Phone: 757.873.1033
Toll Free: 888.873.1033
Email: grichardson@goodmanco.com
Web Site: www.goodmanco.com/hr

Chapter Two

SUPER LEADERS THINK, ACT AND ACHIEVE THEIR WAY TO SUCCESS

William Austin, Ed.D.

Introduction: We Need a Leader!

Consider the example of King Alexander, who over twenty-three hundred years ago led his troops across a scorching, desolate plain. After eleven days in the desert, he and all his followers were near death from dehydration and thirst. Alexander pressed on. At midday, two scouts brought him what little water they had been able to find. It barely filled the cup, but to all who looked at it, it represented the most priceless commodity on Earth. Alexander's troops stood and watched as he poured the water into the hot sand. Alexander looked at his followers and spoke with conviction: "It is of no use for one to drink when many thirst." Being a super leader, he knew that he had only one thing to offer his followers to help them overcome their situation and peril: inspiration! Alexander aspired to significance and those he led followed him into history. To this day, his name is hardly remembered as Alexandros III Philippou Makedonon, rather he is known throughout the world as Alexander the Great. His strength of leadership character is spoken of so often but emulated in far too may circumstances.

The moment has come for super leaders[1] to emerge in our corporations, not-for-profits, service agencies, healthcare, education and government organizations. Contemporary organizations are full of people with leader titles, leader responsibilities, leader prestige and leader power; yet few organizations have leaders with devoted followers fulfilling worthy missions, surpassing expectations, transforming lives and continuously improving the morale of each and every employee.

Leadership is one of the most fulfilling endeavors an individual can choose to pursue. An effective and inspirational leader can have a very rewarding and positive influence over the lives of other people. It is the journey to super leader status that is the greatest reward, not the prestige, money, power or glory that is so often sought as an end. Leader satisfaction is found in the struggle to develop followers, to act and to succeed, not in the accomplishment of attaining constructed leader status for personal gain. The contemporary notion of the leader, in the postmodern sense, has become a competition over which set of truths should dominate rather than a contemplation over which truths provide meaning and essence to our followers. Once this latter notion is accepted and embraced, the realization of super leader status can commence.

The realization of super leader status is an aspiration more than a definitive destination. The super leader represents inspiration, noble intentions, style, refinement, definition of purpose and strength of character. It is an ideal more than a concrete prescription for action or transformative behavior; it is an ideal type of behavior that few, if any, can sustain for an extended period of time (largely due to our inability to become anything more than human). Super leader status is the ability, within the mind of each of us, to conceive within ourselves a level of grandness that transcends our current self-conception and ability. During this journey to seek enlightenment, truth, trust and continuous self-improvement, we will fortunately find leadership challenges, succeed at them and gain personal, professional and financial rewards. The challenges exist for each of us in

---

[1] The term super leader in this context is used in the Nietzschean sense of the *ubermensch* or "over (man) leader." The super leader is defined as the potential and the grandness within us; to think of ourselves as a parent to something greater than our current selves. (Solomon & Higgins, 2000) It represents something to work or strive toward; it is not a concrete state of being that can simply be obtained. The opposite of the super leader is the constructed leader who defines his/her ability by current conceptualizations, definitions of reality and other limiting, normative behaviors or attitudes.

the companies, communities and nations we serve. Our organizations are screaming out for leadership, for vision, for a mission worthy of pursuit and for something and/or someone to believe.

The Contemporary Leadership Gap

The greatest challenge facing contemporary organizations is the total lack of leadership that plagues their direction, decisions and daily operations. As an organizational leader and a consultant, I have little difficulty in locating the supervisor's office in any of the organizations I am privileged to serve. I immediately begin looking for the symbols of deference and power. I look for the biggest desks, the largest conference tables, the most expensive furniture and the best window views. Since I have personally never been invited to consult with or speak to an organization where everything was perfect, I always start working with the individuals proudly displaying these proven symbols until I can locate the organization's hidden potential of leadership and shared powership base.

While meeting with one organization's top management team, to learn its potential, I was treated to coffee served in magnificently designed mugs, to a most comfortable chair and to the most frightening conversation I had had in many years. The company's second in command was right there to share his personal perspective on management and organizational deference. He began to explain in beautiful prose how the organization was run, the pitfalls, those individuals of whom I should beware, how he would trick his employees into assisting me in my work—all while he openly shared his disdain for my service and presence. Disturbed, yet intrigued, I began my normal probing.

Why would he need to trick people? Why not just ask them for cooperation and help in making the organization better? He explained that people were, by nature, interested in disrupting the normal operation and management of the firm, so he had spent twenty years fooling them into moving his agenda forward. He had instilled so many rules (which he mistakenly referred to as policy) that movement and advancement toward success were defined out of existence. In fact, his management by rules (or what I call bureaucratic malaise) was so entrenched that no person at the firm could possibly be successful. Even members of other divisions of the firm could not achieve because cooperation with his unit was impossible, therefore stagnating the entire operation of the company. Although our friend might be the most obviously disruptive, overtly manipulative and divisive manager I have met to date, his practices of heavy-handed management are not at all uncommon at some level in most organizations.

Looking at this example, one might believe that this manager is leading his organization to ruin (and he is); however, in a macro sense this would be an inaccurate supposition. In fact, this manager is using bureaucratic mechanisms to sustain power in an organization that should have never let him near the controls. He is not a leader at all, he displays no leadership qualities, and his very mental model is the antithesis of leadership. His practices are leading the organization to disaster; however, to think of these practices as a form of leadership is a crucial mistake made by many constructed leaders. Far too many managers believe they are leaders because of their position, title, power or ability to exercise control. None of these common attributes of an organization epitomize leadership; rather, they are tools that can make a leader great if he has them at his disposal.

Recently, our organizations have been taken over by an unprecedented level of uninspired bureaucrats, supervisors without the vision to see past the end of their respective noses and corporate scoundrels more interested in their own greed and advancement, not the organizations they serve. The people who serve our organizations in middle management—professionals and staff positions—have become increasingly disenfranchised, uninspired, tired and the embodiment of malaise. These constructed leaders thus create an existence out of pretending to be the leaders until real leadership emerges from within or outside the organization.

The uninspired bureaucrats have taken to developing an unending system of policies, rules and regulations that diminish the creative process. These rules and regulations evolve beyond guiding policies and enter into proscriptive management so constricting that the life of the organization is strangled from existence. The bureaucrats are so uninterested in engaging with other people in the creative process that they develop rules that they believe define complex problems out of existence. The central issue is that problems remain below the surface, bubbling in confined spaces until eventually they erupt with a volcanic force that severely wounds the organization. Hospital management, higher education management, government agencies and HMOs all provide ready examples of this type of organizational leader base. Super leaders are required, by their nature, to diminish the power of the bureaucrats, for they realize, as Saint Augustine of Hippo once proclaimed, that there is no obligation among people to follow any unjust law or rule created by man. As super leaders have no obligation to obey these rules, they realize the need to free their followers from constraint before the followers are severely damaged.

The visionless leaders often are people with drive and ambition enough to become the leaders. They rise through manipulation, coercion, ascribed birthrights, longevity, accident or other unnatural means into positions of organizational authority and power for which they have no ability. They are very capable people who have been promoted one too many times. They may have good intentions; however, they do not possess an ability to lead, to inspire, to set divisional or organizational goals or to move the organization forward. The organizations for which these constructed leaders provide oversight often stagnate for years, until some competitor removes the leaders from business or a board removes them from power. The "old boy network" often allows this abomination of nature to remain in power far too long. Some of the organizations that I believe best demonstrate a failure to show a vision toward greatness include Silo, Bethlehem Steel and CompUSA. (Collins, 2001) It is not that these are necessarily poorly run companies; rather, they have failed to move toward a level I would personally define as innovative or success oriented. In the end, the failure to succeed should always be defined as the ultimate accountability measurement for the top leader of the organization.

The corporate raiders enter an organization with the goal of increasing profits at all cost, usually at the price of the values and mission of the organization. Raiders are there with one purpose: to become richer, to embody greed and to convince others that the sole purpose of an organization revolves around money instead of service. These organizations are pillaged and raided into nonexistence or to a point where they do not serve the communities where they emerged. Enron, Tyco and, in the past, Singer, all provide great examples of what occurs to these organizations when the corporate raiders have completed their change efforts.

Numerous books have been written to demonstrate the differences between being a leader and being a manager. Being a leader in an organization does not necessitate hierarchical authority from position; however, leaders that possess traditional predefined authority will find their leadership efforts more fruitful. The successful organizations of the future will find a method to get their natural leaders into key management positions while simultaneously getting their best managers to become better leaders. The duality, and often adversarial self-conception, of the leader/manager role is becoming more complex as our organizations move from production and being service centered to being learning centered.

Leaders today must inspire people through symbolic action and the realization of goals—some real but many representational. Super leaders realize that people react more to meaning and less to the negative motivating forces geared toward the realization of ill-conceived goals. Success-based super leaders create an entrepreneurial spirit of planned change through a focus on innovative practices and processes by publicly outperforming competitors and by investing in intellectual capital. A renewed spirit in your company will naturally emerge from a growth in its leadership potential.

Fewer people are choosing leadership tracks. Many contemporary leaders are weak in spirit, ability and ideas, and too many leaders have years of experience as a symbol rather than years of successful experience as a reality. Many contemporary leaders believe that their experiences in other positions have prepared them for their current roles. This fallacy is to your advantage because many people fail to realize that all new leaders start with the same tenure of experience, regardless of the number of years they have managed to survive their current or previous organizations. Constructed leaders do not choose to grow, to develop and to reformulate past assumptions and perceptions. The super leader's ability to succeed is realized through an ability to grow, to learn, to develop, to take risks and to challenge the contemporary definitions of reality. The combined effect of all of these examples is a leadership gap so severe and so broad that the limits of achievement are the limits of your conceptualized goals and determination.

Learning to Lead

Prior to assuming that you are a leader, you might benefit from a simple test of leadership within your organization. All leaders should ask four simple but essential questions that determine their current leadership potential:

1. Do I have followers?
2. Can I inspire my followers into action?
3. Will people sacrifice for my ideas?
4. Can I make this happen?

The easiest way to determine if you are a leader is to determine if anyone is following you. If you have a determined course of action and have stated it publicly and no person is in voluntary agreement, then you are not leading. You cannot be a leader if no one is following you; you are something else, something more basic and less prestigious. Often, managers who have obtained power through position use their authority to force and coerce people into following their directions. (If they believe this is leadership, then they are sadly mistaken.) There is an even simpler test of this phenomenon: Do you use the power of your desk to impress people? When a subordinate comes into your office, do you move to a neutrally seated position, or do you use the symbolic power of your desk and office to dictate orders?

Your position is not the genesis of your leadership; it is merely a means of accessing power, resources and the talents of employees. To determine your current leadership status, you must determine your ability to inspire and influence through mind and action the agendas of others. If you are constantly being asked for your opinion and perspective, if you are being sought out as the expert, if you are admired and desired as a part of any team and if you have people who express publicly their belief in your ability, then you are a leader and can put these techniques into immediate usage. For it is the desire and duty of a super leader to influence others by choosing values, aiming for excellence in thoughts and deeds, embracing personal integrity, developing the courage to change and finally, helping others to reach their maximum potential. (Blanchard, 1999)

The next step is to determine if you can inspire your followers into action. Can you express an idea, get people to adopt it, convince them to voluntarily and willfully act to achieve it and stay with them to see it through the course? If the answer is yes, then you may ask the even harder question: Will people sacrifice for my ideas and my desired course of action? Are the people who follow you willing to sacrifice (e.g., their reputation, time with their families, their trust, money, effort, etc.) to make your agenda a reality? The previous question is really about trust and trustworthiness. Are you the type of person who is trustworthy, possesses integrity and does not quit or abandon others? To be a leader, people must be willing to follow you, they must be willing to act on your lead, and they must be willing to trust you enough to take a risk in losing something to make your leadership goals a reality.

Once you have determined the answers to these questions, the emphasis falls completely from the relationship between your followers and you, to an emphasis on you alone. If you have followers, you will want to convince them to remain loyal and engaged. To do so, you must determine that you have the ability to make their collective as-pirations occur. Although this ability is normally defined in terms of functional authority, control over organizational power systems, re-ward-giving capabilities and title, the reality is that these symbols of prestige are products of your individual ability to think, to inspire others to action and to achieve the results that reward yourself, your followers and your organization.

Think, Act and Achieve

How can you think, act and achieve your way to becoming the leader of your organization? Your first step is to realize that most or-ganizations are currently in need of innovation and improvement at the leadership level. It is not that their current leaders are necessar-ily inept or incapable; it is the recognition that there are few, if any, superior organizations where constant change and innovation are not necessary to maintain excellence or to just survive. Success is found in the awareness that you can conceive a better future, a better workplace, a better "mousetrap" and a better reality that will put you, your followers and your organization on the path to excellence and accomplishment.

Think

At first glance, thinking seems like a relatively simple idea. So how can thinking be a competitive advantage over current leaders or others trying to climb that often-referenced corporate ladder? The answer is simple: Most people never stop to think. They don't envi-sion a future, they don't develop strategies, they don't set goals, they don't monitor progress and reevaluate, and frankly, they just don't think. Take a look at the leaders in your current organization. Are they known for their ability to think? Do they often appear to be in-novative and perceptive or to possess a global understanding? Are they empathetic, or do they understand the consequences of their de-cisions? Although there are leaders who think in many organizations, overall, the norm for most people is that their leaders are not known or admired for their perceptive qualities and abilities.

Why do so few people and leaders think? The answer is simple. First, most people do not develop an ability to be analytical. Second, thinking time is often mistakenly viewed as a luxury they cannot af-ford when trying to balance busy lives and careers. Most people elect to spend free time in an activity other than in deep introspective and/or analytical contemplation. Many managers view it as a waste of time. In fact, many organizations have trained their employees to view this behavior as offensive, disruptive or as a form of shiftlessness.

Learning and thinking about what has been learned are the first essential components of excellent leadership. Your first objective should be to learn everything you can about your company (or the one for which you plan to provide leadership). Study every enterprise and component of the organization (whether you will lead that area or not, since your division will need to interact with all others to achieve success). Gather any and all information about the organization, learn it and commit it to memory. Next, study your industry (or the business your organization is in). Who are the best firms in this industry? What do the best firms do differently or better than your organization? Do people like working for your competitors? If so, why?

Once you have committed the operation of your organization to memory and studied other successful companies in your industry, you can begin the hard task of thinking. First, consider your organization as a whole or at a global level. What can your firm do to improve its competitive advantage? How can your company change its operations to improve immediately? What should it change over the next three years to improve its operation five years from now? What business should the organization be in twenty years from now, and what changes would have to be in place today to reach the future you envision? Congratulations, you have just created a vision for your company and begun envisioning a future for yourself as a leader.

Now consider the division you work within at the company. How can this division improve immediately? What changes are necessitated? How can your operation improve to be more cooperative with other divisions at the firm? What changes can be made immediately to improve work efficiency and employee morale simultaneously? How can your division improve itself over the next five years? What are the five key initiatives that would need to be put into action?

Finally, you need to answer some more basic questions about your ability to lead. What can you do to communicate these thoughts to others in your division and at the firm? What would you need to do to get others to believe in your ideas and to implement them? How might you create a sense of urgency in the organization to get your ideas and thoughts at center stage? Have you tested (i.e., shared with others) your ideas and considered the feedback of your fellow employees? How do you see yourself as a leader in your organization? What position will you hold, and how will you use power and authority to make your company a better place to work? How would you reward people for hard work and success?

What goals would you like to achieve over the next year for your company? What goals would you like to achieve for yourself over this next year? What goals would you like to achieve over the next five years for your company? What goals would you like to achieve for yourself over the next five years? Finally, on a piece of paper you plan to carry with you everywhere, write down the leadership goals that you expect to accomplish over the course of your life. You have done well and already accomplished more than most people will ever do. Now it's time to couple your brain power with action, for success is achieved in the accomplishment of these essential goals.

GOAL SHEET		
Goal Level	Timeline	Goals
Self	One Year	
	Five Years	
	My Life	
My Organization	One Year	
	Five Years	
	My Life	

Now that you have thought, pondered and evaluated, you must go back and judge each goal and desire against one essential set of criteria—your personal values. Do your goals and desires complement your beliefs, values and principles? If any goal is in violation of your principles and values, it is not worth the effort of achieving. Do your desires and goals help people or hurt people? If your goals and desires do damage to others, regardless of whether the ends might in some abstract sense justify the means, then your goals are not worth achieving. Super leaders act superior, not to other people but to lesser values and principles that are unworthy of them. For example, greed hurts other people, it hurts you, it hurts your company, and it is not a value worth believing; it is, therefore, an idea that is too far below a super leader to pursue. If you wish to exercise influence over other people, then you must become a person who has a stimulating and encouraging effect on other people. Greater ends defined by better means will be the thought goals of any person trying to reach the status of a super leader. All else is rather mundane, ordinary and unfulfilling.

Act

Super leaders understand the power of action and ground all action in the context of what they believe and value. Their values and beliefs become the guiding forces of their decision making, prioritizing and the actions that they elect to take. Super leaders take action, and they inspire others to take positive, proactive action as well. Leading requires the ability to think through a vision and inspire others to join you on the attainment of that vision. Leadership requires an ability to create within the hearts of your followers the desire to act; in such cases, the leader examines the situation and looks for an opportunity to solve an immediate issue through the involvement of many stakeholders. Inspirational super leaders study and think through the circumstances, choices and potential outcomes of their decisions before taking action. They take calculated risks, maintaining the values of honesty and integrity, while simultaneously believing in the ability of their followers. The super leaders know that if they set course and direction, their inspired followers will amaze them with the ingenuity with which they complete tasks, goals and the entire journey. Super leaders rely heavily on action since they require the results to gain more followers, more trust and more responsibility in leadership. Finally, to truly inspire their followers to further action, super leaders share the bounty of accomplishment while sheltering the followers from all blame for leader mistakes.

The super leaders realize that they grow both through failure and success, that their true accomplishments occur after they have fallen from success and that all glory is fleeting. The super leaders develop within their mental psyche an Amor Fati (a love of fate). They accept with great enthusiasm whatever happens, whatever people do and whatever happens to their respective lives. They know that they cannot control the world but can control life's outcomes and that they have an ability to influence these outcomes toward the positive through action. The super leader realizes the power and mystery of action, which has a real potential to lead to success over failure.

Super leaders are never fearful of action or the consequences actions may require. They develop a true love of life and all of life's pleasures, pains, failures and successes. To love fate is to embrace leadership with a goal of enjoying the journey of life and the responsibility of leadership. A leader will develop a love of fate, thus possessing a complete sense of character and the self-confidence to be bold, to drive forward and to take the serious risks of action, purpose and spirit necessary to succeed.

Many constructed leaders fail because of an inability or lack of desire to act. These leaders are afraid of action; they fear that their deeds will be punished, that their actions will cause failure (which they try to avoid all costs), and these constructed leaders do not realize that they cannot control or influence fate by any means. Other constructed leaders fail because they constantly react to opportunities and challenges without preparation. These leaders decide all action by majority vote. They fail to develop new ideas and live in a constant fear of change. The overactive constructed leaders try anything once; they try everything on the backs of their followers without a chance to recuperate and without any sense of hesitation. These leaders mistake vision and thinking with action. They never consider and ponder consequences, instead living by a motto of "Keep trying and eventually, I will find success." The followers of the overactive leader are engaged at first but later check out, quit or lose interest due to lack of accomplishment and/or exhaustion. The super leader is proactive, as she knows the value of action in the context of a well-thought-out plan and a well-devised strategy of action, and she has a real desire for achievement for her followers.

Once the leader learns to love the fate that life will provide and works to develop a proactive course of action, that leader will become truly effective and, by most standards, a truly bold and exemplary (if not, at times, dangerous) person. This super leader does not regret action or resent others, does not live in fear, does not regret life but accepts its conditions. For the super leader, it is life itself, not the achievements or successes of that life, which provides his/her leadership and self-worth with meaning and value. How can a leader come to live without fears, to live in the moment with a forecast of the future and to joyfully embrace the fate of life that emerges?

Super leaders can do this because they understand the concept of eternal recurrence; or, more simply, they fully understand what Winston Churchill meant when he said, "Never, never, never, never, give up!" Super leaders have the heart, courage, integrity and character to see their goals through to fruition. They use their ability to understand eternal recurrence (as defined by Friedrich Nietzsche) to find the courage to endeavor to persevere and achieve victory in the journey of life. The central idea of eternal recurrence is that the sequence of events of life and/or leadership recurs over and over, again and again. Each opportunity for action and its subsequent success or failure is a series of recurring phenomena. How many times have you heard of an example of some person hitting rock bottom, only to bounce back to even greater levels of success? Leaders should realize that they must be fearless in taking risks and can be audacious in action since there is always a second chance, third chance, fourth chance, ad infinitum.

When leaders realize that any one decision is not the end of the world, not the defining moment of their respective lives and not the definitive point of their leadership potential, they free themselves to take action and succeed. The principle of eternal recurrence ensures each leader that he will have an infinite number of opportunities to succeed as well as an infinite number of opportunities to overcome setbacks. Far too many people live in fear, live within the predefined constructs that limit action and achievement. Our society is defined in terms of an endless pursuit of conformity and safety, a negation of greatness in favor of mediocrity and is socially constructed to limit the personal achievement to only a few. You may chose to be one of the few successful people, to never be defined by conventions, by a job, by a career or by a set of social standards that others use to limit your potential. What would happen if you rebelled, if you broke free, if you thought and acted as if today were your last chance at greatness (knowing full well that another chance is only moments away)?

No single failure or success is eternal; rather, the events that create the outcomes of success and failure are the eternal constants. Therefore, one cannot rest on any individual success, just as one cannot be destroyed by any one failure. Neither success nor failure should define or immobilize us; instead, the definition of our leadership ability should be found in our relation to the world in thought and action. A super leader is capable and acts to rise above the outcomes of his/her action. Super leaders view proactive, thought-derived actions as the essence of life and as the norm for which to strive and achieve. A person living as a super leader will realize that positive outcomes will naturally emerge from proactive, thought-based, positive actions.

"L'audace, l'audace, toujours l'audace," as originally stated by Frederick the Great, and later often quoted by General George S. Patton, Jr., is the essence of the super leader's charge of never giving up or giving in to defeat. A super leader understands the need for a virtuous existence and lives by this motto of audacity, audacity, always audacity. Unfortunately, the current usage of the term "audacity" is linked to negative connotations such as insolence, arrogance, carelessness or thoughtless action. However, if used in the classical sense (as meant by Patton and Frederick), the term signifies a greater, more positive connotation: fearless, daring, boldness and freedom from conventional restraints. (Axelrod, 1999) The super leaders develop an intrinsic understanding to love their fate, to free themselves from fear because of eternal recurrence and to act with a boldness rarely employed and the audacity to achieve.

Achieve

How to best measure achievement is one of the most difficult challenges that any leader must face. Often, leaders choose to measure their personal accomplishments in terms of getting work done, in terms of a bottom line or in terms of their own personal accomplishments (i.e., rising up the corporate ladder, increasing salary, prestige, power, etc.). Accomplishment or achievement cannot be measured for a leader in these terms (although they are extremely important to the organization and the leader's life); these are effects of the leader's actions but not the defining reality of the leader's potential for achievement. It is in the realization of the leader's ability to motivate, inspire and create value for the followers that the true leadership potential is best defined and measured.

The super leader inspires people through action and the attainment of goals—some real, some symbolic. Within the leadership process itself, super leaders begin to see the value of managing impressions and symbols while building trust in a socially constructed world. Super leaders rely more on reaching the highest levels of integrity and personal accountability than on continuously measuring success against mere numbers of subordinates, material possessions, power, wealth, income or prestige. They realize that people react more to meaning and less to the negative motivating forces of unrealized, ill-conceived goals or the successful acquisition of tangible and intangible possessions. Super leaders see achievement in terms of their ability to make the lives, mental frameworks and working conditions of their followers better.

The definitive impediment to the achievement of super leader status is found within the leader's character, for if the leader chooses power, privilege and money over passion, duty and service, then the leader will ultimately fail. More power, privilege and prestige are not rewards (as commonly believed); these effects merely represent the ability of the leader to accomplish more, to take on more responsibility and to strive for more thoughts, actions and achievements that will benefit followers. The danger of personal ego will always preoccupy the leader. At times, the leader will mistakenly come to believe that achievements come solely from his/her ability and not from the collective ability of the organization and his/her respective followers. Although it is important for the leader to possess courage, a positive attitude and self-confidence, he/she should not be delusional and arrogant, thus losing the loyalty of the followers.

Leadership at the highest level requires that both tangible and intangible expectations are set for the organization and its departments as well as for each individual follower. Prior to setting these expectations (which should clearly define the level of accomplishment desired), the leader should set and proclaim clear expectations for herself. When a leader sets high expectations for herself, she then has the right and responsibility to expect more from her followers. Without clearly stated expectations, no leader can require accomplishment from herself or her followers. When expectations are thought out and acted upon, well-defined achievements can become simple potentials that naturally become part of the leader and followers' expectations.

The path to achieving the status of super leader is a chosen journey, a chosen destination that cannot be found by accident, by luck or by any instrument of good fortune. The actions of super leaders will lead to success, to prosperity and to great ends as a matter of providence derived from living an audacious, inspiring, risk-inclined, forward-focused life. The super leader achieves far more because the heart becomes virtuous, the spirit embraces courage, actions encourage the hearts and minds of the hopeless, words speak with integrity, respect and honesty, a strength of character defends and uplifts all followers, and the leader's antagonism undoes the tyranny of the iniquitous. Achievement is found in aspiring to lead from inspiration, from a greater set of principles, from the realization that the road to real leadership is paved in actions that are coupled with personal values.

Reaping the Bounty of Success

The ultimate success objective of your leadership is to set new standards by listening to the needs, hopes and desires of others and by making informed decisions that will advance your organization. The success you seek can only be found in your ability to assist others in achieving their goals. Once others have accomplished and achieved their goals, they will realize the rewards of following you, your leadership ability, and your ability to work toward the betterment of others.

Prior to any fruitful discussion of success, it is essential to understand the real and valid nature of failure. Most leaders mistakenly view their failures in terms of failed projects, a declining bottom line or the lack of implementation of their ideas. These are the effects of failure not the causes or origins. In reality, I can name each of my failures personally; each has a unique and distinct name. At the core of each of my failings (which are manifested in failed outcomes) is a person or small group of people, each of whom has a name, a face and a spirit that I have impaired by my inability to lead him or her to success. Ideas and projects never fail—people do. To fail at leading is to provide no inspiration, motivation, support, information or communication and/or to not manifest a realization of the ability of each and every individual person who has provided you with the gift of his or her followership.

Your best and most fruitful rewards will come in the awareness that you have provided a unique service to each individual that has followed you. For super leaders have served followers and created better organizations, better departments, better workplaces and hopefully generated more fulfilled lives for those whom their leadership talents complement. The essence of super leaders is that they serve, and their benefit is realized not by aspiration or goal attainment but by their ability to remember and follow their conscience, values and humanity. Super leaders leave a legacy that endures because of their character, integrity and conscience. All other constructed leaders develop a set of skills and practices that work, but they fail to endure.

The final reaping of success in leadership is the legacy you can leave to your organization, your followers and your memory. The true test of your leadership's impact is a study of what happens when you are no longer the leader of the group. If that group sustains momentum, continues to grow and improve, continues to move forward (based on your past influence) and remains successful, you have gloriously succeeded and known a triumph few individuals will ever know. Your legacy will naturally emerge from your character and conscience. Your conscience should navigate your leadership journey, as it is well-formed and universal, set in the values of respect, honesty, humanity, equality of contribution and reward and is in the presence and desire for a life that succeeds within a world that is fair. Your ability and success in using your values to establish a model of follower-based leadership will provide you with a high ground of superiority based in the principles and values of service, equality and accomplishment.

Once you have realized your leadership potential, set the expectations, served each and every follower and created a positive, proactive legacy, stop and examine your current situation and you will realize the bounty you have reaped. Your will note two things: First, your position within the organization and your level of responsibility have both improved and increased since you began your journey. Second, look at your salary and bank account; both will have improved as the journey has progressed. The goal of leadership cannot be material possession and economic advancement; rather, the acquisition of material goods and the increase in fame and money are the outcomes of your great work in leading others to a better life and being.

As your leadership potential rises and your realization of success takes place, the real hard work begins. Now you must develop a mental state of continuous growth, innovation, creativity and momentum. For instance, consider the average board game that simulates business, life or work and consider that the greatest joy within the game comes at the challenge of the climb. Once you have achieved any level of success, the game begins to become boring and monotonous and the excitement diminishes. The realization of success is where the fun and adventure take place; sustaining the momentum becomes the more difficult task.

Super leaders are those people who can think to create a better workplace and more success, can act to achieve positive results and can succeed while maintaining the momentum of success. The super leader realizes that risk is warranted since the phenomenon of eternal recurrence constantly provides new and more opportunities to succeed. The super leaders value human existence and serve the person found within each of their followers, they release the limitations of their egos, and they set new expectations of excellence for themselves and for their followers to achieve. To strive to be a super leader is to search for the superiority of your potential self over your current self, to judge your personal limitations and overcome them and to realize the value and talent of each individual you are fortunate enough to lead. When you define success in terms of the accomplishment of others, you will know true success, and all the credit, power, money and fame you have earned will naturally materialize.

Summary

Your future and the ability to lead others is found in your ability to continuously improve and develop your potential. This leadership strategy is highly effective because super leaders hold the line on vision and direction. They pledge to accomplish a set of goals and then stay true to their word. You will know you are a super leader when you bang on a desk, look your followers straight in the eyes and state clearly and concisely where you and the organization are going. From the moment the words leave your mouth, you know full well that you and your followers have the ability to overcome all obstacles in achieving your goals.

SELECTED BIBLIOGRAPHY

Austin, W. (2002). *Strategic Planning for Smart Leadership*. Stillwater, OK: New Forums Press, Inc.

Axelrod, A. (1999). *Patton On Leadership: Strategic Lessons for Corporate warfare*. Paramus, NJ: Prentice Hall Press.

Blanchard, K. (1999). *The Heart of a Leader*. Tulsa, OK: Honor Books.

Collins, J. (2001). *Good to Great*. New York, NY: Harper Business.

Greenleaf, R. K. (2002). *Servant Leadership: A Journey Into the Nature of Legitimate Power and Greatness*. New York, NY: Paulist Press.

Heidegger, M. (1991). *Nietzsche: Volume III: The Will to Power as Knowledge and as Metaphysics*. San Francisco, CA: Harper Collins Publishers.

Solomon, R.C., & Higgins, K. M. (2000). *What Nietzsche Really Said*. New York, NY: Schocken Books.

William Austin, Ed.D.

Dr. William "Will" Austin, the youngest community college president in New Jersey state history, has served others as a keynote speaker, consultant, businessman, elected leader, and author. As an energetic mind provocateur that informs and inspires audiences into a frenzy of proactive action; through high-content, memorable, value added, service based presentations. Will doesn't just speak about leadership, planning, and success; his actions embody it. As a higher education leader, he has assisted individuals, companies, and groups in setting goals and achieving them. In humorous storytelling seminars, he shares experiences and successful strategies of numerous contemporary leaders. His ideas on strategic planning and leadership are taught in graduate schools throughout America and in Europe.

William Austin, Ed.D.
Principal
PMC, LLC
draustin@thusspokewill.com
www.thusspokewill.com

Chapter Three

LEADERS *MAKE* TIME TO LEAD

Dr. Warren Linger

Taking time to do anything assumes that time is there for the taking. But when was the last time you had two hours just waiting for you to take them? If you're a leader or an aspiring leader, the answer is probably "never." The solution, then, is to make time a priority—to spend it on the most important projects that will improve your work, your personal life or the lives of other people.

The problem is that we often can't find time. How often have you heard someone (or yourself) say, "I just don't have time to improve the system"? Nobody has time to make the system better. The world is set up to fill the time we have. Every time we finish a task, the next task catches our attention, the next person walks into our office, the next phone call rings, or the next e-mail tells us that it is the most important item on the planet and needs our attention now.

The challenge is that at some point, we must say "no" to all these outside interruptions and make time to improve the world around us. There are three keys to accomplishing this goal:

1. Make time for your leadership priorities every day.
2. Use that time to achieve your best, most productive work.
3. Work on your highest leadership priority.

Those who cannot master these skills will have great difficulty becoming leaders.

Leaders make a little time every day to get the most important items done. Let me share an example with you. A while back, I was leading a large seminar on time management in Houston, Texas. In the seminar, we began to discuss the importance of protecting a block of productive time to complete one's most important priority. A group that was sitting toward the front of the audience started to nod, roll their heads and roll their eyes.

At break, I asked them why they had such a strong reaction to the topic. It turned out that the members of this group all worked in the same department. They had a co-worker (whom I will call Sally) who was very protective (the group described her as overly protective) of her time and did not let anyone else interrupt her when she was working on important projects.

They were not happy with her because they could not get any help from her when she had her "caution" tape in front of her cube. Because caution tape (the substance officials use to keep innocent people away from accidents or danger) is bright yellow and on it are the words "CAUTION" or "WARNING" it let everyone in the office know that Sally was working in her peak efficiency period. One problem the group mentioned was that it seemed as if Sally was working on an important project almost every day.

At the end of the seminar, Sally's manager (whom I will call Joe) and I started talking about productivity. I asked where Sally was, and he said that she was on a vacation that she had won from the company as a reward for being so productive.

I then asked Joe how he felt about Sally's protectiveness of her high productivity time. Joe said that he didn't like it but that he put up with it because Sally was the department leader. He said, in fact, that she was almost twice as productive as the next most productive worker. Joe eventually admitted that he saw the benefits of Sally protecting her time and that he was going to help the rest of his employees create their own highly productive moments.

Sally was a master at making time for that most important project. She knew what it was, and she guarded her time to work on it. Often, people tell me that they don't have one or two hours to put into their most important projects. But making time doesn't start with two hours; it starts with twenty minutes every day and building up to one hour then two. I'm only talking about two hours a day; the rest of your time can be used on meetings and other things that must be done yet are not as productive when it comes to improving work systems.

You still say that you don't have two hours every day. I once had a client who believed that, but after several months, he had finally managed to free up two hours every day. He told me that it was like someone had turned on the lights and that he could see what he needed to do and where he was going to lead his company. He said it was the most valuable lesson he learned that year, and he wondered how he had gotten along for so many years without using this productivity tool. Now that the lights were on, he could see where he needed to lead. I told him that he was the one who had turned on the lights by making time to see what needed to be improved and then improving it.

Leadership can be described in various ways. According to a leading global consulting and training firm, leadership is setting examples for others and being seen as responsible. In his book *Leadership*, former New York City mayor Rudolph Giuliani mentions characteristics of leadership: persistent learning, relentless preparation, and developing and communicating strong beliefs. *Entrepreneur* magazine defines leadership as "communicating with diverse audiences, making decisions that may be unpopular, making sure your message gets through, and setting quality and service standards that will survive after you are gone." None of these leadership tasks can be done without making the time to make them happen. Leaders make productive blocks of time every day to work on their most important leadership projects.

The tools you read about in this chapter should be considered supplementary to your existing time-management skills. I am assuming that most of you reading this chapter have such skills and use daily planners. Also, I am assuming that you have taken time management courses and reviewed ways to improve your use of time. Everyone should make an effort to improve their time management skills at least once a year, but it is better to do this quarterly.

Leaders Make Time Every Day

Plan, prioritize and schedule leadership time.

At this point, you are probably wondering, "How do I make this time? My boss/colleagues/customers will never give me that time!" I have news for you. You're right. No one will ever give you that time. You must take that time from somewhere in your already busy schedule.

There is a difference, however, between planning time and scheduling time. When we say "scheduling time," we mean actually marking the time on your calendar and considering it as taken. You should treat this time as if you were meeting with the most important person on the planet (you!). This is nondiscretionary time, during which you should have no other choices about how you are going to spend it.

The following graphic shows a great leadership week. You can see that the leader has scheduled time for leadership tasks before the week begins. Here you can see leadership time is scheduled every day of the week, and most of the time is scheduled during his or her peak productivity time. This kind of schedule is an objective to strive for, as it is difficult to achieve this kind of productivity at the beginning. This kind of performance often takes practice. As Zig Ziglar says, "if something is worth doing, it is worth doing poorly until you can do it well."

Optimal Productivity Work Week

	Mon	Tues	Wed	Thurs	Fri	Sat
7:00 AM						
8:00 AM		Prep Time	Wed Meeting		Prep Time	Prep Time
	Prep Time	Power		Prep Time	Power	Power
9:00 AM	Power	Productivity	Prep Time	Power	Productivity	Productivity
	Productivity	Time	Power	Productivity	Time	Time
10:00 AM	Time	Block	Productivity	Time	Block	Block
	Block		Time	Block		
11:00 AM			Block			
12:00 PM				Appointment		
1:00 PM	Lunch	Lunch	Lunch	Lunch	Lunch	
2:00 PM						
			To Do		To Do	
3:00 PM		Meeting	Project	To Do	Project	
	To Do		#2	Project	#5	
4:00 PM	Project			#3		
	#1					
5:00 PM						
6:00 PM						
7:00 PM						
8:00 PM						

Figure 1. Example of a Power Productivity week. (I have included Saturday because in Hong Kong, where I live, most people work five and a half days a week.)

Leaders look at scheduling productivity blocks on their to-do lists as essential parts of their day. One leader told me that doing this was a reflection of her leadership ability. This means that the more time you make to be a leader, the better leader you will be. This is what it takes to be a leader. If you don't make the time, nothing will change. If you change nothing, are you really a leader?

Defend your productive block of leadership time.

There are times when you have to set aside time for your productive block, but there are also times when you will need to defend the productive block against interruptions once you're working. This can be one of the most challenging steps in becoming a leader.

One of your primary defenses is learning to say "no" to others' requests for your time. One day, I was giving a friend a ride to work. She was about to chaperone eighty students at Disneyland for a two-day, two-night "Senior Grad Night" celebration. During the entire fifteen-minute ride to her school, she kept saying "no!" When I asked her what she was doing, she said she was practicing her "no's". "For what?" I asked. She said she knew the students would ask for more than she was able to authorize and she was preparing to be stern without being overbearing. The lesson: practice saying "no" out loud.

How do you say "no" tactfully and skillfully? There are several ways, but the important thing is to practice. Let's say you have practiced and it still doesn't go well. Do what you did when you were learning how to ride a bike. Get back on and try it again. If saying "no" doesn't work the first time, keep trying until you find a way that works. Then you will have to keep trying new ways, because others will now be ready to counter what you said the last time.

I'd like to suggest an effective, five-step process for saying "no." Again, as with all the tools I give you in this chapter, you will have to vary your style and see what works best for you.

> 1) Say "no" quickly and firmly. It is easier to say, "I found some time to help you" than to say, "Sorry, I know I said I may have some time to help you, but..." If you say "no" all the time, however, you are not seen as a leader.

> 2) Thank the other person for asking you. Say, "Thank you for asking me to help" or "I appreciate your thinking of me."

3) Reaffirm that you cannot help the other person by saying, "…but I cannot help."

4) Account for your time or priorities. This may seem like you are making excuses, so be careful.

5) Become a consultant and help the other person brainstorm for alternative solutions.

The most important steps are the first and last. Say "no" first so that others won't think that you can help. The last step is important because when you say "no," you become the "bad" person, but when you are helping others solve their problems, you are now a consultant who is on their side. Remember to not be too helpful or take too much time, or they will see that you really could have helped them with their requests.

Here are some other ways you can say "no":

- "I cannot help you, but why don't you try Joe down the hall."
- "I am overcommitted right now, but I am sure you can find someone who will be more effective than me."
- "I have a meeting/task/project, so I cannot help."
- "Thank you for showing confidence in me, but I cannot help you."

You might also try using "Yes, but later" language.

- "I will be finished with this project in two hours and would love to help you then."
- "Thank you very much; I will start on it in two hours."
- "This priority I am working on will take two hours. Can you come back to me then?"
- "I am really busy right now. Please send me an e-mail and I will get back to you in two hours."
- "I can do that for you. Looking at my schedule, I can have that done by the end of the day."
- "Right now, I am working on X. Can I get back to you in two hours?"

Remember that most definitions of leadership all have a communications component. Many people think they can communicate well, but most of the time this is not true. One must practice one's communication skills over and over to truly be effective. At the beginning of my career, I led public speaking training for Dale Carnegie and Associates in San Francisco and have taught and coached public speaking ever since. People often ask me what they need to do to become effective communicators. The conversation usually goes something like this:

Q: What do I need to become an effective speaker?
A: Practice.
Q: I know that, but what else do I need to do?
A: Along with practice, the second most important thing to do is practice more.
Q: I know, I know, but can you tell me what I must do to be a really good communicator?
A: In addition to practice and practice more, you need to practice even more.

My Tai Chi instructor told me once that if people were not willing to practice the foundations of Tai Chi, he was not willing to show them additional postures, because these people do not want to become great at a foundational level (a house is only as strong as its foundation). Learning new postures instead of perfecting foundation moves is like trying to dig a well by digging many shallow holes in many different places. To dig a well, you need to dig straight down until you hit water. In this case, effective communication is your foundation, so keep practicing.

Take a communications class and read as many books on the subject as possible. Most important, though, is to practice using new words and being persuasive. These two skills do not come naturally to many people. Some think, "You either have these skills or you don't." This is nonsense. Great persuaders make time to practice. If someone is stopping you from getting your work done, it is time to be a leader and persuade him or her not to interrupt you. My suggestion is to keep improving your relationship skills, your crisis management skills and your negotiation skills.

It is important to manage relationships just as you would manage a bank account or a company budget. If you don't keep a balance on the account or keep track of your budget, neither the bank nor the company will give you any more money. Likewise, if you are giving support, guidance, development and positive assistance to others, they usually will give you the things you need. Sometimes all you need is for them to wait a couple of hours before you help them with their requests.

Use Your Time to Achieve Your Most Productive Work

How do you transform your time from simply productive into highly productive?

What time of day are you at your best? Can you remember the last time you were in that highly productive state where you were challenged yet still getting things done? Can you recall completing your work and afterwards saying to yourself, "I feel good"?

Leaders set aside time to work on their most important projects, usually the time of day when they are at their best. This is their prime time. Most people have one, two or sometimes three peak productivity times each day. Because only one of these times is actually your best productivity period, you want to set aide that time to do your best work.

According to research conducted by Mihaly Csikszentmihalyi, when we are completely engaged in an activity, our life fulfillment improves, and we experience higher levels of motivation, satisfaction and activation. This state of awareness is called "flow" because people in this state describe their minds' and bodies' activities as being so automatic that they seem to be flowing. Also, when people are totally submerged in their work or other tasks, they forget about the world around them.

This state may only last for a few seconds, or it may last much longer, but those who experience it describe finding peace in the projects they are doing. The key is in being challenged enough to be totally involved in an activity. The challenge must be sufficient for you to not be bored but not so challenging that you become frustrated.

There are four states of productivity: optimal, anxiety, boredom and apathy. The optimal condition is when the skills and challenges are both above average. The anxiety condition is when one's skills are not able to handle the challenges presented by the task. The boredom condition occurs when one's skills are greater than the challenges presented by the task. The apathy condition is where neither one's skills nor the challenges are up to the task.

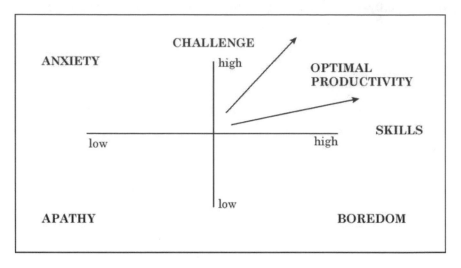

Figure 2. Simple Model of Optimal Productivity (adapted from Flow in Sports by Jackson and Csikszentmihalyi).

When challenges and skills were matched and at their highest, participants in Csikszentmihalyi's studies reported that their positive sense of self, or their self-esteem, was also highest. The researcher found that because increases in challenges and skills seemed to precede feelings of improved self-esteem, we need to develop skills and face challenges first. Also, the findings suggested that this increase in self-esteem made the individuals in the studies strive for more high-challenge, high-skill situations, creating a cyclical effect of feeling good and wanting to do better.

The research shows that it takes twenty to thirty minutes for most people to achieve their optimal level of performance. This highly productive state lasts for about two hours, after which time we start to fall off in productivity. If you let yourself get interrupted during that first twenty minutes, you will have to start over and take extra time to get back to your peak state of performance. It takes warm-up time to be at your best.

Let's look at the four keys to making your time highly productive:

1) Plan ahead to stay in your peak productivity state.

It takes planning to make sure you can use your productivity block to achieve your best results. Take a few minutes before you begin your project. Look at your priority tasks and make sure you have all the materials you need before you start with your project. Have different sub-projects ready in case you hit a snag. You can even break your productivity time into several plans.

Plan A: You start to develop a plan to improve your time usage in the office. After fifteen minutes, you realize that you need a productivity report from your boss, Sally. Instead of interrupting your power productivity time, you go to...

Plan B: Now you switch to using the reflective thinking process (this is outlined on page 66) to find a way to improve the communications between your department and the accounting department. Your employees are being interrupted by accounting several times a day to answer questions. You work through the process, develop three possible solutions and outline the actions needed to get the solutions implemented. Now you have twenty-five minutes left, so you go straight to...

Plan C: You know that you need to negotiate with your employees more effectively, so you pull out your book on negotiation skills and practice (by saying the words out loud) language that will help your employees feel that they have won concessions, yet also feel happy to do everything you ask.

2) Make sure you have no interruptions.

Allow absolutely, positively *no* interruptions. Every time you are interrupted, you have to start over to get into that peak productivity state. Am I saying that if you have a short interruption you cannot get back into the your peak state? No, but it most often takes a while.

When I worked as a human resources clerk in a law firm, I thought I was a great employee, because I would drop what I was doing to help anyone who came to me with a question. It didn't matter that it wasn't my job. It got to the point that everyone seemed to come to me because they new they could get my help. However, I found that I was not doing my job and was getting nothing done. I had to learn how to say "no" to others and make them feel happy that I could not help them. I wasn't so good at this at first, and even many years later, I am still perfecting this skill.

Some of you are thinking that there is no way that you can get one to two hours of uninterrupted time in your office. But I have seen clients who sit in meetings and do absolutely nothing for two hours and then say, "I can't leave the office to get two hours of work done." Often, I see executives work late because in the evening (when no one else is around), they can get more done than they do all day long. Sometimes, you might have to get out of the office to stop the interruptions. Of course, I am assuming that leaders will actually work on their most important projects when they're out of the office and not run errands or do other non-priority tasks.

Where can you go? In my seminars, people share very creative ideas about where they go to get work done. You could go to a coffee shop, a conference room, an empty office, the library, a park or the custodian's closet (if the custodian works at night). What if you can't get out of the office? Then practice your communication skills, to help others feel happy about leaving you alone.

3) Start small and measure your progress.

I often see people get really excited about their peak productivity time. They make comments like, "I am going to start this tomorrow and make two hours a day for the rest of the year." However, I advise starting small, working for just thirty minutes at first. Then work up to your peak time of one to two hours.

It is also important to know where you are as you are involved in your task. Think of it as knowing score. But while it is important to know the score, you shouldn't spend too much time thinking about the score.

What do the following people have in common when they are at their best? Michael Schumacher, when he is driving his Formula-1 race car. Serena Williams, when she is playing tennis. Tiger Woods, when he is playing golf. I know, these leaders have many traits in common. When they are at their best they all know their position or the score yet they have all of their attention focused on the activity that brings them to their goal.

They must concentrate all of their attention on the ball or what they are doing and not think about the score, or else they will miss the next corner, the ball, or their next shot. You must learn to do the same when you are working in your highly productive moment.

To be most effective, you want to make score keeping rules that fit your life and help you be productive. What do I mean by rules? For example, I have kept track of my time in quarter-hour increments for almost nine years now. Based on my history, I know that I will be inaccurate in my time estimates about ten percent of the time. With this in mind, I have a goal that I will complete five, ten-hour days every week (after ten hours, I find I don't get much else done). Since I know I am usually ten percent off, I work about fifty-five hours a week to allow for inaccurate estimations of my time.

There are two areas where you will want to keep score. First, keep track of the work you do during your power productivity periods, and second, keep track of how many hours per week you can achieve in your power periods. An example score would be, "This week, I had four days with one uninterrupted hour per day."

If my goal was to get five hours this week, my score would be eighty percent. Another example would be, "I finished two and a half of my three projects this week, so I give myself eighty-three percent." If you are working on a creative project, you may want to judge yourself by working for the entire two hours without an interruption. This may give you a one hundred percent score, whereas working for one and a half hours will only give you an eighty percent score.

Make the rules obvious so you can give yourself instant feedback. They are not intended to put pressure on you but to give you guidance. The old saying goes, "You can't win if you don't know how much time is on the clock."

Have your own personal self-rewards ready, and give them to yourself after you finish. In her book *Get Clients Now!*, C.J. Hayden reminds us that we need to have a reward and that we need to be able to accept that reward when we accomplish a task. Rewards might include that double scoop of ice cream or that whole milk mocha with regular espresso (this is big if you normally have low-fat, decaf latte.) If you have completed eighty percent of your goal for the entire month, give your self a golf lesson. One client I was working with told me that for every month she met eighty percent of her productivity goal, she gave herself one day at Disneyland with her kids.

When I was young, I was on a bowling team. After our weekly match, we added our scores and averaged them with the our previous scores to see if we had performed better or worse than before. This can also be a valuable tool to help you see how you are doing when it comes to making time for your power productivity periods. This will give you a target to beat.

For example, every month, try to double the number of hours per week you spend in your power productivity periods. You can also average the amount of work you complete. Sometimes, this will be very subjective; you may just have to choose a number between zero and ten every week and average the results over a period of weeks. Or you can average the number of interruptions you have during your productivity period, which will give you a lower target to shoot for the next time.

4) Keep yourself positive and be around positive, productive people.

What can you do to stay positive and improve your power time average? When you are in your moment of power productivity, concentrate only on what you are doing and what comes next. The mind has a tendency to wander, so let go of that idea that just came up, or quickly write it down so you can let go of it and get back to work. Remember that only you have the power to make changes in your life. It takes personal initiative to change your attitude to one of success.

What to do:
- Find better ways to be productive.
- Reduce the number of steps needed to complete a project.
- See items or concepts in a new way.
- Take charge and stop the boss (the customer) from stopping you.

What not to do:
- Do not let go of your positive attitude and self-discipline.
- Do not let anyone interrupt you.
- Don't get emotional if, right away, you are not able to restructure your time and use it to work on your highest priority.

Try to only be around people who maintain control of their time and demonstrate leadership qualities. Stay away from those who complain about not having time to get things done; these are people who let time lead them. People tend to rise to their peer group's level of expectation, so surround yourself with those who have positive attitudes.

Work on Your Highest Priorities

At any given moment of any day, a leader can tell you exactly what the most important items on his/her to-do list are. So how do you, as a leader, decide which are your most important priorities? After all, this is one of the most important decisions you have to make, whether it's in your business, your family, your church or any other community organization.

As with anything in life, if you plan your route, follow your plan and make adjustments as you go, you will successfully arrive at your destination. In business, your destination is improving the processes, systems and products within your company; planning your route involves learning how to set time management priorities in your everyday tasks and communicating those priorities to the rest of the organization.

In my project management seminars, I talk about the three drivers that control our lives: time, money and quality. Conventional wisdom says that you can only choose two at a time. For example, I tell the participants in my seminars that they can have the work done fast, they can have it done inexpensively, or they can have the work done with high quality. But they may only choose two; they cannot have all three.

Let's use money as a more specific example. Everyone says they would love to win the lottery, but most people who have won the lottery would tell you that instantly receiving a large amount of money makes life much more difficult. Yes, they have that grand, euphoric feeling at first, but after that feeling wears off, they usually end up in more debt and feeling less happy than they were before they won the money. In fact, surveys of lottery winners and paraplegics reveal no differences in happiness levels between the groups, one year after the event. Don't get me wrong; I want to win the lottery, but I know that with that money comes a lot of responsibility.

The lesson is that winning the lottery might satisfy one's time and money concerns, but it won't necessarily result in a higher quality of life. On the other hand, when people take time to learn from other wealthy people how to deal with money, they develop a respect and appreciation for their money, and they seem to have a much higher quality of life. Remember drivers effect priorities.

I should also take a moment to point out what priorities are *not*. A priority is not something urgent that just comes up—the colleague/boss/report who comes into your office and demands your attention. Often, we drop what we are doing because it makes us feel important. Ask yourself, is it more important to help someone with a problem or to develop a system that will prevent the problem from happening again? Leaders spend their most important time preventing problems from happening. Followers spend their most important time solving problems.

Priorities are also not the dust bunnies under your desk or the filing that you have been putting off or something that you've known was coming for the last three weeks and "suddenly" needs your attention. This is called procrastination, which likewise will not help you make a better work environment or improve your life.

Finally, priorities are not "busy work." We often have projects that keep us busy but do not improve our lives or the lives of others. These projects make us feel comfortable, and we know the rules and challenges. The problem, however, is that we are not improving anything. A few characteristics of busy work:

- We know the rules.
- We know it is a priority.
- We are organized when we do it.
- We have self-discipline when we do it.
- It does not make us or our lives any more efficient.
- It takes our time away from improving the system.
- It makes us think, "This is the way we have always done it."
- It causes others to say, "This is the way you should be doing it."
- It makes us feel good.

The important point to remember—busy work is not a priority. Do busy work when you are not in your most productive time of day. Also, do it when you think you will be interrupted because it is easier to get into the flow of busy work.

I remember when I was working for the accounting department of a particular organization. One of my projects was to complete a weekly report. When I left the firm, they decided not to replace my position. What happened to that report? The boss decided that she did not need it any longer. But if she didn't need it after I left, then why did she need it while I was there? Had she just been giving me busy work?

When determining whether a task is busy work or not, ask yourself, "Do I really need this?" If the answer is "no" or "I *might* need this *someday*," then stop doing it, unless there are legal or safety reasons for continuing the project.

Genuine priorities can be grouped into categories: top tier, second tier, third tier and fourth tier. These projects should be split according to the 20/80 rule. Twenty percent of the time you should be doing the top tier projects that will have eighty percent of the impact, the ones that will change you or your work or will make the world better for someone else. Therefore, at least one day a week should be spent working on top tier projects. And only *one* project at a time can be the most important; if you finish that one, then the rest of your block is free for planning your next projects.

1) Top tier leadership projects include:
- Planning and refining vision, mission and values for you or your organization
- Being creative and doing what you dreamed of, things that people have successfully done in different areas of application, things that people tell you can't be done
- Improving systems to slash the overall time or costs required to complete a project or increasing the quality of the output
- Developing or updating your goals
- Changing the outcomes you had planned in the past that no longer seem realistic
- Finding solutions to problems when others have said, "This can't be changed"
- Increasing your passion for being a great leader. Passion for leadership is like a muscle; the more you flex it, the stronger it gets. If you don't flex your muscles, they waste away.
- Increasing your passion (like developing a muscle) for improving the organization or the systems within the organization
- Creating systems that decrease the amount of work or the time taken to do the work

2) Second tier leadership projects include:
- Developing your purpose
- Developing the value of the new systems
- Determining the benefits of improving and streamlining

3) Third tier leadership projects include:
- Practicing and improving your leadership skills
- Practicing your communications skills
- Developing communication programs
- Practicing and preparing to sell your ideas
- Recognition planning

4) Fourth tier leadership projects include:

- Implementation planning for new projects
- Delegation planning
- Collaboration planning
- Resource planning

As I said before, your priority projects improve a process, product quality or cost effectiveness. Projects on which you should not focus your highly productive leadership include:

- What others have told you to do or assigned to you.
- Tasks that fit the description, "This is the way we have always done it."
- Things that won't make an improvement/difference in yours or others' lives

But what if you don't know how to solve the problem or improve the system? John Dewey, a leading educator and philosopher, developed a great method of reflective thinking. Although he developed the method many years ago, it still works today. I have modified it slightly to suit the business improvement environment.

1. Clearly define the improvement you want to make or the problem you want to solve.
2. Brainstorm to create a list of needs for making the improvement or solving the problem.
3. Brainstorm to create a list of possible solutions for the improvement or the problem.
4. Select the best possible solution or solutions.
5. Create an implementation plan. Also anticipate what may stop implementation of the solution so you can be ready for the problems that will inevitability arise.
6. Take action to implement the plan.
7. Gather feedback as you take action and determine what is working and what is not working.
8. Adjust your plan based on the feedback you receive from your actions. This may mean that you will need to return to step number one and start over.

The natural tendency is to jump ahead to step four and come up with a solution. By starting with the first step, however, you can have a better understanding of the problem. By going all the way though step eight, you can be sure the problem is solved. When I first learned this method, I thought it took too long, but soon it became a habit to think this way every time things didn't seem to work or didn't work as well as I would have liked.

To be a leader remember to:
1. Make time for your leadership priorities every day.
2. Use that time to achieve your best, most productive work.
3. Work on your highest leadership priority.

Dr. Warren Linger

Warren Linger has been recognized as an outstanding professional trainer and speaker who evokes passionate responses from those attending his seminars and workshops throughout the world. Warren's involving, motivating, entertaining, interactive, and dynamic presentations are filled with high impact, useful information designed to give solid direction and help to those who want help achieving higher levels of success and leadership in their lives. Being an architect who created an international training and speaking firm, Warren understands that everyone has different needs. Warren has devoted his life to learning understanding and developing ways to help individuals and organizations achieve ultimate experiences in achieving their goals and dreams.

Dr. Warren Linger
World Class Value Training and Speaking
Linger Research International, Inc.
606 Kinwick Centre
32 Hollywood Road
Central, Hong Kong
Direct +852 2854-2720
www.linger-research.com

Chapter Four

STRATEGIC LEADERSHIP STARTS IN THE HEART

Patti Branco

The world stands in awe of those with the ability to lead. Leaders capture our minds and imaginations, often becoming celebrities for their life's work, despite humble beginnings.

Consider Mother Teresa, who devoted herself to serving the poor. Through her example, the "angel of Calcutta" left an unmatched legacy of love and compassion, touching millions of lives for good.

Colin Powell, raised in utter poverty, rose through the ranks of the military and government service. Driven by a deep desire to make a difference for his family and for the world, he has become one of the most respected leaders in the world.

Leaders raise the bar for their professions. They shatter previously held expectations and limitations.

Vince Lombardi, for instance, set the standard of excellence among coaches, possessing a desire to win like no other. The most prized trophy in professional football bears his name, a lasting tribute to his accomplishments.

President George W. Bush moved beyond privilege to a life of service, motivated by an undaunted passion for this wonderful land we call home and by his faith in God and his family.

Are Leaders Born or Made?

Leaders like the ones above differ from one another in countless ways. But they share a common feature: profound passion. Leaders own their passion and make no apologies or excuses for their deeply-rooted convictions. They are fervent about their missions, and those missions drive them.

Can this passion be developed? Or do leaders emerge from the tender protection of their mother's womb with a destiny to lead ingrained in their DNA?

I believe leaders are born and made. While the necessary ingredients to lead may already be deep inside each of us, these innate leadership skills can be unleashed with the proper care.

Leaders Close to Home

Whom do you know that demonstrates strong leadership? Is it a boss, a friend or a family member? Who seems to enjoy a Pied Piper-like charisma that moves others to action effortlessly and positively?

Imagine having the ability to manage a work team with enthusiasm and a commitment to your goal. Think about the problems that could be resolved when a group pulls together behind a respected and powerful leader. It is possible, and this chapter will share some proven methods of developing leadership and management skills.

The Fallacy of Leadership Training

Corporate boardrooms are abuzz with the benefits of leadership training. But leadership training alone does not create effective leaders. Only when you combine it with management skill development will you likely achieve the results you seek—namely employee retention, job satisfaction, loyalty and increased productivity.

Leadership, after all, is the frosting on the cake of competent managing skills. Don't believe it? Ask yourself the following question: Can a successful, organized and competent manager survive without leadership attributes? Most definitely. Can a dynamic and charismatic leader prevail in a corporate setting without management skills? Usually not.

Managers vs. Leaders

To help my clients grasp the difference between a manager and a leader, and to determine where they or their team members fit on the "leadership scale," I often ask them the following questions:

When you walk into a room of your direct reports, do they suddenly become quiet, or do they enthusiastically invite you to join in the conversation?

If invited in, you are more of a leader than a boss!

When you have a tough goal or deadline, do your team members get behind you and make it happen, or do you sense that they secretly hope you fail?

A competent leader will always have the full support of his staff!

Do you manage based on your own style, or do you make it a point to really understand your people before deciding on a management strategy?

A leader cares and is sensitive to the needs of her people.

Are you tough but fair? Structured, but flexible?

Strong leadership means more than being a "nice person."

Do you go by the book but freely explain the consequences of not doing so?

Rules are important; communication is equally so.

Do you understand that your responsibility to manage or lead a team does not include the luxury of liking or disliking anyone, that you must treat everyone the same?

Without absolute fairness, you can't even consider yourself a leader.

Developing Management Skills

Being a competent manager paves the way to becoming a powerful leader. Competence begins with knowing what needs to be accomplished and not playing favorites. Some managers are overly concerned with being liked. This desire inevitably impedes their ability to lead and manage effectively. Likability is often confused with leadership qualities. But you will never please everyone all of the time. Pandering to this natural insecurity will make you appear weak and malleable. Period. Accept that and move on. (You are entitled to respect, but that is earned rather than demanded.)

The first step in developing management skills is to ensure that your actions are governed by integrity. The commitment to integrity results in a comfort level that allows flexibility. Why? If you avoid the slightest perception of impropriety, your reputation as one who takes the high road will precede you. Cut corners and bend too many rules or be inconsistent in your values, and you will be on the company radar screen as a loose cannon, someone to be watched—or worse, phased out.

Becoming a Top-Notch Manager

Managing is not about power but effectiveness. To be a successful manager, you need to keep your ego in check and learn everything needed about the rules governing human resources. This includes regulations issued by your state, city and, most importantly, your firm; your firm may interpret the state and federal rules differently, either more strictly or more leniently, as companies often prefer to add their own spin.

Bear in mind that if you have been promoted through the ranks, you may need mentoring to learn what you need to know as a manager. Here are other methods of developing the skills of a top-notch manager:

- Research company policy by reading the employee handbook. This is an often-overlooked tactic for becoming a better manager.
- Learn about the senior team and what is most important to them. Companies, like families, have different cultures and goals. Make sure they know you, too. Be warm and outgoing when meeting in the halls or elevators.
- Learn how to recruit talent and how to interview appropriately. Improper interviewing and the selection process as a whole seem to be ever-expanding sources of lawsuits. If protection of your firm is tops on your list, you will be highly valued by your superiors.
- Make sure you dress the part, that your hair and grooming is consistent with what is acceptable in your firm. Your manners should reflect good breeding. A major recording studio might have different expectations than a private bank. Know the score!
- Be on time, use time management techniques effectively, and keep an organized work area. Maintain accurate records and files.

- Communicate like a pro. Use handwritten thank-you notes whenever the opportunity arises. Be sensitive to the support staff and everyone else you encounter. Use e-mail and communication software to the maximum extent possible, especially if your firm has made a significant investment in technology. Block time each day to reach out with through various methods, including phone, fax and voice mail messages.
- Learn something new every day, and read a book a month, minimum. Don't stagnate. Grow, blossom and move through your career with increasing finesse and confidence.
- Keep a journal and encourage your direct reports to do the same. At the end of the day, spend ten minutes wrapping up thoughts and ideas that were sidelined during the day.
- When times are tough, be mindful of the timeless advice I once received from Deborah Bernot, my mentor and boss for many years and the president and leader of a $30 billion bank investment program. She reminded me, "Light always shines in the darkness." In my darker moments, that comment was my strength. I learned many years later that it was biblical.

Attending Leadership University

Once you establish competence as a manger, it is time to work on your leadership skills. Remember, everything you need is inside.

The first thing to do is examine how you view your people. It's important to know your people are and what's important to them. Satisfied employees will provide the wind for your sails.

This is where the adage, "God gave you two ears and one mouth," is critical. Be a good listener. Fight the urge to interrupt and make early comments.

Fairness isn't always easy to accomplish. As humans, we often tend to like some people more than others. Departing from the luxury of selection based on personal taste is the earmark of a great leader.

If I asked you today about your top people, how much could you tell me? Pick your most valued employee, and try to answer the following questions about her (or him):

- What is important to her? Does she have kids to pick up after school? Is she concerned with her job performance?
- Where did she work before coming to your firm? Where does she live? How long is her commute every day?

- Is she caring for a sick parent? Does she have a handi-capped child?
- Is she happy, sad or indifferent?
- What does she do in her leisure time?
- Does she rent or own a home?
- Are her children good students? Are she and her spouse try-ing to have children and can't?
- What does she look like, and could you describe her accu-rately?
- What kind of car does she drive?
- What music does she like?
- What is her favorite sport?
- When is her birthday?

Now run through the same exercise using your least favorite em-ployee. Did you know the answers? The first step in effective leader-ship is to know who your people are and what motivates them. The second step is to effectively utilize the information you glean for eve-ryone's benefit.

Many questions—like marital status, sexual orientation, age, etc.—cannot be legally asked; however, it is acceptable to learn this information through the course of normal conversation as long as you don't use any of it to discriminate in any way.

For instance, suppose someone confided in you that she was try-ing desperately to become pregnant. If that confidential information influenced your decision to promote her or led to a negative conse-quence for the employee, you would likely be in violation of federal law, putting both you and your firm at serious risk.

Building a Team That Views You as a Leader

The following exercise is one of the most enjoyable aspects of de-veloping leadership; it gives you instant rewards and sets the direc-tion for your new goals.

Plan a meeting for a day when everyone who works for you can attend. Have a nice lunch brought in and do a few extra things to make it special. This is not a meeting to convey negative news or any-thing remotely uncomfortable.

Open the meeting by announcing your plan to become a better manager, to learn more about them and to build a stronger team. De-clare your desire to accept all input, both positive and negative.

Plan a couple of team-building exercises that will foster relation-ships among team members. One method is to pair them off and instruct one person to interview the other. Select three things in advance—such as favorite movie, secret passion, most admired person, etc.— that each interviewer should learn about his partner. After the first group is finished, ask everyone to switch roles. When all the team members have been interviewed, ask each person to stand and give a three-minute talk on the co-worker he or she interviewed. The idea is to get them talking to one another. Another fun game is to ask everyone to bring a baby picture, post the photos on a board and have a "Guess Who This Is" activity. That is always a fun team builder.

The Essential Moment of Truth

In order to improve as a leader, it's essential to solicit feedback from your reports. This requires bravery and nerves of steel. At some point in your team meeting, pull a flip chart to the center of the room and select a leader for this exercise. Announce to the group that you are going to leave the room so they can talk about you. Ask them to make a list of things on the flip chart that you could do better. Tell them that this is their chance to vent and speak honestly. Encourage them not to seek approval by writing complimentary things. Also, remind them not to list things that are out of your control but to focus on things that you can change.

After about forty-five minutes, return to the meeting and spend time going over the results. Resist the urge to be defensive. It is such a natural reaction, especially if something that you do has been misunderstood. You will have plenty of time to work this out later.

At the end of the meeting, open your appointment book and schedule one-on-one meetings—over lunch, if possible—with every direct report. During each meeting, plan to complete the get-to-know-you exercise and raise a couple of points brought up when you were out of the room.

When making one-on-one field or office visits, use a notebook to record everything you can about each person—from birthday to favorite sports to music—after his or her respective meeting. Make a page for each employee and keep it updated. They will be amazed that you are keeping track of things and showing a personal interest.

This notebook need not be kept a secret if it makes you uncomfortable to do so, and it should never contain anything illegal or private. It is a journal for you to remember the important things in a conversation and to guarantee follow-up. I have always preferred to keep my notes private; it is your choice.

When you know your direct reports well enough to answer the questions listed earlier, you are truly on your way to becoming a leader.

Intuition Is A Gift

Emotional Intelligence starts with recognizing how emotions affect our actions. Daniel Goleman, one of the leading researchers in the field of emotional intelligence, asserts that the rational mind takes a moment or two longer to register and respond than the emotional mind. The first impulse, he claims, is in the heart, not the head.

If Goleman is correct, then shouldn't our intuition serve us well in all situations? I think intuition is always there to guide us, and I have personally experienced this. As a manager seeking solutions, logic would often override my intuition in an important decision. Later, reflecting on the outcome, the discarded instinctive response may have afforded a better solution. I am certain that if you ponder this, you will realize that it has probably happened for you, too.

I have used my emotional intelligence throughout my career, even before it became a buzzword. As a successful manager of an investment program in a $30 billion bank, my good fortune and effective management were often attributed to the fact that I was female. I always had a vision, to the point of being called a dreamer.

Vision is what inspires us, say James A. Belasco and Ralph C. Stayer, authors of a 1993 leadership book called *Flight of the Buffalo.* They stated that "Long-term successful companies stand for more than just profit and big salaries." Sounds like emotional intelligence to me.

I was part of a management team that consisted of eleven people (one for each state in our territory). I was the only woman and the number one manager not only in sales but also in employee retention and customer satisfaction scores. They often teased me about having "the woman's touch" or a "good gut" when explaining my successful recruiting.

Years later, I realized that my intuition had always served me well when it came to hiring, firing and retention. Intuition and emotional intelligence guided my coaching and training as well as my decisions on whether or not to give raises or promotions. Emotional Intelligence helped me know when to be extra sensitive and when to increase pressure. It has served me well on every project I have encountered. In fact, the only complaint that ever showed on my annual review was that I often reacted based on feelings rather than facts but that there was also no harm done in the process.

Through the years, our firm performed studies such as left brain vs. right brain, Herman brain tests and DiSC. In all of these, I was assessed as right brained, a creative thinker, spiritual and less logical than the rest. Yet I won awards for leadership, remained a top performer and was enthusiastically engaged in the welfare of my team. I was a puzzle. It was my intuition, also, that made me realize the importance of being a competent manager as well as a spirited leader. Instinct encouraged me to seek mentoring and knowledge whenever and wherever it was available.

This hallmark of my ability to lead will live forever in my heart. When I finally decided to head out on my own, my entire team held a going away dinner in my honor. I was surprised to see every single employee there. As I left to pull out of the parking lot, my convertible top down to accommodate all the flowers I received, there they were on the corner, in downtown San Francisco, singing "Happy Trails to You," oblivious to the group of onlookers that had gathered.

You probably guessed that I cried all the way home. What else would you expect from an emotionally intelligent manager?

Recognizing Your Inner Leader

We all have intuition, feelings and perceptions. Successful people often engage this gift without realizing it exists.

Leadership requires a total activation of our hearts. As I said before, leadership is frosting on the cake of competence. Leadership from the heart makes life easier and more enjoyable. Your team will support you, walk on hot coals for you and cover your back. If you are a dynamic leader, you will find immense pleasure in your work, higher value in people and less stress in your life.

Heart-centered leadership involves tuning into feelings that may be buried, especially for men (sorry, guys). Men are taught to be tough; women, gentle. Although the Baby Boomer generation is a more sensitive lot, there is still a lot of machismo in the male corporate world.

Leadership, like managerial competence, demands fairness in all things. To achieve fairness, a leader must have an open mind and be a good listener. A leader is able to care and routinely practices the Golden Rule. A leader gives credit to the team and reciprocates with communication, recognition and advancement.

Make it a point to read up on emotional intelligence. Dig deep within yourself and objectively study who you are. List your strengths and weaknesses. Ask friends and colleagues to describe them also. Do their assessments of you resemble your self-assessments?

Remember to trust your intuition; it is the greatest gift, and it is there to guide you.

A Word on Navigating Human Resources

It is interesting how many "human" resource departments deal with the duties of their world as though there weren't a human being in sight. HR can become a labyrinth of rules and regulations, interpretations of the law and administration of the company policies and procedures. Along the way, the people for whom the policies were created are forgotten.

Human resource departments are usually involved in every aspect of your day-to-day activities as a manager—from hiring practices to the company picnic, from the first advertisement for an employee to the termination of a top performer who has been the subject of praise for the past several years.

Yes, you need to be certain that you follow personnel policies in place and comply with all state and federal regulations. You also need to make sure that your managers and direct reports have the knowledge and the skills needed to act on your behalf and in the best interests of the employees and of the firm, thereby avoiding awkward and litigious situations.

Bear in mind that your human resource department is concerned with the following:

- Are employment contracts and agreements thorough and consistent?
- Is there an employee manual, and is it required reading for all new employees?
- Is your compensation plan profitable for you and for the retention of quality help?
- Are job descriptions clear and specific?
- Are consequences for not meeting those requirements spelled out and enforced fairly and professionally, in writing?
- Are performance reviews done regularly and uniformly?
- Are retirement plans and benefits available?
- Is there a written vacation policy?

One might wonder: With all of this detail regarding administration, how can leadership be engaged? By aligning yourself with your firm's HR department and educating your people as to why it is important, you gain legitimacy and credibility. Both are essential for strong leadership.

Avoid Miscommunication

Make sure you speak the language. I had often referred to the aforementioned attitude of compliance as "carrying the company banner." One time, a new employee called me about three days after a meeting and said that she had looked high and low but was unable to locate this company banner. She then asked if I could direct her to one. Although we both had a good laugh, it was a reminder to make sure we were all speaking the same language.

I once worked on a project where everything discussed regarding HR was offered with a wink or a rolling of the eyes. The manager referred to HR as "they." This only made the manager look small and the employees disrespectful and confused. Embrace your company culture and convey that to your team. They will fall in step and emulate your own positive attitude.

As for using your emotional intelligence when hiring and recruiting, how can you not have a feeling one way or another about a candidate? Simply incorporate those feelings into your decision making without overlooking the proper HR processes. It is possible to use all of your talents when selecting a candidate.

A good leadership tack when hiring is to make sure the person being considered will fit in with the rest of the group by bringing the team into the interview process. Have a couple of your top people do a second interview. This will serve two purposes: It will make them feel important and capable of assisting you, and it will help you to identify a worthy candidate.

Dealing in the intuitive world can create problems with the black and white world of HR; and vise versa. There is not a lot of room to negotiate in this area, but there is always a place for instinct used correctly and wisely.

Utilizing Recognition and Rewards

The best motivator is recognition. Finding people doing something well and making a big deal about it is the cheapest and fastest way to increase performance. I once worked for a firm that only sent out a sales report at the end of the month. On report day, everyone was either jubilant or embarrassed, but by the next day, it was all over.

I immediately started reporting weekly, then daily. I made positive notes to the people leading the pack and never criticized those at the bottom. Seeing their names last was reminder enough that they had work to do. I sent voice mail broadcasts out to announce the top five people and to further publicize the results. This turned out to be a method that immediately increased business.

Privately, I would write encouraging notes on reports to those struggling saying, "I know you are having a bad month. Let me know if I can help out." Or "This is better than last month. Keep it going!"

Each and every one of us has a child inside, and it can be fun to let the kid out to play. My office manager used happy face stickers and all sorts of little stamps to make comments in individual notes. He would send an "Attaboy" note along with a small bag of M&M's. What always amazed me is that our six-figure employees loved it! On a super busy week or during travel, if we neglected to send notes out, we would get calls asking if we had forgotten.

When our management team realized how effective these little rewards and recognitions were, we initiated awards for team spirit, best mentor, most improved and most flexible. I consistently gave my people more and more to strive for and more opportunities for the old pat on the back.

Whatever business you are in, find ways to track as many aspects of good behavior as you can. Publish them consistently and across every department. Keep your people in the limelight as often as you can. If there is a company newsletter, make sure your department gets a little space for news and updates. Other departments will begin to learn what your department does, and during unfortunate but necessary corporate realignments, your people will have a good chance at being relocated within the firm.

Other best leadership practices:

- Encourage team members to bring problems to you, along with solutions.
- Allow them to make decisions and think processes through independently.
- Create simple recognition awards and present them in a group setting.
- Communicate by multiple methods frequently (phone, e-mail and broadcast messages).
- Hold regular, purposeful meetings and encourage employees to participate in the planning.
- Remember birthdays and anniversaries as much as possible.
- When a problem arises, make no judgment until all the facts are studied.
- Stop fixing. Let people be responsible for the jobs they were hired to do.
- Remember common courtesies such as saying "Hello," "Thank you" and "May I help you?"
- Handle serious problems quickly, or delegate them to a more suitable department.
- Know the company policies. Understand and follow HR policies.
- Read at least one personal growth book every month.
- Keep your own life balanced and stress free, and encourage employees to do the same.

Include Stress Reduction in Your Plans

Experts say stress can occur in both positive and negative situations. Believe it or not, there are stories of lottery winners having heart attacks after learning they won millions. As an effective leader, you can reduce the day-to-day stress for your team members in the following ways:

- Instill confidence through training and coaching.
- Recognize the smallest accomplishments with praise and positive feedback.
- Encourage life balance, reaffirming belief in the need to have a life outside of work.

- Champion physical activity by finding deals on local gyms or providing in-house fitness facilities, if the budget allows.
- Never discuss one employee with another. It will get out.
- Help employees manage their time by teaching them to use time-blocking methods and other time-management techniques.
- Make time for everyone, and show no favoritism.
- Make eating lunch mandatory.
- Bring in an expert to discuss desk yoga or other relaxation techniques.
- Let your people know you aren't perfect and that you care about their success.
- Before you deliver bad news of any kind, think your delivery through carefully.

Maintaining Life Balance

Without balance, there is stress. Life can be divided into three areas that need your attention and tender care: family, faith and work.

Family

Family includes those most dear to you. It can be a spouse (with or without a houseful of children), your church, your community or anything in between. It may be that puppy that awaits your return every day.

Faith

Faith is your belief system; it is the glue that binds you to your passion. Everyone believes in something, because without faith, we would travel aimlessly through life. Even the famous atheist Madelyn Murray O'Hare was impassioned about her nonbelief and thus had faith in her convictions (poor thing).

My belief system lies in God and a higher calling. I am of the mind that giving begets, and it has always lifted me to exactly where I needed to be. I believe that faith, propelled by a powerful attitude and unfailing mindset, can accomplish anything.

What drives you? What gets you up and out in the morning? It might be something spiritual. It may be something worldly or love for your family and children. It might be a combination of all of these. Be in touch with yourself enough to know who you are and what you stand for.

Be careful, however, never to judge others in light of your own inner passion. Let others choose their own paths, and sell your own belief system by example. This is a personal matter that's better left out of the workplace.

Work

Keeping in mind that you are striving for leadership qualities, your choice of work must be of the highest order. Seek an opportunity that lifts you and allows you to do good deeds. Any job or position that feels wrong will not fulfill you but impede your progress toward being a leader.

And don't make the common mistake of overidentifying with your position at work. Are you an attorney or a husband and father? Are you a vice president of marketing or a wife and mother? Keep you priorities straight.

Leading by Example

If you consider yourself a leader, then your natural expectation is that people will follow you. Your people will look to you and your own behavior as a guideline to follow. They will look up to you, support you and look for direction.

That's the good news. The bad news is that they will copy your style whether your behavior is good or bad. After all, if you take two-hour lunches, why shouldn't they?

You could say, "Because I'm the boss, and I said so." But that is about as far away from leadership as you can get. The solution is to set an example for what you expect, and it will be followed without question.

I once worked on a project in a financial institution. I was only the project manager/consultant, but it drove me nuts that most people drifted in between 9:30 and 10 a.m. I never commented on this, for it really wasn't my place to do so. However, I started arriving at 7:30 a.m., which is easy to do on location, away from home and other responsibilities.

By the conclusion of the project, most of the office was coming in much earlier, saying how pleasant it was to work before the phones began ringing. I will always remember that as a simple reminder about leading by example.

Time Blocking

Leaders are usually in control of their own time, using it wisely and purposefully.

One of the best and most effective methods for managing time is time blocking. It's the simple act of making appointments for your prioritized activities.

When a future leader is planning her time blocks, she should have at least fifty percent of her time assigned to activities that involve contact with her workers.

If you let your day be dominated by administrative duties—mail, reports, issues—you will never get out of that ivory tower office. You must proactively choose to put your people first and worry about the administrative duties after that.

That is why time blocking works for leadership development. You can plan and do exactly what needs to be done, and if a task is incomplete on Monday, there will be a little time scheduled on Tuesday, Wednesday and so on, to finish the job.

Allot time in the schedule for flexibility and to handle issues that can crop up outside of your control. Overscheduling your activities will create frustration and discouragement.

Write out your list of activities, prioritize it, and then book time for each activity in writing. It will take a while to get into the groove, but eventually, you will feel an amazing sense of freedom and accomplishment. There are many time management tools on the market to help you keep track of your time and appointments.

A Final Word on Integrity

In otherwise ethical situations, you might be asked to put your ethics on hold momentarily. Don't do it. Wrong choices would include anything that is immoral, illegal or even remotely connected to activities that are. You know what they are.

If it is a manager or your boss making such a request, report the indiscretion to human resources immediately. Why? The minute you don't play, you are blacklisted. Reporting the infraction will protect you, once recorded. Also, keep accurate notes of the situation. Consider Enron and their infamous accounting firm. That situation could have ended before it began had more ethical people been willing to speak up.

Not snitching may be a sign of coolness in fifth grade, but in corporate America, your first loyalty should be to the company that signs your checks and puts food on your family's table.

Some businesses breed bad behavior by the sheer nature of the business. I hail from the brokerage sales and investment industry, where pressure is frequently placed on ethics, and aggressive salesmanship is too often the rule. Imagine hearing that you must either generate a certain amount of revenue through commissions earned by investing someone's life savings or you are out of a job.

This really does happen, but fortunately there are many more good than bad apples. Ideally, the advisor learns to market to and find clients that are enthusiastically interested in investment products and services. The majority conduct their business in this appropriate manner.

But what of the advisor with a family to feed, who has had a bad month through no particular fault of his own and hears a dire warning due to low production, alluded to above? What will he do when someone who is not suitable to take an investment risk sits down at his desk with cash? Is he pushed beyond his integrity to perform?

If this advisor has established integrity and always takes the high road, he may be out of a job. As difficult as it might be to find another job, it would be far easier than breaking the law and having something come back to haunt him years later.

For example, before I was a manager, I was a financial advisor and faced a situation that caused me to leave several months' salary on the table. A client was on the brink of purchasing almost a million dollars worth of a certain investment, something he requested, based on his own research. At the midnight hour, just before we entered the trade, he asked what his "cut," or rebate, was.

I was new and green and an idealistic people pleaser. I thought there must be a way to accommodate him; after all, we would make a very good fee on this transaction, and it was his selection! Regardless, my boss made it clear that rebating was a serious violation and that the best we could do was offer to discount future commissions on trades, something that was an acceptable practice.

This didn't fly with Mr. Dealmaker, and he proceeded to do business with another firm in the area. Two months later, we witnessed the market crash of 1987. I heard through the grapevine that Mr. Dealmaker had taken major losses and took the broker with whom he wound up doing business to arbitration, saying that he had only invested with that broker because—are you ready?—the broker bribed him with a refund of his commissions.

That broker is out of the business now. I thank my manager at the time, Paul Robinson, for his wisdom and sage guidance, because this industry has been the work I have loved for almost twenty years.

Putting It All Together

You obviously desire to become a leader or you wouldn't be reading this book.

I hope you realize by now that although some leaders may be born to lead, others are developed along life's path.

Only you can reinvent yourself to inspire and motivate. When you do so, you will reap the benefits as well. It is within you to command respect and admiration rather than fear and disdain. You can become a respected leader, one that shepherds her employees to their highest potential.

And while most of what you need is within, the actual process requires you to look outside and to learn about each and every person that relies on you as his or her manager. It isn't about you alone; it is about the group as a whole. Your management style must become chameleon-like, ever changing. Rather than expecting everyone to conform to your wishes and demands, no matter how worthy, try instead to adapt to the personalities and styles of the people you are managing.

Remember this acronym when you need a leadership tune-up:

L - Listening
E - Ethics
A - Accountability
D - Dedication to mission, team and company
E - Enthusiasm
R - Recognition
S - Sensitivity
H - Humor
I - Integrity
P - Progress toward goals

"Your talent is God's gift to you. What you do
with it is your gift to God."
Leo Buscaglia

About The Author

Patti Branco

As founder and president of Management & Training Solutions, an L.A. based consulting firm (1999), Patti Branco is a respected and well known financial services industry expert, developing dynamic leadership and sales management, high energy presentations and roll-up-your-sleeves project management in the financial services industry. She enjoys rich experience and 20 successful years in senior management in the financial services arena, primarily the bank, credit union and brokerage industry, once responsible for the success of over 70 investment center employees and multi million dollar budgets in a thirty-billion dollar bank, Cal Fed. Patti walks the walk and runs the race, and has assisted companies large and small to develop business, people and peak performance. She is often called upon as a source for information from major publications including NY Times, USA Today, the Chicago Tribune and the WSJ Online. Her consulting experience includes clients such as Morgan Stanley, Pentagon Federal Credit Union, Cal Fed Bank, Allstate Financial Services, L.A. Times, Conseco Insurance Company, Los Angeles Bar Association and Union Bank of California. She is an active member of the National Speakers Association, Past Programs Chair & Vice President of the Board for the Greater Los Angeles Chapter of the NSA, and FastTrack Chair for the NSA/GLAC Apprentice Program.

Patti Branco
7623 Van Buren Street, 2nd Floor
Ventura, CA 93003-2575
Phone: 805.671.9998
Fax: 805.671.9964
Email: BrancoPublished@aol.com
Web Site: www.PattiBranco.com

Chapter Five

SEVEN STEPS TO COMMUNICATE EFFECTIVELY
AS A LEADER

Cheli Cerra, M.Ed.

I paced up and down the hallway and glanced at the wall clock. Thirteen minutes to go. I took a deep breath and held it for several seconds. I exhaled. The stress technique that I had learned from my husband began to take effect. I was calm, I was in control, and I was the new CEO of the organization. No one could stop me now. I was invincible. At exactly 2:47 p.m., I began to walk toward the large auditorium, my speech memorized and my gait steady. I took a breath, opened the doors and stepped in. The meeting would last exactly twenty-seven minutes. What I would learn was a lesson in leadership that I would never forget.

What happened? I was the new CEO. I was very happy and excited to be there. Unfortunately, though, my audience didn't feel the same enthusiasm that I did. I stood at the front of the room, looked at the crowd and began my "rah rah" speech. We were going to do great things together, I began. I told them of the painstaking analysis of data that I had made. I told them of the goals that I wanted to work with them in putting together That's when I realized that no one was paying attention. After twenty-seven minutes, I ended the speech. As I walked out of the auditorium I thought of Henry Ford's saying, "Failure is the opportunity to begin again more intelligently."

When I arrived home that day and began to talk to my family, I discovered that no one was really listening there, either. At that moment, I decided that I was going to come up with some techniques that would help me communicate effectively, both at home and at work. You see, whether it's in the boardroom or your family's living room, your communication style impacts everyone around you.

We all have our own perceptions of everything that goes on in our lives. As individuals, we are unique, and that is what makes us special. But this uniqueness can also affect the way we give and receive information. In junior high, I remember playing a game where the "leader" would say a phrase and pass it along to the rest of the group. By the time the phrase reached the end of the line, it was nothing like what had been said at the beginning. The phrase was entirely changed, twisted and made no sense. Knowing how things are said and interpreted by others is important when it comes to leading an effective and profitable organization. You need to make sure that your message is heard correctly and that you are not misquoted, misinterpreted or misunderstood.

Communicating well is an art. Have you ever seen a savvy communicator at work? It is equivalent to watching a conductor direct a symphony. Being an effective communicator takes timing, practice and understanding. There are also seven key concepts that need to be understood along the way. I have personally come upon these through experience, research and practice. Understanding and practicing them will provide you with the astute leadership skills necessary to transform organizations and keep your family life in balance.

Organizations undergo change, and how they cope with that change, in large part, determines whether they succeed or fail. Of all the kinds of organizational transformations, changes in leadership are among the most common. They often bring with them the need for additional communication within the organization. A new leader needs to employ savvy communication skills immediately because how he communicates and how he is understood is critical to his success.

Step into an organization that has a leader who practices these seven key concepts and you will see an organization that runs like a fine Swiss watch. Communication is like a relationship—it requires work. It also requires a good foundation with a clear set of guidelines and objectives.

Master the art of effective communication by:

I.   Knowing the process
II.   Understanding the audience
III. Understanding the barriers
IV.   Promoting feedback
V.   Artfully listening
VI.   Receiving the outcome
VII. Receiving message validation

I. Knowing the Process

Understanding the communication process—or how information flows between people and within organizations—is the first key step to becoming a savvy communicator. Within most organizations, it tends to flow in one of three ways: from the top down, from the bottom up and sideways.

Communication flowing from the top down is usually intended to let employees know of policies, procedures, instructions and job information. Many times, this type of communication is not always successful, especially coming from new leadership. Let's face it; how much information should you provide, and what is really viable? Too much information and you may begin to overwhelm your people; too little and they may feel that you are withholding information. The key to having successful downward communication is having other channels through which to positively communicate. To be effective, communication that goes from the top down must take into consideration the message that is intended, how it is told and whether it has relevance to the audience.

For top-down communication to really work, the bottom-up communication must work as well. Bottom-up communication provides information on how well the employees are doing their work, how they are getting along with each other and how they are contributing to the betterment of the organization. The importance of having a channel within an organization to gauge what is going on in the trenches is a leadership lesson that I learned firsthand. A responsive leader is able to deal with problems before they become monumental obstacles, because her company's communication processes work and her people are always in the know. An example of bottom-up communication—one that works very well in many organizations—is the suggestion box.

The third process by which communication flows is sideways. A message being delivered between colleagues or employees is one example. This type of communication is very important to an organization. It is vital for getting teams to work together and for communicating information within departments.

Which leads us to the grapevine. The grapevine is an informal channel of communication that tends to carry more accurate information than inaccurate and that flows throughout the company in all directions. Is it useful for communication? Absolutely. The grapevine is fast, accurate and usually has a lot of factual information. Go to the water cooler or the employee lounge and you will see this process in action:

"Did you hear that so-and-so was promoted?"
"I can't believe it!"
"I heard that…"

It is essential for effective leaders to understand and utilize this process for the well-being of the organization. If I had taken time to hear what was going on in the grapevine in my own situation, I would have had a red-flag alert to the problems looming on the horizon.

II. Understanding the Audience

The second key step in effective leadership communication is understanding the audience. Knowing your audience's background and culture will help you craft your message for its most effective delivery. Are you speaking to a group of your peers (other leaders), your managers, your workers, your family? Crafting your delivery for your target audience is critical.

I recall the story of a leader who learned to speak Spanish so he could deliver his message to the Hispanic audience within his organization. Since his organization was located in Miami, the Hispanics there were predominately Cuban. He spoke well and was well liked and funny. Then, however, he traveled to California, where the Hispanic culture is predominately Mexican. As he prepared his opening speech to the organization there, he decided to use the same funny phrases and anecdotes that had worked for him before. He bombed. Why? Because dialects within cultures are different. A word or phrase in one culture may be funny while in another, the same word or phrase can be insulting. This business leader lived in Miami and learned to speak Spanish from a Cuban teacher. The phrases that he used were funny in Miami, but in California they were insulting. He never recovered from that speech and ultimately left the company. A lesson to be learned: Always do your homework.

III. Understanding the Barriers

So you understand the first and second steps. You believe that all is going well. But then you hit a wall. Which brings us to the subject of barriers, the third key concept in effective communication. As a leader, understanding the nature of barriers can prepare you to be successful.

There are two types of barriers in communication—external and internal. External barriers are distractions that occur due to outside influences—a telephone ringing off the hook, an intercom announcement, a car alarm. They interfere with the communication process by competing with it. When you have an external barrier, it is very difficult to focus until it is dealt with.

Internal barriers arise from within communicating parties and can lead to miscommunication. One example is anger. Going back to my twenty-seven-minute speech, I was unaware that there were several people in the group who were angry because of a change in leadership. They, in turn, expressed their anger by ignoring me. If I had done a little bit more research beforehand, I would have been privy to this fact and taken the steps needed to address the problem.

Another form of internal barrier is not using appropriate words or vocabulary to get the point across. Your audience should be your cue as to the vocabulary level and words that need to be used.

IV. Promoting Feedback

The fourth step to effective communication is promoting feedback. In an organization, the purpose of feedback is to clarify communication between parties. It should be descriptive, specific and appropriate. It should take into account the needs of the sender, the receiver and the situation.

Leaders need to give feedback to their employees, but they also need to provide an avenue by which feedback can be given to them. They need to encourage it. Ken Blanchard, author of *The One Minute Manager*, has his employees meet with their managers once every two weeks for one-on-one meetings that usually last a half-hour each. What is different about these meetings is that the employees set the agenda. Talk about promoting feedback!

Feedback can be communicated verbally or nonverbally. In the example of my speech, the audience was distracted because they were angry, and I perceived this through the nonverbal way in which they were conducting themselves. This feedback sent me the message that I had to end the meeting quickly, before it was too late. By doing this, I was able to salvage the message, deal with the problem and reconvene the team to deliver the message again.

Author Carl Rogers did a study on communication and came up with five categories of feedback that take place during conversations. They are listed in order of occurrence:

1. **Evaluative** - when we make judgments on the other person's statement.
2. **Interpretive** - paraphrasing by explaining what the other person's statement means.
3. **Supportive** - attempting to assist the other communicator.
4. **Probing** - trying to gain additional information, continue the discussion or clarify a point.
5. **Understanding** - attempting to discover what the other person means by her statements.

To achieve communication, leaders need to listen and understand first before they try to figure out what someone is saying.[1]

Timing is everything when it comes to feedback, especially when the more instantaneous it is, the more valuable it is. But providing feedback to an emotionally charged audience needs to be handled with care. It is better to wait and go with your gut. My gut instinct told me to end the speech in a professional manner. What do you think would have happened if I had become defensive? What message of leadership would I have conveyed to the group? Not a favorable one in the least.

Being an astute leader means that you are always in the feedback loop. In the book, *1,001 Ways to Inspire Your Organization, Your Team and Yourself*, David E. Rye talks about motivational strategies and understanding how people think, what turns them on and what turns them off. Leaders need to constantly increase their awareness of everyone within the organization.

---

[1] http://www.nwlink.com/~donclark/leader/leadcom.html

Here are some tips on conducting feedback effectively:

1) Always start with a positive when having to discuss a negative.

Once I was conducting a performance evaluation on an employee and needed to bring up several points that he needed to work on. I began the meeting by providing positive feedback regarding a program that he had been involved with. I then went into what needed to be worked on and ended the feedback session by asking, "What resources do you need to enable you to correct the problems?" This provided an avenue for him to discuss how he was going to correct the problems that had been put on the table.

2) Provide a way for employees to give feedback.

When I ran a K-8 public school, I managed 240 full- and part-time employees, plus the parents of the 1,500 students who were enrolled at the school. A feedback box was put in the office, where anyone could drop off an idea, a concern or a problem. This resulted in many issues being resolved before they escalated into serious problems.

3) Provide positive feedback in formal and informal settings.

Effective leaders master the art of providing positive feedback. Let's say, for example, that you have a big project or meeting that needs to be put together. You have several key people who go the extra mile, and the outcome is a success. At the next staff meeting, you might mention these key people and thank them publicly for helping make the project the success that it was. Or even better, you could send them each a personalized note saying, "Thanks! Great job! Really appreciated it." Taking time to give positive feedback will make a big difference within the culture of your organization. It's not about money but motivating people from within, making them feel that they are important.

By providing a venue for feedback, many problems can be dealt with quickly and simply. This tactic can also be carried over in our personal lives. What about your family? When was the last time you gave them positive feedback? Are you a parent? Understanding the concept of feedback will clear up many miscommunications that you may be having with your children (as well as your spouse) and provide you with a clear road to happiness.

"When you know something, say what you
know. When you don't know something, say
that you don't know. That is knowledge."
Kung Fu Tzu (Confucius)

V. Artful Listening

The fifth key concept on the path to effective communication is artful listening. Listening is a vital communication dynamic in organizations, although many of us find it to be a challenge. I, for one, am always trying to perfect this skill.

We all have likes, dislikes, wants and opinions and are usually quick to state them. But to listen well is an art; so much so that when you begin to get really good at it, you know what the person is going to say even before he says it. As a leader, this gives you an edge.

So how do you become an artful listener? You act as if you already are one. Begin to believe that you are an artful listener, and in time, you will be one. This is one of the most difficult skills to master, but know that listening is coupled with higher levels of effective leadership. When you master the art of listening, you attain a high level of leadership effectiveness.

Here's a simple technique that will help you become a good listener: Practice patience. Sure, it is difficult to intently listen while someone goes on and on and on about something this is irrelevant, insignificant or totally out in left field. But as Jack Canfield said in the book *Conversations With Millionaires*, by Mike Littman and Jason Oman, "Everybody's doing the best that they can with the knowledge, the awareness, and the consciousness they have." Understanding this statement will be a turning point for many. How many times are we more interested in promoting our own point of view than in understanding or even listening intently to someone else's point of view?

Let's look at two scenarios. In the first, imagine being involved in a conversation, waiting like a vulture to pounce on the first momentary pause so you can take over the floor. During this conversation, you are not listening; you are waiting for the precise moment to take over. Or worse yet, what if you are waiting for that pause so you can attack the messenger? In your mind, you are going over the rebuttal, the attack, the precise words that will deflate the other person and make you the victor.

Now consider this scenario: You are involved in a conversation, and you are actively listening. As the other person is speaking, you think about her words; they linger in your brain, forming pictures, and you wonder what the other person is thinking and feeling as she speaks. You make sure that you understand her point of view before you respond. You wait until she is completely finished, and when the moment is right, you restate and rephrase what she has said, sending a verification message back to the sender. The sender acknowledges the message.

In the first scenario, the supposedly "active" listener was only hearing the words. In the second scenario the active listener was truly listening for the message. To master artful listening, we must be actively involved in the conversation process as described in the second scenario.

Here are several tips for mastering artful listening:

1. Think about what the person is saying, his feelings and the message behind the words (not the meaning of the words themselves). Good listeners think of what the message is conveying.
2. Look at the body language.
3. Use eye contact; look directly into the face of the person speaking.
4. Be nonjudgmental. You don't need to agree with everything the person is saying, but you do need to respect others' feelings and beliefs.

"The reason why we have two ears and only one mouth is that we may listen the more and talk the less."
Zeno of Citium, c. 300 B.C.

VI. Perceiving the Outcome

The sixth step is perceiving the outcome. It is important for leaders to have realistic expectations of the outcome of their message. Otherwise, communication can break down, be misunderstood and split in several directions. This is where miscommunication, hearsay and gossip come into play. They make up a dangerous precipice on which no leader wants to walk. A slight misstep on this path and you may fall into the dark abyss.

To keep the outcome of the perceived message in view, you need to go over the key concepts and fine tune any elements that may be keeping your message from being perceived in the clearest manner. Planning is essential. Do your homework. It will save you time in making sure that a crystal clear message is perceived in a crystal clear way.

Let's go back to my speech. The intended outcome of my message was for everyone to know that I had a commitment to them and to the organization. The real outcome, however, was a barrier of anger and negativity. Had I been privy to all the background information beforehand, I would have perceived the outcome and never given a speech like the one that I delivered.

VII. Message Validation

Understanding and mastering the six concepts detailed thus far leads us to the final process in the communication chain. The seventh step is receiving message validation. Message validation occurs when your message is understood by the person receiving it. This can be your organization, your team leader, your child or your spouse. Validation can take the form of a simple conversation, a smile, a nod, a paraphrasing of the message or a promise to ensure that a specific desire is carried out. Within an organization, message validation is the key to everyone working in unison and harmony.

You may be thinking about those twenty-seven minutes during which I pretty much bombed with my staff. What did I do afterward? A lot of homework, a lot of listening and a lot of small group discussions. I didn't address the staff for a couple of weeks, until I had taken care of the issues that needed to be discussed. —. I practiced an "in-the trenches" approach to the seven key concepts that I have outlined.

Eventually, I received message validation in the form of a staff that was open and receptive and a positive environment in which decisions were made together for the good of the cause. This may sound impossible. But let me tell you about the organization that I led. It was a public school. When I was asked to take over as CEO, I had a $5 million budget. But the budget was $60,000 in the red, there was organizational chaos, and there was a looming thirty-day deadline for a new project that involved construction of a building and implementation of a program. Along with all that, a new staff needed to be hired. Talk about getting to work! But work we did. We worked to repair the faults in the system and unite the organization. We set a goal of success, opening the new building and hiring a new staff within the thirty-day deadline.

Yes, I received message validation in many different ways—ways that were intrinsic as well as performance based. The bottom line, which we all can understand, was that we got the budget into a positive state. But the more important bottom line in public education is achieving excellence. One day, I convened the staff to announce that we had attained the highest rating for a public school within the state of Florida. And we achieved it in less than ten months. Personally, that was the best message validation I could have received.

Cheli Cerra, M.Ed.

Recognized as "The Right Choice" by *Women's Day Magazine*, and featured on numerous radio shows throughout the country, Cheli is committed to helping teachers and parents come together for the success of children. Her keynotes, seminars, coaching programs, and presentations have provided strategies that empower her audiences to action. She will captivate you by teaching the lessons learned from her in-the-trenches experience in public education. Cheli is the founder of Eduville, Inc., a company that provides resources and strategies for parents and teachers to help their children achieve school and life success. Her website http://www.eduville.com, is full of tips, techniques, and strategies useful for anyone interested in helping a child succeed. Cheli is also he co-founder of School-Talk, an educational communications company and the co-creator of the School-Talk Series: *Teacher Talk! Parent Talk! School Board Talk! and Principal Talk!,* books on communication for educational success. For more information go to http://www.school-talk.com.

Cheli Cerra
9737 NW 41 Street, #356
Miami, FL 33178
Phone: 305.437.9916, office
1.877.741.8116, toll free
Email: cheli@eduville.com
www.eduville.com
www.school-talk.com

Chapter Six

SELECTING THE RIGHT PEOPLE FOR THE RIGHT WORK

Peter A. LaChance

Matching People with Work

Many recent books on the subject of leadership stress the importance of matching people to their work to optimize organizational performance. In *First, Break All the Rules,* authors Buckingham and Coffman present the concepts of behavioral talents and non-talents, and they recount the benefits of working with people according to their natural talents. In *Leadership is an Art,* author Max Depree writes, "We do not grow by knowing all of the answers, but rather by living with the questions." This refers to corporate bias toward experience, skills and knowledge and away from potential, creativity and curiosity. In his book *Good to Great*, Jim Collins writes that matching people with their talents is a key differentiator separating great companies from the pack: "Get the right people onto the bus and in the right seats, and get the wrong people off the bus!"

Traditionally, leaders delegate matters of recruitment to the HR department. They also rely on the HR department for advice on identifying existing people for new roles. *All* **business leaders need to read this chapter: CEOs, COOs and division and department heads, including HR department heads.** The message delivered here can make a huge difference in the success of your business. Successful business leaders do not "delegate and forget" matters of such great strategic import!

How do you determine who the right people are for particular work? Let's look at the model used by the vast majority of modern companies to recruit new employees and select existing employees for new work. First, for each position, you develop a selection process based largely on the experience, skills and knowledge that you determine an archetype, or model employee, would have. Second, you only accord minor consideration to "soft," less concrete attributes like temperament and attitudes. Using this approach, ninety-five percent of the people you hire will have great relevant experience. So what's wrong with this model? Well, at first, nothing appears to be wrong, because the resulting outcomes from using this model won't be apparent for a while. In time, you'll notice that your failure to focus your attention on attitudes and temperament will lead to performance problems. Overall productivity and performance will be lower than you expected and fall short of your CEO's demands. Morale will be low, and turnover will be high. Also, the number of employees with whom your company has recurring discipline and performance problems will be higher than it ought to be. Lastly, ninety percent of the people you fire will be dismissed because of their attitude.[1]

What does this say about popular modern personnel selection processes? It certainly does not appear that customary HR processes result in successfully and consistently matching the right people to the right work! According to a recent study reported in the Harvard Business Review, using traditional recruiting methods, the best interviewers in the world have a success rate of only fourteen out of 100!

Using the Work-Matching™ process, you can improve your prediction about a person's *fitness for a role* by matching his or her temperament traits to the mix of temperament traits required to excel in that work. Work-Matching™ involves applying a temperament assessment tool to help select employees for roles using a behavioral perspective. Temperament assessment tools like the *MBS Survey* that we use and the team-building program, *Management by Strengths,* take the understanding of temperament a step further by helping existing work groups to communicate better. By recognizing the different temperament traits and communication styles, your

---

[1] Resource Associates Corporation, *Concept Speech for Affiliates*

company can improve its selection process *and* solve communications problems that your employees are experiencing.

Any employee can perform several roles in his company, given the necessary education, training, experience and attitudes. However, in our experience, temperament is often the key differentiating factor that results in consistently good performance in a role. When an employee's temperament is suited to a certain kind of work, he has latent potential for excelling in that work. Even if he has limited skills and knowledge for the work, watch out! Get out of his way! It won't take long for him to acquire the skills and knowledge necessary to outshine his experienced counterparts. When leaders perform the Work-Matching™ process across their organization, they match their existing talent pool to its most productive use, in turn maximizing overall performance.

Companies spend a lot of time and money on team building and trying to improve internal communications in an attempt to fix problems largely created by slotting the wrong job candidates and employees into the wrong roles. The process of Work-Matching™ will save a company a lot of trouble and money. It begins with determining the model profile—the mix of temperaments required to excel in that work. Then you profile the temperament of your employees, seeking to find reasonable matches to the model profile. When you identify people who reasonably match the model but who aren't trained for the particular role, you should consider training them. It is more cost-effective to train *behaviorally compatible* employees for new positions that call for their talents than to recruit experienced people from outside the company.

What is Temperament?

To understand the Work-Matching™ process, it is first necessary to discuss the mix of traits that make up a person's temperament profile. Even more fundamental to the understanding of this process is appreciating what we mean by "temperament." According to Michael Postlewait, CEO of MBS, Inc. (which stands for Management by Strengths), "Temperament makes up the core of a person's nature. You are born with it; your parents could identify it within you at an early age. Temperament also serves to define the style with which you communicate with others, which is why some assessment tools refer to *communication style* rather than *temperament*. When you have a better understanding of a person's temperament, you are equipped to work more effectively with that person, because he or she will be comfortable with you."

Designing a Model Profile

What is meant by "the mix of temperaments required to excel in a job"? It's really a matter of common sense. Here are some examples:

- Does the work require diplomacy or a candid communications style?

- Will employees do better in the job if they are outgoing, or is it better if they are a bit contemplative?

- Are empathy and listening important to success in the role, or do self-starters who may sometimes be compulsive perform better?

- Is constant attention to detail the key to success in the role, or is "thinking outside the box" more important to success?

Personality profiles are frequently used by HR professionals to assess candidates for employment or as part of team building. However, a person's *temperament* is even more basic. Experts often refer to temperament as *nature* and to personality as *nurture*. That's because many factors contribute to forming a person's personality, mostly during early development. Factors contributing to personality are environment, upbringing, education, creed, job skills and temperament. Michael Postlewait puts it this way: "A person's temperament is the foundation upon which his personality is built. It is his psyche, his soul-ish self, or nature."

There is a lot more to successfully understanding a person than just understanding her temperament; temperament assessments can only provide a general description. Experiences, intelligence, maturity, values, education and religion are all important aspects of who people are; a temperament assessment cannot measure these. Looking at one of these profiles is like looking at the outside of a house; you don't know every detail about it, but you know where the front door is so you can enter it. This analogy is a subtle one. Personality profiles tell you quite a lot about what's inside the house, but if you don't know how to gain entrance to the house, all that information is rather useless! Information about a person's temperament is fundamental to understanding how to best utilize the talents she has to offer.

The Origins of the Study of Temperament

In the fifth century BC, Hippocrates[2] professed that knowing a person's dominant temperament means that one can largely understand that person. He theorized that every person has a dominant temperament, falling into one of four categories:

- Choleric
  o Having an irritable temperament
- Sanguine
  o Having a cheerful temperament
- Phlegmatic
  o Having a calm temperament
- Melancholy
  o Having a depressed temperament

Modern Day Temperament Assessment Tools

In recent times, systems for classifying and profiling temperament have been refined. By studying and testing large populations of subjects, statistical methods have made these assessment tools accurate and reliable. In the days of Hippocrates, they would not have known how to quantify the complex interplay between the four temperament traits – explaining the *mix* of temperament traits that each of us has. We each hold a complex combination of these traits. A temperament profile reveals a person's most basic nature in terms of lev-

---

[2] Hippocrates is sometimes called *The Father of Western Clinical Medicine.*

els of prevailing and counterprevailing magnitudes for each of the four temperament traits.

You can choose between several temperament assessment tools, but for simplicity, we will discuss the Work-Matching™ process in terms of the MBS Survey and the resulting MBS Profile Report, available from MBS, Inc. We prefer this tool because of its ease of administration (ten to fifteen minutes), its accuracy and its simple yet powerful one-page output. For the sake of our readers who are clinicians, the MBS tool utilizes a one-to-five Lichert scale rather than popular "yes/no" or "least/most" methods. For the rest of us, this means that it is sensitive and accurate.

The four temperament traits measured by the MBS assessment tool are:

Directness

Extroversion

Pace

Structure

Note that we've highlighted the first letter of each temperament trait, because the MBS system uses the letters "D," "E," "P" and "S" when graphically displaying a person's temperament. (See the example MBS profiles that follow.)

Comparison of the MBS temperament system to Hippocrates's system

- ♦ **Direct** – loosely corresponds to "Choleric" in Hippocrates's description.
- ♦ **Extroversion** – loosely corresponds to "Sanguine" in Hippocrates's description.
- ♦ **Pace** – loosely corresponds to "Phlegmatic" in Hippocrates's description.
- ♦ **Structure** – loosely corresponds to "Melancholy" in Hippocrates's description.

Person A

The graph on the left depicts the temperament profile of Person A, having:

- Two prevailing traits (above the centerline)– **E**xtroversion as the dominant trait, followed by **D**irectness.
- Two counterprevailing traits (below the centerline)– **P**ace and **S**tructure.

Person A's dominant trait is **E**xtroversion, but that indicates only a part of his overall temperament. To determine with greater certainty how he will perform in a role (given the right skills, knowledge and experience) it is important to account for the position of all four temperament traits in the grid. The total picture defines how Person A is naturally wired to excel in certain roles, including tactical sales.

Person B

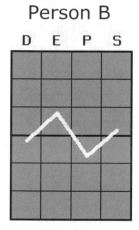

The graph on the left depicts the temperament profile of Person B, having:

- Two prevailing traits (above the centerline)– **E**xtroversion as the dominant trait, followed by **S**tructure.
- Two counterprevailing traits (below the centerline)– **D**irectness and **P**ace.

Like Person A above, Person B's dominant trait is **E**xtroversion, but the types of work that naturally suit Person B will tend to differ from the work suiting Person A. The profile for Person A is a model profile for tactical sales, such as retail sales, whereas the profile for Person B is better suited to jobs requiring diplomacy and a nonthreatening style (**D** below the centerline) and the ability to work within established guidelines (**S** above the centerline). Sales support is an example of such a job. Both Persons A and B would prefer to work with people as part of a team or with clients (because **E** is their dominant trait). While either might succeed in sales, of the two profiles, Person A has the more natural sales temperament (high **E** and **D**).

The position of each trait relative to the centerline denotes whether it is a prevailing trait (above the centerline) or a counterprevailing trait (below the centerline). For example, a person whose Directness temperament trait falls below the centerline (low D) exhibits opposite behavior from that of a direct person. High Ds tend to be decisive, candid and outspoken; on the other hand, low Ds tend to be modest, diplomatic, and they appreciate support in making decisions. It is important to consider a person's counterprevailing temperament traits; as we stated earlier, the position of all the traits in the temperament profile is important in deciding how well a person is wired for a role.

Prevailing Temperament Traits

- Directness - as a prevailing trait ("D" above the center line)
  - Strengths: decisive, self-confident, candid, authoritative, self-motivated.
  - Weaknesses: outspoken, abrasive, don't realize how strongly they come across, more interested in results than people.
- Extroversion - as a prevailing trait ("E" above the center line)
  - Strengths: friendly, optimistic, talkative once they're comfortable, enthusiastic, like to work in teams to accomplish tasks.
  - Weaknesses: tend to think they've told you something they haven't, constantly selling—often themselves, too talkative, caught up in how things appear.

Strengths or Weaknesses?

As we discuss the specific characteristics of each of the temperament traits, both prevailing and counterprevailing, it is important to remember that, regardless of whether the trait is above or below the centerline in the MBS graphs, the trait is a *strength*. However, this is only true if a person is in control of her temperament. When we lose control of our TEMPER-ament, these same strengths can work against us and appear as weaknesses.

- Pace - as a prevailing trait ("P" above the center line)
  - Strengths: warm, considerate, calm, steady, harmonious, cooperative, dependable, empathetic, good listeners.
  - Weaknesses: don't like to be rushed at the last minute, stubborn, have a long fuse, but when they blow, watch out!
- Structure - as a prevailing trait ("S" above the center line)
  - Strengths: careful, accurate, good with details, loyal, good organizers, they're usually right.
  - Weaknesses: their way is the ONLY way, critical of new methods or ideas, sensitive to criticism, although they are self-critical.

Counterprevailing Temperament Traits

- Directness - counterprevailing ("D" below the center line)
  - Strengths: nonthreatening, nonconfrontational style, willing to delegate authority.
  - Weaknesses: too low-key, difficulty taking charge, needs support in making decisions.
- Extroversion - counterprevailing ("E" below the center line)
  - Strengths: able to work alone or one-on-one, think before they speak, creative and introspective.
  - Weaknesses: shy, withdrawn, appear unfriendly, abrupt.
- Pace - counterprevailing ("P" below the center line)
  - Strengths: able to productively rush at the last minute, like variety.
  - Weaknesses: impatient, always hurrying, poor listeners.
- Structure - counterprevailing ("S" below the center line)
  - Strengths: flexible, able to delegate details, independent.
  - Weaknesses: poor attention to details, difficulty with rules or systems that interfere with accomplishing their goals.

Applying Work-Matching™: Understanding the Four MBS Temperament Traits

For Work-Matching™ to work well, you must carefully develop model profiles that suit your company's culture, its industry and its marketplace. Then, you have to reevaluate these models continually, to ensure their relevance to ever-changing conditions within your company, its industry and its marketplace.

In the following pages, you will learn about the characteristics of each of the four MBS temperament traits. Using these guidelines along with the example that follows, you can develop Work-Matching™ model profiles for the various roles in your organization.

Once you've developed model profiles for your organization, you will have a valuable tool in matching the right people to the right positions. Remember though that it is just that ... a valuable "tool". A model temperament is not the only variable in a successful Work-Matching™ formula. Companies should not sacrifice proper interviewing techniques and thorough investigation into the performance claims of candidates. It could probably go without saying, but as we emphasize the importance of considering a person's temperament to their projected success in a given situation, we need to be careful not to discount relevant past successes in favor of the "model profile". We should also be open to the very real possibility that there may be more than one valid "model profile" for a given job. Also, it is important to remain flexible. For instance, we shouldn't discard a candidate simply because their Extroversion falls slightly below the centerline, whereas the "model profile" has the E slightly above the centerline.

Because there is not enough space here to provide more examples and a lot of the finer points, we recommend that you work through the "Frequently Asked Questions" section at the end of this chapter and contact us for our answers, so you can learn by doing. With enough care and experience, successful managers will come to know the power of the Work-Matching™ process.

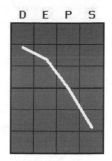

Directness

Overview

The focus of the **Direct** person is on getting results, being in control and solving problems.

You know people whose **Directness** is their *dominant* temperament trait (i.e., the highest trait prevailing above the centerline). They're the ones who take charge, wanting to lead rather than follow. High **D** people have a direct style of communication ... they get right to the point. Sometimes their direct style can be misunderstood as criticism, when really all they are doing is saying what is on their mind in a very direct way.

Application of Directness to the work

Is the work generally performed better by people who exhibit natural *candor* and *decisiveness* (prevailing **D**), or is it the work generally performed better by people who are naturally *prudent, diplomatic* and *supportive* (counter-prevailing **D**)?

Guidelines for positioning **Directness** in a Work-Matching™ model	
Very High	Very outspoken, blunt, brusque, intimidating. Thrives on challenge. Makes decisions and stands firm on them.
High	Outspoken, demanding, determined, persistent. Likes challenge. Comfortable making decisions.
Moderately High	Straightforward. Comfortable making most decisions.
Moderately Low	Tactful, diplomatic. Appreciates support with decision-making.
Low	Reserved, discreet. Will seek support with decision-making.
Very Low	Prudent, often modest. Will seek support with decision-making. Cautious.

Examples of work suited to *high* Directness

It is always important to consider the position of other traits. However, in general, the following work is often well-performed by high **D** workers, who are driven, candid and self-starting:

- Managers
- Supervisors
- Entrepreneurs
- Troubleshooters
- Authority figures

Examples of work suited to *low* Directness

Again, it is always important to consider the position of other traits, especially when dealing with traits located below the center-line. The dominant trait plays a larger role in the Work-Matching™ process. However, in general, the following work is often well-performed by low **D** workers, who possess a nonintimidating style:

- Diplomats (with Extroversion or Pace)
- Customer service reps
- Teachers
- Routine technical workers (not troubleshooting)
- Counselors (with Pace)
- Support staff (with Structure)

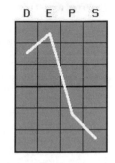

Extroversion

Overview

The focus of the **Extroverted** person is on people and teamwork.

Everyone knows someone who has Extroversion as his or her *dominant* trait (i.e., the highest trait prevailing above the centerline). Extroverted people are talkative, friendly and outgoing. They LOVE to talk. High **E** people have a persuasive style of communication; they naturally tend to talk you into things. They're most creative when working with others, and they thrive on being part of the team! They are interactive.

Application of Extroversion to the work

Is the work generally performed better by people who exhibit natural *sociability* and *cheerfulness*, who are *outgoing* and *persuasive* (prevailing **E**), or is the work generally performed better by people who are naturally *modest, private* and *serious* (counterprevailing **E**)?

	Guidelines for positioning **Extroversion** in a Work-Matching™ model
Very High	Very enthusiastic and outgoing. Actively encourages the participation of others. Strongly persuasive and optimistic. Seeks opportunity and status.
High	Enthusiastic, loves teamwork. May hold back at first, but quickly gets accepted. Seeks participation from others and likes to be noticed. Persuasive and optimistic. Likes status.
Moderately High	Holds back until accepted. Pleasant, prefers when others participate and enjoys teamwork. Mildly persuasive and optimistic.
Moderately Low	Mildly reserved. Okay working in groups but does not actively partake in group discussion if the group is newly formed.
Low	Prefers to meet one-on-one rather than in groups. Can be abrupt under pressure.
Very Low	Modest, private, sometimes shy. Prefers to plan and make decisions alone. Often abrupt under pressure.

Examples of work suited to *high* Extroversion

It is always important to consider the position of other traits. However, in general, the following work is often well-performed by high **E** workers, who prefer frequent interaction with internal and/or external customers, often as a member of a team:

- Sales of all types
- Entertainers
- Work requiring teamwork

Examples of work suited to *low* Extroversion

Again, it is always important to consider the position of other traits, especially when dealing with traits located below the center-line. The dominant trait plays a larger role in the Work-Matching™ process. However, in general, the following work is often well-performed by low **E** workers, who prefer to work alone or one-on-one:

- Analytical workers (technicians, engineers, scientists)
- Detail-oriented workers (accountants, bookkeepers, craftsmen) (with **S**tructure)
- Contemplative workers (religious, writers, certain academicians)
- Mentors (with **P**ace)

Pace

Overview

The focus of the **P**aced person is on timing, harmony and cooperation.

It's easy to recognize someone who has **Pace** as his or her *dominant* trait (i.e., the highest trait prevailing above the centerline). **P**aced people appear laid back, relaxed and easy going. They don't rush; they just move along in a smooth, "under control" manner. High **P** people HATE to be put under pressure, so they naturally avoid pressuring others. High **P** people are naturally considerate, helpful and cooperative.

Application of Pace to the work

Is the work generally performed better by people who exhibit natural *harmony* and *stability* (prevailing **P**), or is the work generally performed better by people who are naturally *urgent* and *exciting* (counterprevailing **P**)?

Guidelines for positioning **P**ace in a Work-Matching™ model	
Very High	Great listener. Likes to plan and get things done on schedule. Very good with routine. Persists to achieve long-term goals. Very dependable and reliable. Extremely empathetic.
High	Good listener, high level of empathy. Good with routine. Dependable. Appears calm and stable under pressure.
Moderately High	Listens well, empathetic, dependable.
Moderately Low	Does not always listen well. Likes excitement but tolerates routine from time to time.
Low	Poor listener.
Very Low	Very poor listener.

Examples of work suited to *high* Pace

It is always important to consider the position of other traits. However, in general, the following work is often well-performed by high **P** workers, who exhibit patience, listening and empathy (identifying with the feelings of others) for the sake of reaching understanding and common ground (cooperation):

- Planners
- Routine work (installers, assembly line workers, certain technicians)
- Customer service reps
- Counselors, advisors, mentors and coaches
- Teachers and trainers

Examples of work suited to *low* Pace

Again, it is always important to consider the position of other traits, especially when dealing with traits located below the center-line. The dominant trait plays a larger role in the Work-Matching™ process. However, in general, the following work is often well-performed by low **P** workers, who like variety; this work frequently requires urgent changes in plans, so it is not routine:

- Managers
- Entrepreneurs (with **D**irectness)
- Tactical sales (with **E**xtroversion)

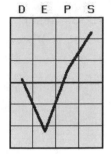

Structure

Overview

The focus of the Structured person is on being right and doing the right thing.

The people you know who are careful, precise and sometimes perfectionists– they're Structured. Someone who has Structure as his *dominant* trait (the highest trait prevailing above the centerline) does things "by the book"–HIS BOOK! They can be resistant to change, not because the change isn't good but because they need some time to be SURE it's good and that it's the right thing to do. They gather facts before making decisions. They ask A LOT of questions. They like to check and re-check. They like to be right!

Application of Structure to the work

Is the work generally performed better by people who exhibit natural *meticulousness* and are *process-driven* (prevailing **S**), or is the work generally performed better by people who are naturally *flexible* and *independent* (counterprevailing **S**)?

Guidelines for positioning Structure in a Work-Matching™ model	
Very High	A naturally good organizer–careful, accurate and precise. A perfectionist. Seldom delegates and will double-check others as well as herself. Very loyal to tradition and processes. Demands solid facts to support change. Justice-oriented.
High	Takes care to be right. Appreciates instructions, processes, standards and constancy. Wants to know what's expected. Doesn't usually delegate, prefers to check the work of others.
Moderately High	Usually careful and conscientious. Micro-picture oriented. Likes constancy and specific praise.
Moderately Low	Exhibits flexibility most times and can delegate work.
Low	Flexible and independent. Tolerates mistakes, often delegates. Open to constructive criticism. Big-picture work.
Very Low	Very independent and flexible. Delegates whenever possible. Very tolerant of mistakes. Takes criticism well. Performs according to her expectations. Big-picture driven.

Examples of work suited to *high* Structure

It is always important to consider the position of other traits. However, in general, the following work is often well-performed by high **S** workers, who respect processes, policies and procedures for the sake of obtaining consistent, quality and reliable results:

- Accountants and bookkeepers
- Analytical, process-driven workers (technicians, design engineers)
- Quality Control
- Maintenance workers (if also high **P**, then routine maintenance)

Examples of work suited to *low* Structure

Again, it is always important to consider the position of other traits, especially when dealing with traits located below the centerline. The dominant trait plays a larger role in the Work-Matching™ process. However, in general, the following work is often well performed by low **S**, independent workers, who are able to look beyond conventional methods. If necessary to perform the work well, low **S** workers are able to (and will) adjust, or break with, established procedures:

- Creative, conceptual workers (artists, architects)
- Salespeople
- Managers (those who make policy rather than live by it)

Using Work-Matching™ to Select the Right People for the Right Work

Different organizations perform different functions in different markets, so it is important to customize your model profiles to suit the work of your organization. For example, the model profile of a salesperson whose employer manufactures military aircraft will differ significantly from the model profile of a salesperson for an automobile dealership. Military aircraft are hugely expensive, and sales normally take several years to close. In contrast, automotive salespeople sell comparatively affordable products to a retail market that presents daily sales opportunities, and their deals typically get closed in a couple of hours.

Military aircraft salespeople need to interact, strategize and negotiate with a broad range of people in the government while also cooperating, interacting, strategizing and negotiating with fellow employees in various departments (engineering, marketing, manufacturing and of course, other members of the sales department). On the other hand, automotive salespeople seldom need to communicate with more than one or two buyers at a time, and internally, they usually only need to interact with their sales and finance managers.

Clearly, the model profile for an airplane salesperson differs from the model profile for an automobile salesperson.

Developing a Model Profile using Work-Matching™

The first step is to answer the following eight key questions about the work being modeled. Don't get discouraged if you don't immediately see how to use the following table. In the next section, we'll walk you through an example, step by step.

Eight Key Questions: *Are most naturally talented workers in this role...*	Very High	High	Mod. High	Mod. Low	Low	Very Low
1. *Straight-talking* and *decisive?*	D+++	D++	D+	D-	D--	D---
2. *Prudent, diplomatic and supportive?*	D---	D--	D-	D+	D++	D+++
3. *Sociable, persuasive* and *cheerful?*	E+++	E++	E+	E-	E--	E---
4. *Modest, private* and *serious?*	E---	E--	E-	E+	E++	E+++
5. *Harmonious, helpful* and *stable?*	P+++	P++	P+	P-	P--	P---
6. *Urgent* and *exciting?*	P---	P--	P-	P+	P++	P+++
7. *Meticulous* and *process-driven?*	S+++	S++	S+	S-	S--	S---
8. *Flexible* and *independent?*	S---	S--	S-	S+	S++	S+++

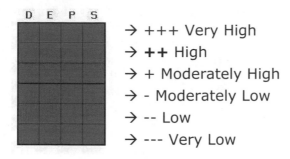

→ +++ Very High

→ ++ High

→ + Moderately High

→ - Moderately Low

→ -- Low

→ --- Very Low

For each two-question set above (i.e., 1&2, 3&4, 5&6 and 7&8), you should arrive at the same answer. If not, reconsider your answers. You may desire to use ranges for some of the traits in the model profile, such as "moderately high to high directness."

First, rate each trait on its own, independently of the other traits. Then go back and adjust your model profile, if necessary, to account for how the combination of traits may interact with each other. (Generally, such interactions are complex and often result in only subtle changes to a Work-Matching™ model profile. One of the Frequently Asked Questions in the rear of this chapter deals with the interaction of temperament traits. There, you will find instructions for obtaining the answers to this and several other good questions.)

Example: Model Profiles for Two Different Sales Roles

Above, we briefly described the differences between the role of a military aircraft salesperson and the role of an automotive salesperson. Use the table above to develop a model profile for both roles, and compare your answers to the following model profile comparison:

Example Work Roles	Directness	Extroversion	Pace	Structure
Military Aircraft Salesperson	Moderately High to High	Moderately High to High	Moderately High to Mod. Low	Moderately Low to Low
Automotive Salesperson	Moderately High	High to Very High	Low to Very Low	Moderately Low to Low

Notice that for most of the traits you only seek to describe ranges. It is important to allow for a span within each trait so you don't miss profiles that don't match exactly but are close enough to consider as matches. Within reason, the overall shape of the model profile matters more than the absolute position of any one trait. That is, when comparing employee or candidate profiles to model profiles, the relative position of one trait to another is more important than absolute position.

A Model Profile for a Military Aircraft Salesperson

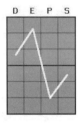

A Model Profile for an Automotive Salesperson

Below is a discussion of the rationale we used to arrive at these two model profiles.

Directness

The model profile for military aircraft salespeople exhibits reasonably high levels of Directness, because they need to make many decisions and maintain control of the long sales process. They need determination and perseverance, focusing on the desired result, to work continuously toward winning a very large sale that will require countless meetings with numerous people over many years. When D is their dominant trait, some of their customer contacts might perceive them to be a little brusque, but there will be sufficient time for them to get to know the salesperson better. (Note: perseverance is also exhibited in the Pace trait, so a person with prevailing P can afford to have a relatively lower D and still suit the role.)

Automotive salespeople need somewhat less Directness; they make relatively fewer decisions, they do not need to impact very many people to close the sale, and they cannot afford to be too pushy, because that may turn the prospective customer away. (Typically, they won't get another chance with the same customer.)

Extroversion

Both models exhibit Extroversion. In general, this trait tends to be quite high in successful automotive salespeople, allowing them to tolerate a lot of "no's" for each "yes" they receive. Extroverts usually talk better than they listen, particularly if their Pace trait is below the centerline. Automotive customers may welcome talkativeness if the information being communicated is helpful to them. In any event, they only need to tolerate it for a short time when purchasing a vehicle. For military aircraft salespeople, Extroversion is also useful, but its application is internal as well as external. These people work in cross-disciplined teams, *and* they have to interface with a variety of people within client organizations. They will have plenty of time to develop internal and external relationships between each sale, so it is not necessary for them to exhibit a "very high" level of Extroversion.

Pace

The Pace trait represents the chief temperament difference between models for the two types of salespeople discussed. People with high P are naturally good listeners and genuinely care about people. They are *relationship* oriented. People with low Pace are self-starters, impatient, and they thrive on chaos, whereas people with a prevailing Pace trait are patient and do not like to be rushed into things. Rather, they prefer to get their work done in a steady fashion (hence the "Pace" descriptor). Automotive salespeople do not need to be as relationship-oriented; their business involves quick transactions with a large variety of people. Low Pace serves them well, acting as a self-motivating mechanism to close the next deal. For military aircraft salespeople, listening and relationship building are important attributes for their work. Self-starting and being flexible with changes are also important, so you don't want Pace in the model to be overly strong. Our model profile for the military aircraft salesperson allows for Pace to be moderately above or below the centerline.

Structure

Models for both salespeople in the example will have nearly the same level of the Structure temperament trait but for different reasons. For both jobs, it is easier for a salesperson to perform his role well if he has a counterprevailing Structure trait. For the automotive salesperson, if S is below the centerline, he is naturally more fluid with creatively structuring a sale around a customer's needs. For the military aircraft salesperson, a counterprevailing Structure trait enhances flexibility in the sales process, to comfortably handle changes in client needs and timeframes as well as to deal with a variety of different people in the client's organization.

You do not want to set the S position in either model too low. Because of the fast-paced, high-volume transactions, auto dealers impose well-defined policies on matters of paperwork and pricing, and automotive salespeople must operate within these guidelines to ensure profitability and to limit liability. Military aircraft salespeople are involved in an analytical sale, and their clients are highly concerned about quality. The military appreciates salespeople who exhibit a knack for details and who understand quality controls, cost controls and the like.

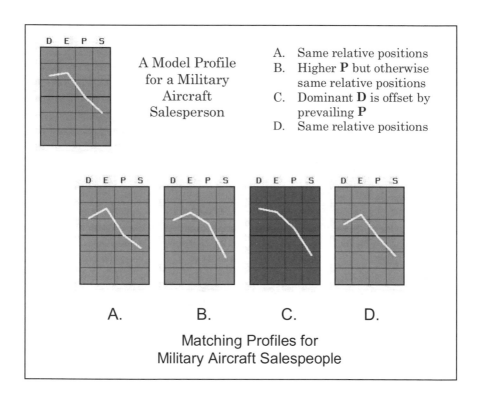

A Model Profile for a Military Aircraft Salesperson

A. Same relative positions
B. Higher **P** but otherwise same relative positions
C. Dominant **D** is offset by prevailing **P**
D. Same relative positions

A.   B.   C.   D.

Matching Profiles for
Military Aircraft Salespeople

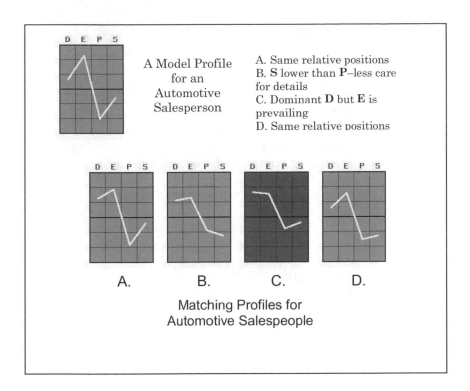

A Model Profile for an Automotive Salesperson

A. Same relative positions
B. **S** lower than **P**–less care for details
C. Dominant **D** but **E** is prevailing
D. Same relative positions

A.   B.   C.   D.

Matching Profiles for Automotive Salespeople

Applications for Work-Matching™

We've discussed Work-Matching™ in terms of its broad application for selecting the right people for the right work. Specific applications for Work-Matching™ include:

- **SELECT PEOPLE FOR FURTHER DEVELOPMENT**
  - o Help ensure that the people you train and develop are willing to learn and are self-motivated to achieve improved results. See the section entitled, "Supe Up the Development of Your Employees."

125

- **DESIGN OPTIMALLY-PERFORMING TEAMS**
  - Form effective work teams by assuring temperamental diversity (i.e., the natural talents of each team member complement the talents of the others, so the team performs a broad range of roles well).
- **IMPLEMENT ORGANIZATIONAL CHANGE**
  - Discover untapped talent in your organization to fill new or vacated positions with known, loyal employees who can perform the jobs well.
- **PERFORM SUCCESSION PLANNING and PLAN PROMOTIONS**
  - Work-Matching™ can greatly assist your management in determining who should be groomed for promotion and succession.
- **IMPROVE COMMUNICATIONS**
  - Understand the temperaments of your co-workers, superiors and subordinates to achieve better communications and fewer misunderstandings.
- **IMPROVE MEETING PRODUCTIVITY**
  - A sound understanding of the temperaments of each meeting participant allows the meeting's chairperson to achieve maximum participation and clearer understanding, in less time.
- **RECRUIT THE BEST**
  - Understanding a job candidate's temperament allows you to ask relevant, targeted interview questions leading to better hiring decisions.
  - Discover alternative opportunities for capitalizing on an applicant's temperament (i.e., perhaps she can fill a role she didn't apply for).
- **MATCH EMPLOYEES TO CLIENTS AND PROSPECTS**
  - Increase your success with clients and prospects by matching the right person to the right opportunity.

Supe Up the Development of Your Employees

The famous behavioral scientist Abraham Maslow created the theory of Maslow's Hierarchy of Human Needs, which is widely applied today by successful organizations around the world. Briefly, his theory states that humans must have their needs satisfied from the bottom of the hierarchy traveling upward to the top in successive stages (i.e., no skipping of stages). The order of the needs hierarchy from the bottom up is: Physiological, Safety, Belonging, Self-Esteem and ultimately, Self-Actualization.

- People who are preoccupied with worry about their health need to fulfill their Physiological needs: They must deal with their problems and/or ease their worries, then progress past Safety and Belonging before becoming willing and eager candidates for development.
- People who are very concerned about their personal and family finances (perhaps they're worried about being laid off!) need to fulfill their Safety needs: They must deal with their problems and/or ease their worries, then progress past Belonging before becoming willing and eager candidates for development.
- People who are anxious because they are not on good terms with their family and co-workers need to fulfill their Belonging needs: They must deal with their problems and/or ease their worries before becoming willing and eager candidates for development.

Typically, when companies select candidates for further development, they do not assess where each candidate presently resides on Maslow's Hierarchy. This is important, because people who are experiencing satisfaction deficits in the needs categories Physiological, Safety or Belonging make poor candidates for development. The most willing and eager candidates for development will reside in the needs categories of Self-Esteem and Self-Actualization, because they are very willing and eager to improve their potential and apply their natural talents to their work!

Importantly, people residing in the top two levels of Maslow's Hierarchy (Self-Actualization and Self-Esteem) may appear not to *need* development; however, because they are self-motivated to improve their potential and apply their natural talents to their work, they make the best candidates for development. **It is critical to the success of your development programs to recognize the difference between the *need for development* and the *readiness for development!*** The following symptoms imply the strong possibility that you need to revamp your company's development process:

- Your company experiences little or no return on your investment in training and development.
- Even some of your best past performers remain stagnant or lose ground, despite your company's development efforts.

Temperament assessments don't measure where a person presently resides on Maslow's Hierarchy; that's determined by being observant and using common sense. But Work-Matching™ is a very powerful self-discovery tool that will help you get your employees to the top of Maslow's Hierarchy and keep them there. Your company will greatly improve the results of its training and development if it selects candidates who are well suited to their work: *Because they know who they are, what they're about, where their talents lie and how to apply their talents to their work, they possess a high potential for self-esteem and self-actualization.* In turn, they are *ready* for development, because they yearn to improve themselves, leading to improved results for their company. Ultimately, development isn't about becoming like others who presently set the benchmark for performance; it's all about *improving who you already are!*

Improve the Effectiveness of Your Recruiting Process

Many organizations use assessment tools to screen applicants; that is, to decide who they should bother interviewing. Screening can land you in court, and from a practical standpoint, you'll miss a lot of good hiring opportunities. Assessments should be used to *assist* your selection process; they don't replace effective interviewing. First, consult with your legal experts on these matters. This book does not provide legal advice! Second, when getting acclimated to this or any other new process, it is a good idea to seek help from an expert. We do Work-Matching™ and leadership development for a living, so please don't hesitate to contact us for assistance. Third, follow these common sense guidelines:

- When seeking job candidates, look to people who are already employed within your organization. Sounds obvious? If you haven't performed temperament surveys on everyone in your organization, you really don't have a road map showing where the hidden talent lies.
- For recruits, assess them *after* the first interview, ONLY if you intend to interview them further.
  - o Don't use MBS or any other tool as a "screen."
- Use the results to generate intelligent questions for additional interview(s) that will verify the match, identify other opportunities for candidates or help you confirm your concerns about the candidate's mismatch.
  - o Always be on the lookout for candidates who may be able to fill other, unadvertised or contemplated positions because of their temperament. It is usually cheaper to develop skills and knowledge in high-potential people than to leave positions unstaffed or filled with underperforming people.
- Many candidates who don't match the model profile can still perform well in a role, because they know how to apply their talents in creative ways. Be open to this possibility! But also realize that such candidates may perform even better in other positions, so discuss other opportunities with them.

FREQUENTLY ASKED QUESTIONS

The following questions provide excellent discussion points. We recommend that you and your colleagues read this chapter, discuss your own answers to these questions and then compare your answers to ours. There is not enough space here to print our answers; however, you may obtain them from electronically from us at no charge:

For a copy of our answers to these questions, please go to our web site at www.WorkMatching.com and complete the electronic form there. Alternatively, send an e-mail to info@WorkMatching.com requesting the answers. Please provide full contact information (contact name, company name, title, phone, fax and address, number of employees).

1. Why is it important to know a person's temperament, or nature, when matching him or her to a work role?

2. Does everyone *have* to fit the model profile for particular work?

3. Can we get into trouble using "profiling?"

4. If some good performers don't fit the model temperament profile for particular work, why bother with Work-Matching™?

5. How do we account for interactions between temperament traits when developing model profiles and assessing employee temperament?

6. For each type of work performed within our organization, why don't we just administer the MBS temperament survey to our best performers and average the results to arrive at model profiles?

7. What do we do about people who don't match the model profile and who aren't performing up to reasonable standards?

8. What about employees who've been great performers in the past but haven't been performing well recently?

9. What happens if we wait until later to implement Work-Matching™?

To take the MBS temperament assessment survey tool, go to **www.WorkMatching.com** and follow the instructions. If you are considering using the MBS tool in your organization, please contact us to arrange a free demonstration. Please provide full contact information (contact name, company name, title, phone, fax and address, number of employees).

We wish to express our sincere gratitude to MBS, Inc., the company that owns the MBS Profile Report temperament assessment tool. The principals of MBS, Inc., Steve Postlewait and Michael Postlewait, generously spent many hours of their time editing this chapter and providing technical advice.

About The Author

Peter A. LaChance

Quintessence provides clients with a unique and truly effective leadership development process. This process grows leaders and achieves improved results through the practical application of behavioral science and goal-achievement methods. The Quintessence leadership process includes its unique WorkMatching™ system, which is a cost-effective and easily employed method designed to select the right people for the right work. Peter has trained and consulted locally, nationally and internationally in many industries, including Security, Insurance, Automotive, Utilities, Government, Engineering, Printing, Software, Financial, Telemetry, Environmental, and Academia. Peter's work has benefited both for-profit and non-profit organizations, ranging in size from $1 Million to $10 Billion in revenue. Peter graduated with honors from Stevens Institute of Technology with a Bachelor of Engineering degree. He also earned an MS degree from Syracuse University and an MBA from Rensselaer Polytechnic Institute with a concentration in Organizational Behavior.

Peter A. LaChance
The Quintessence Corporation
484 Stony Hill Road
Yardley, PA 19067
Phone: 1.888.35.LEADER (1.888.355.3233)
Fax: 215.790.6276
Email: Peter@TQC.com
www.TQC.com

Chapter Seven

ETHICS-BASED LEADERSHIP

Nobby Lewandowski

It is a struggle for one to develop a meaning for the word "ethics." Webster defines it as "the philosophical analysis of human morality and conduct; a system of conduct or behavior; moral principles." Richard Daft (*The Leadership Experience*, Harcourt Publishers, 2002) suggests that "ethics is in the soft, almost impossible to measure realm of human meaning, purpose, quality, significance and values." Daft compares the world of business with the realm of ethics. Business, he claims, can be dissected, diagnosed and compared whereas ethics does not lend itself to precise interpretation, comparison and evaluation. It is my opinion that the intensity of world competition tends to create a separation between the worlds of business and ethics, but recent scandals have led to the recognition that the two must be brought much closer together.

Two of the major components of ethics are integrity and character. I remember once reading the saying, "As I have watched you live as you believe, I have learned the meaning of integrity." Wouldn't it be great if our leaders could imagine those words on their tombstones, living on forever? Maybe if we lived by ethical behavior, integrity and character, the world would be a better place.

So how does one recognize a leader who behaves ethically? Perhaps one way of defining a leader is to describe the behaviors that one hopes to observe in such a person. The following checklist will aid in the description and development of one who attempts to lead others in an ethical manner.

Ethical Leaders...
- accept responsibility for their decisions and actions, protecting the reputation of their families, company and professions, avoiding even the appearance of wrong doing and taking action to correct or prevent the unethical conduct of others.
- consider others equal to self in a caring, kind, compassionate, respectful and helpful manner.
- use their power to serve others in a fair, open-minded and just manner, being willing to admit mistakes and change position when appropriate.
- align their vision with that of their followers, remembering the maxim, "You cannot lead people where they do not want to go."
- pursue excellence in meeting their professional duties, staying well informed while seeking to improve their competencies.
- coach, stimulate and develop followers to think independently and creatively.
- obey just laws, express informed views, respect democratic processes and make certain that others have the information needed to perform their roles in the organizations and societies in which they live.

America today appears to be overmanaged and underled. By definition, most managers typically plan, organize, budget and control their workers rather well. Many, however, have taken the low road and manipulated employees and other important stakeholders into believing things that are just not true. Leaders, on the other hand, are those managers and others who possess high levels of integrity, which earns the trust of their followers. This ethical behavior, in turn, assists everyone on the team or in the organization to realize his or her mutually agreed upon mission and goals. I often use the saying, "Without integrity, you can never develop trust, and without trust you can never develop people."

The question arises as to why the American public has recently lost so much confidence in its so-called leaders. Why has the unethical and often immoral and illegal behavior of those in positions of trust undermined and disgraced these people and the organizations they represent? Adding to the problem is the fact that media frenzies often reduce confidence, even in those who adhere to ethical and moral principles throughout their work, family and spiritual lives.

The purpose of this chapter is to introduce readers to the types of ethical dilemmas that confront most managers, leaders and other professionals at some point during their careers. Perhaps through the use of real examples and their outcomes, valuable insights can be gained; questions will be answered, guidelines provided and future ethical traps avoided. When a real example is presented within this chapter, try to define the ethical dilemma, put yourself in the position of the people who are confronted with the problem and then decide what you would have done had you been the responsible leader.

Our first ethical dilemma takes place at a major university in the Midwest. Its basketball team had won several national titles during the 1990s, but recently, the president of the university was notified that its fabulous five players had accepted more than $600,000 in gifts and other payments from a wealthy alumnus during their playing days. How would you have handled this shocking news of NCAA violations if you were the university president? What ethical principles are involved? What are the potential impacts of your decision on your respected and world-famous university?

The university president, upon learning of the unethical behavior of the key athletes, immediately had her custodians tear down the team banners celebrating impacted victories, repaid $450,000 in postseason receipts and gave up the scores of all victories between 1995 and 1999. She also said at a news conference, "There is no excuse for what happened. It was wrong, plain and simple. This is a day of great shame for the university." Perhaps the president was using a common, although somewhat simplistic, definition of ethics in her decision making: "Ethical decision making is deciding between what is right and what is wrong and always trying to do what is right."

Unfortunately, ethical decisions are not as simple as they used to be. In modern times, these decisions have often become the difference between *right* and *right*. Preston Townley, in his speech "Business Ethics: Commitment to Tough Decisions" (Vital Speeches, January 1992, pp. 208-211), states, "It ought to be fairly easy to choose between right and wrong by relying on principles, but business activity often demands that we select from alternatives that are neither wholly right nor wholly wrong."

Consider the following example that occurred over a decade ago within a large manufacturing company in the central part of the United States. An international sales manager for the company telephoned his vice president from a warehouse in Baghdad. He claimed that an Iraqi purchasing agent was demanding a "token of appreciation" (better known as a bribe) for doing business and that all of the companies competing for the business had offered this token. Now the ethics code of the company stated that no bribes would be offered in return for business. Further complicating the situation was a U.S. law known as the Foreign Corrupt Practices Act that forbids U.S. companies from offering bribes. In spite of these constraints, The U.S. sales manager was told by his supervisor to "Get the business; I do not care how, and don't tell me how you did it."

The sales manager, wanting to keep his job, I suppose, then paid a million dollars for a fictitious advertisement in a Baghdad newspaper, with the money diverted to the Iraqi purchasing agent. The sale was made. In this situation, ethics, morality and U.S. law were all intertwined in global intrigue. Most U.S. business people do not understand the complications of decision making when dealing with foreign cultures that do not subscribe to the same ethical principles and laws found in the United States. (Footnote to the case: The only way this transaction became public and totally embarrassed the manufacturing organization was through an IRS audit that uncovered a $75,000 kickback from the bribe money taken by the international sales manager, who was later fined, fired and jailed).

Philosophers' Lessons on Ethics, Briefly Stated

Philosophers have been discussing ethics since the time of Plato and Socrates. Many modern day philosophers consider ethics to be the science of conduct, the fundamental rules by which good people live their lives. Some consider ethics to be equivalent to values that guide how we ought to behave—values such as honesty, respect for others and their property, fairness, accountability, etc. Statements concerning how these values are applied are often referred to as ethical principles.

It would certainly be a better world if we all followed the three "Rs":

Respect for self

Respect for others

Respect for all our actions

Ends-Based Thinker

Discussions about ethics sometimes lead to definitions of three types of thinking that might be used by a leader. This leader considers the consequences of an action on all relevant parties. She bases her decisions on the utilitarian view of the greatest good. Decisions are made on the premise that the end result should be the greatest good for the greatest number of people involved. She would authorize termination of 700 workers on the premise that it would save the positions for thousands of additional employees. The ends-based thinker normally defends the public or common interest over personal gain.

Rule-Based Thinker

This ethical leader bases his decisions on established rules, regulations, laws and policies, without consideration of the consequences or impacts on others. This type of thinker believes that rules are the best way to achieve fairness and consistency, believing that rules apply to everyone equally. A rule-based thinker might ignore the problems of a physically challenged worker, saying that everyone must meet corporate standards of performance in spite of age or stature. For example, if a landscape company has a policy that all beginning workers must be able to carry a chain saw to the top of a tree for purposes of trimming the branches, then all job applicants must pass this test. Perhaps this employment hurdle has been in place since the company was established. Forty years earlier, the test was probably logical, legal, fair and ethical. However, as times have changed, new laws relating to equal opportunity and affirmative action would probably make the policy obsolete and, if not illegal, at least unethical.

Care-Based Thinker

The third type of ethical thinking is based on caring and compassion. This type leader brings a sense of fairness and balance to the decision making process. Decisions may even favor weaker stakeholders. Mercy tends to take precedence over justice. The care-based thinker often turns to more exemplars for guidance. Perhaps care-based thinking was involved with many of the decisions regarding wayward clergy, where mercy for the perpetrator took precedence over justice for the victim.

As one examines the complexity of ethical decision making in light of the three types of thinking outlined above, it becomes painfully clear that leaders may face horrific quandaries as they attempt to follow moral values and ethical guidelines in dealing with daily decisions. Consider the dilemma faced by world leaders as they struggle with the problems of evil dictators who prey on their people as well as present dangers to the rest of the world. A president must ask himself over and over, "Do I attack and risk the lives of innocent people or do nothing and wait for what appears to be the inevitable murder of my own people"? This has to be the greatest of burdens that could be placed on any one individual.

Rushworth Kidder, in his book *How Good People Make Tough Choices* (Prima Publishing, 1996), describes four classical dilemmas that leaders face.

- The good of the individual versus the good of the community.
- Truth versus loyalty.
- Short term versus long term.
- Justice versus mercy.

As you think about your future leadership responsibilities, consider the difficulties you will undoubtedly face as problems arise and you must decide among these four conflicting goals. I like to use the analogy that management is to checkers as leadership is to chess. Managers have policies, rules, contracts and regulations that they can fall back upon when the going gets tough. Leaders, however, have personal values, compassion, caring and fairness that will enter and cloud their decision making. One can master the rules of checkers and beat most opponents. Few, however, become masters of the game of chess. Perhaps this is why we have so many managers in the world of business and so few leaders. While coaching many companies, I have seen that managers do things right while leaders do the right things.

Is There a Common Morality?

Based on my research and practical experience, it appears to me that there is a common body of moral rules that might be helpful in responding to the ethical decision making dilemmas similar to those presented in this chapter. For example, for a person to be considered ethical, it seems necessary for him to keep his word. Codes of ethics stress the importance of doing what you say you are going to do. Taking this rule a step further, it is also important to behave in the same manner in which you are asking others to behave (i.e. walk the talk). If upper management is asking employees to use both sides of the paper to reduce office supply costs, then upper management must follow the same practice.

In one large organization, the president once stated that all associates would, from that day forward, be treated equally. He then proceeded to have a parking garage built for use only by his vice presidents and himself. Certainly, the president has a right to have a garage built for his senior managers, but trust can soon be lost when statements or promises are made to which one does not personally adhere.

Another common moral principle is that we all have a right to expect that violence is not an acceptable means of settling a dispute. Leaders and others should be able to act cooperatively with one another, because they realize they do not have to fear for their physical safety. A third common rule of morality is that we should expect that when we are in trouble, others will offer some form of assistance. This is referred to as the principle of mutual aid. Isn't it true that most of us have an innate desire to help others? Along this same line, common morality demands that respect for others involves accepting their interests as important and taking their concerns seriously. *Leaders listen.*

Respect for property is a critical aspect of common morality and ethical behavior. Property rights for organizations and individuals lead to the moral principle that anyone may own property, which provides a foundation for how business is transacted in a free society.

Ethical Myths

Carter McNamara, in his article "Complete Guide to Ethics Management: An Ethics Toolkit for Managers," 2001, identifies numerous misconceptions regarding business ethics. Those most relevant to this article are noted below.

MYTH NUMBER ONE
Business ethics is more a matter of religion
than a matter of leadership.

Diane Kirrane, in "Managing Values: A Systematic Approach to Business Ethics" (*Training and Development Journal*, November 1990), claims that changing personal values is not the purpose of a business ethics program. Rather, business ethics is the management of people with different values and the conflicts that will inevitably arise among them.

MYTH NUMBER TWO
Business ethics is a discipline best taught by
academics, philosophers and clergy.

This type of thinking leads many to believe that ethics is a movement having little to do with the daily realities of modern business decision making. The truth is that ethical decision making is a practical tool, absolutely essential to the survival of an organization. Consider the tremendous upheaval created by the lack of ethics among top business leaders during 2002. A world-renowned consulting and auditing firm, which is no longer in business, lost its clients and its reputation due to the inappropriate, unethical and possibly illegal "cooking of the books." Certain individuals within this long-respected firm lost sight of the dilemma caused by conflicts of interest to include situations where auditors are often asked to play the role of consultants to the organization they are auditing.

One of the nation's largest energy firms was riding the crest of an economic wave. People with capital had good reasons for investing in this company, including the fact that *Fortune* magazine listed it as the most innovative company in the country in 2001. It was also listed as the second most admired company in the country for its quality of management. But Enron failed because of a lack of integrity—the basis of trust. Because others lost their trust in the organization, it failed. Its market capitalization crashed from $70 billion to less than $1 billion in just ten months. As Steve Priest of the Ethical Leadership Group (see Steve Priest, "A Matter of Trust", *The Chicago Tribune*, January 18, 2002) points out, underestimating the importance of trust is not just a corporate problem. Today there are too many examples that remind us that trust is the key to success for individuals and institutions. Ethical leadership based on trust is the basis for saving corporate America as well as personal careers.

MYTH NUMBER THREE
Business ethics is superfluous since it only
asserts the obvious: "Do good."

Many managers assert that the ethics codes to which an organization aspires are not necessary since all members of the organization are honest. These managers are quick to speak about the Golden Rule, integrity, respect and courtesy. However, when presented with complex ethical situations, these same managers realize there is a wide and gray area when trying to apply ethical principles. Consider the recent case at the United States Naval Academy, where scores of midshipmen were caught cheating on a difficult electrical engineering examination. The academy has one of the strongest honor codes of any organization, yet its members felt it was appropriate and necessary to circulate a stolen copy of the test prior to the day of the examination. If the graduates of the academy felt it was necessary to get advanced information on a difficult exam in order to achieve their goal of a commission in the United States Navy, what types of behaviors would these future leaders follow when they eventually assumed civilian positions in American industry? I doubt that anyone can defend the position that codes of ethics are superfluous in light of such an example occurring in one of the nation's most respected military academies.

MYTH NUMBER FOUR
Business ethics is a matter of the good guys
preaching to the bad guys.

Some members of upper management claim the moral high ground while lamenting the weaker ethics of their employees and lower level supervisors. However, experienced leaders realize that good people can make bad decisions, particularly when stressed, confused or even a bit greedy.

Consider the case of the chairman of the number one online job-search site, Monster.com. He oversees a database of more than twenty-two million resumes. Despite his expertise in helping people list their resumes on his site, his own credentials are lacking the most important element: accuracy. According to his listed resume, the chairman holds an "executive MBA" from the Harvard Business School. ("Look Who Inflated His Credentials" *Business Week*, January 27, 2003.) The problem is, there is no such degree. Harvard does not offer the executive MBA. The only MBA it awards takes the customary two years (attending school full time) to earn. According to a spokesperson from Harvard, the only work the chairman of Monster.com completed at Harvard was a nine-week summer certification. The chairman took a salary of $950,000 from the company in 2001.

Now consider the impact of this expose on the employees of the organization. The top manager of the United States' largest job-search firm misrepresented his own credentials. With such behavior on the part of the chief executive, should the company expect more from its own employees? In the words of Ralph Waldo Emerson, "What you do speaks so loudly, that I cannot hear what you say." Learn to see things as they really are, not as we imagine they are.

The case of the Monster.com chairman brings up a very important point. Research indicates that twenty-five percent of all resumes contain incorrect (false) information. Before you place a resume on the web or circulate it widely to others, be certain that it is completely accurate. Falsification of resume or application information is grounds for immediate dismissal from an organization. The law will uphold this cause for termination. Employers are becoming increasingly aware of the tendency to "stretch" qualifications and achievements and are watching the data very carefully, especially in these difficult times when layoffs and terminations are more prevalent. Consider the once-trusted football coach who was just two resume falsifications away from one of football's dream jobs—head coach at Notre Dame. He lost a multimillion dollar pay package and a credible reputation by submitting a resume that was less than truthful.

Stress, confusion and greed are not excuses for unethical actions; they are the causes. Therefore to encourage development of an ethical workplace, all leaders, managers and employees should work together to help each other remain ethical and to work through ethical dilemmas together. John Donne once said, "No man is an island." There is nothing wrong with a leader who seeks counsel from trusted employees before making a difficult decision, especially when conflicting interests are involved.

I often use acronyms in my talks. The one that fits here is (T.E.A.M.). Together Each Accomplishes More. One of the team members will probably bring everyone into focus in a difficult situation, which is a win for the organization.

MYTH NUMBER FIVE
Ethics cannot be managed.

In reality, ethics are always managed, but very often, this management is indirect. For example, the behavior of the organization's founder or current head is a strong moral and ethical influence on the behavior of employees. Organization priorities (market share, profit maximization, cost cutting) are strong influences on ethical behavior. There are many instances of managers asking employees to alter documentation to indicate less scrap, more positive research results, greater tonnage out the door, etc. in order to make themselves and their departments appear more profitable or effective. As managers ask others to cheat, they set the tone for the rest of the organization. They actually are managing ethics—downward. Just as in the case of the chairman at Monster.com, employees watch the actions of their upper management, and often, it is a case of "monkey see, monkey do."

MYTH NUMBER SIX

None of our managers have ever broken the
law; therefore, we are a highly
ethical organization.

A manager can operate within the limits of the law yet can still be unethical in her behavior. Take, for example, the captain of a university golf team whose roommate, team member and best friend admitted in confidence that she took money for playing in a sanctioned professional tournament. Now we have an ethical dilemma. The golfer broke no law except the code of professional ethics that says no varsity athlete shall take money for playing professionally while still a member of a university or college team. Of course, the captain of the team owes it to her team and coach to report the infraction, but in order to do so, she must betray the confidence of her best friend. What to do? This is a case of truth versus loyalty. But loyalty to whom? Is it the individual or the university that will suffer the most if the truth becomes known? In actuality, the captain never reported the infraction, but the truth became known anyway, the violator was dismissed from the team and an apology was made to the national organization. So the captain gained little from withholding embarrassing information from her superior, and the team lost a key player, even though no laws were broken. This example illustrates the point that actions can be legal but still unethical.

MYTH NUMBER SEVEN

Ethics management has little practical relevance in the workplace.

On the contrary, research indicates that organizations that rank high on the scale of ethical conduct have significantly outperformed the stock market average. *The New York Times* (July 27, 1987) reported a study, conducted by the Johnson and Johnson company, of thirty business organizations that were considered to have above average ethical standards. While the overall stock average (as measured by Dow Jones) had risen fivefold between 1957 and 1986, the stock value of the thirty so-called highly ethical companies experienced a twenty-threefold increase in value.

There are many other benefits of leading an organization that is ranked high in ethical behavior. A few of these benefits, as mentioned by Carter McNamara, include the following: Attention to business ethics has substantially improved society over the past fifty years. After years of employee exploitation, intimidation and harassment, society reacted and demanded fairness and equal rights. Antitrust laws were instituted, government agencies were established, unions were organized, and laws were written. Yes, this environment was changed by laws, but the laws were enacted by humans who felt the need for more secure and respectful places of employment.

Ethics programs provide a moral compass to guide leaders through times of chaos and turbulent changes in technology, economics, politics and social upheaval. These programs help to align employee behavior with ethical values preferred by upper management and leaders of the organization. This alignment of values and strategies promotes teamwork and dialogue regarding values in the workplace, which can lead to openness, integrity and community.

Ethical organizations support employee health and significance. *The Wall Street Journal*, (April 11, 1991) explains that a consulting company tested a wide spectrum of executives and other supervisors on matters of ethics. Their most striking finding, according to the article, was that those scoring the highest on the ethics test were more emotionally healthy and satisfied with their work environment.

Logic suggests that it is far better to incur the cost of ensuring ethical practices now than to incur costs of litigation later. A major intent of effective human resource policies is to assure ethical treatment of employees in matters of hiring, evaluation, discipline, benefits and termination. Drake and Drake (*California Management Review*, Vol. 16, pp. 107-123) argue, "An employer can be subjected to suit for breach of contract for failure to comply with promises. Therefore, the gap between stated corporate culture and actual practice has significant legal as well as ethical implications." Managing ethical values in the workplace strengthens the coherence and balance of the organization's culture, improves trust in leadership and relationships among individuals and groups, supports greater consistency in standards and qualities of products and services, and it encourages greater sensitivity to the impact of the organization on its internal messages and external environment.

There are numerous benefits in the development and implementation of ethics programs. Unfortunately, research indicates that these programs are not stemming employee misconduct. Workers are seeing but not necessarily reporting widespread illegal and unethical conduct in the workplace, despite many corporate ethics programs. This was reported in a study of more than 2,300 employees by KPMG LLP, New York (*The Wall Street Journal*, May 11, 2000). More than seventy-five percent of those surveyed said they had observed violations of the law or company ethical standards in the previous twelve months. Many of the employees taking part in this survey indicated a willingness to report misdeeds, but sixty-one percent thought management would not take appropriate disciplinary action.

Among other things, workers noted sexual harassment, conflicts of interest, employment discrimination, deceptive sales practices, unsafe working conditions and abuse of the environment. A KPMG executive stated, "People are not reporting misconduct because they are not encouraged to do so." The study also discovered that cynicism, low morale and indifference were to blame for the misconduct. Based on this study, and some of the blatant violations of ethical standards since the time of this study, I conclude that ethics programs in and of themselves will not stem the tide of deceit and corruption in organizations. It is also important that leaders provide rewards or incentives for adhering to ethical standards. This would reinforce the importance of the ethical programs.

I conclude this section by quoting Bob Dunn, president of the San-Francisco-based Business for Social Responsibility, who states, "Ethical values, consistently applied, are the cornerstones in building a commercially successful and socially responsible business."

Ethics Training

One important way to raise a leader's awareness of the critical nature of ethical dilemmas and their impact on the organization is to discuss actual case studies related to the industry in which he or she operates. An excellent source of such case studies can be found at The Institute for Global Ethics, www. globalethics.org.

Here is one sample case from the Global Ethics database:

"As a young, three-year manager of a chemical plant, Alex learns that a team of internal auditors from his firm's home office will descend on his factory in two days. He prepares his staff as best he can.

The day before the auditors are to arrive, one of his assistants discovers some disconcerting news. It appears, the assistant says, that Woody, a thirty-year veteran of the plant, has been systematically altering accounts for years. Month by month, Woody has been shipping products to customers without billing them and then billing customers without shipping anything.

Alex is stunned. Seeking an explanation, he learns that the practice has nothing to do with fraud. Woody was not lining his own pocket. He was simply trying to be helpful. His goal was to smooth out the cyclical nature of the orders so that month by month, the figures sent to the home office appeared level and consistent, with no peaks and valleys. On balance, Alex finds no money has been lost or gained. It all balances out in the end. He also finds that the amount is not immense in that the funds affected are only about five percent of the plant's annual sales.

In one sense, Woody's adjustments have benefited Alex, who has been complimented by higher management for his astute forecasts and for meeting his targets so accurately. But Alex also knows that if these practices were to come to light, Woody would be fired instantly and he himself, though unaware of the practice until now, might have some tough explaining to do. After all, Woody has been fudging records and misstating corporate revenues to management, shareholders and the IRS.

As Alex sees it, he has an ethical dilemma rather than a legal imperative. There is no doubt in his mind that the practices must stop. His question, however, is how best to stop them. He sees his dilemma as one involving justice versus mercy. Adhering strictly to a sense of justice, he could inform the auditors of his recent discovery the moment they arrive. Or seeking a merciful outcome that would protect the career of a long-standing and very loyal employee, he could try to buy a little time, enabling him to deal with the situation internally, quietly and with compassion. Deal with it he must. But how and when?"

The following case is adapted from the article "State Employees Accept Gifts, Violating Ethics Code" by A.W. Huggins, *Akron Beacon Journal*, June 30, 2000:

Employees of the Ohio Department of Human Services' computer support division were reprimanded for accepting gifts, including $280 leather jackets, from a company receiving a state contract. The department's deputy director endorsed the gifts and praised the computer items he had purchased from the company providing the jackets. The Ohio Inspector General stated, "These actions clearly give the appearance of impropriety and a potential conflict of interest." Another network services manager attended a party hosted by a vendor trying to win a contract with the Human Services Division and accepted gifts. He also attended golf outings offered by other computer vendors. Investigators learned that a $5,200 "appreciation dinner" had been provided to the employees of the computer support group.

When managers accept gifts, endorse parties or attend vendor-sponsored athletic events, they send a powerful message to all employees: "What we do is fine for you to do." Perhaps this message can be more clearly stated: *"What we allow, we teach."*

Using this type of case in an employee training or leadership development program creates a wonderful opportunity for discussing ethical issues and dilemmas without embarrassing (hopefully) any particular person within the organization. Dialogue does not necessarily teach new values, but it certainly reminds people of the values they already possess and how difficult it is, sometimes, to live up to them.

Practical Tools for Addressing Ethical Dilemmas

I have noted on several occasions that ethical decision making is often a complex and stress-producing task. It would be remiss of me if I did not provide a few useful tools for addressing such dilemmas. I do not claim originality for the three tools that follow, but I have taken the liberty of altering and editing them to assure consistency with my own beliefs.

One approach to dealing with a difficult ethical situation is to refer to some sort of checklist. A sample checklist is provided below and is adapted from a similar list developed by Doug Wallace and Jon Pekel of the Fulcrum Group.

1. Have I sought out and received as much information as possible related to the decision that I must make?
2. Have I communicated with everyone who has a right to have a voice in this decision as well as the action plan that must follow the decision?
3. Have I anticipated the consequences of this decision for those who will be significantly affected by it?
4. If I were in the position of one of the people who would be significantly impacted by the decision, would I perceive the decision to be fair, timely and consistent with the ethical policies of the organization?
5. Is this decision consistent with my own values and ethical standards?
6. Would I want this decision to be the basis of a universal principle applicable to all similar situations?
7. How would I feel if this decision were to become public and disclosed to everyone I know, including my immediate family?

Another popular ethical checklist was first published by Laura Nash in her article "Ethics Without the Sermon," *Harvard Business Review*, (59). Again, I have made minor adjustments in the list to update the material and to bring it into conformity with my own thinking and the intentions of this chapter Questions that should be asked in addressing an ethical dilemma might include:

1. Is the dilemma defined accurately and completely?
2. How might the dilemma be defined by a person who would be impacted by my solution?
3. What is the origin of this dilemma?
4. To whom must I give my loyalty in arriving at a solution to the problem?
5. What are my motives in making a decision regarding this dilemma?
6. Whom might this decision possibly injure or embarrass?
7. Can I discuss the situation with the affected parties or the people responsible for the problem in advance of my decision?

8. Do I feel that my resolution of the problem with endure over the long run?
9. Can I disclose my decision to my superior and family without qualms?
10. Under what conditions might I allow for exceptions to my position?

The reader might find value in using the following ethics quiz as a discussion starter or group exercise during an ethics training forum or class. Most of the items on the quiz are commonly experienced situations that are faced on a day-to-day basis by practicing managers and leaders.

An Ethics Quiz

People of character will encounter circumstances in which the correct answer is not simply right or wrong. Gray areas exist in most situations where human beings are involved. The dilemmas outlined below point out the complexity of modern living and the difficulty of leading with integrity. In order to focus your own thinking regarding very difficult ethical and moral issues, you may want to respond to the questions listed below. Place an "A" next to the items you agree with and a "D" next to items with which you disagree. Compare your responses to those of a close personal friend or mentor, and where disagreement between you exists, discuss the possible reasons why the two of you do not agree.

1. _____ Employees should be expected to inform on peers who are involved in activities that may damage the reputation of their organization.

2. _____ There are times when a leader will have to overlook contract violations in order to get the job accomplished in a timely manner.

3. _____ Some people are naturally good; some are naturally bad.

4. _____ To be a successful leader, it is necessary to be ethical.

5. _____ The pursuit of self-interest and the issue of ethical conduct are compatible.

6. _____ Most leaders will use the same ethical standards no matter where they might find themselves in the world.

7. _____ Most business firms use unethical behavior when facing very severe competition.

8. _____ There are times when a person must withhold embarrassing information that could hurt the company from his or her immediate supervisor.

9. _____ In order to protect career development potential, it is important to do what a manager requests, even though I may have doubts about whether it is an ethical form of behavior.

10. _____ True leaders should be very goal oriented; therefore, the end result usually justifies the means used to achieve that result.

11. _____ Exceptions to organizational policies, procedures and moral codes of conduct are a way of life and therefore, should be allowed.

12. _____ When applying for a position, I would cover up the fact that I had been fired from a previous position.

13. _____ There is no problem with conducting personal business on company time.

14. _____ To make a needed sale, I might stretch the truth about actual delivery date.

15. _____ It is acceptable to read the e-mail messages of fellow workers if they are printed out and inadvertently left lying on the office printer.

16. _____ I would accept a permanent, full-time position, even if I knew I wanted the job for only seven months.

17. _____ I would check company policy before accepting an expensive gift from a supplier.

18. _____ To be successful in any organization, it is usually necessary to ignore ethics.

19. _____ I would never accept credit for the ideas of a peer or subordinate.

20. _____ If I felt physically attracted to a job candidate, I would recommend hiring the individual, even if I thought he/she were not as qualified as another candidate.

The quiz outlined above could be used in many college courses and programs as a reminder to young professionals regarding their responsibilities as tomorrow's leaders. Three new leadership programs at Kent State University have been added to the curriculum through the efforts of Professor Robert D. Smith of the College of Business Administration. Two of these programs are titled Learning to Lead Through Life—one designed specifically for freshmen, the other for juniors and seniors. A third leadership course taught by Professor Smith was introduced in the MBA program five years ago.

Each of the undergraduate Learning to Lead programs serves as the foundation course for a Certificate in Leadership and places heavy emphasis upon ethical decision making for leaders. Case studies, videos, role playing, brief lectures, guest speakers and modern texts and readings introduce ethics, honesty and integrity into nearly every class meeting. Hopefully, this approach to leadership development emphasizing ethical decision making will assist in molding competent and honest managers and leaders for the future.

Conclusion

Many young people beginning their careers feel that achievement at any cost is what really matters to their organizations. They watch their managers and follow the often unethical examples of their peers and superiors. Their values are tested early. One recent graduate was asked to make telephone calls and misrepresent herself as a student intern in order to generate information about a competitor's distribution system.

One of John Grisham's best selling novels, *The Firm*, tells the story of a young law school graduate who is recruited by a large law firm into what appears to be a dream career. A high starting salary and perks, including a home and luxury automobile, entice the new lawyer to join the partnership. One huge drawback for the rookie lawyer is that he is gradually trapped into crossing the ethical line, a line which he discovers is incredibly difficult to walk back across.

Stretching the imagination a bit, we find an analogy in the cunning of a real life boa constrictor, one of the deadliest of all snakes (*Journal of Business Ethics*, Summer 1993). Most of us believe that the boa drops from a tree onto its intended victim and rapidly crushes the victim to death. However, this is a false perception. The boa actually places two or three coils of its body around the chest of its prey. Then each time the victim exhales, the boa simply takes up the slack. After only a few such breaths, there is no more slack. The prey suffocates and is then swallowed by the snake. This phenomenon of nature, whereby the victim becomes the unwitting accomplice of its own destruction, is not confined to the land of reptiles. It also exists in the worlds of law, business, religion, politics, medicine, education, athletics and research, as we have noted throughout this chapter The boa lives within all professions. Our task is not to take that first step (breath), which is the beginning of our demise. My grandmother, paraphrasing Sir Walter Scott, had a simple way of expressing this important ethical point: "What a woeful web we weave when *first* we practice to deceive."

When confronted with an ethical dilemma, such as the ones I have used as examples in this chapter, you may choose among the following courses of action: You can elect to not be concerned about it and eliminate it from your thoughts. You could object verbally or in a memo, sometimes referred to as "blowing the whistle." You might decide to go along with it to get along with others. You could walk away by quitting the organization. You might negotiate with the appropriate party or parties to assure an ethical solution to the dilemma. Whichever course of action you choose, keep in mind that you will be living with your decision for the rest of your life. Most people find that ethical lapses are not easily erased from their conscience. Regardless of your decision, keep these guidelines in mind:

Watch your thoughts; they become words.

Watch your words; they become actions.

Watch your actions; they become habits

Watch your habits; they become your character

Watch your character; it determines your destiny.

(author unknown)

My purpose in writing this chapter has not been to teach or preach morality but rather to assist the reader in recognizing what one should think about when confronted by an ethical dilemma. Based on my years of managerial, coaching and public speaking experiences, I have suggested the types of situations that can easily cross over the ethical borderline. People from all walks of life have faced dilemmas similar to the actual situations described in this chapter. The selected situations are intended to assist the reader in recognizing alternative considerations when confronted by an ethical dilemma.

Nobby Lewandowski

Nobby had been active in sports since childhood and received combined athletic and academic scholarships to both Benedictine High School and Kent State University. He went on to pitch professional baseball, but at that time salaries were too low to support a growing family. Capitalizing on his bachelor of Science degree in Business Administration from Kent State University, Nobby obtained his Master from Case Western Reserve University where he majored in Banking and Finance with a minor in Taxation, and gained his CPA Certificate in 1964. In 1970, he co-founded and was Managing Partner of an accounting firm and ultimately led the firm to its current status among the "Top 25 Largest Accounting Firms in Northeastern, Ohio." At the age of 55, Nobby retired from the firm on July 1, 1992 and devotes his time to civic and charitable endeavors, along with involvement in outside business ventures and public speaking engagements. He serves on several corporate advisory boards and boards of directors. He has presented his seminars on Leadership, Integrity, and Success, on marketing professional services and accounting practice management to several professional groups. Offering a broad range of topics suitable for a variety of audiences and environments, Nobby is a truly gifted, and unconventional, public speaker who motivates and inspires in a highly entertaining format. From the moment he begins to speak, or maybe sing, he captures the attention of those in the audience and keeps them enthralled, energized and encourages. Nobby guarantees he'll leave audiences with much more to think about than when they arrived.

Nobby Lewandowski
3637 Medina Road, Suite 350
Medina, OH 44256
Phone: 330.723.1424
Fax: 330.722.7753
Email: nobby@apk.net

Chapter Eight

ENLIGHTENED LEADERSHIP IS BASED ON SELF-ACCEPTANCE AND POSITIVE BELIEFS

Dr. Bill Newman

The Stark Reality of Current World Leaders and Their Reflection of Our Global Condition

The proliferation of weapons of mass destruction, controlled by world leaders entangled in self-deception, risks the lives of more people than at any time in history; thus, the need for enlightened leadership is more urgent than ever! We recently witnessed the world's hunger for such leadership in Baghdad, Iraq, after United States and coalition soldiers helped the people there topple the statue of their former leader, Saddam Hussein, on April 9, 2003. The celebration of the Iraqi people following this event signified their jubilation over the termination of the threat of their leader, who embodied the most severe and horrific consequences of leadership corrupted by deception and self-deception.

Current events have unveiled the murky depths of Saddam Hussein's self-deceit and its destructive consequences for the people of Iraq. Several major world leaders voiced opposition to George Bush and Tony Blair waging war on Hussein, based on the Iraqi leader's development and use of weapons of mass destruction and his support of Usama bin Laden. It was not a surprise that we received opposition from the leadership of China, because we already knew of their sale of military equipment (such as missiles) to Hussein. But surprise and concern were also expressed by other world leaders—Vladimir Putin, the president of Russia, Jacques Chirac, the president of France and Gerhard Schroeder, the chancellor of Germany. While it is known that these three countries have done business with Saddam Hussein, the veil of leadership involvement has yet to be completely lifted. However, evidence is progressively mounting to expose the deceit of Putin and Chirac. Soon after entering Baghdad, coalition forces found Russian antitank rockets, although it is currently unclear whether Putin knew about their sale to Hussein. Chirac's possible deceit was exposed on April 16, 2003, when coalition troops found French-made missiles in Al Kut, Iraq. Only history will reveal the true breadth and depth of their influence and their motives for so strongly opposing the leadership decisions of the U.S., Great Britain and their allies.

The blatant and outrageous deception used by Saddam Hussein to hide biochemical and nuclear weapons from inspectors and to hide the truth from his people through the control of Iraq's media, was only an external, surface display of deception, masking the internal disease of self-deception. There now appears to be a similar external display of deception by the leadership of Russia.

On April 14, 2003, Fox News reported that top-secret Iraqi intelligence documents found in Baghdad indicated that Russia had funneled spy secrets to Saddam Hussein and that Moscow was still training Iraqi spies in fall 2002, in violation of U.N. sanctions. According to the *London Telegraph*, the captured documents also showed that the Kremlin gave Hussein lists of assassins who could make "hits" in the West and that Iraq and Russia had signed deals to share intelligence and help procure visas so that these agents could travel to Western countries. One document also suggests that Russia believed Iraq had a nuclear weapons program—at the same time the Kremlin was publicly denying such a contention. The Arabic documents also suggested cooperation between Russia and Iraq that was far more extensive and recent than previously reported. There were even copies of Christmas cards exchanged by the Iraqi and Russian intelligence chiefs, the report added. A U.S. official described the reports as "plausible."

If true, the documents could raise grave doubts about U.S.-Russian relations and President Bush's belief that he looked into Russian president Vladimir Putin's "soul" and knew he could trust the Russian leader. They also raise new questions about Russia's motives when it formed an "axis of the unwilling" with France and Germany to block U.S.-British efforts to persuade the U.N. Security Council to get tough with Hussein. Recently, these documents raised further questions about Russia's motives when President Putin invited President Chirac to join him and Chancellor Schroeder for a meeting in St. Petersburg, Russia, to discuss the restructuring of postwar Iraq.

Bush has complained to Putin that Russian companies sold Iraq military gear (possibly funneled through Syria), such as satellite jammers that were intended to interfere with U.S. weapons. Russia denied the charge.

The *San Francisco Chronicle* reported that documents found in the personnel files of Iraqi intelligence agents showed that they had received spy training as recently as September 2002 from the "Special Training Center" in Moscow. One agent's file—found in an annex to Iraq's Mukhabarat spy agency—indicated that he had completed "acoustic surveillance" training and received a diploma with Russia's double eagle insignia, the report said.

Such training would have been in violation of U.N. sanctions.

Other documents—mostly intelligence reports from anonymous agents and the Iraqi embassy in Moscow—show that Russia and Iraq also agreed to exchange information on Usama bin Laden. One document, dated March 12, 2002, said that the Russians warned Iraq that if it refused to comply with the United Nations, it would give the United States "a cause to destroy any nuclear weapons," the *London Telegraph* reported.

While the people of Iraq celebrated the defeat of Saddam Hussein in the streets of Baghdad, Iraq's U.N. ambassador, Mohammed Al-Douri, was speaking to news reporters in the streets of New York City. As he walked away from them he said, "The game is over." He knew the game of deception that he, Saddam Hussein and the other Iraqi leaders were playing in the world had been exposed and terminated. However, it is unlikely that he was aware of his own self-deception, which led to his choice to play a game of deception with Saddam Hussein.

Similarly, Hussein was severely self-deceived and consequently blinded to the extent and the evil of the human suffering he had caused the people of his country. His self-deception may have started in early childhood, a maladaptation stemming from the physical abandonment of his father and the emotional abandonment of his depressed and suicidal mother.

The Global Plight of Self-Deception

Fortunately, such extreme self-deception is not as common as the everyday self-deception that affects our lives and determines our experiences. As a clinical psychologist, I provide marital and family therapy to help people solve the problems that prevent them from functioning effectively. As a consulting psychologist, I provide management consulting and executive coaching to help companies find solutions for improving performance and growth with sustained results. Families and marriages fail to function successfully for the same reasons that companies do—because they are both organizations of people. The same self-deception, or resistance to solutions, that is present among fathers, mothers, sons, daughters, brothers and sisters, is present among co-workers in companies.

Self-deception can blind a person to the true cause of his problems—his own self. Once blinded to these problems, any solutions he thinks of only exacerbate the problems, further undermining his relationships.

Self-Deception in Business Organizations

Understanding self-deception is key to effective leadership, because effective leadership leads to good solutions and good results in relationships. The extent to which one is self-deceived determines the extent of his effectiveness or ineffectiveness as a leader.

As a management consultant and executive coach, most of my work over the past twenty years has focused on different types of "people problems," such as workers who are major impediments to teamwork and issues of communication, motivation, performance, management and leadership. And they are all caused by the same thing—self-deception, the most detrimental of all the problems in organizations.

Self-deception is an individual's inability to see that he has a problem. It is an unawareness of one's damaging affect and impact on others. Think of it as "being in the dark." For example, suppose someone in an organization is demeaning, disdainful or scornful in verbal and nonverbal ways toward co-workers he deems "incompetent and lazy." These people are then uncommunicative and uncooperative with this person, which causes a problem within their department. When the man is confronted by the manager about his behavior, the response is, "I'm very dedicated and work hard at my job! I don't have the problem; they do!"

This person sees matters only from his closed perspective and is deeply resistant to any suggestion that the truth is otherwise. He is blind to the truth that he has a problem or is in the dark. This kind of self-deception is a disease in organizations, spread by a germ that we all carry to some extent. This germ causes a multitude of people problems and kills leadership! My work as a consultant and executive coach helps organizations focus on isolating and neutralizing this germ. Only then can an organization move out of the dark of self-deception and into the light of successful results through enlightened leadership—which is effective leadership.

Enlightened leadership occurs when leaders relate to their people in a manner that communicates high regard and great respect for them. When a leader honors his people, they feel valued and are more likely to respond in positive ways. Their responses lead to improved performance and productivity in the organization. Dr. Robert Hartman, a Nobel Peace Prize nominee in 1973 for his work in axiology (the formal system of identifying and measuring value), reported that people in an organization will withhold forty percent of their work capacity until they feel valued and cared about by leadership.

People can sense how others feel about them. Great leadership radiates sincerity, kindness, care, compassion and honor. If a leader makes a mistake and says, "I'm sorry," but her tone of voice, eyes, facial expressions, posture and level of interest do not convey the same sentiment, then her people will find her apology disingenuous. People detect hypocrisy and can always tell when they are being manipulated or outsmarted. People can sense the blame emanating from beneath the veneers of niceness, and they usually resent it. A leader is then ineffective when he insincerely tries managing others by inquiring about their family members, practices active listening or uses any other skill to be more effective. People know when they are highly regarded and respected and are inspired with devotion and commitment to the organization when treated this way by their leaders. Leaders who relate to people this way will see improved performance and productivity, because their people love working with them. These effective leaders do not always say or do the right things, but they always get results.

Conversely, there are leaders who negatively affect and influence people. These leaders may do all the "right" things interpersonally and apply all the latest skills and techniques to their communications and tasks, but they do not inspire results. The people of their organizations resent them and their tactics. These leaders fail because they provoke people to resist them.

People skills are never primary in effective leadership. Whether people skills are effective or not depends on something deeper than behavior and skill. The deep choice that determines effective leadership is self-deception—whether the leader chooses to be in the darkness or in the light. No matter what a leader is doing on the outside, people respond primarily to how he is feeling about them on the inside. And how the leader is feeling about his people depends on whether he is in the dark or in the light when it comes to their well-being.

While the outward behaviors of leaders may often seem the same, their inner experiences may be entirely different, depending on whether they are in the dark or in the light. "In the light," then, means the leader sees himself and others more or less as they are, as people with the same needs and desires. "In the dark" means that he sees himself and others in a systematically distorted way; he sees others as less than he is, as mere objects with needs and desires somehow secondary and less legitimate than his own. One way, he sees himself as a person among people. The other way, he sees himself as a person among objects.

Good companies grow into great companies when the leadership develops a culture in which people are encouraged to see others as they are. When people are being seen and treated straightforwardly, they respond accordingly with commitment and enthusiasm for success.

Great companies do not minimize the importance of hiring people who are intelligent, hard working and skilled, who demonstrate the right behaviors, attitudes and values. Great companies understand that these assets grow greater when employees are viewed by their leaders as people. Great companies also understand that self-deception is a particularly difficult and complex problem. The extent that the company is infested with the disease of self-deception is the extent to which they cannot see the problem. Most companies suffer from the disease of self-deception and are lost in the darkness of it.

Being Versus Doing

The leaders of great companies understand that the people of their organizations respond to how the leaders really feel about them—not what they do. But the distinction is not a behavioral one.

160

We are human beings, not human doings; or, as was most eloquently stated by Teilhard de Chardan, "We are spiritual beings having a human experience."

For example, a leader who recognizes a manager for high performance is engaging in a soft behavior. On the other hand, a leader who confronts a manager's lack of commitment is engaging in a hard behavior. But there are two ways to be hard as a leader—acting in the dark or in the light. The distinction is not the behavior; it is the way the leader is *feeling about others*. If the leader is in the light, she is seeing others as people, and when she gives people hard encouragement in the light, she is encouraging more performance, productivity and commitment. The alternative is to give hard encouragement in the dark, which stirs up resistance and ill will.

Although great leaders are still sometimes in the dark, their successes have resulted from the many times and ways they have chosen to be in the light in their company. This enlightened leadership catalytically inspires the people they lead to also choose to be in the light, to contribute to their companies' successes. The point is not to strive for perfection but to get better in concrete and systematic ways that improve the company's performance, productivity, profits and growth—the bottom line. This enlightened leadership mentality at every level of an organization is what makes a good company become a great company!

Beginning With the Germ and Ending With the Disease

If self-deception is the disease that infests organizations and impedes the development of enlightened leadership, then what is the germ that causes the disease? To answer this question, we must first understand that when we are in the light and seeing others as people, we have a very basic understanding of them. This understanding is that like ourselves, they have needs, cares, hopes and fears. Sometimes, as a result of this understanding, we get ideas about things we can do for them that we think might help them. Therefore, when we act contrary to our sense of what is appropriate or what we feel we should do for others, we betray our own sense of how we should act. This act is self-betrayal, the germ of the disease of self-deception.

Self-betrayal is very common. It occurs when we have the choice to honor our convictions to do for others but betray them instead. For example, self-betrayal occurs at work when you have information that would be helpful to a co-worker, but you keep it to yourself; or when you need to stay late to finish work for someone but go home instead;

or when you are in an elevator watching someone rush to the door with an outstretched arm and you do not try to stop the doors from closing.

The Blame Game and the Provocation Situation

When we betray ourselves, we begin to see the world in a way that justifies our self-betrayal. For example, after we betray ourselves, we may use someone else's faults as justification for our own misbehavior. The other person's faults become relevant only after we fail to help the other person. Therefore the sequence of self-betrayal goes as follows:

1. When we act contrary to what we feel we should do for another, it is an act of "self-betrayal."
2. When we betray ourselves, we begin to see the world in a way that justifies our self-betrayal.
3. When we see the world in a self-justifying manner, our view of reality becomes distorted.
4. When we betray ourselves, we enter the dark.
5. Over time, being in the dark becomes characteristic of us, and we carry it with us.
6. By being in the dark, we provoke others to be in the dark.
7. In the dark, we invite mutual mistreatment and obtain mutual justification. We collude in giving each other reasons to stay in the dark.

When we betray ourselves, we start seeing things differently. Our views of others, ourselves and our circumstances are distorted in a way that makes us feel okay about what we are doing. Over time, as we betray ourselves, we come to see ourselves in certain self-justifying ways. Eventually, we end up carrying these self-justifying images with us into new situations, and to the extent that we do, we enter new situations already in the dark. We do not see people straightforwardly, as people. Rather, we see them in terms of the self-justifying images we have created in our minds. If people act in ways that challenge the justifying images, we view those acts as unimportant. However we see them, the people are just objects to us.

And if we are already in the dark regarding someone, we generally will not have inclinations to do things for them. Therefore, when we get the feeling that we should help someone, it is not necessarily evidence that we are out of the dark. Rather, it may be a sign we are deep within it. If we seem to be in the dark in a given situation but cannot identify a specific feeling that we have betrayed, that is also a clue that we may already be in the dark.

In such cases, it may be useful for us to examine whether we are carrying self-justifying images. Almost anything can be transformed into a self-justifying image, most of which are perversions of otherwise good things, when seen in the light. For example, it is great to be a good leader. That's exactly what we should be for our managers. And it is great to think of co-workers and to be as helpful as we can in our areas of work. But this will not happen if we have self-justifying images about our colleagues. Certainly, it is good to think of others, but who are we *really* thinking of when we distinguish ourselves as the sort of people who think of others? Obviously, we are thinking about ourselves. In such cases, our self-justifying image lies to us. That image seems to tell us we are focused on others, but in having that image, we are actually focused on ourselves.

When we are in the dark of self-deception, we are transmitting blame to others. And most people are already in a defensive posture, ready to defend their self-justifying images against attack. If we are in the dark, blaming others, our blame invites them or provokes them to be in the dark as well. They then blame us for blaming them unjustly. But because we feel justified in blaming them, we feel that their blame is unjust and blame them even more. But of course, they are in the dark also, so they feel justified in blaming us and feel that our further blame is unjust. So they blame us even more, and so on, and so on.

When two or more people are in the dark with each other, mutually betraying themselves, they are in collusion, which means they are actually condemning themselves to ongoing mutual mistreatment. This becomes a dynamic process of mutual self-deception and self-betrayal. While in the dark of self-deception, nobody sees clearly, and we are all blind to the truths about ourselves and others. We even become blind to our own motivations. We are also blind to how the dark of self-deception undercuts our efforts to obtain the outcomes we want.

Awareness for Fairness

When people within organizations are in the dark, they invite others to be in the dark as well, which leads to conflict. In turn, conflict leads to a loss of performance, productivity and profits. The company wants results, not losses, and successful results cannot be achieved in the dark. The dark keeps us from focusing on results, because in the dark, we are focused on ourselves. People in the organization whom you think are results-focused really are not when they value results primarily for the purpose of creating or sustaining their reputations. They do not feel that the results of others are as important as their own, so they walk over people, which has destructive consequences.

When we provoke others to join us in the dark, we may withhold information, which gives others reason to do the same. We try to control others, which provokes all the more the very resistance that we feel we need to control. We withhold resources from others, who then feel the need to protect resources from us. We blame people for being too slow, and in so doing give them reason to feel justified in slowing down all the more. And so on.

Through it all, we think that all our problems would be solved if Chuck would not do this or Susan would not do that or if XYZ department would just cooperate or the company would wake up and change. But this is an illusion, even if Chuck and Susan, XYZ department and the company need to improve, because when we blame them, we are not doing so because they need to improve. We are blaming them because their weaknesses justify our own failure to improve.

One person in an organization, by being in the dark and failing to focus on results, encourages his or her co-workers to fail to focus on results as well. Collusions spread far and wide, and the result is that co-workers position themselves against co-workers, teams against teams, work groups against work groups and departments against departments. People who came together to help an organization succeed actually end up delighting in each other's failures and resenting each other's successes.

As I mentioned earlier, most of the organizational issues I address as a consultant and executive coach in corporations are common people problems, such as fear, stress, resentment, poor communication, conflict, mistrust, low motivation, inadequate accountability, misalignment, low morals, lack of teamwork, low engagement, reactive attitudes, low levels of commitment and bitter gossip. Whatever form the problem takes, the origin is usually self-betrayal. Self-betrayal is the germ that creates the disease of self-deception, and it has many different symptoms. Companies die or are severely disabled by those symptoms, because the people who carry the germ are unaware that they are carrying it.

In all organizations, many people fail to do things for co-workers when they feel that the co-workers should do those things themselves. And when that happens, they experience self-betrayal. A foundational self-betrayal is one's failure to do what he is hired to do—focus on helping the company and its people achieve results. I have found that the key to solving most of the people problems that beset corporations lies in their discovery of how to solve the problem of self-betrayal!

Trust Versus Mistrust and Collusion With Illusion and Delusion

Each time I consult with an organization about its problem with achieving the results it wants, I always begin with an evaluation of self-betrayal within the corporate leadership. Sometimes, it originates with the CEO or president and other times with vice presidents and senior managers. The leader may be so enthralled with her magnificence, that she may not allow brilliance to shine in anyone else in the leadership team. The leader may think she is so brilliant that, in order to prove her brilliance, she treats employees as less capable. The leader may be so obsessed with being superior that she makes sure nobody else appears to have the same capacity to achieve results that she does.

With such self-justifying images telling this self-betrayed leader that she is magnificent, brilliant and superior, collusions are provoked with her executives, managers and other employees. This leadership choice to be in the dark creates an excuse for other employees to justify their own self-betrayals with their co-workers.

For example, the more a leader takes responsibility for his team's performance, the more mistrusted the other team members feel. This in turn leads to many different kinds of resistance. One way other team members may resist is by giving up participation in or contribution to the team. Another way may be through defiance of the leader by doing things their own way. The most extreme way to resist is to quit the company.

A leader in the dark misinterprets these responses of resistance as the incompetence of the executive team and the other workers. He therefore reacts in the dark by being more controlling when issuing instructions and developing more policies and procedures. The executive team members then react with even more resistance, because the leader's choice demonstrates further evidence of disrespect for them. This dynamic process is perpetuated in a circular fashion, going around and around in the organization, because the leaders and the other workers provoke each other to be in the dark and in so doing, provide each other with mutual justification for remaining in the dark. Collusion in the organization becomes pervasive and insidious when this dynamic of destruction infects the organization with self-betrayal. When a leader is in the dark, he provokes the very problems he complains about. Then the best executives leave the company, and the leader, always feeling justified (because he is in the dark), deludes himself into believing that he was not a very effective executive.

Leaders in the dark also make the mistake of doing their best to "cope" with others. This is just as insufficient as trying to change the other person, because it is just another way to continue blaming. So is leaving. In certain situations, leaving may be the right thing to do, but it will never be sufficient, because ultimately, one must learn to leave one's darkness as well. Communicating in the dark is also a way of blaming. A leader may improve his communication skills, but the skills do not hide his blame. In the dark, whether someone is a skilled communicator or not, he is still communicating in the dark, and that is the problem.

No matter what skills a leader may teach others, he can be acting either in or out of the dark at the time. And using a skill in the dark is not a way out of the dark. This explains why skill training in non-technical areas often does not have a lasting impact. Skills and techniques are not helpful if they are taught in the dark, because they just provide people with more sophisticated ways to blame. The people problems that most leaders try to correct with skills are not due to a lack of skills but rather to self-betrayal. People problems seem unchangeable not because they are unsolvable but because the skill interventions that are commonly used are not solutions.

Finally, if a leader tries to change her behavior, it will not free her from the dark. Every change in behavior is just a change in her style of being in the dark. Whatever changes she thinks of in the dark are changes from within the dark and are therefore just a perpetuation of the original problem. Other people remain objects in her eyes. Because the dark itself runs deeper than behavior, the way out of the dark and into the light has to be deeper than behavior, too.

From Darkness to Light—The End of the Plight

So what is the leader's way out of the dark? To understand the answer to this question, it is important to understand that the leader's choice to be in the dark is a metaphor for how he resists other people in the organization. When resisting, the leader's self-betrayal is active rather than passive. In the dark, the leader is actively resisting what the humanity of others in the organization calls him to do for them. In the darkness, everything a leader thinks and feels is part of the lie of the darkness. The truth is found in the fact that the true leader changes in the moment he ceases resisting what is in the light—the others in the company!

From Enlightened Leadership to Transformational Leadership

Although the leader can do nothing from within the dark to get out of the dark, he can, during moments in the light, make choices to reduce the number of in-the-dark moments and heal in-the-dark relationships. The nature of a leader's experiences with others while in the light invites the leader to question his virtue. That is, the leader questions whether he was, in fact, as much in the light as he assumed. When this dynamic occurs, it transforms his views of others. Then the process of transformational leadership and enlightened leadership begins to be developed.

Transformation and enlightenment in life are both miraculous and common. They happen often in our lives, typically in small ways that are quickly forgotten. Suddenly, because of the basic "otherness" of the people who continually stand before us and because of what we know as we stand in the light, our darkness is diffused by the light from the humanity of others. At that moment, we know we need to honor them as people with high regard and great respect. Also in that moment of being in the light, we see others as people with needs, wants and concerns as real and important as our own. At that moment, we are out of the dark!

When we are out of the dark, it does not mean we are suddenly showered with burdensome obligations. That is because our basic obligation to see others as they are occurs, in many cases, by the fundamental change in our way of being, which happens when we choose to get out of the dark and into the light.

To stay in the light, it is critical that we honor what our in-the-light sensibility tells us we should do for other people. However, this does not necessarily mean that we should do everything we feel would be ideal. We have our own responsibilities and needs that require attention, and it may be that we cannot help others in the company as much or as soon as we would like to. We can do the best we can do in the situation we are in, because we want to see others as people.

We live insecurely when we are in the dark of self-deception, because we are desperate to justify ourselves by demonstrating thoughtfulness, nobility or worthiness. We become overwhelmed when we always have to demonstrate our virtue. When we are feeling overwhelmed, it generally is not because of our obligation to others but our desperation to prove something about ourselves. A leader feels overwhelmed, overburdened and overobligated far more often in the dark of self-deception than in the light. When this happens, a leader cannot truly focus on results, because he or she is too self focused.

The success of a leader depends on being free of self-betrayal. Only then does the leader invite others in the organization to be free of self-betrayal themselves. Only then is the leader creating other leaders—executives and other co-workers whom people will respond to, trust and enthusiastically want to work with. Then a process in the company can be developed whereby the leaders help others to see that they are in the dark of self-deception and are therefore not focusing on results. Next, the leaders can develop a system—an effective way of thinking, measuring, reporting and working in the light to focus on results—that keeps the company out of the dark of self-deception more than the company has been before. As the leaders of a company lead their people away from the darkness of self-deception, the company will be able to identify and develop a specific plan of action that minimizes the basic workplace self-betrayal. This enlightened results system will minimize self-betrayal in the workplace and maximize the organization's bottom line. It will work in a way that significantly reduces common people problems in the company.

Enlightened Leadership

Whether or not you successfully inspire your organization to greatness will depend on two choices you must make as a leader. The first is to understand the information I have discussed about transformational and enlightened leadership. The second, and more important, choice is to live it! While I cannot make you live it, I can influence your understanding and knowledge of the information with the following summary of insights and strategies:

1. Self-betrayal leads to self-deception and living in "the dark."
2. When you are in the dark, you cannot focus on sustainable results.
3. Your influence and success as an enlightened leader will depend on being in the light.

4. Do not try to be perfect. Always try to be better.
5. Do not use the terms "in the dark or "in the light" with people who do not already know them. Always use the principles in your own life.
6. Do not look for others' choices to be in the dark. Do look for your own.
7. Do not accuse others of being in the dark. Always try to stay out of the dark yourself.
8. Do not give up on yourself when you discover you have been in the dark. Always keep trying to be in the light.
9. Do not deny you have been in the dark when you have been. Always apologize and keep moving forward, trying to be more helpful to others in the future.
10. Do not focus on what others are doing wrong. Always focus on what you can do right to help.
11. Do not worry whether others are helping you. Do be concerned over whether you are helping others.

The key to understanding self-deception or resistance to solutions is asking, "How can people simultaneously create their own problems, be unable to see that they are creating their own problems and yet resist any attempts to help them stop creating those problems?" This reality is the origin of most organizational failure. This is the reason many organizational problems seem so unmanageable and unchangeable. At the heart of these problems are self-deceptions, which are resistant to solutions.

As an enlightened leader, you now have the transformational tools to replace the self-deceptions that resist solutions. You are now ready to inspire greatness in your organization and to achieve the sustainable results you have always been capable of obtaining. As you continue choosing to be in the light, the results you want will be yours! When you first choose to be and then to do, you will have what you want. This is enlightened leadership!

Transformational Leadership

Transformational leadership, the kind that inspires the greatness of an organization, begins with your own personal transformation. Personal transformation begins with clarity about your identity, purpose and values. You connect with your highest self when you align your values, because you create congruency between who you believe you are, what is most important for you to do with your life and what is most important to you in your life. Your action of alignment is your choice for self-acceptance! When you passionately act upon your identity, purpose and values through your vision and mission, you will achieve the personal transformational results that you can then apply to your organization as the transformational leader!

Self-acceptance and Self-esteem

As an enlightened and true leader, you first lead yourself before you can effectively lead your organization. You begin with the consciousness of who you are and the courage to accept and be that person. Your choice of self-acceptance is an action of self-value and self-commitment that emanates from the reality that you are alive and conscious. As a powerful leader, the development of high self-esteem grows from your seeds of greatness, which are your identity, purpose and values. These seeds of greatness are your self-esteem, germinated by self-value, cultivated by willingness to experience and watered by self-compassion—your actions of self-acceptance. Your actions of self-acceptance nourish the seeds of your self-esteem.

Self-esteem and Self-image

Low self-esteem is the first obstacle to becoming a highly effective, enlightened and true leader. This experience is caused by a low self-image that is caused by unconscious negative beliefs about yourself. These beliefs create a weakened mental state and a loss of power which perpetuate ineffective behaviors with others and yourself. However, your consistent choices of self-acceptance will create a new life experience of empowerment, which strengthens your mental state and increases your self-esteem. Your self-image becomes positive, optimistic and strong. Your behaviors change, because you become confident in your competence. You mentally shift from conscious competence to unconscious competence because your consistent choices of self-acceptance create consistent experiences of high self-esteem. In other words, your repetitious, conscious choices of self-acceptance create conscious feelings and thoughts of high self-esteem. Eventually, these lead to actions, which become the habits of highly effective, enlightened and true leaders.

Positive Versus Negative Beliefs

The second obstacle to becoming a highly effective, enlightened and true leader is your unconscious negative beliefs about your life experiences. The day of my two near-death experiences in the desert of Baja California Sur, Mexico, taught me that what I do not know can kill me! That is, what I believe unconsciously may affect my choices for actions that could lead to death! I literally almost lost my life twice on that same day because of my negative belief that I could not trust others with something as important as my life. However, when I saw the face of death before me as I lay in the hot sand, under the scorching desert sun, and had the thought, "I'm going to die," I made the ultimate choice of self-acceptance! I also heard the voice of a life force resonating deep within my soul saying, "I will live! I will survive!" The voice compelled me to stand up and keep moving. I stood up again and began to walk in the direction of a dried riverbed.

My choice for self-acceptance at that moment in the desert was a choice to live, because I valued my life; I knew who I was, and I knew my purpose in life! While I had the self-esteem to act on self-acceptance and survive in the face of death, I lacked the consciousness to trust another human being to prevent those near-death experiences.

My extraordinary act of self-acceptance propelled me to a new height of self-esteem and consciousness that expanded my awareness of choices in the face of extreme adversity. I became aware, through this ultimate experience of self-acceptance, that if I can first trust myself with something as important as my life, then I could also trust in the teamwork of others to survive together in a life-threatening experience.

More likely, your unconscious negative beliefs may affect your choices of actions that could figuratively lead to death—death of a dream, a personal or professional vision or mission, a great idea, a career, a relationship, a team or even the death of your business.

Great Leaders Inspire Great Organizations

Whatever death experience you may have had as a result of your unconscious negative beliefs, you can change it and prevent it from recurring by accepting yourself for choosing this experience. Your self-acceptance of the experience will increase your self-esteem, which will expand your consciousness or awareness of alternative choices that can lead you in a new direction of increased growth and performance. Then you will be in strong and powerful state to lead others in your organization with enlightened leadership.

Your future behaviors or choices of action as a highly effective leader are shaped by both your unconscious, low self-image, which causes your low self-esteem, as well as your unconscious negative beliefs about your life experiences. Either can become an obstacle to becoming an enlightened and true leader. Both obstacles can be overcome by the same solution: leading yourself first by rejecting self-deception and acting on self-acceptance! Then you will cultivate the greatness to lead yourself first, to truly inspire and to lead the greatness that exists within your organization!

About The Author

Dr. Bill Newman

Dr. Bill Newman is CEO of Executive Beacon, Inc., an executive development company that works with executive teams and their leaders who want to maximize results in growth and performance. Bill is a consulting psychologist, executive coach, and expert in leadership development who speaks professionally. As a consultant, facilitator and speaker, Bill helps CEO's, presidents, and other executives to develop, inspire and lead the greatness of their corporations for the enduring results they want. . Bill's customized executive development programs, keynote speeches, and business presentations address leadership, management, peak performance, change, stress, sales, and corporate trust. For over seventeen years, his international programs have been so effective for producing sustained results in corporate growth and performance, he has been featured in business magazines such as Forbes, Inc. and Success; major newspapers such as U.S.A. Today, and the Wall Street Journal; major radio stations such as National Public Radio, Morning Addition; and major television stations such as CBS T.V. Internationally, Bill has appeared in newspapers, radio programs, and television programs in Montreal and Toronto, Canada. He has also been featured in magazines and newspapers in both London, England and Paris, France. Bill is a member of the National Speakers Association and a member of the New England Speakers Association.

Dr. Bill Newman, CEO
Executive Beacon, Inc.
Hamilton Gateway Building
5 Market Square, Suite 101
Amesbury, MA 01913
Phone: 1.800.908.2009
Fax: 978.834.0990
e-mail: Bill@ExecutiveBeacon.com
web: www.executivebeacon.com, www. ExecutiveBeacon.com

Chapter Nine

LEADERSHIP: THE SUCCESSFUL USE OF CONFLICTING PRINCIPLES

Sam Allman

"The opposite of a correct statement is a false statement. But the opposite of a profound truth may well be another profound truth."
Niels Bohr, Nobel-Prize winning scientist

I couldn't believe the pain I was in. No one told me being a sales manager would be this hard. I figured all I had to do was act like a salesperson—make a connection to my customers, in this case, to my constituents, and influence them into becoming peak performers. All it was is selling.

Had I broken a cardinal rule of leadership: Never become too close to your people? The vice president of sales had told me that my people liked me too much!

There I was, driving to a meeting I dreaded. I was on my way to fire Scott, a guy I had visited in his home. I had stewed over this decision for weeks. It kept me awake at night. But, it was time. Scott was not performing. He knew it and I knew it. He simply had quit taking care of his customers. They were consistently calling me and complaining. Sure, Scott's performance began to drop, when he discovered his wife was having an affair with a fireman. I certainly understood marital problems; been there, done that.

At first I empathized with Scott, told him to hang in there and do the best he could. I certainly wasn't going to kick him when he was down. But, six months of poor performance was enough. We had a very serious discussion 30 days earlier. He knew what would happen if he did not improve

The meeting ended worse than I expected. When I told him of my decision, he started to cry. He told me he had already lost his wife, now he would lose his new house. He begged and pleaded for another chance. I had delayed this decision so long that now I had no choice. In order to keep my job, I had to make this decision.

As a leader, I felt that I had failed. As I reviewed the situation in my mind, I wondered, "Did I leave Scott alone too much?" I thought that's what empowerment was. Should I have micro-managed him more? Should I have neglected my other constituents to save him? Did I just hire the wrong guy? Should I have become a tough, demanding taskmaster, demanding that he respect me, rather than *like* me?

I was a great salesperson. I think I was an above-average sales manager. If I had understood then what I know now about the paradoxical nature of leadership, I believe I could have been an even better leader for Scott and all my sales staff at the time.

Accept and Finesse the Paradoxical

"There ain't no answer.
There ain't going to be any answer.
There never has been an answer.
That's the answer."
Gertrude Stein

The longer I study leadership, the less certainty I find in it.

One book tells me to be a servant leader. Another says my style should be tough and mean. One leader achieves success by persuading his followers to respect him. By contrast, retired U.S. Army Gen.

Norman Schwarzkopf, who led American forces in the 1991 Gulf War, found that success depended on his loving his troops, and their loving him in return.

The struggle I have is that most approaches tend to simplify leadership to five or six easy steps—but being a truly great leader is never that easy.

The weird fact is: *all* the experts may be right. My research and experience reveal that successful leaders use widely *different* styles and strategies to produce *similar* successes. If that be true, how can we leaders know which leadership strategy is the most effective?

First off, consider what Sir Laurence Olivier, one of the 20th Century's greatest actors, said about acting: "You have to have the *humility* to prepare, and the *self-confidence* to carry it off." It's a crucial life lesson — one that many leaders learn late — it takes a lot of time and thought to know which strategy to use at the right moment.

Opposition and contradiction are a natural part of human experience. We have a word for seemingly contradictory statements that may nonetheless be true. It's "paradox" - from the Greek word "paradoxon," meaning "something beyond belief, incredible, or contrary to expectations."

When we think about it, how can two conflicting statements both be true? It's incredible.

"All truths are only half truths."
Alfred North Whitehead

History offers many examples of two opposite principles being true. Think of the U.S. Constitution with its checks and balances, and even our two-party system, which makes pluralistic democracy possible. Think of art, where Romanticism opposed Classicism, a conflict at the heart of most literary movements. Consider how reason opposes emotion, and law limits freedom.

You may ask, "How does this impact my leading? What does this have to do with being a leader?" The simple answer is: at every turn. Leadership, given the apparently paradoxical nature of the universe itself, cannot ever be a simple, clear set of unequivocal propositions. Paradox is the rule and not the exception.

Your greatest struggles emerge from the conflicts between priorities and principles. Examples include customer satisfaction vs. profitability; thinking long-term (visions and strategies) vs. thinking short-term ("How am I going to pay my employees on Friday?); employee satisfaction vs. employee accountability; and giving time to your business vs. time for family.

When YOU face such paradoxes, do you punt or cope? Successful leaders live in paradoxes. Consider Abraham Lincoln as described by Donald T. Phillips in his book *Lincoln on Leadership*:

- Charismatic, yet unassuming. (How could you <u>do,</u> or <u>be</u> both at the same time?)
- Consistent, yet flexible. (How is this possible?)
- The victim of pervasive slander and malice, yet immensely popular with the troops. (Loved and hated at the same time?)
- Innovative and willing to take risks, yet patient and calculating.
- He fired many generals, yet first gave them ample time and support to produce results.
- He claimed not to have controlled events (his policy was "to have no policy"), yet he did control events to a large degree by taking charge, being aggressive and extraordinarily decisive. (Which is true or are they both true?)

Of course, opposition wasn't any easier for President Lincoln to manage than for us.

Smart leaders recognize the paradoxes. They've studied leadership and know the opposing principles. They accept the need to struggle with them. An ancient Jewish prophet remarked, "There must needs be opposition in all things."

The Power of Paradox Arises from the Power of Conflict

Opposites not only coexist, but can even enhance one another. Take pleasure and pain, for example. Scratching an itch is both. Not pleasure, *then* pain, or pain *then* pleasure, but both at once. Just as the day follows night, our capacity for joy is born <u>in</u> sorrow. Of all the polarities, none is more daunting than life and death. The shadow of death gives life its potential for meaning.

The friction between individuals often generates tension and discomfort, disrupts interactions and even destroys relationships. Between couples, it can lead to divorce. Between countries, it can lead to war. Between a corporation's departments, it can distort communication and degrade cohesiveness.

However, when well managed, such conflict or abrasiveness can generate *creative* tension and *original* thinking. Disagreements can *magically* produce ideas that can lead to better results. It's the power of conflict and diversity.

In my home, I struggle with the diversity my wife brings to our relationship. With a strong ego, and being male, I hate being told what to do and how to do it. When my wife makes suggestions, if I am open to her feedback and advice, many times we arrive at a better solution than just relying on my input. She makes me better. She brings that creative tension to my paradigm and I bring it to hers. Our diversity brings the creative tension, but the power of synergy springs out of our unity.

Creative tension calls for the development of leadership styles that focus on first identifying, and then incorporating *polarized* viewpoints and priorities. By doing so, you sharply increase mutual understandings and the probabilities for unexpected juxtapositions – the spark for ingenuity. Effective strategic thinking is seldom born of a quiet birth. The absence of visible tension and dissension in an organization often signals decay. In the best companies, the debate is raucous. Thus, ironically, by means of a process evolving from disagreement, conflict or abrasiveness, you build a corporate culture of heightened sensitivity and harmony.

> "It is possible to fashion various mechanisms
> for coping with conflict. Better yet would be
> for the organization to fashion a culture that
> appreciates the creative power of conflict
> and seeks to harness it."
> *Michael Hammer*

It helped me to approach this challenge when I compared paradoxes to adjusting the water temperature of my morning shower. In the shower, we adjust the knob until the temperature feels right. We are "finessing" the hot and cold water into the best blend. If, while you shower, someone changes the dynamic by flushing, what must you do? You re-adjust, to accommodate the change. Even so, in leadership: blend and apply, finesse the conflicts until you achieve a better result.

Your challenge is not hopeless. Difficult! But not hopeless. I invite you to view the *"Power of Paradox"* or the *"Magic of Conflict"* as an opportunity for synergy, an opportunity to produce ever-greater results. In this chapter, I evaluate four of the most perplexing contraries that add power to your leadership.

PARADOX I:

Vision (Thinking Long-Term) and Taking Control of Today (Thinking Short-Term)

> "Where there is no vision,
> the leaders perish."
> *Proverbs, The Leaders Bible*

Becoming a Visionary Leader

I believe a lack of clear vision (of the long-term) underlies nearly all business failures.

By contrast, entrepreneurs know exactly what they want <u>today</u> – freedom and independence with a respectable paycheck. They see tomorrow only vaguely.

> "Every day at IBM was devoted to business
> development. We didn't do business
> at IBM, we built one."
> Thomas Watson Jr.

Leaders without vision live in the moment. As my friend, Dan Newbold says, "What frustrates us most in our life is to give up what we want most for what we want now." Are you into instant gratification ... you want it, and you want it now? Or, are you willing to pay short-term pain for a longer-term gain?

Company owners who have no clear picture of their future can't today's actions to promote the company's future. They don't know in which direction to bend! How much better to visualize the future and then think and act today in ways that move the company inexorably toward your vision of a great tomorrow!

A landmark study reported by Harvard University determined that the most important quality of successful people was the ability to think "long-term." Successful people think in long segments of time. Unsuccessful people think in short segments of time.

What is the time perspective of a drunk? His next drink. What's the time perspective of a homeless person? "When will I eat, and where will I sleep tonight." What about the average blue-collar worker? His next paycheck, or "Thank goodness, it's Friday."

The time perspective of the average American? "I want it, and I want it now." Maybe that's why 70% of us spend more than we make.

What is *your* time perspective?

Social scientists who have studied children find the same principle holds true. According to Benjamin D. Singer in *Learning for Tomorrow*, nearly all kids who have no vision of their future live at risk. Their short-term perspective makes them feel that fate will direct their future. Feeling powerless, they do little to rise above their state. His research revealed that IQ and socio-economic status do not determine success. Rather, envisioning a hopeful future does.

You may remember the example of Mr. P.S. Lang's promise to sixth-graders in a Bronx low-income, largely black-students school. He promised to pay for the students' college education if they'd graduate from high school. Until then, only 25% of the sixth-grade students in that school had been graduating from high school. Almost no one attended college. However, he gave these students a vision of their future and hope. As a result, 92% of the students (48 of 52) graduated from high school. Of those, 40% went to college.

The power of vision helps us to develop discipline... doing what we ought to do, when we ought to do it, whether we feel like it or not.

What is a vision, but the clearest possible picture of a <u>future desired result</u>—what you want the results of your leadership or life to look like when you're done.

> You have to know where you're going. You have to
> be able to state it clearly and concisely. In addition,
> you have to care about it passionately. That all
> adds up to vision: the concise statement or pic-
> ture of where the company and its people are
> heading and why they should be proud of it."
> *Peters and Austin, A Passion for Excellence*

For entrepreneurs, thinking long-term is driven by the question: "How much will my business be worth when I'm ready to retire or sell it?"

Bottom-line, if you spend your days preparing to sell your business, even if that date is years away, you are a visionary.

In my seminars, I ask entrepreneurs, "Do you own a business ... or just a job?"

How can you tell? Would someone be willing to pay you its value as a "going concern," or just pay the liquidation value of the hard assets? If someone would pay its "going-concern" value, you own a business. If not, you own just a job.

> "In the coming decade, vision will be the critical
> executive skill. It's not mystical. It doesn't take a
> 'special person.' Vision is a statement of what you
> want your organization to be. It conveys a picture
> of where you want to go and how you want to get
> there. It is a simple-to-understand, inspirational,
> focusing statement. Then, it's lots of actions. The
> 'vision thing' is much more 'down-and-dirty doing'
> than fancy plans and words. Then, isn't that what
> management has always been about?"
> *– James A. Belasco*

Peter Drucker said, "The best way to predict the future is to create it." So, what's your vision? Can you articulate it, so every employee can plainly see it? If you can't, beware. Remember the scriptures say, "Where there is no vision, the leaders perish."

Living Today as If It Were Your Last

Yes, vision is critical, but doesn't it make *equal* sense that you ought to live *today* as if it were your last? You only go around once in this life, so grab the gusto while you can! We may *dream* of a great future: "Someday, I'll be happy ... when I get the right employees, double my profits or expand my business." But those remain *dreams* unless we act on them TODAY. Today is the only moment of time we have within our control.

"The past is behind—learn from it.
The future is ahead—prepare for it.
The present is now—live in it."
Thomas S. Monson, Church Leader

Life is about enjoying the moment, learning to live for today, for there will never be another quite like it. Those who live by vision alone would do well to stop spending so much time chasing life's big pleasures, while neglecting the little ones. We should never put off the things that are important to a later time. Simply put: never put off happiness for the sake of achievement.

In *leadership*, it's about taking control of the only moment of time that you currently have. Being a successful leader is not determined by fate nor good fortune, but by a succession of successful days. When you put together a succession of five successful days, you have a successful week. Fifty-plus successful weeks get you a successful year. Without any progress today, a vision remains but an empty dream.

"The ability to convert visions to things is
the secret of success."
Henry Ward Beecher

If the No. 1 cause of business failure is lack of vision, then the No. 2 cause is the lack of focus on the right things. Johann Wolfgang von Goethe aptly said, "The things that matter most must never be at the mercy of the things that matter least."

In my consulting practice, I find many entrepreneurs lose focus on the important things by letting the day-to-day business operations run them. When we lose sight of what's important, our aim is to stay busy, and we accomplish nothing.

How would your spouse and employees answer this question: *Do you run your business ... or does it run you?*

If it runs you, you're in crisis management, fire-suppression. You can't progress much.

"One of the measures of a manager is the ability to distinguish the important from the urgent, and then to refuse to be tyrannized by the urgent, to refuse to manage by crises."
R. Alec McKenzie

How many times have you spent your today in being *busy*, but at the end, you hadn't accomplished much that you'd call *important*? You'd just put in your time.

The good news is that you have as much time as the richest person in the world—1440 golden minutes a day. You can spin whatever you desire out of TODAY.

"Out of it you have to spin wealth, pleasure, money, content, respect, and the evolution of your immortal soul. Its right use, its most effective use, is a matter of the highest urgency... all depends on that."
Arnold Bennett

I'm not suggesting that you work harder, or longer, or simply more efficiently. There is nothing so wasteful as doing with great efficiency that which doesn't have to be done at all. I am suggesting that you focus on results. That means focusing on doing the right job before focusing on doing the job *right*. As Stephen R. Covey says, "First things first, second things hardly at all." The main thing is to keep the "main thing" the *main* thing.

If you understand the Pareto principle, also called the 80/20 rule, you will find key areas in your business where you need apply only minimal efforts to produce dramatic results.

The Pareto principle asserts that a minority of effort usually leads to a majority of the results. Applied to business, this principle has one theme: to produce the most results with the least expenditure of time, effort and assets.

Rarely does luck produce significant results. Leaders produce results because they plan to do the things that *cause* results. Luck comes when preparation meets opportunity. Fortune favors facility first.

So what do you do? Ten minutes of planning will save hours in execution. Every evening before retiring or every morning before you begin your day, you remind yourself, "What is my vision? Where do I want to go?" Then, you say to yourself, "What can I do today that will produce the results I want?"

If I were managing a store again, I'd focus on increasing the productivity of my salespeople - their closing rate, average ticket and their credit sales. I'd train them better. I would make them feel cared about, while at the same time I would impose quotas and hold them accountable for results. I would spend more time in business development, working on my systems, eliminating steps and mistakes, so that their execution would run smoother.

I would learn something every week. Johnny Wooden said, "It's what you learn after you know it all that counts." Fifteen years ago, I went to my first time-management class. It changed my life and it can change yours.

Again, leaders will *wander* in all their doing – unless they have a clear and vivid vision. A leader without vision, or one who can't take control of it, will become a crisis manager. His day and his entire life will be controlled by the moment. He will always be in the reactive mode - the mode of 95% of business leaders. The paradox is that vision is not enough.

Of course, your plan should include time to meet emergencies. "Stuff happens" or "Compost occurs." Great leaders know that occasionally they will have to call an "audible." They can't control the wind, but they can adjust the sail.

Still and all, their day is governed by vision. That's why visionaries, who control their days, change the world.

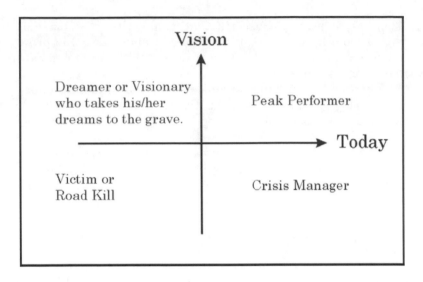

PARADOX II

Finessing Leadership and Management

All leaders must resolve a particularly tough paradox: the conflict between leadership and management. How do you separate the two? Steven R. Covey, author of *The 7 Habits of Highly Effective People*, advises, "You lead *people*, and manage *things*."

John P. Kotter, a retired professor of organizational behavior at Harvard Business School, defines the two a bit differently. He says management is about coping with *complexity*, while leadership is about coping with *change*. In his book, *What Leaders Really Do*, Kotter elaborates in the following table:

LEADERS Cope with *Change* by ...	MANAGERS Cope with *Complexity* by ...
Setting direction—developing a vision of the future, and strategies aligned with the vision, to produce the change.	***Planning and budgeting***—setting goals, determining detailed steps to achieve the goals, allocating resources to reach them.
Aligning people—communicating the new directions to those who can create coalitions that understand the vision and will commit to achieve it.	***Organizing and staffing***—creating an organization structure and a set of jobs for accomplishing the plan, staffing the jobs with qualified individuals, communicating the plan, delegating responsibility, and devising systems to monitor progress.
Motivating and inspiring— keeping people moving in the right direction despite any obstacles, by appealing to untapped human needs, values, and emotions.	***Controlling and problem-solving***—monitoring results (versus plan) by means of reports and meetings,

Both Covey and Kotter believe that leadership relates more to *vision and people*, while management relates more to *detailed planning and implementing*. Even so, both of them require the skills to deal with tasks <u>and</u> people.

Do you want to be both a leader and manager in your company? Would you prefer to be one or the other, and hire someone to take your less favored role?

Many executives are called "sales manager" or "store manager," but the term "management" has sometimes been denigrated. High-technology conglomerate United Technologies has written: "People don't want to be managed. They want to be led. Whoever heard of a 'world manager?' A 'World Leader,' yes. We know of Educational Leaders, Political Leaders, Religious Leaders, Scout Leaders, Community Leaders, Labor Leaders, and Business Leaders. They lead. They don't manage. The leader's carrot always wins over the manager's stick. Just ask your horse. You can lead a horse to water, but you can't manage him to drink.

"If you want to manage somebody, manage yourself. Do that well and you'll be ready to stop managing, and start leading."

The paradox: management is a critical part of leadership. I think management gets a bad rap. After all, without management, leadership lacks structure. Management makes a company efficient and profitable. Managers make quotas, meet deadlines, give and take orders, evaluate others and get the most out of themselves. A manager maintains the stability, control and the status quo.

Leadership is about change and improvement. A leader inspires constituents to dig deep and to give more. Management buys their arms and hands. Leadership captivates the constituents' heads and hearts. A leader sets standards, exceeds goals, initiates actions, and draws the most out of others.

While the leader empowers, the manager controls. Leadership changes the world, and management maintains it. The fundamental purpose of management is to keep the current system functioning. The fundamental purpose of leadership is to produce useful change — especially non-incremental change. You need both leadership and management.

As John Kotter has observed, it's possible to have too much or too little of either. If you have neither leadership nor management, you'll find a rudderless organization, no direction and no expectations. Strong management with no leadership tends to entrench an organization in deadly bureaucracy. Strong leadership with no management risks chaos, and imperiling of the organization.

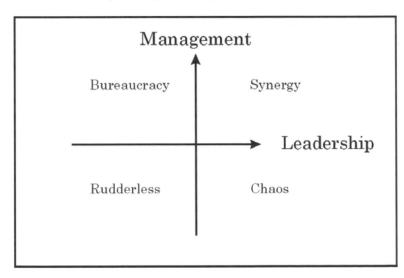

Thus, I'm not saying that leadership is good or that management is bad. Rather, they are different because they serve separate purposes.

The best leaders have the ability to finesse the struggle between leadership and management. The friction between the two concepts helps the leader bring about optimal results through synergy.

How should a leader finesse the crucial balance between management and leadership? Each constituent and situation requires its own blend. It's important to use the kind and degree of management or leadership that the employee, in whatever situation, requires. Management guru Ken Blanchard calls that strategy "situational leadership."

Suppose you're a parent with a young child. Is it better to tilt more toward management or toward leadership? Answer: consider what the situation requires. A young child needs to be watched over so that he doesn't run into the street, wander off or eat something dangerous. A child needs direction with careful tutelage. In many ways, a new employee in an organization needs similar guidance.

Yet how many of our sales managers leave new salespeople to themselves ... with little more guidance than, "If you get confused, just remember the fuzzy side goes up."(That's what the owner of a carpet store would say.) Perhaps that's why "unrealistic expectations" represent the No. 1 cause of employees' failure in the workplace.

When guiding small children and new employees, begin your training with greater oversight and narrower restrictions. Teach values (corporate or family), culture and establish standards. Yet, closely supervise, to assure understanding of the rules and compliance.

Later, as teenagers become adults and new employees learn the system, they need less direction and supervision. You can shift the dynamic between management and leadership. You can verify their learning and compliance. From the management realm, the only remnants are the controls of the family's or company's systems, values, mission and standards of performance.

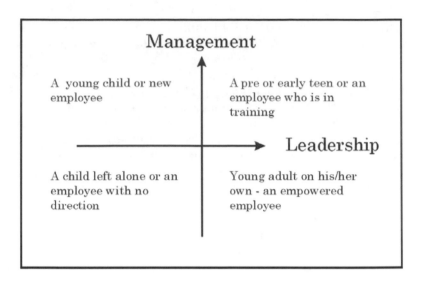

Management

A young child or new employee

A pre or early teen or an employee who is in training

Leadership

A child left alone or an employee with no direction

Young adult on his/her own - an empowered employee

Paradox III

Accountability and Connection, or Getting Constituents to Like You <u>and</u> Respect You

A leader has been defined as "someone with followers." Therefore, a "supposed leader" without followers is <u>no</u> leader. In his book, *Gung Ho,* management guru Ken Blanchard says, "A leader is a person you would follow to a place you would not go by yourself."

Both definitions imply that the willingness to follow (follower-ship) is a choice. A leader's power cannot be demanded, it can only be granted. With wages, you can buy an employee's hand, but you can't buy his heart. Whether the economy is good or bad, we are dealing with a largely voluntary workforce. Volunteers won't work for bad bosses or follow bad leaders.

As a leader, you are responsible for the productivity of your team. Fact: *Employee* satisfaction causes productivity and customer satisfaction...and customer satisfaction causes profit growth. In the 1990's, Sears analyzed complex math-data to determine if, and how, employee loyalty pushed the bottom line - up or down. Its conclusion: "For every 5% increase in employee satisfaction, there is a resultant 2% increase in customer satisfaction, returning up to 1.8% in net profit." (*Harvard Business Review*)

What lies at the heart of employee satisfaction? According to the Gallup Organization, employees follow leaders they like and to whom they feel connected. It comes down to how they are treated and whether they feel connected to the leader.

Related to these findings, nearly all peak performers had a best friend at work. Consequently, effective managers seek ways to become trustworthy friends with their employees. Not necessarily a social relationship, though it could be, but at least an open, trusting relationship where bad news can be shared as safely as good news.

"There are two classes of [leaders] – [leaders] by education and practice, these we respect; and [leaders] by nature, these we love."
Ralph Waldo Emerson

You will gain your followers' loyalty only if they both like you and respect you. Remember, loyalty cannot be demanded, only granted.

Naturally, if a leader comes too close to his constituents, he will find it difficult to hold his constituents accountable for results. He may retreat from good business decisions that would hurt people's lives. When such leaders fail to demand accountability, their constituents lose respect for them. Unfortunately, some managers leap to the other end of the spectrum: they choose to keep a distance from their constituents. They seek respect *at the expense of* being liked.

However you balance the two, remember that lack of accountability invites mediocrity and complacency. If employees are not held accountable for their performance, they may lose respect for the boss. In my seminars, we learn that many leaders fail because they don't:

- Hold constituents accountable for results.
- Fire unproductive employees.
- Demand that their constituents take their vision seriously.
- Correct unacceptable behavior.

CAUTION: Do not confuse respect with fear. Don't try to push employees past respect *for* you and into the realm of fear *of* you. W. Edwards Deming has shown that fear actually sabotages peak performance and productivity.

What are the consequences of not being both liked and respected?

If followers don't like you and don't respect you, they will be openly critical and will seek to sabotage you.

If they like you, but don't respect you, they will follow you for a while, but only at a distance. Why at a distance? Would you follow an incompetent leader into battle? Maybe, but you wouldn't follow too closely.

If they respect you, but don't like you, they will undermine your projects and even your career.

Why didn't Saddam Hussein lead his troops? Would you lead troops, if you knew that the soldiers you were leading had guns and didn't like you?

However, if they both like *and* respect you, they will serve you as loyal employees. They will feel your concern for their welfare and your confidence in their ability to produce great results. Your support will empower them to reach new heights.

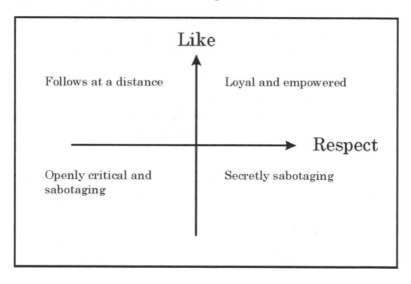

Finessing these two contraries—being liked and being respected—is one of the most difficult paradoxes to manage in leadership. Niccolo Machiavelli said it well in the 15th Century: *"There is no other way of guarding oneself against flattery than by letting men understand that they will not offend you by speaking the truth; but when everyone can tell you the truth, you lose their respect."*

PARADOX IV

Prepare Carefully, Then Finesse at the End

You read, you think. You plan and envision. Then you act in a single moment with decisiveness. Though it's always too tough to finesse paradoxes effectively, we know it can be done.

Accept, don't fight, the existence of contradictory principles, strategies and priorities. F. Scott Fitzgerald said, "The sign of a first-rate intelligence is the ability to hold two opposing views in the mind at the same time and still have the ability to function." Use your intelligence to address both views. When you do, it's beautiful — the friction or conflict between the opposing principles usually enhances leadership and performance. Paradoxes and polarities are not enemies, but rather beneficial forces. Paradoxes invite us to find better solutions. The better approach is to accept paradox, try to understand it and make it part of our reasoning.

> "Every coin, I now realize, has at least two sides, but there are pathways through the paradoxes if we can understand what is happening and are prepared to act differently.
> *Charles Handy, The Age of Paradox*

In the past, high tolerance for uncertainty was found only in geniuses like Leonardo da Vinci. Now, as change accelerates, all leaders need the ability to thrive in ambiguity. *Poise* in the face of paradox is key not only to effectiveness, but also to sanity in a rapidly changing world.

Welcome the conflict or friction between ideas as a source of better ideas. Let the friction between opposites enlighten your group to produce better decisions, styles and strategies. Be willing to study polarized viewpoints and priorities. By doing so, you'll sharply increase the probability that you'll generate unexpected synergy. That's the power of diversity.

The wonderful irony is that out of any process keyed on welcoming disagreement, conflict, and differing viewpoints, you develop a corporate culture of heightened sensitivity, harmony and synergy. I know that friction between individuals and groups can cause discomfort. However, creative collaboration between people sponsoring different ideas can produce better ones. Instead of seeing it as conflict, see it as a means to creativity and improved results. Applying both of the opposing strategies can lead to better results.

You don't want abrasion when you run your car's engine or try to move a group of people forward, but you do want it when *designing* a car and searching for better ideas *before* the group moves forward. "In great teams, conflict becomes productive," writes Peter Senge, author of *The Fifth Discipline.* "The free flow of conflicting ideas and feelings is critical for creative thinking, and for discovering new solutions that no one individual would have come to on his own." Truth may be found in the tension between the polarities.

Don't accept experts' simple formulas without considering the potential contradiction. In business literature, we find many successful management formulas. For every formula, however, there's an opposite and equally successful formula. Don't accept any expert's formula until you study and understand it. Consider using or finessing both contraries at the same time.

"To remain whole, be twisted. To become straight, let yourself be bent. To become full, be hollow."
Tao Te Ching

Accept the fact that no one style, strategy or answer works in every situation. The message of polarities is that there's no single, always-right action. What worked last time may not work this time. You may have been caught in the common trap of the tyranny of the OR. Avoid the logic that tells you to do either A or B. Instead, embrace the genius of the AND — the paradoxical view that allows you to pursue both A and B at the same time. As a parent, I learned along time ago that what works with one child may not work with another. Even though each child was raised in the same home, each responds to different strategies and tactics. As children are different, so are constituents.

Look for value within each of the opposites. Instead of fighting and trying to destroy paradox, we should celebrate it. When confronted by a problem, leaders would be wise to carefully consider all sides of the issues involved, no matter how paradoxical or absurd. Look for the value inside each.

Finesse them together, and adjust as needed. Remember you always have at least two choices: do this or do that. Cope ... and endure the confusion. Be poised. We rarely succeed by mixing equal amounts of each principle. Remember the shower? We have to continually adjust, based on how hot the "hot" is, how cold the "cold" is, and if anyone has flushed. Be ready to call an "audible" and finesse the shower knob.

"The way of paradoxes is the way of truth."
Oscar Wilde, Playwright,
toast of London, convict

Leading is difficult.

"Life always gets harder toward the summit—the cold increases,
responsibility increases."
Friedrich Wilhelm Nietzsche

Extracting maximum power out of two opposites is the challenge of leadership, mastered by few. By sharpening your recognition, finessing and struggling with paradox, you will enhance your leadership and enjoy showing others how to succeed.

Samuel D. Allman

Sam Allman began working at the age of 9, installing carpets with his father. He continued working in the floor covering business, as a salesman in his twenties, as a store owner in his thirties and as territory manager, regional sales manager and Vice President at Mohawk Industries in his forties. Through his business career, he became an expert in the paradoxes of life and the challenges they create. Working from his principles, Sam has teamed with major corporations to create corporate "universities" that have transformed training from a "cost" to a "profit center". He has taught managers how to lead, manage, supervise, motivate and coach. And he has taught sales employees how to increase sales, sales margins and customer loyalty. Sam received his BS from Long Beach State University and his Masters from Brigham Young University. Together with his wife, Jessie, he has ten children and 15 grandchildren. Today, he leads Allman Consulting and Training, including among his clients, Mohawk Industries, Home Depot, Lowe's, and Sears.

Samuel D. Allman
5150 Stilesboro Rd., Suite 100
Kennesaw, Georgia 30152
Phone:770.425.2142
Fax: 678.355.0177
Email: samallman@aol.com
Email: sam@allmanconsulting.com
www.allmanconsulting.com

Chapter Ten

ORGANIZING YOURSELF TO LEAD EFFECTIVELY: POWER TOOLS FOR LEADING YOUR TEAM

Lynn Hayden

Leadership is often depicted as some mysterious power, some charismatic gift or some strategic vision belonging only to special human beings. But I believe leadership is a skill that anyone can learn and improve upon—a rather homey skill, like cooking.

So are there any tools out there that can help you improve your leadership skills? Stocking your "leadership kitchen" is first a matter of discerning what utensils you need and then setting about acquiring them. The right tools will assist you in becoming a more skilled leader, more knowledgeable about yourself and more able to relate to and motivate your staff.

I'm speaking of "power" tools—from little gadgets to big machines—tools that will *em*power you and your staff. A wise cook knows a stove isn't enough for a good meal; you also need little utensils like measuring spoons or graters to do the job. Depending on the situation, the same concept applies to leading and managing people.

I'm talking about fundamental human skills, so I believe it's most valuable to share with you not only the challenges that my clients have faced as they have sought to become better leaders but how we responded to them together to create customized solutions.

As you read about a few of my clients' leadership and organizational challenges, ask yourself: "Do I know someone like this person?" Then ask yourself further: "Could that someone be me?"

Before I introduce you to a few of my clients, I should emphasize that I began to do seminars in time management/work organization and individual consulting nearly twenty-five years ago. My first client was myself. I had always believed in cultivating these skills, and I found myself always helping others to be better organized. Friends and colleagues were constantly asking me, "How do you manage to have so much free time for yourself? How do you keep your drawers and closets so spare?" So I figured, "Why not share with lots of people what I've learned about these mundane yet important challenges?"

Over the years of working in this self-improvement kitchen, I've also developed a philosophy: "Have it your way." By that, I mean enjoy your meal! Enjoy the learning process of getting organized and learning to lead more effectively. I'm not the kind of consultant or trainer who makes your decisions for you or sells you a one-size-fits-all program or pushes a system. Everything we work out is custom-tailored to your temperament, needs and aspirations. Why? Because I've discovered—sometimes the hard way—that if leadership and management practices aren't customized to your style and your priorities, you won't practice them after I leave. They'll be half-baked—just one more day planner that lies in the desk drawer (causing, not eliminating clutter). You'll revert to your old, comfortable, suboptimal habits, because the techniques never became integrated into your day. After all, to become good at anything—like cooking meals—you need to practice your skills. The same is true for leading and managing. And to do that, the practice must suit you and make sense to you.

Now to my clients. The six clients of mine that you'll be meeting can talk you blue in the face about exorcising the devils of clutter and procrastination, the fine arts of mapping, tracking and prioritizing assignments, using Post-Its, keeping a phone log and a to-do list, and the rest of the leadership tools in my kitchen drawer. More importantly, they can also tell you about the attitude shift that helped them get more out of their work life and their life's work.

In consulting both individual clients and corporations—from New York to Texas, Singapore to Guatemala—I've found that all leadership problems fall into three huge piles: time, space and people. Invariably, the piles overlap and interact, so I've organized and simplified them here for illustration. But the following cases, like most cases, were much more complex than my limited space here permits me to explain.

Case #1: The Detail Monger

Wrestling with Guatemala's future—and always racing the clock—is Ricardo Stein, the executive director of the Soros Foundation in Guatemala (Fundacion Soros, Guatemala). Ricardo is a man very much aware that he can't afford to waste a single moment.

In the office by 7:30 every morning, Ricardo's typical day is a blur of high-level meetings, speech writing, phone calls and whatever else is in store. Yet, looking back, he can see how he was once far from making the best use of his time and talent.

Ricardo was an academic with real world experience. A self-described "big picture" thinker who, at fifty-four, was at the top of his game, Ricardo found himself trapped. Instead of giving free reign to what he did best—think—he was tied up for hours a day answering phone calls, mail, e-mail and wading through piles of paper. What a waste!

As is my custom, I began by asking a series of seemingly innocent questions about his daily work habits. Ricardo recounted our conversations to a friend of mine: "Lynn wanted to know the first thing I did every morning. Why did I keep my papers in piles on my desk, which, while neat, were not necessarily organized? How did I process my mail? Did I plan my day? And so on.

"There was one question, though, that really threw me for a loop. She asked me why I took notes. I told her, 'So I can remember, right?' She told me, 'Wrong. You take notes so you can forget. Which means by taking the time to write something down—a task, an idea—you now have conserved your brain power for a more valuable mental activity, which is decision making.' It was a pivotal moment—a total change in my thought processes."

No, it wasn't easy to work with Ricardo! Getting organized has been an arduous journey for him. But he told me on my last visit a few months ago, "It's been so freeing." Why? What changed?

He began planning each day. He became convinced of the importance of sitting down alone for ten to fifteen minutes at the end of the day to plan the next day. He began blocking and delegating. He's no longer a prisoner of e-mail, phone calls or the piles of mail that used to take him hours to go through. Now he delegates that job to his secretary, and then they sit down together to review needed items together. As for phone calls, he now chooses a specific time of day to answer them. That liberated him to no end.

He also began handling the flow of paper. The neat piles on his desk have become boxes on his shelf. Now he culls through his clips and intended readings periodically. If he has not gotten to something within sixty days, it's gone.

Instead of constantly playing catch-up, he feels he's more in control of his work and life. And now he has more time for higher-order thinking. He had mistaken orderliness for order. Now he has the time and space to plan ahead and not have his day eaten up by the small details.

Richardo's Challenge: Space

Tool #1: The Managerial Menu

Yes, Ricardo Stein turned out to be a handful. A skeptic by nature, he took nothing on faith. Most people will give something new a try. Not Ricardo; he first has to be convinced. He had a well-stocked kitchen, but no meals were being finished. He had all the ingredients and kitchenware, but he wasn't following a recipe.

To put it plainly, he was mired in details, not protecting time for the big picture. It's not easy to get a detail monger to raise his sights from the shoestrings toward the stars—even though Ricardo is a brilliant man, who had a rich vision of where he wanted to take the organization. That's not enough. You need to do mental uncluttering so that you can consistently glimpse the vision unfolding. In terms of being a good chef in the kitchen, you need what I call a "managerial menu." By that, I simply mean you need to organize and delegate in an orderly sequence that matches your rhythms.

With more responsibilities than the time to accomplish them, Ricardo liked the idea of mapping or blocking out his day. Instead of trying to juggle ten things at once, he devoted a predetermined time to specific tasks, such as answering phone calls, replying to e-mail, meeting with staff and setting aside time to read or just think.

Planning forces you to consciously think about how you're spending your time. Instead of finding your day shot and none of what you wanted to accomplish getting done, you approach each day knowing that at least some of your high-priority tasks will get your undivided attention.

The other advantage of blocking out your day is that it allows you to schedule some of your most mentally challenging tasks for when your mind is hitting on all cylinders. Why waste your best hours doing the sort of mindless ongoing housekeeping all of us have to do? Reserve your prime time for the things that are most important.

Ricardo has made terrific strides. He still struggles with letting go of papers. Like most bosses, no one is making him toe the line. No one is going to march into his office and tell him his desk is a nightmare or give him the ultimatum: "Either get organized or get out."

Remember, we're talking about a visionary here, a truly innovative leader. He wanted to be more effective, so we identified his challenges and worked with tools and techniques to enhance—not drastically alter—Ricardo's own unique style.

Shopping List Check-off Reminders

√ Organize and plan to create time for pondering.

√ Delegate to overcome myopia and envision long-term possibilities.

√ Don't juggle details; stay connected to your Big Picture.

√ Notice what your clutter is interfering with or distracting you from.

Case #2: The Great Communicator (*Not!*)

With its 360-degree reviews, which use everyone in the company you come in contact with (above, below, all around) to pinpoint the areas in which you're most wanting, computer giant Dell is no place for anyone whose feelings bruise easily. As such, Diane Candler's professional life was an open book.

No one questioned her brightness, energy or commitment, but the word around Dell's Round Rock, Texas, campus was that she just wasn't up to the job of keeping tabs on her team of supercompetitive, but raw, MBA hotshots. She had already been put through the mill of organizational training, but nothing seemed to be working. With her management career on the line, Diane jumped at the chance to work with me, when Dell's management hired me as a consultant.

We hit it off right away. She later reported to a colleague of mine, "Lynn doesn't try to cram some cookie-cutter system down your throat. She asked me lots of questions to better understand what system I was using and what I was trying to accomplish. Over a number of visits, she came up with a system completely customized for the way I work."

Following my advice, Diane began mapping or blocking out her day for specific activities, including a scheduled time to meet with specific team members. She remembers it this way: "Before, I was always looking so harried, a yo-yo in and out of their offices all day long. That's all changed now. The scheduled meeting time Lynn prescribed serves two purposes. It tells my team when I'm available but also lets them know that it's not a productive use of my time, or theirs, to be constantly interrupting each other."

It wasn't long before team members began noticing that they were dealing with a newer and improved model. At my urging, Diane began keeping an 8 1/2-by-11, three-ring binder, in which she kept track of individual team member assignments, among other things. "I would write myself a Post-It note and stick it in onto their individual pages in the staff section, so I could follow up with them at our scheduled times."

As Diane learned, communicating to subordinates which projects have a higher priority—what she calls "criticality"—also made her more sensitive about her own supervisor's shortcomings as a manager. She was always guessing which projects had the higher priority. On some projects, he'd expect an immediate turnaround but never told her ahead of time. Now she was better able to understand where he was coming from.

Making sure assignments didn't slip through the cracks wasn't the only virtue of this new tracking system. "It helped me get a better feel for each team member—who needed more hand holding, and who was more independent and didn't need as much follow-up," she says.

Indeed, her new stick-to-itiveness paid quick dividends. Gone were the whispers of recrimination and ridicule from subordinates. She recalls, "It wasn't like I was eavesdropping. Believe me, in Cubeland [her word for Dell's open-cubicled floor plan], you hear everything. I could hear them saying, 'You know, she's going to be following up.' It was almost instant respect from my team. They had noticed I was more organized, that I had a plan for the day, that I wasn't as frantic as I'd been before. It was like night and day."

Diane's Challenge: People

Tool #2: The Executive Egg Timer

Diane really took to the program. She was eager, hard working, conscientious and committed to having a tidy office. Clutter wasn't her problem. Her problem was that she was just too scattered, either too available or unavailable to her staff. And there were problems with follow-through. She just needed the executive egg timer.

Diane had a tendency to mismanage by not attuning herself to the needs of her team. She either micromanaged or practiced a hands-off policy—two extremes. She realized she could better coach her team by meeting their needs, not by doing what she subjectively judged to be the best way to go about a task. That meant adjusting herself to each of her staff members so that she erred by neither micromanaging nor by benign neglect. She needed to balance her flair for spontaneity and serendipity with sensible, other-sensitive scheduling.

The executive egg timer is a handy and versatile tool that functions not just as a stopwatch but also as a grandfather clock or even a wall calendar. By that I mean that scheduling meetings is not a matter of keeping an eye on the passing second but rather getting to know a staff member and discerning what that person needs from you in order to do his or her job better. Mismanaging is doing what you prefer, which is self-indulgent and not leadership.

Out of my kitchen tool drawer for leaders came a recommendation for blocking out her day—when she would be available to individual team members and when she wouldn't. No more "catch as catch can." No more spontaneously popping in and out of each other's cubicles. No more constant interruptions. Maybe she would meet each team member only twenty minutes every other day, but the routine would leave everyone less frazzled by constant interruptions.

It also had the virtue of leveling the playing field by putting her in her workers' place. Some would be more reluctant to bother the boss while others would be pounding on her door constantly. This way, everybody got a piece of her time.

What's more, the regular and planned meetings sent an important signal to her team. It let them know that she was involved. Too many people confuse good managing with police work. But it's a lot more than just keeping tabs on people. It's about staying involved, following up and intervening early enough to spot problems before it's too late. It means giving team members encouragement when you sense they're deflated. To me, good managing will always have an element of coaching, trying to help bring out the best in people. It's not easy, and very few of us can bring it off without some coaching ourselves.

Of course, good managing does involve keeping track of people's work. Diane's hit-or-miss ways were clearly not working. She was trying to keep five people with five projects at different states of completion straight in her head. I said to her, "Even if you could keep it all straight in your head, why leave it to memory? That's a form of mental clutter."

Instead, I recommend using an organizer. Long-time clients still call their loose-leaf binder (8 1/2-by-11) the "Hayden Organizer" or just the "Hayden Book." I prefer the name "control center," not just out of modesty but because it underscores its importance. The control center has divisions for everything from e-mail and phone numbers to notes from meetings and random thoughts to staff assignments and highlights of conversations. I suggest taking the handy and portable organizer everywhere and using it as a desktop reference.

Armed with her control center, Diane was better able to keep track of employees, their assignments, the different stages of completion and each assignment's priority rating. The last is crucial. Sometimes a manager will forget to tell a worker that a previously high-priority assignment has been shifted to the back burner. The employee keeps going full tilt, only to find out all the hurry-up wasn't necessary and that another, more urgent, project will now require an even quicker completion. The employee feels like his or her time has been wasted, and the manager loses credibility.

The control center is the air traffic control tower of your life. You need it, because even with good pilots, planes will crash without a good system in place.

Shopping List Check-off Reminders

√ Lead your team by adjusting to their individual needs and coaching them to understand your own.

√ Customize your staff scheduling.

√ Beware the extremes of rigidity and indulgence of spontaneity; your staff needs predictability and flexible planning.

√ Remember that your success as a leader is based on what your team does, not on what you do. They are your scorecards.

Case #3: The Misprioritizer

To everyone around him, Roland Hernandez looked like the picture of professionalism. Brainy, hard working, dedicated and public-spirited, the Texas state director of the National Assessment of Educational Progress (NAEP) was a man on a mission. He'd written his doctoral dissertation on school reform; it addressed how "total quality management" could transform a big, lumbering, faceless bureaucracy into one where the school culture put customers first.

Moreover, unlike a lot of theorizers, Roland actually lived what he preached. To him, public service meant just that—prompt, courteous and efficient service. Especially prompt, "mañana" just wasn't in his vocabulary.

So what's wrong with making yourself available to your customers or making sure phone calls, mail and e-mail get answered right away? Nothing, if your job is an emergency 911 operator. Plenty, if constantly putting out brushfires means you're neglecting other, even more consequential, aspects of your job—not to mention the havoc it wreaks on the rest of your life.

"To me, putting the customer first always meant never putting people or responsibilities off," says Roland. "It meant answering phone calls and e-mail as they came. But most of my own work wasn't getting done until after the center closed, and that wasn't fair to my wife and family.

"Lynn showed me I could get more accomplished if I set aside a part of my day to answer phone calls and e-mail. It felt strange, even slightly irresponsible, at first. After all, I'd written my dissertation on putting customers first. The idea of using voice mail and getting back to people several hours later didn't seem right. But Lynn convinced me that it was enough that people could trust that I would get back to them by the end of the day."

It didn't take long for Roland to see the difference. Without the constant interruptions, he found his own work was getting done during normal office hours. He was so taken with the results, that he spoke to his wife about my suggestions. "My wife's a professional, too, and we both agreed we weren't giving enough time to each other and the kids. You know, work can consume you if you let it. So it's important to find the right balance. Becoming better organized and efficient is a good way to find that balance."

Roland's Challenge: Time

Tool #3: The Super Strainer

I could have left well enough alone. After all, with an orderly office, a filing system, a calendar and a to-do list, Roland would never have qualified for the twelve-step program called "Messy Rooms Anonymous" (yes, it does exist.); his "symptoms" were more subtle. Roland suffered from chronic overavailability. It was causing a terrible strain, not just on him but on his family members and his colleagues. To relieve this strain, I recommended the Super Strainer, which acts as a sieve that strains out all the chaff—the pulpy, indigestible parts of your day—thus easing the stresses and strains. It restricts the inflow and thereby limits access, so that other people don't distract you with low priority items and you don't succumb to self-distraction. The solution to misprioritizing invariably includes limiting your availability so that you focus on who and what matters here and now. You don't try to do everything, which is the malady of the excessively conscientious person. Unlike Diane, Roland's problem was not so much about leading a team and coordinating its efforts as it was about maintaining his own personal focus and learning better to lead and manage himself.

Some people's work habits are such that they end up letting a lot of things slide. Not Roland. If anything, he's too conscientious. The truth is, like many busy people, he had too much to do. I tell my clients that in today's world, it's more important to decide what you're *not* going to do. It's a kind of triage—deciding where time and energy can make the most difference. It's just not humanly possible to do everything you'd like to do. Of course, you could do what Roland was doing—coming in early, staying late and taking work home. But that's a recipe for emotional burnout. You have to set your priorities. For someone as service-oriented as Roland, it requires a major attitude shift.

Roland was a brilliant thinker, yet he wasn't getting around to the special projects he felt called to do. I asked him, as I do all my clients, "What are the things you're going to be evaluated on? Where, if you had the time, could you make the most difference? What's going to make you stand out? In other words, what's your *big picture?*"

I was quick to add that I wasn't recommending that he not answer the phone or e-mail—just relegate them to their proper place. I recommended that he schedule himself twenty to sixty minutes a day to focus exclusively on his major project. "Twenty minutes? How much can you get done in only twenty minutes?" he asked. I replied, "You'd be surprised. Think how many new words you could memorize if you were trying to learn a new language. Or what if you had twenty minutes to practice your golf game or write a letter? Besides, researchers have found that even a relatively short period of concentration can plant the seeds for the unconscious mind to cultivate."

My advice: Think about how you're using your day. Instead of working unconsciously—I call it being on automatic pilot—think carefully about sifting your priorities and organizing the flow of your day. The feeling of being overwhelmed by work is more often caused by a disorganized approach than by the amount or difficulty of the work. By having critical information readily available to you when you need it, you can increase your ability to manage your time, people and projects. This can only be done effectively if you match your organizing tools with your work style and needs.

Shopping List Check-off Reminders

√ Beware of overavailability to others.

√ Limit your distractions by carefully limiting others' access to you.

√ The ineffective leader reacts to problems; the effective leader responds to challenges and learns from them.

√ Develop a master list of your goals, and organize your to-do list to support their completion.

√ Make full use of short periods of concentration.

Case #4: The Pile-Loving Pack Rat

Call it pride or just plain stubbornness. Will Lowrance knew his fridge was overstocked and admitted that he didn't know there was rotten lettuce behind the fresh quart of milk. He had a full fridge with a lot of inedible, spoiled stuff. He needed to clear out his fridge!

"I was one of those people who kept everything," says Will, a sixty-two-year-old lifelong teacher and school administrator, working in recent years as a troubleshooter for the Texas Department of Education. "I was convinced that the minute I threw something away, I'd need it."

As always, my response was, "In all probability, that's exactly what's going to happen, but it doesn't do you much good to hold onto something if you won't be able to find it. In fact, there's really no difference between having it and not finding it and not having it all."

Somehow, though, he'd managed to convince himself he didn't need any help. I had to fight him to get him to throw away all the moldy stuff, to set expiration dates on the perishables, to rotate his stock and to start using a garbage disposal; in short, to toss the junk food of paper clutter in order to digest fully the meaty memos.

"I actually thought of myself as an organized person," says Will. "I thought I had a legitimate filing system and I knew how to manage a calendar. But it didn't take long for me to see that I wasn't nearly as organized as I thought I was," he concedes. "I ended up throwing out two thirds of the paper I had convinced myself that I had to keep."

But it wasn't just the piles of paper. "My calendar was one of those linear to-do lists that wasn't letting me devote my energies to the things that mattered most. As for time management, I was letting other people call the tune, controlling my day rather than pro-actively taking charge of my time. Again, following Lynn's advice, I started blocking out my day, setting aside certain times for certain things. One of those things was setting time for myself; just closing my door and thinking."

Will's Challenge: Space

Tool #4: The Scouring Pad

After initially coming up with every excuse not to get together, Will relented, and once he made up his mind, he was on board. What a character. Will, who has since been elected the mayor of Hillsboro, Texas, had two problem areas: general organization (primarily a filing system) and a haphazard approach to time management.

Will was simply clogged, both by stuff and by appointments. He suffered from "collectivitis." He was the classic Mr. Collector, who engaged in overcollecting because he always could imagine a scenario in which he might need whatever item he was stockpiling. He just couldn't trust and let go.

Much of what we had to do was simply start from the beginning and assess, item by item, what he really needed at that moment. We based that on what he had needed in the past and how likely present trends would continue and serve as predictors of his likely needs in the future. So we started with "zero-based clutter busting" in order to break through the defenses of the pack rat, which are related both to material and to time.

Uncluttering and unclogging, both physically and mentally, was a big task. It meant developing "simple-mindedness"—cultivating an attitude of simplicity, namely that the essentials will suffice and that he would be able to get what he needed when he needed it. But in order to get simpler, we had to use a scouring pad. The strainer wasn't enough. We had to do deep cleaning (and then use the garbage disposal!).

Will agreed with my assessment. So through the files we plowed. With every scrap of paper I'd ask, "What's this for? Does it have a purpose? Is it just a feel-good item? Does it have any current relevance or future purpose?" I don't believe in backing up the truck and indiscriminately pitching everything. As I see it, people wouldn't collect all their stuff if it didn't have some meaning to them. Besides, I think it's good practice to get in the habit of forcing yourself to make a conscious choice about what stays and goes.

As for managing time—even a more pressing challenge now that he's a mayor—I recall sitting down with Will and his secretary. My advice was that they meet every week to go over his calendar and projects, to be sure, when blocking out his day, that he made time for meetings with himself—private time for being creative, for strategizing, for brainstorming.

I targeted Will's to-do list for redoing. Like so many others, he had one of those everything-but-the-kitchen-sink lists. Instead, I told him, "Reserve your to-do list for actual tasks that can be accomplished in one day. Don't make the mistake of clogging up your daily to-do list. It's the quickest way to feel defeated. And you'll never give yourself the satisfaction of completing the list."

Certain tasks fall under the category of goals or long-term projects; for example, writing a new policy and procedures manual. Writing the manual, however, will inevitably mean breaking things into smaller, bite-size, doable activities. Getting hold of a copy of the old manual, for example, would qualify as a to-do list item.

"And remember," I added, "Don't try to keep it all in your head. Even the best of memories are spotty. Besides, it's another form of mental clutter." My advice: Clear your mind for more important things. You can store information anywhere. Reserve your mind for what is most important—making stellar decisions.

Shopping List Check-off Reminders

√ Beware: Overaccumulation can overwhelm you.

√ Practice zero-based clutter-busting to effectively organize your environment by first culling and then purging.

√ Make sure that the information you have at your desk and in your files is retrievable with the minimum amount of effort.

√ Note that the compulsion to keep is rooted in fear.

Case #5: Mr. No-Hugs

Alex Van Der Zwaard is a thirty-five-year-old Dutch banker. He's a senior manager overseeing a team of twenty-five sales people in the trust and estate planning division of Meespierson Asia. We crossed paths when he attended one of the two-day workshops that I regularly teach at the Singapore Institute of Management. As Alex remembered, "I've taken more than my share of senior management workshops where I've fallen asleep. They were either too technical or too abstract. Lynn's workshop was a revelation to me. In simple English, she showed me how certain habits can become a hindrance to effective work and living."

Alex could be pretty hard on himself. "I think I'm one of the worst administrators you can think of. I'm much stronger on the commercial side." Strong or not, he finds himself managing a group of high-powered sales people, a task made a lot harder by his own, quite noticeable disorganization. "My desk was simply a mess, and they—to put it mildly—would frown at my filing and administration. Lynn showed me what I could do improve my work space; how to design a system to file everything so that my desk would not be so disorganized."

Like so many managers, Alex found himself constantly fighting the clock, never having enough time to get to all his responsibilities. "I was spending most of my day responding to e-mail, he says. "It was time-consuming and irritating. Thanks to Lynn, I'm scheduling the e-mail for predetermined times and those requiring lengthy responses closer to 5:00."

The most important issue facing Alex was building the morale of his team. "Lynn put me in touch with the importance of giving my subordinates more pats on the back. She asked, 'What gives you joy at work?' I realized that money is certainly important but so are achievement and recognition.

"I feel like I'm on top of the world right now; more effective because I'm more in control, thanks to the practical, common-sense tools she gave me. Overall, my life has more balance now, with more time for other things. I've become more conscious of how easy it is to waste time if you don't organize your day. I just needed someone to hold up the mirror."

Alex's Challenge: People

Tool #5: Party Favors!

Alex came away from our workshop with a newfound appreciation of the need to give his salespeople more pats on the back. I wasn't surprised. I'm forever running into old-school type managers who think professionals shouldn't have to be babysat. Their attitude is, "What do you mean I'm supposed to tell them they're doing a good job? They get paid don't they?" The truth is that people don't pour heart and soul into their work just for the paycheck. You're dealing with human beings, and human nature being what it is, people like to feel they've accomplished something and that someone appreciates their work.

Alex's problem, I told him, stemmed from that old-school idea that leaders and managers get more out of their workers if they remain stern, aloof and withholding. That's how Alex appeared to his staff—the Super Rationalist, Mr. Insensitivity. Alex was not socially adept. He was much more comfortable doing e-mail than he was in the give and take of personal conversation. Nonetheless, what many of his staff members needed was more face time—more meetings, more emphasis on developing a personal relationship with him as a supervisor. He just needed to open his heart a little more. He wasn't insensitive; he was simply unaware of some of the negative effects of his communication style. He needed a more personal touch that included smiles and laughter and thinking through what I call the "seating chart of his staff table;" even giving out party favors to break the ice, to make him seem more approachable and more human. Alex was an example of a great cook who could ruin a meal because his guests didn't feel they were in a comfortable environment. The quality of the food isn't enough. The ambience of an office will make people feel good or bad about the work they're doing. Alex had to become less of an impersonal boss and more of a mentor and guide.

The reason is that leading is not the same as bossing. One is about commanding obedience; the other is more akin to coaching, and a good coach can be both a taskmaster and a cheerleader. Leading is determined by two factors: technical and people skills. How you organize and how organized you are will determine how effectively you can carry out those skills. And perhaps even more importantly, they affect how other people perceive you.

In fact, a manager who is more approachable—staying involved, setting up regular times for meetings, looking out for things that can help a team do a better job (sharing an article you cut out of the paper, with a personal note attached from you) and offering praise for a good effort—gets more out of his team.

One of the virtues of setting a regularly scheduled meeting is that it provides a less threatening way to check up on how each person is doing. People are only too eager to talk about the projects that are going well. But if they start hemming and hawing about a project, that's your signal that they need help. Very often, encouraging them to talk it out will break the logjam. This is where good coaching is essential. Instead of this meeting being an inquisition, you want people to think of it (and you) as a support system, trying to bring out the best in them.

"It was a revelation to me," says Alex. "Lynn showed me in plain, simple language how my management style hindered effective leadership and living."

Shopping List Check-off Reminders

√ Don't demand that your team become you; help them be themselves.

√ Leadership is getting things done through other people.

√ Let your team know what you need from them to get your work done.

√ Your role is to do everything you can to help your people succeed.

Case #6: The People-Pleasing Put-offer

Susan Kaderka had the opposite problem as Alex: She was too sensitive to the needs of others. Susan is one of my long-time clients, dating back to the late 1970s. A professional writer with very little prior managerial experience, she found herself in charge of a fairly large research staff at the Texas Department of Agriculture. She felt overwhelmed.

"By temperament, I'm inclined to want to concentrate on one thing at a time," says Susan. "But as a manager, I didn't have that luxury. I had to juggle a lot of different things. I'd have two or three meetings in a row on totally different subjects. I still struggle with this. But Lynn's check-ins help me stay on top of things."

Today, Susan manages a staff of fifteen as a regional director for the National Wildlife Federation. After twenty years, here's how she summarizes her ongoing challenges.

Getting a handle on chaos: "I need to maintain a sense of calm. By devoting time to planning ahead, I'm able to think about the bigger picture. When I take the time to plan ahead, I know I will not have my day eaten up by trivia, by wall-to-wall activity."

Planning the day: "I'm more in touch with the many ways we sabotage ourselves—meeting other people's priorities and pleasing them, not me. It's a tough habit to break when you work under people and over people and you depend on them to get your work done and you care about their good opinion. In my case, instead of concentrating on personal higher-priority projects, I got bogged down taking phone calls, e-mail. Now I protect the first hour of the day. I learned what Lynn stresses, that creativity requires freshness—in the office or in the kitchen—so I use my freshest hours!"

Using the control center: "I now keep a running account of lots of things going on at the same time. You don't have the problem of remembering 'Where was I?' It's a way of compartmentalizing things and keeping them at your fingertips."

Wrestling with procrastination: "My biggest struggle is with putting things off. I probably always will, but now I work on the hard projects first by slicing things into smaller pieces. It isn't about being a more efficient machine. Working smarter means having the time for a more balanced life."

Susan's Challenge: Time

Tool #6: The Slicer-Dicer

Like many highly competent people, Susan bit off more than she could chew. That caused her always to be champing at the bit. In working on her tendencies toward procrastination, we honed her skill for slicing and dicing her work into manageable chunks.

You need manageable chunks for good managing. Sometimes the slicer-dicer isn't enough. Very often, the procrastination habit is a reflection of poor priorities—a problem that we've already discussed—but it means that other kitchen utensils must be relied upon. Sometimes, you have to move a task from the front burner to the back burner. At other times, an unimportant matter should just be put in the microwave and given a few minutes to keep it warm and up to date. Do it now! Devote the most time to what matters most. Don't always solve your problems. Dissolve your problems! Don't simplify by condensing or squeezing more into less space or time. Do it by selection. Pick out your priorities and drop or defer the rest.

So don't cram more and more into the same available time; rather, set priorities. Use a carving knife, if necessary, to trim the fat and keep the real meat. This is all about working smarter, not working harder. If you chunk it small, you will get clarity and momentum. If you plan, you will be able to cut through the piles and do what counts most. Planning is a power tool for managing multiple projects. Studies show that one hour of planning saves four hours of work!

Of course, Susan is far from alone in her struggle with putting things off. It's right up near the top of clients' complaints. Our society is groaning under the near universal curse of procrastination. And why not? If all work were enjoyable, exhilarating and easy, there wouldn't be anything like procrastination. We don't have to be pulled kicking and screaming to watch a beautiful sunset or read a good book. It's the pleasure principle. We put off what we don't like, what we find hard to do or what we fear we may fail at.

Still, natural or not, avoiding the disagreeable and the difficult doesn't have to be inevitable.

It takes a lot of self-awareness not to run and hide when you feel a lump in your throat and a knot in your stomach. It's really painful, and most people's first inclination is to take refuge in the familiar, the mundane, the less threatening—anything to take their minds off what they know they should be doing. Instead, they resort to making phone calls or answering e-mail. The mind games we play on ourselves are endless. The kicker is that we'll turn around and say, "Such and such made it impossible for me to get to my work!"

Of course, at a certain level, that's true. There will always be other things to do—phone calls to answer, meetings to attend, the problem employee. Something is always coming next.

Some of those things will even qualify as urgent. But the most successful people know the difference between urgent and important and guard against being sucked into the daily clamor for their attention.

I tell people to break assignments down into more psychologically manageable pieces, even if it's only fifteen minutes at a time, and to slice the job into more easily doable tasks, just as they would cut a salami roll into smaller bites. With bite-sized pieces, you'll start to create a momentum that can carry you to the end.

The real payoff will be this: The next time the panic button gets pushed, you'll be able to turn it off more quickly because the unknown is now more familiar territory. Remember, the last thing you want to do is avoid the work altogether. Try as you might to push it out of your conscious mind, you'll only end up torturing yourself.

Shopping List Check-off Reminders

√ Be on the lookout for areas of procrastination.

√ Combat the procrastination habit by slicing it into bite-size pieces.

√ Remember that the payoff ratio for time spent planning is four to one.

√ Carve off your fatty nonpriorities to leave the real meat.

Parting Thoughts

You've just met six people who learned to better manage their time, take more control of their space and better exercise their leadership responsibilities. And you've been introduced to six tools to help you manage your own time, space and relationships, which are, after all, the stuff of your life.

Wouldn't you like to be better organized if that would help you do what you truly want to do? We all want that, so I'll share with you a final story.

I'm a Dakota farm girl. I recall how each farm would have a huge pile of rocks and boulders. Clearing the land back then involved pulling out huge rocks by hand. It was backbreaking work. So the pile served to remind the families—and those who came after them—that it took a lot of sweat and blood to make that place what it was.

No wonder, then, that the people I see hold onto their piles of paper as if their lives depended on it. Those are their rock piles. Those are their lives. But unlike the farmers in those days, you can put your piles of rocks aside and move on.

Yet for me, the image of farmers carving a future out of the wilderness also serves as a powerful inspiration for change. Why? Because getting organized is about clearing a path to the future. It's about becoming conscious and protective of your time. It's deciding what you must do, and when you add the element of responsibility for leading other people, the stakes extend beyond yourself. Do you want to have the time and energy for things that matter most? It's your choice.

About The Author

Lynn Hayden

Lynn Hayden is a management consultant based in Austin, Texas. She specializes in personal management and work organization systems, delivering training sessions for a broad array of audiences and industries. In her work with both government agencies and private corporations, she regularly conducts seminars in Guatemala, Singapore and Hong Kong. She is a member of the National Speakers Association and the Singapore Training and Development Association. Her trademark is to partner with her clients by providing customized solutions that equip them with the ability to personally achieve their goals. Lynn brings expertise that is grounded with easy-to-implement strategies. She has helped individuals and departments increase productivity by designing individual systems that addresses personal organization, paperwork flow, and information retrieval; systems that track and monitor people and projects; and systems that aid in developing management and leadership skills. Lynn's individual clients include administrators, teachers, attorneys, salesman, artists, entrepreneurs, students, real estate agents, directors, public officials, among others. She has personally worked with people at every level of an organization—boards of directors, advisory councils, managers, supervisors, line staff, clerical staff and volunteers. Lynn empowers individuals, teams, and companies to achieve results.

Lynn Hayden
Lynn Hayden & Associates
3611 Claburn Drive
Austin, Texas 78759
Phone: 512.349.0113
E-mail: lhayden@austin.rr.com

Chapter Eleven

PREPARING WOMEN TO LEAD

Alison R. Brown

This chapter is dedicated to those chosen to
lead and to those who do the choosing.

Boys and Girls

Think for a minute about the different types of toys that boys and
girls are encouraged to play with, the role of sports in the lives of our
youth and the rules that may apply to one gender but not the other.
Consider that girls may be more relationship oriented, while boys
may be more competitive and focused on rules that protect their
rights. Times are changing for current and future generations of
youth. So where does all this leave the adults that are in the workforce now, leading organizations and making decisions that affect and
influence employment?

Women and Men

From a historical perspective, the responsibilities of women have
traditionally included family, household chores and childbearing.
When women began to work in manufacturing environments and as
teachers, their roles expanded. In the companies I work with and

have interviewed, one thing has remained consistent: Leadership competencies are not gender specific. But understanding how men and women have been socialized gives insight into the way things are and how they got that way. The entire process is a contributing factor to where companies, educational institutions, boards, families and communities find themselves today. One of the difficulties for women has been, and continues to be, that they spend more time on family responsibilities than men do. As a result, women are sometimes not considered for promotions or are viewed as not being dedicated to their jobs.

Spectator Sport

The basis for the way society functions in the United States has a foundation in the world of sports. There are veterans and rookies, winners and losers, and generally one star on the team. We use terminology like "leveling the playing field." Today we have company scorecards and executive coaching, and women have stood on the "sidelines" for a very long time.

In 2002, I was featured in the third volume of a book entitled *Mission Possible*, along with Pat Summitt, basketball coach for the University of Tennessee Lady Vols. Coach Summitt exemplifies the way to build team unity and demonstrates what it takes to have a winning team. When her team doesn't win, she handles the situation very graciously. There are many women in corporate America who have the skills needed to succeed but do not have access to high-visibility opportunities and assignments that offer the best education. The roles women have traditionally had in the work environment are, in part, based on the way they are perceived by the individuals making the decisions.

In the Eyes of the Beholder

Decision makers have certain perceptions when it comes to promoting females into middle and senior management positions. For example, once women are promoted, there perhaps may be a power inequity brought about by the sheer numbers of men competing against them. It would be a mistake to underestimate the influence of such perceptions. Women are sometimes categorized or labeled if they are aggressive, assertive, outspoken, opinionated, detail oriented, sensitive, not assertive enough, too quiet, etc. Once a label is attached to a person, it takes energy and effort to see that person in a way that contradicts the label. During the training sessions we've conducted for corporations, management has come to understand the impact its thinking and behavior has on the productivity and the profitability of its companies.

Let's say you're in a situation where your children are older and more independent and that the mindset in the corporate world is starting to change, which will lead to a transformation in organizational culture. The skills it takes to raise your family, run a household and care for a sick family member are transferable to the work environment, although they are not always seen that way. Prior to and during your employment, you have spent time in the home making decisions, balancing the budget, coordinating schedules, providing assistance with schools and community organizations, raising funds, communicating instructions, giving discipline, delegating responsibilities, building relationships, managing conflict, building consensus, listening intently, multitasking, being creative and thinking of ways to manage financial resources. Decision makers need to be open minded and have the willingness to view these skills as assets that can add value to the organization.

Companies that are successful at promoting women into leadership positions generally:

- Understand the business case for doing so
- Develop a pipeline for aspiring women
- Monitor and manage the pipeline
- Understand the challenges women are faced with

Women moving into higher positions within their organizations need to understand:

- Organizational culture
- How to balance professional and personal goals
- How to collaborate
- Effective leadership behaviors, skills, qualities

Understanding the culture of the organization and being able to function effectively within it is important to your success. Dee Ann Neri, director of employment and employee relations for US Bancorp, feels she is very fortunate to work for a dynamic, fast-growing company that encourages development and maximum opportunity, and celebrates success. "With our fast growth, I have been forced out of my own comfort zone, which has helped me to stretch my potential," Neri says. "Knowing I have the support of our management team has allowed me to take risks and to learn and grow with each step. As a leader, I try to instill that same support and encouragement in my management team," she adds.

Business Case

Statistics reveal that 49.5 percent of the total workforce is made up of women. Companies are realizing that they need to attract, retain and develop the talents of women. This involves mentoring, leadership training, recruiting and childcare. The dilemma is that none of these approaches in and of themselves create significant amounts of change over the long term. With a combination of approaches, however, there is greater chance of identifying the opportunities for women as well as the challenges that can keep the organization from reaching its objectives. The approach to leadership should be done just like it is in a training program—systematically. Identification of root causes, goals, business objectives, assessments and measurement are ongoing methods for developing leaders.

A McKinsey Company study involving seventy-seven large U.S. companies, 400 corporate officers, and 6,000 executives concluded that "Companies are about to be engaged in a war for senior executive talent that will remain a defining characteristic of their competitive landscape for decades to come. Yet most are ill prepared, and even the best are vulnerable." From a training, OD and HR perspective, it will be a challenge to attract, select, develop and retain leaders, given the current circumstances.

(Source: Training and Development, March 2000, Five Steps to Leadership Competencies by Robert Barner)

The Pipeline

For some organizations, having a sufficient number of women in the pipeline may give a false sense of the effectiveness of their recruiting strategy. A pipeline that is full doesn't mean you have a significant number of women in various stages of career development or that they are being adequately prepared to take on leadership roles. Monitoring the process ensures that the participants are progressing at the necessary pace and that they will be ready to step into the leadership roles when the positions become available. Key talent needs to be identified, developed and promoted.

Higher education faces the same challenges as the corporate world when it comes to promoting or hiring women for top leadership positions. Around 1900, the proportion of women on college faculties was 20 percent, increasing to 25 percent by 1940. By the 1960s, the percentage had declined to 22 percent. Currently, more than one third of full-time faculty members are women, while more than half of the undergraduate student population is made up of women.

Richard Simpson, managing partner for Columbus, Ohio-based Bricker & Eckler LLP, spoke about their challenges in the recruitment and retention of women of color. Although the law firm wants everyone to succeed, many women and people of color don't always buy into the degree of effort it takes to become a partner. Most are part of two-income families. The 70 to 80 hour work-week required of partner-track associates for the first several years of employment causes the law firm to lose them to other choices—not to other law firms. The firm is considering several options for keeping people in the pipeline.

The retention issue demonstrates the importance of learning the expectations of new hires and clearly communicating the expectations of the organization. It is also one of the indicators that reinforces the necessity of constantly developing new leaders. A desire to learn and lead are both important factors in the short- and long-term success of the individuals and their organizations. Corporate downsizing, however, has made it difficult for companies that would like to promote internal candidates to senior positions. Retirement and turnover also disrupt the leadership process and emphasize the need for systematic mechanisms, constant monitoring and ongoing development.

Gender Communication

The majority of communication comes from nonverbal cues rather than verbal ones. People tend to listen to men more than women during meetings or when a customer wants to resolve a complaint. Women tend to explain things in detail, while men want the bottom line. People allow the firmness of a handshake or a person's body posture to determine his or her strength or weakness. And how we communicate as adults is directly related to our socialization as children.

To Play or Not to Play

In some instances, business continues to be conducted on the golf course. Should women learn to play and be willing to participate in golf outings? The women I interviewed had mixed responses to this question. Some were very adamant about their refusal to learn to play. They believed you could still advance to the upper levels of a company without playing golf but were of the opinion that the process may be more challenging. Others felt pressured to play in order to fit in and be considered as a team players, realizing that business was being transacted while people were in a relaxed environment.

Then, of course, not all male executives play golf, and optional activities are now available at conferences to accommodate the generations that may desire more physically strenuous activities.

International Assignments

Cultural barriers exist for female managers in the U.S. as well as internationally. The work environments in this country are made up of a variety of cultures. In the 1980s, research revealed that only 3 percent of the managers working overseas were women. The prejudice of foreign employers was cited as the number one barrier to North American female managers working overseas. Despite this, there has been substantial growth in the number of female expatriate managers.

Catalyst, the leading research and advisory organization working to advance women in business, with offices in New York, San Jose, and Toronto, conducted a study regarding women and international assignments. Men and women who had worked overseas or had been given global responsibilities participated in the study. More than half the men and women surveyed said they would have liked to have received an education in how to work and live abroad; only one third actually received this type of education. Such training should address the culture, values and traditions of the host country, how these conditions may affect the manager and how potential problems should be dealt with. The training should not be used to discourage women from international assignments.

More and more women are entering the job market in different countries. This is the result of several factors, including the desire for self-fulfillment. In spite of the number of women in professional and managerial jobs in this country, women make up only 6 percent of the expatriate work force. Women's levels of interest in foreign assignments is increasing and is viewed as necessary for high-level promotions. Corporations hesitate to send women overseas because they are operating under the assumption that women won't be successful in certain cultures.

(Source: Catalyst, Passport to Opportunity: U.S. Women in Global Business, 2000)

Organizational Culture and Ethics

Ethical behavior is considered one of the most important values that make up an organization's culture. Courses in ethics are taught in many business schools. Some examine ways to build ethical environments that will discourage students from sharing exam answers and duplicating textbooks.

Ethics guide us morally and govern our behaviors as to what is right or wrong. Ethics set standards that dictate how we should conduct ourselves and make decisions. At the early stages of moral development, children make decisions and behave in certain ways to obtain rewards or avoid punishment. There is a relationship between the culture they grow up in and how they respond to the culture of the work environment.

For example, I grew up in a household with parents who believed in discipline. There were rules to be followed and consequences for not following them. We did not question what we were told to do. Good grades were expected. Household chores were assigned and had to be done before we could enjoy any recreational activities. My parents, both of whom worked full time, always knew where we were and whom we were with. On graduating from high school, I worked eighteen years for a company that functioned exactly like my home. When I began my career in 1977, work-related assignments were given, along with specific instructions. Any deviation from the expected way of doing things was not viewed positively. People were not empowered to make decisions without management approval.

Top management provides the leadership and sets the example for the ethical values under which the organization operates. Once the values are determined, there are a number of ways to communicate them, such as speeches, company publications, policy statements and behaviors. Employees learn about values, beliefs and appropriate behaviors from managers in the same way children learn from their parents. Although comparatively fewer in number, leaders have the authority and power to influence most aspects of their employees' day-to-day operations.

Personal Values

Values shape the way we think and behave. Examples of values are honesty, humor, loyalty, professionalism, respect, balance, creativity and health. Organizations, departments and individuals within organizations all have their own sets of values. One of the keys to success is knowing what those values are.

According to Dr. Morris Massey, when our values collide, we divide. When values are not aligned, the results are turnover, absenteeism, low productivity, low morale and high levels of stress. So much of the conflict you see in organizations is rooted in differing values:

Organization places a high value on working fifty-plus hours a week.

You value leaving work at 5:00 p.m. to watch your child play sports.

Department places a high value on competition among employees.

You tend to be more team oriented.

Employee Perspective

What characteristics do employees want in their leaders? One of the surveys we conducted in 2000 revealed that respondents want leaders to:

- Have good communication skills
- Give feedback timely and constructively
- Provide encouragement and support
- Lead by example
- Have words and actions that are aligned
- Be trustworthy and accountable

Trust is one of the most challenging aspects of the leader-employee relationship. There are different types of trust in professional relationships, and each party goes through several stages of development. Trust is developed gradually as the parties move from one stage to another. The level of trust can mature to a point where each party knows the needs, preferences, thoughts and behavior patterns of the other as well as how to compensate for the other's limitations and interact in a way that maximizes his or her own strengths. Instability is a direct result of trust that is violated. The process of repairing trust is longer than the process of building it.

Qualities of an Effective Leader

Leaders need to be efficient and effective. Efficiency is achieved when the resources required to achieve an objective are weighed against what is actually accomplished. Effectiveness entails achieving a stated objective. Managers must balance both. They must be effective in getting the job done while being efficient in containing costs and conserving resources. In the organizations we have worked with, we have found that effective leaders are able to manage change, build team cohesiveness, develop the talent pool, give credit where its due and support people who have made mistakes.

"The most effective leadership style is one that is positive, open and direct while at the same time encouraging growth and questions from the team," says Neri. "Fostering an environment where managers feel they can run their line of business and have the support and guidance they need is critical to our organization's success." According to the 1998 National HRD Executive Survey, leaders should exhibit consistent leadership behavior and clearly articulate a clear vision of the future.

Being in a leadership role means having the responsibility of getting things done with and through others. "One of the toughest challenges is that being seen as a leader takes some time, and you have to establish credibility with your team and among your peers," Neri adds. "Often in today's business environment, time is of the essence, so you have to learn to work multiple fronts, one of which, I believe, is leading by example. Combining this with being honest, open and fair helps confirm the respect and view of your leadership."

It is also important to live up to the expectations of peers and superiors. In a staff survey we conducted, leaders were found to have poor communication skills, the inability or unwillingness to give feedback in a timely manner, the tendency to play favorites, an insensitivity to cultural differences and an overall lack of leadership qualities.

Companies that nurture their own leaders have consistent behavior among managers at all levels. Organizations seek managers with skills in Internet commerce, cross-cultural communications and change management. Executing strategy, putting the right people in the right jobs and understanding the external environment are some of the problems facing leaders. Companies struggle to move faster to market, deal with shrinking profit margins, develop ways to motivate people and deal with culture change

The ability to think strategically is another important aspect of leadership. One of the things I have always enjoyed about chess is that it requires me to think about my future moves and those of my opponent, the risks and benefits involved, the outcomes and long-term effects. Without realizing it, I learned to think strategically. Leaders who are able to think in this manner see their organizations in the context of world trends, events, emerging opportunities and obstacles.

Leaders vs. Managers

Leading and managing are not the same thing, although the words are used interchangeably. Managers are focused on today's business. Leaders are implementing changes that transform the organization, prepare it for current and future competition and provide the vision that defines where the organization is going. Leadership is a responsibility that does not end when the work day is over. Generally, the majority of management responsibilities are handled during the course of the work day. After developing the vision, leaders empower managers to develop and implement strategies that support the overall goals of the organization. Some of the comparisons between leaders and managers are:

Leaders	Managers
Have followers	Have employees
Measure qualitatively	Measure quantitatively
Think globally	Think linearly
Effective with people	Efficient with systems

Dealing With Change

Change is a slow process. It could easily take two to three years before the impact of a change is apparent. In the meantime, approximately 50 to 70 percent of all restructuring and quality improvement initiatives fail because the people implementing them quit during the process. Every change that is introduced is inconsistent with the existing ways of doing things. It then becomes a contest to see which is going to win—the existing (dominant) way of doing things or the new way.

For women who are relationship-oriented, the task of dealing with change may be an uncomfortable one, because the results of implementing a change relate directly to the conversations that are taking place within the organization. Consider the benefits of the change, compared to the consequences of not doing it. You need mechanisms in place to know that the change is bringing about the desired or expected results.

Integrity

Being a person of integrity means leading with honesty and accountability. As a leader, people listen to what you say but are always waiting to see what you will do. Excuses and justifications for not following through on a commitment or promise are sure ways to sabotage your career. If you've not been able to keep a particular commitment, explain why. When no explanations are given, your relationships will eventually become damaged beyond repair. People who are affected become cynical, resigned and angry, and they feel betrayed.

There are numerous occasions at work when we have to demonstrate and explain to others what's in it for them so they will care, be engaged, complete their tasks and support company goals and objectives. People of integrity think differently and reach for standards that are beyond self-serving. They constantly ask themselves, "What's the right thing to do?" rather than, "What will I gain by doing things this way as opposed to the alternative?" Consistent behavior exhibited by executives and managers at all levels creates commitment and accountability and conveys a message that is unified and cohesive. As a result, employees understand the goals, values and direction of the organization. On a day-to-day basis, employees are more aware of how to accomplish their tasks, deal with problems and make decisions consistent with organizational objectives. This style fosters trust that is lasting and enables the organization to continue moving forward.

Mentoring

Mentoring is a tool for evaluating your current competencies, identifying competency gaps and developing strategies to acquire new and required competencies. Mentoring has always existed in organizations, at least in an informal capacity. People generally tend to gravitate toward individuals or groups with which they believe they have things in common.

Recently, I wrote an article on mentoring that was published by the Society for Human Resources Management (SHRM) in a 2003 issue of *The Advisor*. And during a recent conference, I gave a presentation on the topic that explained the purpose of the mentor/protégé relationship, the benefits of a formal program, the reasons programs fall short of their objectives and the effects of different teaching and learning styles. One key to the success of the relationship is the mentor's willingness to explain the informal rules and to be straightforward in telling the protégé what she needs to do to get ahead.

Korn/Ferry International and the Columbia School of Business conducted a study that found that eighty percent of high-level black and female professionals lacked formal mentors. Approximately thirty percent of those who achieved career advancement to the upper ranks did so without being involved in an informal mentoring process.

When mentoring programs are structured properly, numerous benefits are extended to the mentor, protégé and the organization. Involvement in the program can give the mentor a new level of motivation, a feeling of continuity, enhanced reputation, financial rewards, fulfillment of her own developmental needs and opportunities to relearn the profession and develop the organization. Protégés gain skill development, motivation, visibility, career advancement, increased likelihood of success, targeted development activity, less time spent in the wrong position and readiness for higher-level responsibilities. The organization experiences improved recruitment efforts, a cost-effective means of improving employee retention, more favorable public opinion about the organization, increased productivity and more efficient and effective training approaches.

In order for a relationship to be successful, mentors should have strong interpersonal skills and the ability to give constructive feedback and communicate organizational knowledge. They should also be willing to share credit, be patient and take risks. Barriers to the success of a program can come in a variety of forms, such as financial constraints or a clash between the mentor's teaching/coaching style and the protégé.

Leadership Assessments

There is merit in using 360-degree assessments as a way to develop leaders and assess their behavior. The assessment results let individuals see themselves through the eyes of others. The feedback is extremely helpful in enhancing skills, advancing your career and improving your overall performance.

While still at my eighteen-year corporate job, I distributed a self-made instrument to my staff of eleven. This was before 360-degree assessments had become popular. Doing something like this was virtually unheard of in the company I was working for. As a supervisor—the first female supervisor in my particular office—I was responsible for giving job performance reviews and was curious about my staff's opinion and perception of my performance. All but one of the results were excellent. Immediately, I went to the person I reported to and asked if I should change or modify my current behavior to try to reach the one evaluator who had rated me as just "fair." He said, "Absolutely not. Don't change anything!" He was of the mindset that when one of his people shines, he shines. He was not intimidated or threatened by anything I accomplished, and he made certain that my achievements were known throughout the division.

When evaluating yourself, answer these questions:

1. Am I accessible?
2. Do I provide ways for people to give input?
3. Do I keep the lines of communication open?
4. Do I listen carefully and remain objective?
5. Do I give feedback to let others know how they are doing?
6. Am I able to make decisions in an objective way?
7. Do I treat others in an unbiased way?
8. Do I deal with problems quickly and effectively?

To Serve or Not to Serve

There are at least 15,000 business boards across the country*. Although women represent only 12.4 percent of the appointments on publicly traded boards, more opportunities are becoming available*. This is due, in part, to the changing demographics of the workplace and customer base as well as some recent scandals that have been disclosed.

When deciding whether or not to serve on a board, consider the amount of time you have to contribute. This will dictate the type of board appointment you should accept. Advisory boards require less time than corporate boards. The former meet only once per quarter; the latter, two or three times a month. Nonprofit boards may have financial requirements, such as fundraising or direct contributions. One of the boards on which I serve as president is for a soon-to-be chartered, small business, federal credit union. Its mission is to meet traditionally underserved business needs. We're creating the prototype for duplication across the country. The project came with some time constraints and financial obligations, of which each of us was made aware at the inception of the project. In this particular instance, our appointments are through the federal government.

(Linda Bollinger of Boardroom Bound; Source: Women's Leadership Exchange (WLE) e-newsletter, February 2003)

Top Thirty Companies for Executive Women

Innovative organizations that are promoting women to leadership positions are being recognized for their efforts. The National Association of Female Executives published a list of its Top Thirty Companies for Executive Women*:

1. Avon	16. Charles Schwab
2. Scholastic	17. Target
3. Liz Clairborne	18. Merck
4. Wellpoint	19. Sears
5. Fannie Mae	20. Gannett
6. Golden West	21. USAA
7. Prudential	22. Dupont
8. New York Times	23. Lincoln Financial
9. Hewlett-Packard	24. Sallie Mae
10. IBM	25. Tiaa-Cref
11. Federated	26. Eastman Kodak
12. Compuware	27. Verizon
13. Principal Financial	28. Bristol-Myers Squibb
14. Aetna	29. Office Depot
15. Washington Mutual	30. Proctor & Gamble

*The Top Thirty Companies for Executive Women is reprinted with the permission of the National Association for Female Executives (NAFE), Working Mother Media, 2003.

I spoke to representatives from Hewlett-Packard, IBM, Principal Financial, Verizon and Prudential to gain some insight as to what each organization has done in order to become a part of the list.

Prudential

"The defining moment came early in my career, within the first three or four years. That's when I started in the management development program and was promoted to a first-level manager," says Sharon Taylor, who, with more than twenty-five years of service, is the senior vice president of corporate human resources and chair of Prudential Foundation. Early in her career, she had a boss who positioned her for her first managerial role—one that she really wasn't very interested in taking. Taylor declined the promotion because she wanted to wait for something else more to her liking. "My boss suggested I try some things that would take me out of my comfort zone," she says. One of the positions she was offered was managing a group of senior employees for whom she had worked previously. She didn't like the work and was not sure she wanted to take the job on.

"Great leaders motivate, ask the right questions, learn new things and add value. They are also open and willing to take jobs no one else wants. Additionally, good communication skills, consulting, problem solving, articulating the vision and making it real for people, and executing the vision all add to the effectiveness," says Taylor.

One of the ways to develop skills is through mentoring. This is done formally and informally at Prudential. The functional and operations areas, for example, have formal mentoring programs as well as business resource groups. The Black Leadership Forum is another group that provides mentoring opportunities for its members at all ranks. The company also recently launched online mentoring for its internal associations.

Taylor views the fact that the organization is global and has diverse lines of business as very helpful. The culture of the organization is focused on bottom-line results and is fast moving. Since becoming a public company, Prudential uses a different business model than in the past. "The company has a commitment to people issues. We know how important this is to our success," states Taylor. "People who don't report to you may now be accountable to you. I'm a natural collaborator and have the ability to bring the right people to the table. I say things so they can be heard," she adds.

Taylor believes women should be open to asking questions, be clear about the things they need and realize there will be more hits than misses. "Through experience and exposure, you start to realize you don't have all the answers—and neither does anyone else!" she says.

Prudential has a commitment to leadership development, offering senior-level coaching and an executive development program. Talent management is also part of the business system. "We are always looking at how we operate, how we get things done and if we are reinforcing the right behavior," says Taylor.

Hewlett-Packard

HP believes in investing in education, training and the development of women in its workforce. The company participates and supports leadership programs and conferences that focus on industry issues and skill building for women. It has been recognized by NAFE as one of the Top Thirty Companies for Women Executives and has been mentioned in *Fortune* magazine's "Fifty Most Powerful Women in Business."

"HP uses a variety of tools, including experiential learning, coaching and 360-Degree feedback to help the professional development of women in our workforce," says Debby McIsaac, who is HP's director of learning and consulting programs for diversity, inclusion and work life. "We also have a mentoring component that is part of the accelerated development process. In this component, a general manager or senior-level manager is partnered with an entry-level or second-level manager."

HP also instituted a job share program as part of its flexible work/life strategy, and in 1997, it committed $4 million over five years to fund four university and K-12 school partnerships. These partnerships began or expanded programs serving African-American, American Indian, Latino and female students who are college-prepared and who ultimately gain employment in the engineering or computer science fields.

IBM

Marie Wieck, vice president of WebSphere business integration for IBM, serves as co-chair of the U.S. Women's Council, which is one of the three groups representing the Americas and thirty-nine worldwide councils. The councils focus on issues that are specific to women working for IBM. "This is a method for supporting women on a regional and national basis," says Wieck. IBM has encouraged the formation of various affinity groups, such as the women's diversity group, individuals with disabilities, and gays and lesbians. Work/life balance, networking and visibility of key roles are focus items aimed at giving women opportunities to develop relationships, enhance skills and let others know what their capabilities are. "The company works to keep women in the pipeline. Employees can work part time, work at home or participate in flextime," states Wieck.

The company also utilizes a technical resource program and an executive resource program. The latter includes a set of eleven leadership competencies, such as breakthrough thinking and building organizational capabilities. In addition to the various education methods, IBM surveys individuals, peers and managers regarding a person's leadership competencies. The combination of these methods has contributed to IBM's success in developing leaders and focusing on the pipeline of women and minorities.

Mentoring is also part of the program. The formal mentoring process involves a discussion between managers and their direct reports as to whether or not each person wants a mentor and what type of mentor is needed, based on the career goals and developmental needs of the potential protégé. Mentors not only provide guidance but also work with protégés to establish ground rules.

"The best leaders are able to adapt their style, depending on the situation," says Wieck. "In a crisis, you want to have an authoritarian style. If you can leverage multiple styles, you have more flexibility. It's important to survey people to find out what their styles are, and how to leverage them." In general, Wieck surrounds herself with a good team. She understands the importance of working with people who "are not like her."

"Some advice I would give to women is to keep your skills current, based on the market and how it's evolving," says Wieck. She believes in the importance of paying attention to the changes in the market and in technology. Wieck has always done work she really enjoyed, and in the process, she has been able to make an impact and continuously learn new things. In the beginning of her career, she looked at the areas that were growing and met with people in each area. She began to understand the thought processes involved while at the same time building relationships. "Approach your job each day as if you were working for your own company. Results come directly from that," Wieck adds.

The Principal Financial Group

The Principal Financial Group is guided by its core values of customer focus, financial strength, people development, operational excellence and integrity. These core values, combined with the commitment of the CEO and management to doing the right thing, have contributed to the selection of the Principal Financial Group as one of the Top Thirty Companies for Executive Women. According to Mary O'Keefe, senior vice president for corporate relations and human resources, the fundamentals of people development and integrity have been crucial in helping women advance their careers.

"From leadership and educational assistance programs to mentoring and flexible work arrangements, we offer a variety of benefits and opportunities for employees to achieve their potential," O'Keefe says. Many women are particularly interested in these types of programs to help them balance work and family—especially in the early years of their careers."

Mentoring at The Principal is both formal and informal. Talent reviews and succession planning help identify people with high potential. O'Keefe actively participates in the mentoring program, meeting with both of her female protégés on a monthly basis. For their part, the protégés work with a series of activities designed to assist in their development. As a result, O'Keefe has been able to provide guidance and counsel and steer her protégés through some of the challenges they have encountered as they have progressed in their careers.

O'Keefe's leadership style is direct. She lets common sense guide her approach to problem solving, pointing out barriers and roadblocks as well as solutions to problems that are brought to her attention. She has an open-door policy. "When people come to me, they know they will get straight, direct information," states O'Keefe. She believes that for women to be successful, it is important to work on not taking things personally and to develop resilience and self-sufficiency. When it comes to advancement, O'Keefe advises women to optimize every opportunity, "even if it's a job you don't want to do," she says.

O'Keefe, who has a school-age child, works at maintaining balance between her job and family by developing outside interests and hobbies. She also encourages a balance among those who report to her. "Helping employees manage their work and life commitments just makes good business sense. We strongly believe that for employees to be productive at work, they need to know they have the opportunities and time to balance their personal lives. This is especially critical in our public environment, where the bar is raised higher each day and where higher performance is part of our culture. We're committed to giving employees the personal freedom and choices to determine how to meet their own needs for work/life balance."

Verizon

Jeannie Diefenderfer, vice president of network services, says the culture at Verizon has evolved over the years, in part, due to an increasing number of women at different levels of the organization. Early on, she saw the clear distinction in how women and men relate to others. "Women have relationships that are like webs, while men have relationships that are hierarchical," says Diefenderfer.

As someone who has worked in the industry for nineteen years, she was able to get to the director level by having informal mentoring relationships with her bosses and with supervisors in other work groups. Mentors approached Diefenderfer because they saw her as a person they would like to encourage and support. "Positive energy, a good attitude, the ability to get the job done, delivering on your commitment, creating relationships laterally and effective interpersonal skills are some of the things mentors saw in me," says Diefenderfer.

Today, Verizon prepares women and minorities for career advancement through mentoring and leadership development programs. Women also find mentors and networking opportunities through the Women's Association of Verizon Employees, a company-sponsored organization (endorsed employee resource) that focuses on workplace and life balance issues.

"Women have to be cognizant of how they tend to receive messages. By nature, women want to be responsible for things. They take blame and give credit," says Diefenderfer. "When something goes wrong, women internalize it more. I try not to take things personally. I'm able to separate the person from the behavior," she adds. Diefenderfer talks to her team in a way that sends a distinct message—that it's all about the business, not any one person.

Challenges for her started when she was hired as a management trainee right out of college. Most of the first-level managers were promoted from the ranks. At twenty-three years old, she found her age to be a deterrent. Diefenderfer chose to focus on communication, particularly her nonverbal communication, as a way of demonstrating her maturity. She was especially mindful of her appearance, dressing very conservatively.

There has always been a strong relationship between her level of maturity and her success. "When you are new, watch how people interact in a meeting or a group," says Diefenderfer. "This helps to get a perception of the existing relationships. At that point, figure out how you can fit in." She realizes that people talk in terms of their own expertise rather than the expertise of others. When someone has a good idea, she can add to it while giving the person credit for contributing the idea.

Leadership: A Choice

Leaders have some commonalities, regardless of their levels within their organizations. By choosing to become a leader, you are, in essence, taking on certain responsibilities. The freedom of choice gives you energy and power that can be channeled into a role, which has the potential for positive influence. Leading in a manner that shows unselfishness, motivation, drive, caring, integrity, commitment and compassion for co-workers, direct reports, colleagues, customers, clients, volunteers and senior-level management has all the ingredients for unparalleled success.

One resource guide is *Mission Possible*, Volume Three (www.almec.com). The book gives leaders at all organizational levels insights into the ways that industry leaders such as Dr. Stephen Covey (7 *Habits of Highly Effective People*), Deepak Chopra (*Grow Younger, Live Longer*) and Pat Summitt (coach of the University of Tennessee Lady Vols) have achieved success in their respective areas.

Alison R. Brown

 Alison R. Brown is the president and principal consultant of **ALMEC International**, which is based in Columbus, OH. Founded in 1995, the company provides management and employee training and development strategies and assessment tools that enable organizations to improve internal communications, productivity and reduce turnover and its effects. Clients include US Bank and the American Red Cross. She is an adjunct professor at Central Ohio Technical College, where she teaches management development courses and has received outstanding evaluations from the students. Ms. Brown is featured in a book entitled *Mission Possible* Volume Three, (www.almec.com) along with Dr. Stephen Covey, Deepak Chopra and Pat Summitt. She is a contributing author to *Real World Leadership Strategies That Work.* Executives from IBM, Prudential, Principal Financial, US Bank, Verizon Wireless, and Hewlett-Packard partnered with her on the project. In the spring of 1993, Ms. Brown was nominated for Ohio Business Person of the Year, a prestigious award that has been given since 1956. She is the President of the Board of Directors for the proposed B.E.S.T. Federal Credit Union (the first of its kind) that is being chartered. The mission of the credit union is to serve the traditionally underserved. The prototype will be in Columbus, OH and then duplicated across the country. Ms. Brown was recently nominated for Small Business Person of the Year, an award given by the Greater Columbus Chamber of Commerce. She is President-Elect of the National Association of African Americans in Human Resources (Columbus chapter).

Alison R. Brown
President and Principal Consultant
ALMEC International
P.O. Box 420
Pickerington, OH 43147-0420
Phone: 614.840.0960
Fax: 614.840.0962
E-mail: alisonbrown@mindspring.com
Web address: www.almec.com

Chapter Twelve

PASSING ON A LEGACY:
THE POWER OF MENTORING

Jack Lannom

In my latest book, *The Leader's Leader*, I describe ten success strategies that every leader should employ to elicit peak performance from the people with whom he or she interacts. Whoever incorporates all ten of these success strategies into his or her leadership style earns the title, the "Leader's Leader."

The tenth success strategy of *The Leader's Leader* system is **Passing on a Legacy**. Great leaders seek to build lives and labor to pass on an enduring legacy of truth, wisdom and excellence. In keeping with this desire, the Leader's Leader will maintain an established program for identifying and developing future leaders.

Leader's Leaders are not as interested in accomplishment as they are in legacy. "Let your lives be excellent!" the teacher in *Dead Poets Society* urged his students. And that is the great desire—some might call it an obsession—of a true leader: building lives, helping others know the joys of learning, growth and self-fulfillment, and teaching the best leadership skills to those who share the desire to become extraordinary leaders.

This role of passing on a legacy is vitally important, because the long-term survival and vitality of any organization is inevitably linked to its ability to clearly and consistently pass on to successive generations of leaders both the beliefs and the behaviors that are essential for success.

Leader's Leaders spend time pondering the question: "How will I be remembered?" A true leader has no desire to be remembered as a no-nonsense, high-command and high-control leader. Great leaders hope to be remembered for championing high discovery, high development, high empowerment and high involvement. They have focused on passing on legacies of truth, wisdom and excellence in all things by their actions, their education and their passion for people.

How about you? When you move on to another organization, or when you finally retire, do you want to be remembered as being merely a tireless worker—someone who worked too hard and made other people work hard with you? Or do you want to be remembered as someone who built an organization that was a model of personal and professional excellence? Have you nurtured a culture of strong relationships that made a lasting impact on people's lives? Or will you merely be remembered as someone whose strong personality kept people in a state of fear and uncertainty?

In Homer's *Odyssey*, Odysseus, the king of Ithaca, went to fight the Trojan War and left the care of his son, Telemachus, to a friend named Mentor. It is from the story of Odysseus and Telemachus that we get our word "mentor." Odysseus gave his child to Mentor for more than an education. Telemachus was heir to the throne, and his father wanted him to be thoroughly prepared to assume his regal birthright and to rule wisely and well. Mentor was to be Telemachus's coach—a teacher, advisor and sage—who would impart the wisdom and the skills that Telemachus would need to succeed.

Today, young leaders need mentors every bit as much as Telemachus. **Mentoring is an edifying, one-on-one relationship in which the mentor diligently seeks to help the protégé achieve his or her highest potential.** History provides several vivid examples of the importance of mentorship. Aristotle mentored Alexander the Great, who became one of the dominant figures of history prior to the time of Christ. Socrates was the mentor of Plato. The concept of mentorship has flourished throughout the years; the master craftsman would have apprentices live with him and learn his particular trade or skill. We can look to the teaching relationships of knights and squires, artisans and apprentices, scholars and students, executives and interns, and the thousands more informal relationships between mentors and protégés in many different arenas.

Jim Collins, in his highly readable and finely researched new book, *Good to Great*, studies the common characteristics of organizations that have achieved sustained, dramatic growth. Collins also provides several examples of companies that have been less successful: these organizations followed one highly skilled or charismatic leader to sparkling success, only to plummet back into relative obscurity shortly after that leader's departure.[1]

Wise leaders do not look to multiply themselves but rather the message—the philosophy that has made their leadership successful. A staff that has learned to work in dependency on the guidance and authority of one individual will be thrown into a state of confusion when a new leader, who may hold different beliefs and utilize different methodologies from his or her predecessor, confronts them. The best way to prevent this kind of trauma is to build a philosophically empowered culture where the organizational values, mission and vision—not one individual—provide the organization with its guiding force.

While transition must always be handled carefully and wisely, in the philosophically empowered organization, the leave-taking of a senior leader will be nowhere near as traumatic, because the new leader—if properly selected and trained—will adhere to the same principles and values that the old one did. Even if the new leader's personality traits are markedly different, his or her beliefs and behaviors will be reassuringly familiar.

The Perpetuation of Life and Leadership

For some time now, I have been asking leaders at the companies I consult with to show me their leadership manuals. The response is usually a blank stare or a sudden aversion of the eyes as the CEO admits that the company has never developed such a manual. Only a tiny percentage of organizations have a defined, prescriptive program for identifying and developing future leaders. There is no system of thought being communicated, no model for leadership being taught, no leadership manual and no personal mentoring of leadership skills. Nothing is passed on from one generation of leaders to the next.

The Leader's Leader who truly wants to mentor (not merely model) excellence will commit to identifying men and women who display the potential to excel in a leadership role and to training and

---

[1] Jim Collins, *Good to Great* (New York, NY: Harper Business, a division of HarperCollins Publishers Inc., (c) 2001), pp. 45-46.

mentoring these potential leaders, who will ultimately carry the baton of leadership excellence into the future. One of the most important things that any leader can do is dedicate time to personally mentoring some of these staffers and to encourage others on the senior management team to mentor other "up-and-comers."

Jim Collins and a team of researchers devoted five years of research to identifying traits that distinguish companies that consistently outperform their competitors. One of their most interesting findings was that ten of the eleven high-performing companies they studied had promoted their CEOs from within the organization rather than bringing in outsiders to inject a new element into the corporate culture. Collins's team concluded that looking outside your organization for new leadership blood to shake things up and promote positive change is unlikely to yield positive results. "In fact," Collins concluded, "going for a high-profile outside change agent is negatively correlated with a sustained transformation from good to great."[2]

One of the most effective ways for leaders to initiate greater impetus toward giving their companies a sustained competitive advantage is to establish a mentorship program. As important as formal classroom training is to the development of professional men and women, it will always be too artificial to provide complete preparation for the demands of leadership. Mentorship is vitally important for transferring life skills from one generation of leaders to the next.

Identifying the Right Mentors and the Right Protégés

One of the best ways to identify the right men and women to place in a mentoring relationship is to monitor your company's ongoing education programs. Which individuals respond eagerly to classroom training? The first indicator, of course, is the level of interest demonstrated during the actual training sessions, but it is even more important to watch how various men and woman employ what they have learned.

Some seeds fall on fertile soil and begin to flower and grow; some seeds fall on barren ground and quickly shrivel and die. **Those who have the desire and diligence to become Leader's Leaders will identify themselves by their actions.** Wait and watch to see who will complete the leadership training program and then begin to incorporate what they have learned into their daily affairs. Praise these

---

[2] Collins, *Good to Great*, pp. 31-32 (emphasis in original).

individuals for their efforts—even the awkward attempts—and encourage them to keep practicing what they have learned. Watch, too, for those people whose attendance and participation in a training program is half-hearted at best or out-and-out resistant at worst. These individuals are clearly communicating that they are not leadership material. They are displaying no desire to commit to making positive changes in their management philosophy or performance.

Talk to the men and women who do respond eagerly to leadership training and find out if they truly value the program. Do they believe in it? Offer your own assessment of their leadership abilities. Talk to them about turning weaknesses into areas of opportunity and building opportunities into strengths and competencies. Their responses will help you begin to identify the natural leaders in your organization. **At this point, your appraisal should be based on desire and effort more than accomplishment.** There will be those who want to study and work and persevere to become exemplary leaders but still lack the knowledge and experience needed to master some of the success strategies of a Leader's Leader. These individuals are prime candidates for enrollment in a mentorship program.

Other potential leaders you interview will be well down the road toward stepping into senior leadership roles. Urge these men and women to pass on what they know, to enter into mentoring relationships with younger or less experienced staffers who display the right attitude to be leaders in your organization but who still need training and attention to master the proper actions.

Those who respond positively to the idea of mentorship are giving final confirmation that they have the potential to be future leaders. This is true of both those who agree to be mentors and those who desire to be protégés. Remember that the Leader's Leader is a teacher, an educator. The idea of establishing a mentor-protégé relationship with another employee will be appealing to the one who truly desires to teach. In the same respect, I have also said that the true leader is one who is a model of lifelong learning. Staffers who have no interest in sitting at the feet of a more experienced hand are uncooperative free agents who are not likely to build the nurturing relationships that are so vital to the long-term success of any organization. **The best leaders will be the best students.** Those men and women who leap at the chance for personal training and improvement have displayed one of the important characteristics of a true leader.

This idea of mentorship must be instilled throughout the organization. There should be specific times scheduled each week for mentors to meet with their protégés on company time and to work with them to help them grow. A consistent, concerted effort to establish and maintain these one-on-one teaching relationships will make your organization the purple tile on the gray wall. Competitive companies remain powerful by gaining strength from within, by building and nurturing caring, sharing, mentor-protégé relationships. Your company will be competitive and productive over time if the quality of the relationships within the company is strong. **The success of your organization's future is in the hands of your mentors.** Leaders who are vitally interested in building lives will build great companies.

The Characteristics of an Effective Mentor

What is the attitude of great mentors toward this role? How do they view their protégés? How will the mentor behave with the individual who comes to him or her to learn to be a Leader's Leader? How can a potential protégé identify the right person to ask about entering into a mentoring relationship? I believe the characteristics that follow paint an accurate profile of a world-class mentor.

Good mentors have a well-defined personal philosophy. They do not repeat nice platitudes; they hold to deeply rooted convictions. I do not believe that maturity reflects a willingness to accept any and every philosophy that is currently embraced by the popular culture, because I believe that men and women who will stand for anything truly stand for nothing. A mentor must have personal values, mission, and vision firmly established, and it must be a healthy, transformational philosophy.

Good mentors have solid character. They've been around for a while, and their beliefs have been tested and proved to be true through years of success and failure, triumph and suffering. There is no integrity gap between their words and their lives. Their philosophy is something they live by and intend to die by. This is not to imply that Leader's Leaders are unthinking and inflexible. To the contrary, they are always eager to listen and learn. Their personal philosophy, however, represents core beliefs that do not waver in the face of adversity or opposition.

Mentors understand that real power is the power that makes other people powerful. Their positional power hasn't gone to their heads. They direct the efforts of others with batons, not baseball bats. They do not intimidate others or use their authority to make staffers feel small or unimportant. Their speech is never patronizing.

Mentors have established a vision for their own personal lives. They not only know what they believe but they know where they are going. They are making for a definite harbor.

Mentors are constantly learning and constantly educating others. To bring their personal vision for success to fruition, mentors have become learners among learners. They do not believe that they have "arrived" at a point of wisdom where they no longer need to learn. When you visit their homes, you find libraries built around the principles that guide their personal and professional beliefs and behaviors. They not only believe in truth, wisdom and excellence in all things, they are students and practitioners of these beliefs.

Mentors have an earnest desire to teach. They don't have to be forced into a teaching role, because they don't view teaching as an onerous job. They love to educate. They enjoy patiently answering the stream of questions that eager students will ask. Mentors teach protégés how to bring out the best in people by teaching them how to bring out the best in themselves. Mentors challenge protégés to stretch for their highest and best, not to settle for their lowest and least.

Mentors are loving servants. They believe their role in the organization is to serve others—regardless of their position in the organizational hierarchy. The words "How may I help you?" are not reserved for external customers but offered freely and sincerely to internal customers as well. The mentor works tirelessly to build relationships of trust and respect with everyone in the organization but especially so with the protégé. The mentor realizes that the quality of education the student will receive is based on the quality of the relationship that the student has with the mentor.

Mentors communicate through attitudes and actions that they believe in their protégés and truly value the teaching relationship. The protégé can then exult in the thought that "My mentor is for me and honors and encourages me like no one else." The mentor possesses the strength of character to ask the protégé, "How do you feel about yourself when we're together?" And the relationship between the two is such that the protégé can honestly reply, "I believe in myself the most when I'm with you." The mentor-protégé relationship is healthy and flourishing, not toxic.

Mentors are models of humility. They understand that negative knowledge is important to a protégé's development, so mentors are perfectly willing to share stories about some of their own past mistakes and failures. Protégés can learn valuable lessons from the mentors' past failures and successes.

Mentors are joyful people. They create an uplifting and edifying culture that celebrates the human spirit. Mentors do not convey an oppressive persona. There are plenty of smiles and laughter in the mentor-protégé relationship; they have fun together! Mentors believe in celebrating people, and they constantly remind their protégés that every human being has exalted dignity and worth.

Mentors are creative people. They have tapped into their own God-given creativity, and they work to expand their own creativity and that of those around them. They help their protégés believe that they, too, are extremely creative. Mentors work to teach protégés the techniques that will improve and enhance their innovative abilities. Mentors teach protégés to challenge the known and defend the unknown, helping them to embrace change—to change before they have to change!

Mentors are always listening. They consistently ask others, "What are your thoughts?" They are secure enough in themselves to assure others, "It's okay to challenge my thinking when you disagree. I want to hear what you think." There is a free flow of ideas.

Mentors have a great desire to pass on the legacy. They teach, encourage and mentor their children, their friends and their co-workers. They are constantly working to pass the baton of truth, wisdom and excellence on to succeeding generations, and they encourage others to do the same. They tell their protégés, "You know how I've taught you. Now I want you to mentor someone else. Become an ambassador of the things I've taught you!"

How to Become a World-class Protégé

Although you can find virtually hundreds of books and articles that offer advice on how to be a good leader, it is extremely difficult to find practical advice on how to be a good follower. What is the mental preparation for being a good protégé? I intend to devote a fair amount of attention to this subject.

I have filled the role of both mentor and protégé many times throughout my career, and I have learned what a protégé can do to bring out the best in a leader and mentor as well as what behaviors should be avoided. These suggestions are very important, because a leader who has been a poor protégé will struggle to be a good mentor. You must be a good student before you can be a good teacher. The knight was once a squire; the scholar was a student; the artisan was an apprentice. One must master the humility of the student before assuming the role of an instructor. This section will outline the "Do's" and "Don'ts" of becoming a world-class protégé. **I begin with the "Do's."**

> **Protégés must have an identity of mind with their mentor about philosophy.** The protégé must value the same beliefs and behaviors as the mentor, so that both mentor and protégé are standing on the same philosophical foundation. If there is going to be fellowship between these two—and it is vitally important to the success of the training that there is—there must be philosophical common ground. How can two walk together in fellowship if they do not agree?

> **Protégés should make every effort to be a delight to their mentors.** Always remember that as a protégé, you are the beneficiary of a tremendous individual kindness on behalf of the mentor. The last thing you want your mentor's prayer at night to be is: "God, please deliver me from this burdensome relationship!" The best protégés will love their mentors and show appreciation. The protégé will share success stories with the mentor. The protégé will, if it is true, assure the mentor that the mentoring relationship is making a profound difference in the protégé's life.

> **Good protégés frequently thank their mentors for their patience and kindness.** Cards and notes are always appreciated. Take your mentor to lunch or dinner to express your thanks. Tell others how much you appreciate your mentor and value the relationship. If your mentor reports to someone else in the organization, be sure to tell that individual how you are

benefiting from your mentor's efforts. Do the same with your mentor's mentor. Always remember that your mentor is taking the time to serve you. Protégés should demonstrate their sincere appreciation by making the teaching relationship enjoyable and rewarding for the mentor.

Always remember that the mentoring relationship is a grace relationship. Mentors and protégés must be gracious with each other. As you come to know each other better, you will come to see each other's faults; we all have them! Protégés should consistently convey the message: "I mean you no harm." A protégé would truly be biting the hand that feeds him if he were to speak disrespectfully of a mentor after that mentor has displayed the humility and transparency necessary to reveal his or her own weaknesses. Likewise, the mentor must never violate the protégé's confidence.

Protégés should watch the example of their mentors closely. The protégé should consistently display a sincere, insatiable desire to learn. The protégé is watching, listening, learning—and asking questions of the mentor. When a protégé sees the mentor doing something that the protégé doesn't understand or is simply not yet capable of doing, the protégé must have the humility to ask "Why?" and "How?" The protégé should be an eternal question box, almost like a child, asking, "Why did you say it that way? Why did you do it differently on that occasion?"

Protégés will also seek feedback on their performance. When a social or professional situation has concluded, the protégé will ask for the mentor's evaluation of the protégé's behavior. The mentor's observations should always be offered with wisdom and respect, and the protégé should readily receive this guidance.

The protégé should honor and respect the mentor based on that individual's superior knowledge and experience. This submissive attitude is not servile, and the worth or significance of the protégé should not be diminished. I am not suggesting that the protégé should idolize the mentor, placing him or her on a pedestal the way a moon-struck teenager fawns over a movie star; nor am I promoting the kind of blind obedience exacted by cult leaders. The protégé should, however, honor the teacher and display a willing, cooperative attitude. The mentor has authority over the protégé, and if the mentor is leading with knowledge and example and the proper use of power, the protégé should treat that man or woman with the utmost deference and respect.

Protégés should maintain an attitude of watchfulness about their own behavior. They will examine their actions and ask themselves often, "Am I respecting my mentor's authority? Or challenging it?" The coaching sessions should be pleasant and helpful; they should not be demanding or taxing for either party.

Protégés should be good listeners, and they honor their mentors by listening without interrupting. The protégé who jumps into a conversation and interrupts the mentor is demonstrating a kind of arrogance. The protégé may think he or she knows what the mentor is going to say, but the mentor may be preparing to develop a completely new aspect of a concept or process that the protégé knows nothing about. My martial arts instructor once gently chided me by saying, "I've taught you all you know, but I haven't taught you everything I know." Good protégés will allow their mentors to fully complete their thoughts.

Protégés will strive not to be argumentative. The teacher is your leader and mentor because he or she knows more than you do. So listen! At the same time, a good mentor will always welcome disagreement, as long as the protégé is voicing an objection out of a sincere desire to learn. Offering a respectful challenge or disagreement to the mentor can be a healthy, learning experience; a bad protégé will feign agreement and learn nothing. On those occasions when the protégé does disagree with the mentor, the protégé will always voice the dissenting opinion when the two are alone and always speak with deference and respect.

Protégés acquire a vision for their own lives from their mentors. The protégé will ask the mentor how the mentor developed a vision for his or her own life and then ask the mentor to help the protégé construct a personal life vision. The protégé might ask the mentor to share where the mentor thinks the protégé should be, personally and professionally, one year from now, five years from now and ten years from now.

Protégés are eager to identify what they need to learn. They want to determine a prescribed course of training and study. A protégé will ask the mentor to be brutally honest in dissecting the gaps in the protégé's knowledge and identifying the skill sets that the protégé needs to develop.

Protégés must take responsibility for their own learning. The protégé must not expect the mentor to spoon-feed everything to her. Just as a mentor will have a personal library of the very best books, audiotapes, videotapes and periodicals, the protégé should begin building a library at home. The protégé will ask the mentor to suggest the materials that are best suited for the protégé's growth.

A protégé should honor the mentor's time by taking good notes, so that the protégé doesn't have to ask the mentor to repeat the same lessons. In addition, the protégé will honor the mentor by asking him or her to speak to a particular subject and then writing down what is said.

Protégés should maintain a desire to learn—even the lessons that may be uncomfortable. Protégés must be willing to allow their mentors to show them their blind spots. Many young professionals are weak in their interpersonal communication skills. It may be that the student fails to let others speak. When someone opens the conversational door even slightly, the protégé may have a habit of stepping in and monopolizing the conversation. Some men and women are so adamant about carrying the conversational ball that others don't even want to be around them because they never get a chance to speak! Wise protégés will frequently ask their mentors to evaluate their communications and listening skills, and they will encourage their mentors to chide them for interrupting.

The protégé should secure permission to call the mentor at any time. If it is granted, the protégé will take care not to abuse the privilege, but the protégé will take opportunities to discuss learning opportunities while they are still fresh in his or her mind.

Protégés must understand that they are being taught in a systemic order and that they are learning why particular patterns and processes of teaching exist. Good protégés will value systemic thinking and apply it to every aspect of their lives. The protégé sees that truth is a system of thought, excellence is a system of thought and wisdom is a system of thought. The protégé learns that the leader's role is not only to improve the performance of people but also to evaluate and improve systems. Rather than shying away from systems thinking because it is "too technical," the protégé is eager to learn how to properly integrate the best business systems with the best human systems.

Protégés are happy to be in the mentoring relationship. They are grateful to their mentors for extending the hand of friendship and experience and wisdom. The protégé recognizes that only a truly world-class organization will offer this kind of learning opportunity. A company that values ongoing professional training is taking a giant step in the direction of excellence; a company that values training and mentoring is operating in the sphere of excellence. The protégé makes every effort to represent the company well and to be a faithful ambassador of the company's values, mission and vision.

Protégés must be willing to be vulnerable. They will express how they perceive their own strengths, weaknesses, goals, needs, values, purposes, visions and challenges, so that the mentors can really get to know how they think. Protégés should openly discuss their perceptions of how they are changing and growing, then ask their mentors if they concur or see a different picture. The question should not be asked or answered as a vehicle for complimentary words but rather as an opportunity for objective evaluation. The only way protégés can grow is if they are willing to reveal their strengths, weaknesses and areas of opportunity to their teachers.

Protégés will never forget that their mentors cared enough to help them grow in truth, wisdom and excellence. Perhaps, one day, a protégé will surpass the mentor in knowledge, skill or professional accomplishment. Leader's Leaders never boast or exult in their own progress or lord it over their mentors. The leader will always remind his or her mentor that the protégé's success is largely due to the mentor's contributions.

Now I offer some "Don'ts" to protégés. This is a list of behaviors that are virtually guaranteed to irritate and alienate any mentor and to hinder or destroy the development of a long-lasting, edifying relationship. Good protégés will evaluate their own behavior regularly, to be sure that they are avoiding these disruptive behaviors.

Protégés must not take over and lead; they always defer to the mentor's leadership. Some protégés, in a desire to "show their stuff," jump into the middle of social situations and force their mentors into a secondary role. Social situations are golden opportunities for the protégé to sit back and learn from the mentor's timing and tact and wisdom.

Protégés must be sensitive to their own behavior when they are with their mentors. There should be no role ambiguity; a good protégé will always defer to the mentor's leadership, even when the protégé might choose a different course. Once again, I am not suggesting blind obedience. The protégé should not assume an "I am nothing, you are everything" attitude. No good mentor likes that. Respectful and deferential at all times? Yes. Obsequious and subservient? No! If a protégé is being encouraged to participate in something unethical, immoral or illegal, the protégé is obligated to make it abundantly clear that he or she will not go down that road under any circumstances.

The protégé must recognize that the mentor may have a different way of doing things, and the protégé should not dispute that particular style. Perhaps the mentor likes to work at a slower pace than the protégé, or the mentor is more task-oriented than the protégé. Perhaps the mentor is direct and the protégé is indirect. All these are questions of style and tactics, and a good protégé will graciously defer to the mentor's wisdom on such issues. The protégé's disagreement could simply stem from a lack of understanding of the subject. If the protégé can't trust the mentor's judgment and leadership, then it's time to find another mentor!

Protégés should not presume to teach their mentors. This is another way of demonstrating respect to the mentor. If the protégé is offering the mentor information, the protégé will preface his or her statements with words such as, "I know you learned this a long time ago, but I wanted to run this idea by you." The protégé should bear in mind that the mentor has probably forgotten more about most subjects than the protégé has ever learned, so the protégé should speak accordingly.

Protégés should never believe that they are above correction. Allow me to be blunt in my admonition to protégés: Don't be a prima donna! The attitude of the protégé toward the mentor should be: "Please correct me when I need it. I understand that the wounds of a friend are faithful. So wound me! Mold me. Lead me. Help me see my blind spots." The protégé will eagerly seek constant feedback and correction. The protégé should want to be told if he or she is drifting off the right path. A good protégé will never sulk or emotionally withdraw when the mentor offers suggestions for improvement or correction.

In the very same way, protégés should not expect that they will always get their way. If the mentor overrules the protégé's wishes, that decision is based on wisdom and a desire to further the protégé's growth. A protégé who becomes resentful under such circumstances is demonstrating a marked immaturity.

Protégés will not take their mentors' time for granted. If a mentor grants permission for the protégé to call at any time— even at odd hours of the night if there is an emergency—the protégé will respect this kind of unlimited access and will remember that the mentor has a personal life and a family and needs energy for these vital responsibilities. The protégé will exercise great care not to abuse the access privilege.

Protégés will not show their mentors up or make them look incompetent. The protégé must be gracious and patient when the mentor makes mistakes—which will happen. When the mentor misquotes something or says or does something wrong, the protégé will be gracious. This is a way for protégés to thank their mentors for being gracious with them. It takes great patience to mentor someone; protégés should be eager to repay that debt.

The protégé will not reinterpret what the mentor says. For example, when the two are together in a social situation, the protégé won't say to a group, "Let me explain that in simpler terms" after the mentor has finished speaking, as if the protégé possesses the ability to express the idea more succinctly or intelligibly than the mentor can.

Protégés will not compete with their mentors. Good protégés will always strive to cooperate with their mentors and work with them. The protégé will not make the mentor's job any harder than it already is. Some protégés can fall into a trap of thinking, "I've read something that my mentor hasn't" or "I've accomplished something that my mentor hasn't." If the mentor begins to believe that he or she is in a competitive relationship with the protégé, the relationship will quickly sour.

The protégé is not the mentor's critic. As I have said, a good mentor will welcome a respectful challenge or disagreement, but the protégé should never adopt a spirit of criticism, as if he or she is waiting for the mentor to make a mistake that the protégé can pounce on. A protégé must never assume the role of "official faultfinder." Again, this is a relationship of grace—a nurturing, edifying relationship. The mentor is giving a great deal of personal time and energy to the protégé. The very least the protégé can offer in return is a positive, respectful attitude.

Neither party will save emotional "stamps." This is good advice for any kind of relationship! Too many men and women are "stamp savers"—like the savers of S&H Green Stamps several decades ago. When these individuals feel they have been slighted or wronged, they say nothing; however, they add a stamp to their collector's book of affronts and insults. Then, one day, the final slight—either real or imagined—occurs, and the stamp saver's book is full. *Boom!* It's time to cash in all those stamps! Months or years of simmering anger erupts, often over a relatively minor issue. Such an explosion can destroy a relationship. To avoid this, both the mentor and the protégé must agree that when an issue arises, both parties have the right and the obligation to discuss it immediately and not let the matter simmer until it reaches a boil. It is always better to clear the air than to allow dark storm clouds to gather over time.

A Mentor and Protégé Up-front Discovery Agreement

I believe that the guidelines I have provided will help potential mentors and protégés to come together and discuss entering into long-term teaching relationships. While the points below do not in any way complete a full review of what has just been discussed, they do provide the important talking points for coming to an agreement on whether to begin a mentor-protégé relationship.

- Do the mentor and protégé align philosophically in their beliefs and values?
- What are the expectations of the mentor and protégé for this relationship?
- In what area(s) does the protégé wish to be mentored? What are the needs of the protégé in these areas?
- Are both parties willing to cheerfully live with each other's mistakes and faults? Have both parties agreed that there will be no "stamp saving"?
- Will the mentor give the protégé permission to respectfully disagree?
- Is there anything that is making either party uncomfortable about entering into this relationship? For example, does either the mentor or the protégé feel reluctant to discuss his or her own weaknesses or failures?
- Have the parties agreed upon a scheduled time to meet and established the length of the mentoring relationship—e.g., six months, one year, etc.?
- Is there anything that the protégé should tell the mentor up front, so as not to surprise the mentor later on, such as the fact that the protégé was previously involved in a mentoring relationship with someone else in the company that went badly? Has the protégé been involved in any questionable behavior that would taint the mentor's reputation in any way?
- Will the protégé commit to making the effort required for learning and growth?
- Has the protégé invited the mentor to graciously correct the protégé's attitudes and actions when appropriate?
- What boundaries should be established? For example, until what time at night will the mentor welcome telephone calls at home?

Conclusion

The entire thrust of the Passing on a Legacy success strategy is to develop leaders by means of mentoring and to help these protégés, in turn, to develop more future leaders, thus passing on a legacy of truth, wisdom and excellence to the next generation. The benefits to the organization that follows such a plan are almost too numerous to detail, but consider these ten summary points.

Ten Benefits that Mentoring Companies Will Enjoy

1. A corporation becomes a nurturing community.
2. The growth of future leaders is expedited.
3. The corporate philosophy is kept from becoming a dead-shelf document. The values, mission and vision are vital and alive and stay at the forefront of everyone's consciousness.
4. Staffers learn to cope more effectively with personal and professional problems, which gives the company greater emotional stability. Resentments are diffused, and the mentoring relationships allow for a catharsis of emotional frustration.
5. Employees' loyalty to the organization is greatly improved. Leadership expresses its commitment to the staff by providing the mentoring program, and staffers respond with loyalty of their own.
6. Employee retention is greatly enhanced; turnover is reduced.
7. Happy, growing employees make for a happy, growing customer base. This, in turn, makes for a happy, growing group of shareholders.
8. Mentoring breathes meaning and purpose into the present leadership staff. Leaders become energized by passing on their wisdom and experience to future leaders.
9. Constant, continual growth becomes a way of life.
10. Mentoring helps the company maintain a razor-sharp competitive edge.

In conclusion, I offer this proverb, which encapsulates the entire Leader's Leader program:

He who knows not and does not know that he does not know is foolish; **counsel him.**

He who knows not and knows that he does not know is ignorant; **teach him.**

He who knows but does not know why he knows is without conviction; **ground him.**

He who knows and knows why he knows is a student; **lead him into deeper waters.**

He who knows and knows why he knows— and, in contradistinction, knows what he does not believe and why he does not believe it—is wise; **follow him!**

What Kind of Mentor are You?

- Mentors make valuable deposits in our human spirit by:
- Giving us knowledge and wisdom
- Helping us develop a unified philosophy of life.
- Helping us create balance in our lives (mental, physical, spiritual, social, financial, emotional)
- Helping us develop ennobling values for our lives
- Teaching us to maintain nurturing, sharing, caring relationships
- Teaching us technical skills and life skills
- Showing us how to have fun, enjoy life and laugh at ourselves
- Providing us with a great example of human excellence
- Pointing us to the high road of integrity, respect and responsibility
- Helping us understand our mission in life
- Helping us draft our vision for the future
- Helping us develop to our fullest potential
- Believing in us more than we believe in ourselves
- Teaching us the importance of keeping our families first on our long list of priorities
- Modeling a gracious and humble spirit
- Instructing us in the importance of developing a spiritual life
- Correcting us when we stray from the philosophy of truth in all things, wisdom in all things and excellence in all things
- Celebrating our accomplishments
- Helping us learn from our failures
- Coaching us in the social skills of honoring, respecting and valuing every human being—without regard to social or economic position
- Introducing us to the greatest books for our personal and professional development
- Teaching us how to respectfully listen to others' points of view
- Helping us cope with crisis and change
- Being our confidant, someone to whom we can bare our souls without fear of harm
- Teaching us how to leave a legacy of truth, wisdom and excellence

Jack Lannom

Jack Lannom is a nationally renowned speaker, author, consultant, memory expert, and Master of Kung Fu. Jack's presentations have been energizing groups for 25 years. His combination of humor, wisdom and inspiration create powerful presentations that have helped individuals and corporations achieve world-class passion, performance and profitability. Jack is a Master in the Martial Arts with black belts in several Kung Fu styles and holds the record for breaking 3,150 pounds of ice with a single blow from his hand. Jack masterfully uses his art to get everyone to focus on the "Power of Focus", and breaking through barriers and working towards each individual's full potential. Jack's PBS television program, "Lannom's Memory Methods" has been shown around the country; and was the first and longest running series of its kind, inspiring millions of people on how to learn. Not only is Jack motivational and entertaining, he gives the audience the tools to remember what he is teaching them! Jack's seminars you will always remember! Regardless of the topic, a Jack Lannom presentation is a high-energy affair, filled with laughter, energy, and passion. Jack has been described as having the humor of Robin Williams, the motivational power of Tony Robbins, and the wisdom of Stephen Covey. His ability to customize his presentations to the audience is loved by his clients.

Jack Lannom
14050 NW 20 Street
Pembroke Pines, FL 33028
Phone: 954.445.2271
Fax: 954.392.1533
Email: jacklannom@lannomlearning.com
Website: www.lannomlearning.com

Chapter 13

IDENTIFYING ENTREPRENEURIAL LEADERSHIP: THE ROLE OF GRAPHOLOGY

Arlyn J. Imberman

As a result of enormous layoffs, people have come to realize that *nobody's job is safe!*

In the 1980s, the Fortune 500—America's biggest and most profitable corporations—announced the layoff of eight million people; in other words, roughly the equivalent of the entire population of New York City!

One of the best ways to characterize layoffs is the way the Bureau of Labor Statistics determines them, by means of events in which at least fifty people from the same company file for unemployment insurance in a five-week period. Here are the data from the last three years as published by the Bureau:

- 1999 - 972,244 people
- 2000 - 1,018,700 people
- 2001 - 1,615,084 people
- 2000 to 2004 - 3 million people

Think about this: No one ever grew a business by dismembering it! Business in America has been forced to take a short-term, quarterly approach; and while this pleases shareholders, it fuels the layoff mentality. Where are *new* businesses coming from?

This is an important question, because small businesses hired more new employees in the '90s than the entire Fortune 500 did ten years earlier. Why are entrepreneurial ventures gaining such importance within the business community?

To answer the question, we must recognize that in postmodern society, the traditional, hierarchical organization has given way to a less formal, more flexible entity. This new model is infinitely more adaptable to constantly changing technologies and markets than the large, monolithic corporation.

The greatest social convolutions of the years ahead may occur in the workplace as companies struggling with fast-paced and brutal competition reshape themselves and redefine what it means to hold a job. The continuing reorganization of the work itself is part of a social transformation as massive and wrenching as the Industrial Revolution.

As management guru Peter Drucker writes in *Innovation and Entrepreneurship*, what is happening in America is a shift from a "managerial economy" to an "entrepreneurial economy." Drucker argues that the nuts and bolts of entrepreneurship can be learned. But learning those skills is really about limiting risk, not creating the desire to gamble. You can't teach that. You can't teach people to be creative *and* driven. Entrepreneurs, as you will see, are not made—they're born.

Entrepreneurs are the creative energy in our society. It is they who create new enterprises and reinfuse the economic system. For this reason, the care and feeding of entrepreneurs should be one of the most important issues any society faces. If we lose or demotivate such people, society will ultimately be the loser.

Before we can adequately nurture entrepreneurs, however, we must have a clear understanding of what makes them tick. We are always looking for new ways to validate graphology (the study of handwriting)—in particular, for business. Handwriting analysis can help us identify and understand these mercantilistic mavericks.

Today, more and more people are quitting the corporate environment to become their own bosses. This being the case, I wondered if there was, in fact, an "entrepreneurial" handwriting. Given that entrepreneurs are a highly prized, idiosyncratic group of people, what implications would such a handwriting typology hold for business?

Why else is entrepreneurship so important today? The answer lies in the fact that the ability to tolerate ambiguity and manage stress, anxiety and risk is a necessity in an environment of increasing complexity and uncertainty. Such conditions, after all, require viewing a crisis as the Chinese do—as an opportunity. (Nanus, 1989)

The entrepreneur, as a risk taker—or, in Peter Drucker's refinement, "a risk manager"—is known for innovation. Routinely required to make successful judgments absent reliable models, they hire and pay workers before they know if consumers will be willing to pay for a product or service. Most of us would rather do nothing under these conditions. We would rather be sure before we jump, but then it is often too late. Someone else has done it—or the opportunity has passed.

For the entrepreneurial type, however, readiness to act is a permanent state of mind. Entrepreneurs take the notion of "Try, try again" very much to heart. Their desire to run their own businesses is so powerful that repeated failures actually heighten their determination, as a quick review of bankruptcy records will show. Ready to act, willing to risk, thriving on applause, yet able to tolerate disapproval and build from failure, the entrepreneur is often in conflict with conventional wisdom.

Most human resources professionals rely upon the traditional employment interview to assess a person's career potential. Ironically, there is actually little or no basis for faith in such an assessment method.

When comparing several interviewers' evaluations of the same candidate, researchers have consistently found interviews to be poor predictions of career potential. And in assessing interview judgments against various measures of actual on-the-job performance, interviews have fared no better.

In fact, reviews of the research, published at periodic intervals, indicate that:

- Different interviewers weigh the same information differently.
- Interviewers can reliably assess intelligence, but few are effective in assessing other traits.
- Interviewers are more influenced by negative or unfavorable factors than by favorable information.
- Nonverbal sources of information—eye contact, mannerisms, dress, etc.—turn out to be more important to forming an interviewer's opinion than what is actually said.

What's more, studies show serious, systematic biases in the employment interview. Sex, race, age, handicaps and personal appearance all have a significant impact on an interviewer's evaluation. Case in point: Women are generally given lower evaluations than men with identical qualifications.

Attractiveness—which helps men no matter what level of job they're applying for—is actually a handicap for women applying for managerial positions. Interviewers tend to assume that a more attractive woman is more "feminine" and therefore, less qualified to take on "masculine" managerial responsibilities.

Beyond this, some of the best candidates—the entrepreneurial type among them—can be terrible interviewees. They might look sloppy, seem idiosyncratic, rough-edged and abrasive or worse, antisocial. Social scientists know that people tend to look for people who will "fit in." The genius entrepreneur may not fit in at all.

Our take-away is this: The qualities smart companies should prize—independence, creativity, courage, energy and drive—are very different from those required to impress in the standard employment interview. What the company should look for and what most human resources departments are conditioned to accept couldn't be more at odds.

Trying to select innovative leaders via traditional paper-and-pencil tests or personality inventories is unlikely to prove successful either. How can companies truly understand a person's character and motivations? Example: Trusting one's own instincts in the face of opposition can stem from feeling betrayed by parents or authority figures. In one person, this can lead to a competitiveness that enables that individual to take risks. In another, the wish to overthrow authority figures can be so extreme that it becomes self-destructive. Distinguishing between the two is not likely to happen by reading a resume, evaluating a written test, conducting an interview or contacting references.

According to the 1998 International Graphology Congress in Zurich, eighty-nine percent of Swiss companies use graphology in making personnel decisions. *The Wall Street Journal* has reported that eighty-five percent of French firms do so as well. Similarly, the Naftali Institute in Tel Aviv reports that seventy percent of Israeli employers turn to graphology for assistance in matters of hiring. What do these countries know that many Americans seem to have missed?

Given that we acknowledge the importance of entrepreneurial leaders in today's global economy, what can we do to recognize such people quickly and celebrate their unique talents? How can we identify them exclusively from their handwriting?

Professional graphologists look at the interrelationship of a number of things—letter formation, size of writing, pressure on the page, margins, signature, speed, fluidity, legibility, stroke, slant, movement and spacing in developing a personality profile of an individual.

There are four ways that people typically connect their letters:

Garland:

This form resembles an open cup. The garland connection indicates someone who avoids friction and is good-natured, adaptable, open to outside influences, tolerant and uncalculating. It is the most predominant of the writing connections.

Arcade:

This form resembles a cup turned upside down. The arcade signifies a person who relies on intuition more than reason and who is formal, reserved and impressed by aesthetics and tradition rather than by intellect.

Angle: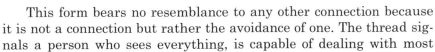

It takes longer to write angles than any other connection. Each stroke demands a pause. The angle connection is reminiscent of a military march. Angles indicate reliability, lack of adaptability, willpower and a desire to impose oneself on the environment. The angle writer may try to adapt but unlike the garland writer, is incapable of doing so.

Thread:

This form bears no resemblance to any other connection because it is not a connection but rather the avoidance of one. The thread signals a person who sees everything, is capable of dealing with most situations and is a nonconformist. This shapeless connection allows the writer to operate free from the restrictions the other forms of connections require.

Unfortunately, there is often not enough time in an interview to find out about the applicants, or the information we do have about them may be biased or incomplete. Graphologists read a hidden language in handwriting that provides extraordinary insights—what I like to call "body language on paper."

To recognize singular signposts in a writing, graphologists do not look for content, neatness or spelling errors. However, graphology does glean a great deal from the zones of a writing.

Upper Zone:

The Upper Zone is defined by the stems and loops of letters such as f, t, l and h. This zone represents a person's aspirations, fantasies and ambition.

Yours sincerely,

Ivan F. Boesky
Managing Partner

This sample indicates that Ivan Boesky, a Wall Street entrepreneur who made a fortune and was imprisoned for trading on inside information, wants to look good and impress others.

Notice that the Middle Zone is neglected and unclear, signifying that he is uninterested in everyday details. The height and prominence of the initial capital letters "I" and "B" are narcissistic balloons filled with hot air and then emptiness, indices of Boesky's ambition and need for recognition.

Middle Zone:

The letters resting on a baseline—a, m, n, o, s, u and w, for example—constitute the Middle Zone. The Middle Zone, the zone of reality, shows how we relate to daily life. If the Middle Zone is well defined, the person has a stable, balanced approach to everyday living.

Look forward to seeing you in Ann Arbor. Milt

This is the handwriting of Milton Moore, a colleague of mine, which demonstrates a well-developed Middle Zone, indicating that the writer is careful, conscientious and perfectionistic.

Lower Zone:

The Lower Zone represents a person's unconscious needs and search for fulfillment, hidden aggression and need for material rewards. See the harpoon in this sample. In the next handwriting sample (Tom Wolfe, the author of *Bonfires of the Vanities*), the Lower Zone is greatly exaggerated, suggesting a strong interest in material security and search for one's roots, to give him a greater sense of identity.

You can envision the three zones in the following way:

- The Upper Zone is the Sky, that which represents our aspirations, fantasies and goals—all that is yet to be realized.
- The Middle Zone is the Horizon, that which we place our feet on—our daily existence.
- The Lower Zone is the Ocean, our unconscious, which is hidden, but influences us nonetheless.

Not all entrepreneurs have the exact same profile. Some are highly ambitious and intelligent and use their ambition as a lens through which their intelligence can be manifested and their goals achieved. Others are very insecure and weak in ego structures and have a tremendous drive to compensate for it. In fact, one of the most common characteristics of the entrepreneurs in our study was the need to compensate for feelings of inadequacy.

Strong movement to the right and strong pressure in a handwriting sample were key to identifying the entrepreneurs' writings, as was originality in the writing connection. They broke away from the Palmer method ("school" writing).

The entrepreneurs also used space in a highly idiosyncratic or unusual way, often somewhat primitively. A small Middle Zone or neglected forms in the Middle Zone often appear, and the entrepreneur compensates with a high, well-defined or exaggerated Upper Zone or exaggerated capitals.

The writing of the entrepreneur may be very regular or irregular in form—signifying impatience and the desire to get things done quickly rather than sitting back and waiting twenty years to accomplish something. Some entrepreneurial writing is not legible, because of the writer's impatience. However, much of it is very legible, because entrepreneurs want very much to communicate. It varies with the individual, but the context, the urgency to move ahead, is the same.

There is a desire to achieve and move ahead that runs through everything. Sometimes the entrepreneurs rush and sprint hastily. Sometimes they make very calculated decisions. But there is always an enormous writing pressure and strong movement to the right. Across the page, the right means the future; and entrepreneurs do not have problems reaching the right side of the page.

By contrast, nonleaders' samples are usually respectful of conventions, more patient and willing to go slow and gradually absorb information and take their time achieving. More rooted in the background of a conservative upbringing, they are inclined to honor the conventions of the Palmer method as they learned it in school, and they are decidedly less willing to take risks.

Among entrepreneurial leaders, disrespect for convention could lead to antisocial behavior at times, because process is less important to them than payoff. And their writing, to a large extent, demonstrates a "hunger" (born of the anxiety or insecurity that they would be found inadequate) that could override all else.

Joseph Schumpeter, one of the earliest economists to recognize and extol the place of the entrepreneur in capitalist society, once wrote, "To act with confidence beyond the range of familiar beacons, and to overcome resistance, requires aptitudes that are present in only a small fraction of the population."

In sum, entrepreneurs had the following traits, which were not found in the nonleaders' handwriting samples:

- Energy and vitality
- A relentless drive
- Could not have been anything or done anything else, even if it meant difficulty with their personal lives
- Willing to take risks
- Resentful of authority, so they had to become the authority
- Interested in outcomes, not process
- Feared being perceived as failures but were not discouraged by actual failures

We have examined eight handwriting samples to look for entrepreneurial traits. Each entrepreneurial leader is paired with a nonleader sample to highlight the differences in writing styles.

Donald Trump—Leader

Sample 1

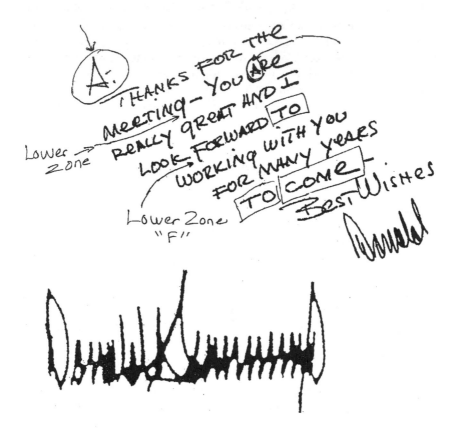

Trump is unafraid of failure. Although he prints, this classic entrepreneur mixes upper and lower cases. The "a" in the word "are" is very aggressive, frequently moving into the Lower Zone. The letter "f" in the word "forward" as well as the "e" and the "g" in "thanks for the meeting" all invade the Lower Zone.

Donald's forceful writing reveals a love of money and a lot of aggression. It is a very energetic, consuming and domineering writing.

Look at the words "the," "are," "to" and "come," and you will notice that the last letters are quite large. This signifies Trump's need to impose himself on others. The sharpness of the "a" reflects his critical nature. The writing is highly angular, and it often floods the page, as does his signature.

Trump lacks compassion. To him, such emotion is not cost-effective. He has amazing resilience, vitality and drive. His writing looks rather like barbed wire. This man is out to win. He continually transmits the message, "Don't cross me." As you know, barbed wire does not bend—it bristles.

Trump has an extraordinary need to demonstrate how strong he is, confirmed by the thickness of his strokes. He needs to impose himself upon the page, as he bends others to his will.

Nonleader
Sample 2

I have just returned from attending a convention in Milwaukee and visiting friends in Chicago, and I am still in the process of going through my mail. I have taken a brief pause to send you this writing sample in the interest of science.

I would be interested to learn how you obtained the names of your scientifically-selected sample for your study. But I suppose you cannot share that method with me.

At any rate all the best with your experiment.

Sincerely yours.

The spacing in this writing is poor. The writer makes a great effort to do what is right. Apparently, this man grew up in a conventional, conservative household, as seen by the copybook, "school" writing style.

The writing does not display enough simplification to qualify the writer as a leader, unless he inherited the business. What's more, there is some indication that the writer has health problems.

A perfectionist, he takes great pains with the spacing of letters, spending too much time in forming letters, such as the "o" in "Sincerely Yours." (CEOs don't have that much time to waste.)

Interestingly, this is an unemotional writing but an emotional person. He reasons things out carefully, as seen in the connections of the writing. The writer's childhood was likely unhappy, with oddly disconnected parents. Maybe this is why he does what is easy and eschews putting himself under stress. A finicky, complaining, introvert, as reflected by the narrowness of the writing, he is never able to fully express his feelings. Moody, he works hard at trying to keep his feelings under wraps and not let others know about them.

Richard Branson—Leader
Sample 3

Branson's enthusiasm for risk derives from something inside him that says, "Do what terrifies you; everything else is boring!"

The Virgin Atlantic Airways CEO's handwriting displays pronounced speed threads, signifying his intensity. A man determined to get want he wants, he arrives at decisions quickly, because he knows what works and what he needs to do to get it.

The "R" in the signature "Richard Branson" cleverly takes the lower stroke of the "R" and transforms it into an "i" in "Richard." Look at how large the capitals are, relative to the other letters, indicating both insecurity and a need to come on strong.

Branson is highly intuitive about people and their unspoken cues and messages. He knows that words can mask thoughts and is adept at taking data and repackaging it for his own benefit. This is seen in the variability and delicacy of his writing.

This is the writing of an original, aggressive salesman who knows how to close a deal. He has the hunger of the entrepreneur. We see indications of this in the "B," which opens to the Lower Zone in "Branson," indicating that he is interested exclusively in money and power. He will never be satisfied with today's triumph; always wanting something more, something better, in part, fuels his success.

There is every reason to be impressed by Branson. He is extremely effective, as seen in the incredible smoothness and fluidity in his writing. The quickly written signature shows he hates to waste time and is completely uninterested in that which doesn't serve a purpose. A man of many interests (although some will be short lived), he disposes of relationships quickly and requires quickness in those around him. He cannot tolerate slowness or incompetence.

A businessman who does what is efficient and expedient, Branson can cut costs and heads, if necessary. Although the latter is not his first choice, he will if he must. He is a true visionary, as evidenced by the speed with which he writes. Case in point: The "i" dot at the end of the signature. Branson must contend with seeing too many things too well. Consequently, he always has the difficulty of choosing from among competing interests, which may at first appear equally valuable or promising.

Branson churns out ideas. To him, success derives from being able to come up with the idea before anyone else, making the idea a reality and setting a standard for others.

Nonleader
Sample 4

Why is this writing not entrepreneurial? There is a softness and lack of intensity to the pressure of the letters on the page. The person has no sense of boundaries, as you can see by the disorganized pattern of the text.

There is insufficient structure or regularity to the core of the writing, which shows a lack of resilience and self-indulgence; neither bode well for leadership traits.

This writing demonstrates a high level of impulsivity instead of a strong, relentless drive and focus, which leads one to believe that this is a person who will not finish what she starts, does not anticipate well and does not have a game plan.

The unevenness in the size and shape of the letters reveals an inconsistency in temperament, energy and discipline, all necessary traits for entrepreneurial leadership.

Warren Buffett—Leader
Sample 5

If Branson is a pragmatist, Warren Buffet is equally unconventional. Forget caution! Warren Buffett is permanently ready for action. Innovation, so to speak, is his middle name.

This writing is not what you would expect from someone who is one of the foremost financial minds of our time. The circularity of "W" in his first name, "Warren," indicates a highly introverted man; that is, the self-encircling "W" means he goes very much within himself. Buffett needs little from others.

Buffett sees things without compassion. A Calvinist, he analyzes things carefully, and rather than being empathetic, he is concerned in creating accomplishments. He looks before he leaps. The "W" is separated from the rest of the word clearly and carefully.

Warren could have been an academic since he made his money in a solitary way. He is an original, highly analytical individual. What is also impressive about the writing is the size of the "W." In spite of the fact that he is an "everyday, regular kind of guy," he is immensely proud of his own accomplishments, as seen in the way he writes his first name. Self-made, despite his wealth, Buffett chooses suits "off the rack" and lives in the same house he bought for his family in 1950.

Emotionally detached, he would have made an excellent strategic, military commander. He enjoys the game of war. Strategic thinking and analysis are recreational for him, and Buffett is extremely good at both.

Nonleader

Sample 6

This is not an entrepreneurial writing because of the very low pressure on the page, the weakness of the stroke, the disturbance of the rhythm and the poor distribution of energy on the page.

There is an inappropriate capitalization of letters, which is the danger sign of duplicity and unreliability in the writer. The waviness of the baseline reveals moodiness and emotional variety. The wide spaces between words show the writer's inability to connect with others and sense of isolation.

The structure of the words has no inner core, as the letters seem to be toppling over on the page. The strokes, extending into the Lower Zone, are very disturbed, as seen in the words "very," "day" and "curtains." The strokes appear to be broken, tremulous or retraced, which indicates an inability to release tension and a searching for roots and stability.

Anonymous—Leader
Sample 7

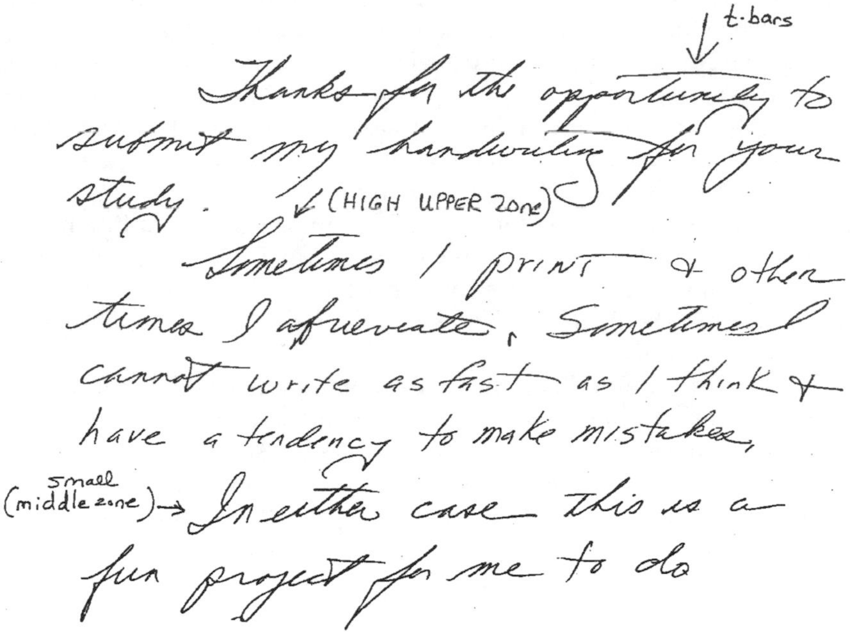

[Handwritten sample with annotations:]

t-bars

Thanks for the opportunity to submit my handwriting for your study. (HIGH UPPER ZONE)

Sometimes I print & other times I abureviate, Sometimes I cannot write as fast as I think & have a tendency to make mistakes,

small (middle zone)→ In either case this is a fun project for me to do

This handwriting of this stock market guru displays a "thready" quality, which shows she is a good salesperson. The words move powerfully to the right, with a strong right slant, signifying her orientation toward the future and her next challenge or goal.

The writer is impulsive and willing to try new things. If one thing doesn't work, she will try something else. Her Upper Zone is high, round and full, which indicates her strong level of aspiration and fantasy.

There is no question that the writer can be assertive. She has carved out a niche for herself, understands how to motivate people and will reward them if they deliver. She understands how the game is played, even though she didn't make the rules. Whatever it takes to get something done, she will do it. While she possesses fine entrepreneurial qualities, these very traits often make it difficult for her as a woman. The pressure of her writing is light. She may not always have enough energy to do all the things she wants to do; and she must have time to recharge.

Her narrow writing means that she was originally an introvert, who has since mastered social skills. Everything is connected in the writing, indicating that she reasons things out. Cagey, logical and shrewd, her writing is fast, displaying the simultaneous use of thread and angle. This means that she is able to navigate her world well and can keep a number of balls in the air at the same time and deals well with stress.

Highly intuitive and able to grasp the essence of a problem or situation, the writer is self-made, practical and the salt of the earth.

What else do we see this in the writing? There is a very strong movement in the Upper Zone, which represents her ambition. The flying "t"-bars are crosses, again reflecting her level of aspiration and need to communicate effectively with others. The strong right slant leads her into the future and propels her to communicate more effectively with others.

Her small Middle Zone indicates questions about her self-esteem or self-concept. In matters of importance, she is inclined to realize her social and political agenda by surrounding herself with dynamic colleagues. The writer validates herself by the personal associations she makes, because she understands these associates' importance and achievements. She also validates others by supporting and helping them. She recognizes the mutual interdependence of her own people around her.

This leader has the ability to adjust quickly and grasp and process information to suit her needs. She is highly resilient and keeps coming back over and over again. She builds and rebuilds like a Phoenix, rising from the ashes and is willing to accept heavy burdens if she thinks there is a chance for success.

The writing is overconnected, which means that she deals with the world through logic, not emotion. When she gets on a track, she is focused and determined to see it through. The high Upper Zone means she is eager to get to where she is going. Although communication is extremely important to her, she is primarily interested in facts, not emotional communication.

Nonleader

Sample 8

But it is when we step outside the arena of our normal circumstances, when we move beyond the familiar emot? and circumstantial boundaries of our lives that our kindnesses, too, move beyond the routine and enter th realm of the extraordinary and exquisite. Instead of being responsible good deeds they become embodiments of compassion.

Why is this writing not entrepreneurial? One outstanding feature is that it lacks angles. It is a soft, small, thoughtful writing, executed in a slow, perfectionistic manner. The pattern is careful, cultivated and sensitive.

The writer is well organized and each line of text is well demarcated from the next. Although goal-oriented, she doesn't identify herself in terms of her goals. There is no aggression present in the writing. An entrepreneur might not always show this care and precision or take the time to put as many words on the page.

She shapes her world in a very different way. The first writing exhibits intense energy and drive, which makes you think the writer wants to break away from the page and conquer new horizons. In contrast, this writing works within a framework. The left margin is too small and somewhat out of the gestalt of the writing. A little anxious perhaps, yet she wants control, and the left margin assures her of that. She is cautious about the future and doesn't make mistakes. Being correct is important to the writer. She doesn't take risks. The writing is upright, which means she wants to keep a sensitive distance between herself and others psychically, socially and physically.

Another indication that this is not an entrepreneurial writing is that the writing is conventional and self-contained. The writer thinks about what she does. There is a nice form level, yet the size changes a bit. This is not an outwardly directed writing but thoughtful and inwardly directed. She is more introspective and more balanced than the average entrepreneur.

In conclusion, there are a number of handwriting indicators that most entrepreneurial leaders share: exaggeration of capital letters, hard pressure on the page, a sharp right slant, and a more idiosyncratic handwriting style. On the other hand, handwriting characteristics among nonleaders revealed a prevalent fear of failure seen in conventional writing forms, narrow margins, slow speed, small capital letters, left trend writing, letters that slant in different directions, a compressed writing pattern and retraced letters.

The following traits did not appear in nonleaders writing samples but typically appeared in the handwriting samples of entrepreneurs—people who are driven, tenacious, outgoing and resilient and who possess other qualities that lead to success in business—and in life.

Risk Taker
- Original letter forms and connections
- Moderate to strong pressure
- Tall Upper Zone
- Good rhythm with rightward movement

Independent
- Simplified forms
- Strong initial letters
- Strong final strokes

Resourceful
- Strong capital letters
- Simplified letter forms
- Garland or primary thread connection

Confident with Strong Self-Esteem
- Good rhythm and form
- Consistent pressure
- Fluid movement
- Large capital letters
- Signature larger than the rest the of writing

Tenacious

- Consistent form and pressure
- Steady baseline and rhythm
- Strong final strokes and overconnected letter forms
- Strong and long "t"-bars that end with a fish hook

Self-Motivating

- Moderate to heavy pressure
- Original and creative forms
- Fast writing
- Good arrangement of words on the page

Outgoing

- Rightward movement
- Larger than average writing size
- Taking up space on a page

Energetic and Ready for Action

- Fast speed
- Original but simplified forms
- Right slant

Forward Thinking

- Tall Upper Zone
- Strong rhythm
- Arcade connection
- Right trend

As Albert Shapiro, professor of management at the University of Texas Graduate School of Business, said, "It is possible that today's bleak and uncertain economic situation will itself generate a new crop of entrepreneurs, because so many people are undergoing displacement." Certainly, we could use more entrepreneurs. For society, as well as the individual, nothing ventured is nothing gained.

The entrepreneur has become the last lone ranger, a bold individualist fighting the odds of the fragile, complex world surrounding him. As we have seen by the analyses presented in this chapter, entrepreneurs use their original and unconventional approach to the world to sniff out opportunities often missed by others. Seen in this light, entrepreneurs, like artists, are ignited by their insecurities, but like many trailblazers, they often leave behind an extraordinary legacy of creativity and, in many ways, profoundly change the lives of those around them.

For them, business becomes the channel through which they display their innovation and artistry. As Wilson Harrell has said, "Our economic future will not long remain in the hands of the Fortune 500. We have a new champion, the American Entrepreneur, who will overcome our current dangers and disasters and will remake America in his or her own image."

I hope that this chapter has presented new possibilities for graphology—how we can use it to gain insight into the complex character of the folk hero of the new millennium, the entrepreneur, and differentiate the leader from the nonleader.

References

Ben-Shakhar, G., Bar-Hillel, M., Bilu, Y., Ben-Abba, E., & Flug, A. (1986) "Can graphology predict occupational success: two empirical studies and some methodological ruminations." *Journal of Applied Psychology*, 71, No. 4, pp. 645-653.

Crumbaugh, J. C., & Stockholm, E. (1977) Validation of grapholoanalysis by "global" or "holistic" method, Perceptual Motor Skills, 44, pp. 403-410.

Frederick, C. J. (1965) Some phenomena affecting handwriting analysis, Perceptual Motor Skills, 20, pp. 211-218.

Galbraith, D., & Wilson, W. (1964) Reliability of the grapholoanalytic approach to handwriting analysis. Perceptual Motor Skills, 19, pp. 615-618.

Keinan, G., A. Barak and I. Ramati, (1984) Reliability and validity of graphological assessment in the selection process of military officers, Perceptual Motor Skills, 58, pp. 811-821.

Nanus, Burt, (1989), The Leader's Edge: The Seven Keys to Leadership in a Turbulent World (Chicago: Contemporary Books).

Nevo, B., (1989), Validation of graphology through use of a matching method based on ranking, Perceptual Motor Skills, 69, pp. 1331-1336.

O'Neil, John., (1993) The Paradox of Success: When Winning at Work Means Losing at Life. (Putnam, New York, 1993).

Oosthuizen, S. (1990) Graphology as predictor of academic achievement. Perceptual Motor Skills, 71, pp. 715-721.

Peeples, E. E., (1990) Training, certification, and experience of handwriting analysts, Perceptual Motor Skills, 70, pp.1219-1226.

Rafaeli, A., & Klimoski, R. J. (1983) Predicting sales success through handwriting analysis: an evaluation of the effects of training and handwriting sample content," Journal of Applied Psychology, 68, No. 2, pp. 212-217.

Rafaeli. A., & Drory, A., (1988) Graphological assessments for personnel selection: concerns and suggestions for research, Perceptual Motor Skills, 66, pp. 743-759.

Schriesheim, C. A. & Neider, L. L., 1989, Leadership theory and development: the coming 'new phase', Leadership and Organization Development Journal, 10, No. 6.

Wellingham-Jones, P. (1989). Evaluation of the handwriting of successful women through the Roman Staempfli Psychogram, Perceptual Motor Skills, 69, pp. 999-1010.

About The Author

Arlyn J. Imberman

ARLYN J. IMBERMAN is President of Emerging Image, Inc., a New York City firm that consults with Fortune 100 and emerging growth companies. As a coach and advisor, Imberman's insights have helped senior managers take on added responsibilities, get the inside track in a negotiation, enhance relationships with difficult co-workers, and build leadership skills and strong teams. Imberman's clients have included Disney.com, Sony Corporation of America, Liz Claiborne, Daimler Chrysler, International Jeweler's Block and Fine Arts Insurance Services, and The Prudential Foundation, among others. With a degree in gestalt graphology and a background in social work, Imberman is a popular guest lecturer. Recent platforms include the Columbia University Graduate School of Business, Oxford University, New York University, The Yale Club, The Knickerbocker Club, and The Young Presidents Organization, among others. Imberman is also the author of *Signature Success: How to Analyze Handwriting and Improve Your Career, Your Relationships, and Your Life*, which has already garnered media attention from The Boston Globe, The New York Post, and WOR-AM Radio in New York.

Arlyn J. Imberman
Emerging Image, Inc.
900 Fifth Avenue, Suite 14-B
New York, NY 10021
Phone: 212.759.3058
Email: Emergim@aol.com

From Chocolate to Morphine

Everything You Need to Know
About Mind-Altering Drugs

Andrew Weil, M.D.
and Winifred Rosen

Revised Edition

HOUGHTON MIFFLIN COMPANY
BOSTON · NEW YORK

For information about permission to reproduce selections from
this book, write to Permissions, Houghton Mifflin Company,
215 Park Avenue South, New York, New York 10003.

Visit our Web site: www.houghtonmifflinbooks.com.

Library of Congress Cataloging-in-Publication Data
Weil, Andrew.
From chocolate to morphine : everything you need to know about
mind-altering drugs / Andrew Weil and Winifred Rosen. — Rev. ed.
p. cm.
Includes bibliographical references and index.
ISBN 0-618-48379-9 / 978-0-618-48379-2
1. Psychotropic drugs. I. Rosen, Winifred, 1943– II. Title.
RM315.W44 2004
615'.788—dc22 2004057677

Printed in the United States of America

Book design by Robert Overholtzer

DOC 10 9 8 7 6

The original title of this book was
Chocolate to Morphine: Understanding Mind-Active Drugs.

Contents

Acknowledgments

Honey Williams and Jeffrey Steingarten helped us in the early stages of our work, as did Woody Wickham and the late Dr. Norman Zinberg.

We are much indebted to Dr. Michael Aldrich and the Fitz Hugh Ludlow Memorial Library in San Francisco. Jeremy Bigwood provided good suggestions and needed infusions of energy. Special thanks go to the late Zig Schmitt for his company, support, and help in finding published source materials.

Leif Zerkin, editor of the *Journal of Psychoactive Drugs,* came up with recommendations for additional reading. Ken and Maria Robbins provided food and information. Dody Fugate of the University of Arizona gave us outstanding assistance.

Friends who helped us complete the manuscript include Richard Carey, Howard Kotler, Dr. David Smith, Sara Davidson, Helen Shewman, Dr. Tod Mikuriya, Jake Myers, Ethan Nadelmann, Jonathan Meader, Sue Fleishman, the late Tim Plowman, and Stanley and Jenine Moss.

We thank the late Dr. Richard Evans Schultes and the staff of the Harvard Botanical Museum for their help, and Anita McClellan, Karen Frankian, and Signe Warner for their part in tying together the many pieces of this work.

For the revised edition of 2004, we received much assistance from Lee Hunsucker and Stephanie Mayer and from the Drug Policy Alliance, especially from Ethan Nadelmann, Marsha Rosenbaum, and Jennifer Johnson-Spence. And we are greatly indebted to Polly Kummel, copy editor extraordinaire.

Authors' Note

MANY DRUGS MENTIONED in this book have three names: a chemical name that describes the molecule, a generic or common name, and a brand name owned by a company that markets the drug. For example, Valium is the brand name of a tranquilizer whose generic name is diazepam. The chemical name of this same drug is 7-chloro-l,3-dihydro-l-methyl-5-phenyl-2H-l,4-benzodi-azepin-2-one.

Because chemical names are long and cumbersome and useful only to chemists, we do not give them. We have tried to stick to generic names, which are printed in lowercase letters and followed, when relevant, by the most common brand names, enclosed in parentheses and capitalized. Thus: diazepam (Valium).

If the brand name is much better known than the generic name, as in the case of Valium, we will use it to refer to the drug after the first reference. Many "street" drugs, such as cocaine, LSD, and marijuana, do not have brand names.

WE HAVE SELECTED COMMENTS about mind-active drugs and accounts of experiences with them from users and nonusers of all ages. Short excerpts from many of these selections appear in the margins of the text. For fuller transcripts, see the appendix, beginning on page 223.

Preface to the 2004 Edition

IT IS NOW more than twenty years since this book first appeared, and we are sorry to say that it is as timely as ever.

Drugs pervade our society, abuse of them is rampant, and the authorities keep doing what they have always done, even though policies of eradicating drug plants, sealing borders, and zero tolerance for users have done nothing but made matters worse.

Over the years, we have received many letters from people telling us how much this book has helped them, from both those who read it as kids and those who read it as grownups and parents. Their responses reinforce the belief that led us to write *From Chocolate to Morphine* in the first place: truthful information about all drugs, presented clearly and nonjudgmentally, cannot cause harm.

We remain hopeful that truthful information will continue to do its work and that, as more individuals increase their knowledge of the real risks and benefits of mind-altering drugs, we will begin to see social change for the better.

We have updated the facts in these pages to reflect current realities. When we last revised the text, no one could have foreseen the epidemic of methamphetamine use in rural America or the popularity of Oxycontin, a medical opiate so favored in Appalachia that it has gained the nickname "hillbilly heroin." The bitter war over medical marijuana is also a recent phenomenon, pitting state and local governments and the will of the people against an implacable federal authority.

We hope that this new edition of *From Chocolate to Morphine* will provide a note of sanity in an otherwise irrational area of our cultural life.

February 2004

1. Straight Talk at the Start

D RUGS ARE HERE TO STAY.
    History teaches that it is vain to hope that drugs will ever disappear and that all efforts to eliminate them from society are doomed to failure.

Throughout the twentieth century, Western society attempted to deal with its drug problems through negative actions: by various wars on drug abuse implemented by repressive laws, disinformation, outrageous propaganda, and attacks on users, suppliers, and sources of disapproved substances. These wars have been consistently lost. More people are taking more drugs now than ever before. Drug use has invaded all classes and ethnic groups and has spread to younger and younger children. Also, more people *abuse* drugs now than ever before, and the drug laws are directly responsible for creating ugly and ever-widening criminal networks that corrupt society and cause far worse damage than the substances that they distribute.

The authors of this book were teen-agers and college students in the 1960s. They had to confront the explosion of drug use of that era and find out for themselves the benefits and dangers of substances that they never learned about at home or in school. One of us — Andrew Weil — has since become an expert on integrative medicine and optimum health. He has a medical degree from Harvard and a rich background of travel among drug-using cultures in other parts of the world, from the deserts of east Africa to the jungles of South America. He draws on his training and his professional and personal experience with most of the substances described in these pages. As a recognized expert, he is frequently invited to lecture on drugs to audiences of doctors as well as students, to testify on drugs in court trials, to write about them for textbooks and popular magazines, and to consult about them with government officials.

The other of us — Winifred Rosen — is a writer, the author of more than a dozen books for young people. The daughter of a psychoanalyst, she has long been interested in psychology and mental health. As a former high-school teacher and veteran of the 1960s, she has talked extensively about drugs with people of all ages and social backgrounds. She now does landscape gardening as well as writing.

We have been writing and traveling together on and off ever since we first met in San Francisco in 1968 (where we both served for a time as volunteers in the Haight-Ashbury Free Medical Clinic). Both of us believe that the present drug problem can change for the better only if society alters its strategy drastically. In this book we are not going to argue for or against drugs and will not side with either those who endorse them or those who oppose them. Instead, we will follow a middle course by presenting neutral information and will ask people on both sides to change some of their basic conceptions about drugs as a result of reading this material.

At the outset, we will insist that readers learn to distinguish drug use from drug abuse. As long as society continues to call all those who take disapproved substances "drug abusers," it will have an insoluble problem of enormous proportions. Real drug abusers are those in bad relationships with drugs (see Chapter 4), whether the drugs are approved or disapproved by society, and, unfortunately, little can be done to help these people, unless they want to change. Once people get into bad relationships with drugs, it is very hard to get them out. For most abusers, the only practical choice is total abstinence or continued abuse. (Some people may prefer that heroin addicts be in methadone treatment rather than on the street seeking heroin, but let us not kid ourselves: the "treatment" is just addiction to another narcotic.)

If society cannot do much about drug abuse once it develops, it certainly can, and should, work to *prevent* abuse. Instead of wasting so much time, money, and energy fighting the hopeless battle against existing drug abuse, society must begin to help people avoid becoming abusers in the first place.

Preventing drug abuse is a realistic goal. Two approaches are possible. One is to teach people, especially young people, how to satisfy their needs and desires without recourse to drugs. The second is to teach people how to form good relationships with drugs so that if they choose to use drugs, they will continue to be users and never become abusers.

The burden of this task will fall mainly upon parents and secondarily upon teachers; it is not a process that can be mandated by law or accomplished by public policy. However, laws and public policies must not undermine the work of parents and teachers by perpetuating irrational ideas about drugs, ideas rooted in fear and prejudice (see Chapter 2). The kind of instruction we would like to see will bear no resemblance to what is called "drug education" today. Drug education as it now exists is, at best, a thinly disguised attempt to scare young people away from disapproved drugs by greatly exaggerating the dangers of these substances. (The Drug Abuse Resistance Education [DARE] program is a perfect example.) More often than not, lectures, pamphlets, and video programs that take this approach stimulate curiosity, make the prohibited substances look more attractive to young audiences than they would be ordinarily, and make authorities appear ridiculous.

Parents and teachers will probably be open to efforts to interest children in alternatives to drugs. Adults will find it harder to support programs that teach young people how to form good relationships with drugs. With drugs so available and young people so disposed to experiment with them, good drug education is vital. The most that responsible adults can do is try to interest children in alternatives to drugs and give them information that will enable them to use drugs nonabusively should they choose to use them.

We have tried to make this book accessible to young people

by keeping our language and ideas simple and straightforward. When we were growing up, information like this was not available to the general public. As teen-agers, we struggled to get the facts, making many mistakes in the difficult process of learning the effects of drugs and adopting rules for living with them. We know how hard it is to grow up in a drug-filled world and hope our experience will be of use to younger generations.

To our teen-age readers we offer some general advice at the start:

You are growing up in a world awash in drugs. All of them can be used wisely or stupidly. Grownups will give you much misinformation about them and will often be dishonest or hypocritical about their own drug use (see Chapter 2). Many of your acquaintances will become involved with drugs, and you will have many opportunities to experiment with them yourself if you have not already done so. The fact that grownups exaggerate the dangers of drugs they disapprove of does not mean that those drugs have no dangers. *All drugs are dangerous.*

The only way you can be absolutely sure of avoiding problems with drugs is never to use them. That is a perfectly reasonable choice and may allow you more freedom than your drug-taking peers. Keep this in mind if you find yourself under pressure to take drugs. You may feel left out of certain groups if you abstain, but you will not really be missing anything. All of the experiences that people have with drugs can be had in other ways (see Chapter 13). If you do decide to experiment with drugs, whether approved or disapproved, make sure you know what the drugs are, where they come from, how they are likely to affect your body, and what precautions you should take to contain their potential for harm (see Chapters 6–11). Remember that forming good relationships with drugs is not easy, and maintaining good relationships takes work. Don't use drugs mindlessly and don't spend time around people who do.

If you are tempted to experiment with illegal drugs, keep in mind that being arrested can bring terrible consequences to you and your family. On the other hand, do not make the mistake of supposing that just because a drug is legal, it is safe. Some of the strongest and most dangerous drugs are legal.

You are less likely to encounter problems if you take dilute forms of natural drugs by mouth on occasion, especially if you take them for positive reasons that conform with rules that you have set for yourself (see Chapter 4). You are more likely to get into trouble if you take concentrated drugs frequently, particularly if you take them to escape feelings of unhappiness or boredom, or just because the drugs happen to be around.

It is a bad idea to take drugs in school. Even if school bores you, you have to be there, and mastering classroom skills is your ticket to freedom and independence in adult life. Drugs can interfere with your education by making it hard to pay attention, concentrate, and remember, or by involving you with people who reinforce negative attitudes about school.

Drugs are likely to be a source of friction between you and your parents. If your parents get upset with you for taking drugs, consider that they might have good reasons, such as valid fears about your safety, health, or psychological growth. Be willing to talk honestly with them and to hear their side with an open mind. Think about how you would feel in their place. What advice would you give your child if you found out he or she was taking drugs? Question your parents about the drugs that they use. Maybe they will agree to give up theirs if you will give up yours. Try to see what your experiences have in common with theirs. What alternatives to drug use can your parents suggest? If you can convince them that your drug use is responsible, you may be able to allay their anxiety. If their fears come from ignorance or misinformation, try to educate them, not by being emotional but by being well informed about the drugs you use. Give them this book to read as a background to your discussions of drug use.

Finally, remember that wanting to change your consciousness is not a symptom of mental illness or an unhealthy need to escape from reality. It is normal to want to vary your conscious experience (see Chapter 3). Drugs are just one way of doing it, though, and if you come to rely on them before you are grown up, you may not be able to appreciate a whole range of nondrug experiences that are more subtle but more rewarding over time. There is no question that drugs can get you high, but they are difficult to master and will fail you if you take them too often (see Chapter 13).

We hope that parents will read this book and use the information in it to help their children. We sympathize with parents. Odds are, you will have to confront the issue of a child's involvement with drugs. Before you react to the discovery that a son or daughter is using drugs, you should keep several points in mind:

A period of experimentation with drugs is today a normal phase of adolescence — a rite of passage that most children pass through unscathed.

Be sure that you have accurate information about the drugs that your child is using before you attempt to give advice. Children today are often well informed and contemptuous of antidrug information that they know to be false. Insisting that marijuana leads to heroin (see pages 142–43), or that ecstasy (MDMA) causes brain damage (see page 127), is a sure way to lose a child's attention and respect for your credibility about drug use.

Examine your own drug use before you question your child's. If your relationships with alcohol, tobacco, caffeine, and antianxiety drugs are not as good as they might be, a position against drug use may have little positive effect on your child. If you use illegal substances, your stand is further weakened by your own violation of drug laws.

It is important to create a climate of trust in which you and your child can communicate openly about difficult subjects like sex and drugs. Good communication is impossible when a parent assumes the role of detective, police officer, judge, or warden.

As we will stress throughout this book, a drug user is not necessarily a drug abuser. Meet your drug-using child with an open mind. Try to remember how you felt as a teen-ager. What forbidden activities did you engage in, and how easy was it for you to discuss them with your parents when you were discovered? Remember that, although the specific issues change from generation to generation, the basic conflicts and problems between adolescents and parents are universal and remarkably constant.

The primary responsibility for preventing drug abuse in your child is yours. Providing models of intelligent drug use is the best way to ensure that your child will use drugs rather than abuse them (if he or she uses them at all). It is well known that alcoholics tend to come from families where one or both parents are alcoholic, but it is less well known that alcoholics also tend to come from families where both parents are teetotalers. Apparently, the absence of a parental role model for successful drinking is the determining factor. The low incidence of alcoholism among Jews has long been ascribed to the integration of occasional social and ritual use of alcohol into Jewish family life. The more you encourage openness within your home and the better your own relationships are with the drugs you use, the more effective you will be at passing healthy drug attitudes and habits on to your child.

Make rules and set limits for your child about drugs. If your child respects you and the ways that you use alcohol, caffeine, and other substances, he or she will welcome guidelines. Be realistic about the rules you make. For example, if you feel strongly that you do not want illegal drugs in the house, you have the right to ban them. Of course, you must realize that your child may then use illegal substances outside the house.

Keep in mind that the main reason children experiment with drugs is to experience other states of consciousness (see Chapter 3). High states appeal to young people as much as they do to adults. Grown-ups enjoy racing cars and boats, hang-gliding, dancing, drinking, smoking, and many other consciousness-changing activities. Don't make your child feel that it is wrong to want these experiences. If you oppose the use of drugs to have such experiences, be prepared to forgo your own drug use. Also, be prepared to suggest alternatives. Alcohol is not an alternative. It is a drug, and the advantage of its legality is more than offset by its many dangers for users of any age (see pages 70–80).

Finally, consider the parallel problem of sexual experimentation, which, like drugs, is an adolescent rite of passage that parents have to deal with. Is it better to provide support for your child by expressing trust and offering reliable information about these issues or to force your child to seek information and experience without guidance and in risky ways? We believe the answer is obvious, in matters concerning sex and drugs alike.

Both of us have taught in schools and colleges and are aware that schools are now popular places for the distribution and consumption of drugs. We know that teachers are likely to be distressed by the prevalence of drug use among children today, especially when they encounter increasing numbers of students who cannot concentrate and have trouble learning because they are intoxicated on one substance or another.

Teachers have a special role in influencing children, but when they have to talk about heated, emotional subjects like drugs, teachers must bow to so many pressures that often they cannot follow their intuition or conscience. Teachers frequently must present drug education programs that are based on incorrect information and irrational attitudes. Acknowledging the falsity of the information may gain teachers the respect of students and allow the teachers to influence drug use for the better, but it may also cost them their jobs. We would like to see teachers inform themselves about drugs and work within the limits imposed on them to make classrooms places where young people feel free to discuss their interest in, experiences with, and conflicts about drugs.

As with successful sex education, to help students feel free to discuss drugs in class, teachers will have to clarify their own attitudes and be prepared to answer questions about their own uses and habits, since students will certainly ask. As in parental discussions of sex and drugs with teen-agers, honesty and consistency will give teachers credibility with their students. Given the political dimensions of the drug controversy, many teachers may just want to avoid the whole issue. We cannot blame them, since we know how vulnerable their positions are. Still, because teachers can contribute so much toward the prevention of drug abuse, we hope that they will try to find ways to change attitudes for the better.

Although we have written this book so that young people can read it, we intend it for doctors, lawmakers, members of the clergy, teachers, and users and nonusers, regardless of age. We have gathered this information from many sources, including our own experience, and, whenever possible, we have included first-person observations by others to create a more balanced overall picture. We have tried throughout to indicate how society can work to prevent drug abuse by encouraging the use of alternatives to drugs and encouraging the formation of good relationships with drugs when people choose to use them.

2. What Is a Drug?

MOST PEOPLE WOULD AGREE that heroin is a drug. It is a white powder that in tiny doses produces striking changes in the body and mind. But is sugar a drug? Sugar is also a white powder that strongly affects the body, and some experts say that it affects mental function and mood as well. Like heroin, sugar can be addicting. How about chocolate? Most people think of it as a food or flavor, but it contains a chemical related to caffeine, is a stimulant, and can also be addicting. Is salt a drug? Many people think that they cannot live without adding salt to their food, and it has dramatic effects on the body.

A common definition of the word *drug* is any substance that in small amounts produces significant changes in the body, mind, or both. This definition does not clearly distinguish drugs from some foods. The difference between a drug and a poison is also unclear. All drugs become poisons in high enough doses, and some poisons are useful drugs in low enough doses. Is alcohol a food, a drug, or a poison? The body can burn it as a fuel, just like sugar or starch, but it causes intoxication and can kill in overdose. Many people who drink alcohol crusade against drug abuse, never acknowledging that they themselves are involved with a powerful drug. In the same way, many cigarette addicts have no idea that tobacco is a strong drug, and many people who depend on coffee do not realize that they are addicted to a stimulant.

The decision to call some substances drugs and others not is often arbitrary. In the case of medical drugs — aspirin and penicillin, for example, which are used only to treat and prevent physical illness — the distinction may be easier to make. But talking about psychoactive drugs — substances that affect mood, perception, and thought — is tricky.

In the first place, foods, drugs, and poisons are not clear-cut categories. Second, people have strong emotional reactions to them. Food is good. Poison is bad. Drugs may be good or bad, and whether they are seen as good or bad depends on who is looking at them. Many people agree that drugs are good when doctors give them to patients in order to make them better. Some religious groups, such as Christian Scientists, do not share that view, however. They believe that God intends us to deal with illness without drugs.

When people take psychoactive drugs on their own, in order to change their mood or feel pleasure, the question of good or bad gets even thornier. The whole subject of pleasure triggers intense controversy. Should pleasure come as a reward for work or suffering? Should people feel guilty if they experience pleasure without earning it or suffering for it in some way? Should work itself be unpleasant? These questions are very important to us, but they do not have easy answers. Different people and different cultures answer them in different ways.

Drug use is universal. Every human culture in every age of history has used one or more psychoactive drugs. (The one exception is some Inuit, who were unable to grow drug plants in the Alaskan tundra and had to wait for white men to bring them alcohol.) In fact, drug-taking is so common that it seems to be a basic human activity. All societies, therefore, must come to terms with people's fascination with drugs. Usually, the use of certain drugs is approved and integrated into the life of a tribe, community, or nation, sometimes in formal rituals and ceremonies. The approval of some drugs for some purposes usually goes hand in hand with the disapproval of other drugs for other purposes. For example, some early Muslim sects encouraged the use of coffee in religious rites but had strict prohibitions against alcohol. On the other hand, when coffee came to Europe in the seventeenth century, the Roman Catholic Church opposed it as an evil drug but continued to regard wine as a traditional sacrament.

Everybody is willing to call certain drugs bad, but there is little agreement from one culture to the next as to which these are. In our own society, all nonmedical drugs other than alcohol, tobacco, and caffeine are viewed with suspicion by the majority. There are subgroups within our society, however, that hold very different opinions. Many North American Indians who use peyote and tobacco in religious rituals consider alcohol a curse. The most fervent members of the counterculture that arose in the 1960s regard marijuana and psychedelics as beneficial while rejecting not only alcohol, tobacco, and coffee but most other legal and illegal drugs as well. Classic heroin addicts — junkies — may reject psychedelics and marijuana as dangerous but think of narcotics as desirable and necessary. Some yogis in India use marijuana ritually but teach that opiates and alcohol are harmful. Muslims may tolerate the use of opium, marijuana, and qat (a strongly stimulating leaf) but are very strict in their exclusion of alcohol.

Furthermore, attitudes about which drugs are good or bad tend to change over time within a given culture. When tobacco first came to Europe from the New World, it provoked such strong opposition that authorities in some countries tried to stamp it out by imposing the death penalty for users. But within a century, its use was accepted and even encouraged by governments eager to exploit its revenue-earning potential. In the past century, Americans' attitudes toward alcohol shifted from nonchalant tolerance to antagonism strong enough to result in national prohibition and back to near-universal acceptance. And the debate over marijuana in the 1960s was mostly a conflict between an older generation that viewed the drug as evil and a younger generation that found it preferable to alcohol.

Students of behavior tell us that dividing the world into good and evil is a fundamental human need. The existence of evil provokes fear and demands explanation. Why is there sickness? Why is there death? Why do crops fail? Why is there war? And, most important, how should we act to contain evil and avoid disaster? One approach to resolving these questions attributes evil to external things and then prohibits, avoids, or tries to destroy those things. This is the process that gives rise to taboos.

Taboos tend to crystallize around those activities and substances that are most important to us. Food, sex, and pleasure are very important, and many taboos surround them — although, again, there is little agreement from culture to culture as to the particulars. Muslims and many Jews eat beef but not pork; some groups in India eat pork but not beef. Homosexuality is taboo in most modern Western cultures but has been fully accepted in the past and is still accepted today in certain parts of the world.

People who adhere to taboos justify them with logical reasons. Jews who do not eat pork like to think that this is because pigs are unclean and carried disease in times past. Many Christians argue that homosexuality is a sin because it perverts God's intended use of sex for procreation. Actually, the reasons for taboos are secondary; the basic process is the dividing of important things into good and evil — a form of magical thinking that tries to gain control over sources of fear. The reasons and justifications come later.

Because psychoactive drugs can give pleasure and can change the ways that people think, perceive the world, behave, and relate to each other, they invite magical thinking and taboos. When you hear arguments on the merits or dangers of drugs, even by scientific experts, remember that these may be secondary justifications of preexisting views that are deep-seated and rooted in emotion. (It is always easy for both sides to produce statistics and "scientific evidence" to support their position.)

Because people have many fears and desires about drugs, finding neutral information about them is difficult. In this book, we try to give unbiased facts about all the psychoactive drugs that people are likely to encounter today. We cannot say that we have no biases about drugs, but we think that we know what our biases are. Our strongest conviction is that drugs themselves are neither good nor bad; rather, they are powerful substances that can be put to good or bad uses. We are concerned with the relationships that people form with drugs, whether legal or illegal, approved or unapproved. We believe that by presenting neutral information about these substances, we can help people, especially young people, come to terms with drugs. Our purpose is not to encourage or discourage the use of any drug but rather to help people learn to live in a world where drugs exist and not get hurt by them.

SUGGESTED READING

The best book on the subject of how societies classify drugs as good and evil is *Ceremonial Chemistry: The Ritual Persecution of Drugs, Addicts, and Pushers* by Thomas Szasz (New York: Doubleday/Anchor, 1975). Szasz is a psychiatrist interested in the assumptions that lead people to call some kinds of behavior sick or wrong. His discussion of drugs and drug users as scapegoats is excellent.

A good general book on psychoactive drugs is *Uppers, Downers, All Arounders: Physical and Mental Effects of Drugs of Abuse* by Darryl S. Inaba and William E. Cohen (Ashland, Oreg.: Cris Productions, 1997). See also *Drugs of Abuse: An Introduction to Their Actions & Potential Hazards* (2004 edition, catalog #203) by Samuel Irwin, distributed by the Do It Now Foundation (www.doitnow .org/pages/203/toc.html) (last accessed April 2004).

A book written for junior-high and high-school students that gives a good overview of the subject is *Mind Drugs*, edited by Margaret O. Hyde (third edition; Brookfield, Conn.: Millbrook, 1998).

3. Why People Use Drugs

D RUGS ARE FASCINATING because they can change our awareness. The basic reason that people take drugs is to experience states other than normal, waking consciousness. Of course, there are many other ways to alter consciousness, such as singing, dancing, eating, fasting, falling in love, laughing, traveling, meditating, playing ball, going to concerts, movies, museums, and plays, mountain climbing, deep sea diving, reading, writing, and fantasizing. The list is probably endless, because it includes nearly all the activities that people put most of their time, energy, and hard-earned money into, suggesting that changing consciousness is something that people like to do.

Human beings appear to have an inborn need for periodic variations in consciousness. The behavior of young children supports this idea. Infants rock themselves into blissful states; many children discover that whirling, or spinning, is a powerful technique for changing their awareness; some also experiment with hyperventilation (rapid, deep breathing) followed by mutual chest squeezing or choking, and tickling to produce paralyzing laughter. Even though these practices may produce some uncomfortable results, such as dizziness or nausea, the whole experience is so reinforcing that children do it again and again, often despite parental objections. Since children all over the world engage in these activities, the desire to change consciousness does not seem to be a product of a particular culture but rather to arise from something basically human. As children grow older, they find that certain available substances put them in similar states. Drugs are attractive because they provide an easy, quick route to these experiences.

Humans have been seeking out and experimenting with psychoactive substances since the dawn of time. The impulse to find and ingest drug plants goes so far back and is so universal that it seems to be intrinsic to human nature and integral to the evolution of human culture.

Many drug users talk about getting high. Highs are states of consciousness marked by feelings of euphoria, lightness, self-transcendence, concentration, and energy. People who never take drugs also seek out highs. In fact, having high experiences from time to time may be necessary to our physical and mental health, just as laughing, interacting with others, and dreaming during sleep seem to be vital to our well-being. Perhaps that is why a desire to alter our normal consciousness exists in everyone and why people pursue the experiences even though there are sometimes uncomfortable side effects.

Although the desire to experience high states is at the root of all drug-taking, on a practical level people take drugs for a wide variety of reasons. These include:

Reinforcing religious practices. Throughout history, people have used drug-induced states to transcend their sense of separateness and feel more at one with God, nature, and the supernatural. Marijuana was used for this purpose in ancient India, and many psychedelic plants are still so used today by indigenous peoples in both North and South America. Alcohol has been used for religious purposes in many parts of the world; the role of wine in Roman Catholic and Judaic rites persists as an example. Among tribal cultures, psychoactive plants are often considered sacred — gifts from gods and spirits to unite people with the higher realms.

Expanding awareness and exploring the self. Curious individuals throughout history have taken psychoactive substances to explore and investigate parts of their own minds that are not ordinarily accessible. One of the most famous modern examples was the British writer and philosopher Aldous Huxley, who experimented extensively with mescaline in the 1950s. His book *The Doors of Perception* is a record of his investigations. The title comes from a line of William Blake's: "If the doors of perception were cleansed, every thing would appear to man as it is — infinite." Some other well-known "explorers" are Oliver Wendell Holmes, the nineteenth-century American physician, poet, and author, who experimented with ether; William James, the Harvard psychologist and philosopher of the late nineteenth century, who used nitrous oxide; Sigmund Freud, the father of psychoanalysis, who took cocaine; William S. Burroughs, a modern American novelist and user of opiates and many other substances; Richard Alpert (Ram Dass), a psychologist and guru, who has extensive experience with LSD and other psychedelics; and John Lilly, a medical researcher and philosopher, who experimented with ketamine. Many others who have followed this path have done so privately, keeping their experiences to themselves or sharing them only with intimate companions.

Treating disease. Because psychoactive drugs really make people feel different, doctors and patients have always relied heavily on them for dealing with the symptoms of illness. Opium, morphine, and alcohol were mainstays of nineteenth-century medicine, used to treat everything from menstrual cramps to epilepsy. (One eminent physician of the day proclaimed morphine to be "God's own medicine.") Tincture of marijuana was also a popular remedy. At the end of the nineteenth century, cocaine was promoted as a miracle drug and cure-all, and coca wine was the most widely prescribed drug for a time. Until recently, diazepam (Valium) held that distinction. This kind of treatment may work by distracting a patient's attention from symptoms and shifting it instead toward the good feeling of a high. Sometimes the medical problem will then go away on its own. Often, however, if there is no treatment of the underlying cause of the symptoms, the problem will persist, and the patient may go on to use the drug again and again until dependence results.

Altering moods.   Many people take drugs to relieve anxiety, depression, lethargy, or insomnia or just because they feel bored.
The view that unwanted moods are disease states that are treatable
by taking medicines has now become widespread in our society.
The chief proponent and greatest beneficiary of this way of thinking is the pharmaceutical industry, with the result that a great
many of the legal medical drugs sold today are aimed at changing
undesired moods. Young people not only see their parents using
drugs in this way but also are influenced by advertisements and
commercials that directly promote such behavior. Many people of
all ages use nonmedical drugs, both legal and illegal ones, in this
fashion.

Escaping tedium and despair.   In the words of Aldous Huxley,
"Most men and women lead lives at the worst so painful, at the
best so monotonous, poor, and limited that the urge to escape, the
longing to transcend themselves, if only for a few moments, is and
has always been one of the principal appetites of the soul."

Facilitating and enhancing social interaction.   Like sharing food,
the ritual of taking drugs together is an excuse for intimacy; coffee
breaks and cocktail ("happy") hours are examples of the way that
approved drugs are used for this purpose. Disapproved drugs may
draw people together even more strongly by establishing a bond of
common defiance of authority. At the big rock concerts and Vietnam War protests of the 1960s, strangers often became instant
comrades simply by passing a joint back and forth.

In different cultures, other drugs perform the same function.
For example, South American Indians take coca breaks together,
much as we take coffee breaks, and chewing coca leaves with a
friend establishes an important social bond. For South Sea Island-
ers, drinking kava in groups at night is the equivalent of an American cocktail party.

In addition to the ritual significance with which drugs are invested, their pharmacological effects may also make social interac-

tion easier. Because alcohol lowers inhibitions, businesspeople often have drinks at lunch to encourage openness and congeniality. Similarly, people on dates often drink to reduce anxiety and feelings of awkwardness. By producing alertness and euphoria, stimulants such as cocaine promote easy conversation, even among strangers.

So important is this function of psychoactive drugs that many people would find it difficult to relate to others if deprived of them.

Enhancing sensory experience and pleasure. Human beings are pleasure-seeking animals who are very inventive when it comes to finding ways to excite their senses and gratify their appetites. One of the characteristics of sensory pleasure is that it becomes dulled with repetition, and there are only so many ways of achieving pleasure. As much time, thought, and energy have gone into sex as into any human activity, but the possibilities of sexual positions and techniques are limited. By making people feel different, psychoactive drugs can make familiar experiences new and interesting again. The use of drugs in combination with sex is as old as the hills, as is drug use with such activities as dancing, eating, and listening to or playing music. Drinking wine with meals is an example of this behavior that dates to prehistory and is still encouraged by society. There are those who say that a good cigar and a glass of brandy make a fine meal complete. Pot lovers say that turning on is the perfect way for a fine meal to begin. Psychedelic drugs, especially, are intensifiers of experience and can make a sunset more fascinating than a movie. (Of course, psychedelics can also turn an unpleasant situation into a living nightmare.) Because drugs can, temporarily at least, make the ordinary extraordinary, many people seek them out and consume them in an effort to get more enjoyment out of life.

Stimulating creativity. Writers have traditionally used psychoactive substances as sources of inspiration. The English poet Coleridge's famous visionary poem, "Kubla Khan," was a transcription

In Xanadu did Kubla Khan
A stately pleasure dome decree:
Where Alph, the sacred river, ran
Through caverns measureless to man
Down to a sunless sea.

— opening lines of "Kubla Khan" (1798), by Samuel Taylor Coleridge
(1772–1834)

of one of his opium dreams. The French poet Charles Baudelaire took hashish as well as opium for creative inspiration. His compatriot, the novelist Alexandre Dumas, joined him in experiments with hashish. The American writer Edgar Allan Poe used opiates; some of the weirdness of his tales probably derives from his drug experiences. Sigmund Freud's early writings were inspired by cocaine; for a time, he actively promoted cocaine as a miracle drug. Innumerable novelists, poets, playwrights, and journalists have found their inspiration in alcohol. Many have paid the high price of becoming alcoholics.

Some traditional peoples turn psychedelic visions into art. In Mexico, for example, the Huichol Indians turn their peyote visions into yarn paintings. Other artists use other psychoactive drugs to help translate their visions into art. Diego Rivera, the best-known Mexican artist of the twentieth century, favored marijuana. The famous American abstract painter Jackson Pollock was a prodigious drinker and an alcoholic; he died at age forty-four in a car crash, the result of driving while intoxicated.

Among the earliest and most enthusiastic users of marijuana when it first surfaced in the United States in the 1920s were blues and jazz musicians, and musicians have been in the vanguard of the drug movement ever since. Some of the greatest jazz musicians were heroin addicts; countless others drank to excess. But nowhere are drugs consumed so conspicuously as in the world of rock music. Jimi Hendrix, Janis Joplin, Jim Morrison, Brian Jones, and Sid Vicious are just a few of the rock stars who died of drug overdoses at a young age. Elvis Presley overdosed at forty-two. Many other great artists, including Eric Clapton, Willy Nelson, James Taylor, and Johnny Cash, came perilously close to burning out on cocaine, narcotics, or alcohol before cleaning up their acts.

Improving physical performance.   Various drugs can enable people to perform out-of-the-ordinary feats. In the ancient Inca empire of Peru, relay runners used coca in order to be able to cover vast distances in the high Andes, carrying news and messages to all parts of the kingdom. Warriors throughout history have fortified themselves with alcohol before going into battle, to boost their courage and decrease sensitivity to pain. Many professional athletes today follow in this tradition, although drug testing has curtailed their uses of illegal stimulants. Baseball players still chew tobacco. Truckers still drive long distances on little sleep and a lot of methamphetamine.

Rebellion.   Because drugs are surrounded by powerful taboos, they are ideal vehicles for rebellious behavior. Breaking taboos is an obvious way to challenge the values of the "establishment." Children quickly learn that they can upset parents, teachers, doctors, and other authorities by taking forbidden substances. Adoles-

> You get into heroin because you have a lot of money in your pocket, and you can't go to video games all the time, and you think life is very trivial and very boring, and you look for other people who think the same.
>
> — seventeen-year-old woman, heroin addict

> I started shooting heroin at the age of twelve and was a junkie till I was fifteen. I went cold turkey eight or nine times, but after each cold turkey I'd see my old friends again, and then I'd go back to heroin.
>
> — nineteen-year-old woman, former heroin addict

cence typically entails the assertion of independence, often by rejecting parental values. It is not surprising that adolescents frequently experiment with drugs. Unfortunately, the attempt to control drug-taking by making some substances illegal plays right into the hands of rebellious children. And, of course, some adults who have not outgrown adolescent traits continue to express rebelliousness in the ways that they take drugs.

Going along with the crowd.   Individuals who would not seek out drugs on their own will often take them in a group, because not to do so would be uncool. Although teen-agers may dislike the effects at first, they often take up smoking tobacco or marijuana in order to fit in and be accepted, much as they might adopt a trendy fashion style that does not suit them.

Using drugs because everyone else is using them is not a good reason, but it is a very common one.

Establishing an identity and getting attention.   Individuals or groups may take up the use of a prohibited substance or abuse a permitted one in order to define and advertise their specialness. Adopting unusual or extreme drug styles may not be wise, but it can be an effective way to get attention and recognition.

People's reasons for taking drugs are so varied that it's sometimes hard to know what is motivating a person to take a particular drug at any given time or why a person would choose to take one drug rather than another. People take different drugs for different reasons at different times. And some people take drugs for no reason, purely out of habit.

SUGGESTED READING

Andrew Weil's *The Natural Mind: A Revolutionary Approach to the Drug Problem* (revised edition; Boston: Houghton Mifflin, 2004) examines drug-taking as a method of changing consciousness and speculates on why altered states of consciousness are important to us.

Society and Drugs by Richard H. Blum et al. (San Francisco: Jossey-Bass, 1970) is a good survey of drug use in various cultures throughout history. In *The Joyous Cosmology: Adventures in the Chemistry of Consciousness* (New York: Vintage, 1965), philosopher Alan Watts gives a colorful picture of states of consciousness induced by hallucinogenic drugs. Watts experimented with these substances as an explorer of the mind and a searcher for religious experience.

Shaman Woman, Mainline Lady: Women's Writings on the Drug Experience, edited by Cynthia Palmer and Michael Horowitz (New York: William Morrow, 1982), is an anthology covering many times and cultures. It gives a broad overview of different ways of using many drugs.

For an account of the healing power of laughter, see *Anatomy of an Illness* by Norman Cousins (New York: Bantam, 1991).

High Culture: Reflections on Addiction and Modernity, edited by Anna Alexander and Mark S. Roberts (Albany: State University of New York Press, 2003), addresses the prevalence of addiction in literature, philosophy, modern art, and psychology, including its effects on many prominent thinkers and writers.

The American Drug Scene: An Anthology, edited by James A. Inciardi and Karen McElrath (third edition; Los Angeles: Roxbury, 2000), is a collection of both contemporary and classic essays and articles on the changing patterns, problems, perspectives, and policies of both legal and illegal drug use.

A good overall textbook about drugs is *Drugs, Society, and Human Behavior* by Oakley Stern Ray and Charles J. Ksir (eighth edition; Boston: WCB/McGraw Hill, 1999).

4. Relationships with Drugs

THE DESIRE TO CALL some drugs good and others bad has given rise to the term *drugs of abuse*. Government officials and medical doctors frequently talk about drugs of abuse, by which they usually mean all illegal substances. In their view, anyone using these drugs is automatically guilty of drug abuse.

But what is drug abuse? To say that it is the use of a drug of abuse is circular and meaningless. We think that the use of *any* drug becomes abusive when it threatens a person's health or impairs one's social or economic functioning. People with respiratory disease who persist in smoking cigarettes are clearly abusing tobacco. Students who are booted out of class because they are too stoned to concentrate are abusing marijuana. Drinkers too drunk to hold down jobs are abusers of alcohol. Addicts who squander all their money on heroin, thereby impoverishing their families, are abusers of that drug. On the other hand, any drug can be used in a nonabusive fashion, even if it is illegal or disapproved. There are many people who consume tobacco, marijuana, alcohol, and heroin without abusing them, that is, they remain healthy and fulfill their social and economic obligations. Drug abuse is not simply a matter of what drug a person chooses to consume; rather, it depends on the relationship that an individual forms with that drug.

Many factors determine relationships with drugs. Obviously, the drug itself is one important factor; there is a whole science, pharmacology, devoted to finding out what drugs do.

Unfortunately, the effects of drugs are difficult to specify. Different people show different responses to the same dose of the same drug, probably because people differ in their biochemistry, just as they do in appearance. Even the same person may respond differently to the same dose of the same drug at different times. Pharmacologists attempt to minimize these variations by giving drugs to animals and people under controlled laboratory conditions. The results of these experiments enable pharmacologists to classify drugs into different categories. For example, they can show most psychoactive drugs to be either stimulants or depressants of the nervous system.

Laboratory experiments also show that the dose of a drug is a crucial variable. High doses of a substance may produce very different effects from low doses. Moderate doses of alcohol will make many people feel relaxed and confident; high doses may cause incoordination, confusion, dizziness, and nausea.

The way a drug is put into the body also shapes its effects. When you take a drug by mouth, it enters the bloodstream slowly, and its influence on the nervous system is less intense than when you bypass the gastrointestinal tract by sniffing, smoking, or injecting the drug. High doses of drugs introduced by one of these more direct routes are likely to be more harmful as well as more addicting over time.

These pharmacological facts can explain some of the variations that we see in the relationships that people form with drugs. For instance, South American Indians who chew coca leaves ordinarily swallow low doses of cocaine and do not become abusers of that stimulant. People who put much larger doses of powder cocaine in their nose or who smoke crack cocaine are much more likely to develop medical, social, and psychological problems. The abuse potential of snorting or smoking coke is far greater than the abuse potential of chewing coca. In other words, people are more likely to form a good relationship with coca than with cocaine, and this difference clearly has some basis in pharmacology.

However, the laboratory is not the real world, and pharmacology can explain only certain aspects of the complex relationships that human beings have with drugs. When people take drugs in the real world, their experiences are often not what pharmacologists

would predict. The reason is that outside the laboratory other factors can completely change the effects of drugs. One such factor is
known as *set;* set is what a person expects to happen when he or
she takes a drug. Expectation is shaped by all of past experience —
what a person has heard about the drug, read about it, seen of it,
thought about it, and wants it to do. Sometimes it is not easy to
find out what people expect of a drug because they may not consciously know their real feelings. A boy smoking marijuana for
the first time may think that he is eager to have a new experience,
whereas unconsciously he may be terrified of losing his mind or
getting so stoned that he will never come down. Such unconscious
fears can determine reactions to marijuana more than the actual
effect of the drug.

Set can also be as important as pharmacology in shaping long-
term relationships with drugs. For example, some people expect
marijuana to make them relaxed and tired and so will use it only
occasionally at bedtime as a sleep aid, whereas others, who feel
that pot reduces their anxiety and makes it easier to relate to people, use it so frequently throughout the day that they become dependent on it.

Setting is another factor that modifies pharmacology. Setting is
the environment in which a drug is used — not just the physical
environment but also the social and cultural environment. During
the Vietnam War many American soldiers got into the habit of
smoking large amounts of the high-grade heroin that was cheap
and easily available to them in Southeast Asia. They rolled it into
cigarettes with tobacco or marijuana and used it primarily to escape boredom, because for many American soldiers Vietnam was,
more than anything else, boring, and because heroin seems to
make time pass more quickly. Pharmacologists predicted that
most of these soldiers would become heroin addicts, but in fact
most stopped using opiates as soon as they came home. It was the
special setting of army life in Vietnam that shaped this pattern of
drug use, and when people left that setting, most of them stopped
easily.

Set and setting together can modify pharmacology drastically. Therefore, talking about the effects of drugs in the real world is not so simple. Effects of drugs are relative to particular people, places, and times. In ancient India marijuana was eaten for religious purposes; people used it for its effects on consciousness in socially accepted ways. In England and America during the nineteenth century, doctors gave tincture of marijuana to sick people as a remedy, and most patients never reported getting high on it, probably because they did not expect to and so ignored the psychoactive effects. In the United States in the 1920s, members of certain subcultures began smoking marijuana to feel high — a practice regarded as deviant by the dominant culture. Many early marijuana smokers panicked, and some even committed acts of violence under its influence. Today, the smoking of marijuana is accepted in many circles, and users think that it decreases aggression and hostility.

The fact that the effects of psychoactive drugs can change so much from person to person, from culture to culture, and from age to age points up the folly of calling any drug "good" or "bad." Although there is no such thing as a drug of abuse, drug abuse is real, and learning to recognize it is important. Only in analyzing people's relationships with drugs can *good* and *bad* have meaning. Some people may be upset by the notion that you can have a good relationship with a drug, but chances are that they fail to acknowledge that many socially accepted substances are, in fact, drugs.

Good relationships with drugs have four common characteristics:

1. *Recognition that the substance you are using is a drug and awareness of what it does to your body.* People who wind up in the worst relationships with drugs often have little understanding of the substances that they use. They think that coffee is just a beverage, marijuana an herb, and diet pills just "appetite suppressants." *All drugs have the potential to cause trouble unless people take care not to let their use of drugs get out of control.* A

necessary first step is to acknowledge the nature of the substances in use and to understand their effects.

2. *Experience of a useful effect of the drug over time.* People who begin to use drugs regularly often find that their early experiences with them are the best; as they use the drugs more and more frequently, the effects that they like seem to diminish. People in the worst relationships with drugs often use them very heavily but get the least out of them. This curious pattern happens with all drugs and can be very frustrating. Frequency of use is the critical factor in determining whether the effect of a drug will last over time. If the experience that you like from a drug begins to fade, that is a sign that you are using too much too often. If you ignore the warning and continue consuming the drug at the same frequency, you will begin to slide into a worse and worse relationship with it.

3. *Ease of separation from use of the drug.* One of the more striking features of a bad relationship with a drug is dependence: it controls you more than you control it. People in good relationships with drugs can take them or leave them. (Dependence on drugs is discussed at length in Chapter 12.)

4. *Freedom from adverse effects on health or behavior.* People vary in their susceptibility to the adverse effects of drugs. Some individuals can smoke cigarettes all their lives and never develop lung disease. Some people can use heroin frequently and remain physically and psychologically healthy and socially productive. Others cannot. Using drugs in ways that produce adverse effects on health and behavior, and continuing their use despite these effects, is the defining characteristic of drug abuse.

Whether a drug is legal or illegal, approved or disapproved, obtained from a physician or bought on the black market, if the user is aware of its nature, can maintain a useful effect from it over time, can easily separate from it, and can remain free from adverse effects, that is a good relationship with the drug.

Bad relationships with drugs begin with ignorance of the nature of the substance and loss of the desired effect with increasing frequency of use, and progress to difficulty in leaving the drug alone, with eventual impairment of health or social functioning.

Any drug can be used successfully, no matter how bad its reputation, and any drug can be abused, no matter how accepted it is. There are no good or bad drugs; there are only good and bad relationships with drugs.

SUGGESTED READING

In *Psychology of Alcohol and Other Drugs: A Research Perspective* (Thousand Oaks, Calif.: Sage, 2001), author John Jung offers a psychological perspective, synthesizing a considerable amount of research on the use of recreational drugs.

In *The Marriage of the Sun and Moon: Dispatches from the Frontiers of Consciousness* (revised edition; Boston: Houghton Mifflin, 2004), Andrew Weil presents a number of case examples of substances and techniques that can make people high. Some involve drugs such as magic mushrooms, coca leaves, and marijuana; others do not — uncontrolled laughter, Indian sweat baths, eating mangoes and hot chilies, and watching an eclipse of the sun, for example. The ways that people think about these substances and activities determine the relationships formed with them.

5. Types of Drugs

PSYCHOACTIVE DRUGS can be classified according to whether they are natural or manmade, produced by our own bodies or by plants, crude mixtures of substances or single, purified chemicals. These differences may influence the relationships that people form with drugs, and users should be aware of them.

Endogenous (In-the-Body) Drugs

The human body, especially in the brain and certain glands, makes powerful chemicals that affect our moods, thoughts, and actions. We call these substances *endogenous drugs,* using a term with Greek roots meaning "made within." Interestingly, they resemble many of the chemicals that people take to change their consciousness.

The discovery of endogenous drugs is a recent scientific breakthrough. By 1950 brain researchers had come to understand that psychoactive drugs work by fitting into special receptor sites on nerve cells, just as keys fit into locks. Only when a drug molecule combines with a receptor that fits it does it produce an effect, such as causing a nerve cell to fire an electrical impulse or preventing it from firing one. This principle is the cornerstone of current theory about drugs and the nervous system.

For example, pharmacologists learned that morphine and heroin attach to special opiate receptors on nerve cells in certain parts of the brain. But why should our brains have receptors designed to fit molecules made by poppy plants? Some researchers suggested that opiate receptors really exist for other substances made by the brain itself — molecules whose shapes happen to be similar to those of opiates. In 1975, this suggestion was confirmed with the discovery of a group of chemicals called endorphins. Endorphins are the brain's own narcotics, producing most of the effects of poppy drugs, including euphoria and reduction of pain.

Endorphins are now under intense investigation because they are likely to reveal much about the workings of our minds and bodies. People who have high tolerance for pain may produce more of these endogenous narcotics. When you wake up one day feeling high and unfazed by the problems that ordinarily get you down, your endorphin system might be in high gear. Some people may be born with an inability to make enough endorphins; they may be the people who find opiates especially pleasant and come to depend on them to cope with the pain and stress of day-to-day existence.

The discovery of endorphins also raised interesting questions. Why have the human brain and the poppy evolved chemicals with similar effects when they are so unlike each other? Is this fact a mere coincidence or does it suggest a deep relationship between people and plants that underlies the age-old inclination to experiment with vegetable drugs? And what does it say about the "naturalness" of taking drugs? It is possible that endorphins and other endogenous agents are the basis of all the highs that people experience, whether obtained with drugs or without. People who get high by meditating or running, for example, may have found ways to stimulate the production or release of their own neurochemicals.

Not only does the body make its own narcotics, it also makes representatives of most of the other categories of drugs discussed in this book. It certainly makes its own uppers in the form of adrenaline and noradrenaline. It makes its own downers in the form of serotonin and GABA (gamma-amino-butyric acid), chemicals that slow down transmission in the central nervous system. Sex hormones can be powerful antidepressants, working better than anything so far concocted in a laboratory. The body probably also makes its own psychedelics — most likely DMT (dimeth-yltryptamine) — since the pineal gland, deep in the brain, se-cretes hormones with a very similar molecular structure. And the brain has its own marijuana analog as well, a compound called anandamide.

Because the drugs that our bodies make are designed to fit ex-actly into receptors on nerves, they are very powerful and efficient at producing their effects. Scientists are just beginning to learn about them and will certainly have much to say on the subject in years to come. It will be interesting to know how the use of exter-nal drugs affects the production of internal ones. Perhaps regu-lar use of a manufactured drug decreases or shuts off the produc-tion of the corresponding endogenous substance and so creates a chemical basis for dependence and addiction.

Natural Drugs

Crude Forms

Most psychoactive drugs come from plants, and there are hun-dreds of plants with psychoactive properties. People have put most of them to use in one part of the world or another at one time or another. Often, drug plants taste bad, are weak, or have unwanted side effects. Traditional peoples who use these plants, such as Na-tive Americans, have come up with clever ways of preparing and ingesting them to maximize the desired effects or make them eas-ier to take. Traditional peoples do not tamper with the chemical composition of the plants, however. For example, South American Indians have found that drying coca leaves and mixing them with ashes or other alkalis increases the stimulant effect of the leaves. To take psychedelic trips the Indians have also learned to make a powerful snuff from the resin of the Virola tree (a DMT-contain-ing plant). In a similar way, Old World natives learned to roast cof-fee beans and extract them with hot water to prepare a flavorful and stimulating beverage.

Crude plant drugs contain complex mixtures of chemicals, all of which contribute to the effect of the whole. Often, the concentration of one chemical will be greater than that of any other, and that one chemical may account for the most dramatic effects of the plant. Cocaine is the main drug in coca leaves and is responsible for the numbness in the mouth and much of the stimulation that coca chewers like. In the same way, caffeine is the predominant constituent of coffee. Doctors and pharmacologists refer to these predominating chemicals as the "active principles" of the plants, which would be fine, except that the term implies that all the other constituents are inactive and unimportant.

Scientists first began to identify the active principles of well-known drug plants in the mid-1800s. They soon succeeded in isolating many and making them available in pure form. Doctors quickly began to treat patients with these purified derivatives. Today, most doctors regard green medicinal plants as old-fashioned and unscientific; they rely instead on refined white powders derived from plants. Because pharmacologists have also lost interest in plants and study only isolated active principles, they know little about how whole plants differ from refined drugs in their effects.

The relationships that people form with plants are different from those that they form with white powders. Crude natural drugs tend to be less toxic, and users tend to stay in better relationships with them over time. One reason for this difference is that plants are dilute preparations, since the active principles are combined not only with other drugs but also with inert vegetable matter. Drug plants commonly contain less than 5 percent of an active principle. (Coca rarely has more than 0.5 percent cocaine.) By contrast, refined preparations may approach 100 percent purity.

In addition, crude plants usually go into the body through the mouth and stomach, whereas purified chemicals can be put into the bloodstream more directly, such as by snorting, smoking, or injecting. (You can't snort a coca leaf.) Harmful effects, both immediate and long-term, are more likely to appear when people put drugs directly into their bloodstream without giving their body a chance to process them.

Finally, the many other compounds in drug plants — often a single plant will contain twenty or more active components — may modify the active principles, making them safer or softening their harsher actions on the body. These safety factors and modifiers are lost when the active principles are isolated from the crude drugs that nature provides.

Natural drugs in whole plant form are the safest types of drugs. They always have lower potential for abuse. If people choose to take drugs, they would be wise to use natural plant forms in order to give themselves the best chance of avoiding problems.

Refined Forms

Morphine, cocaine, and mescaline are all examples of drugs that occur in plants but are commonly available in refined form as white powders, sold both legally and illegally. Some of them, such as mescaline, can easily be synthesized in laboratories, but even when they are, we can still call them natural drugs because the molecules already exist in nature. Others, such as cocaine and morphine, have more complex molecular structures. Chemists can make them in laboratories, but it is not cost efficient to do so. All the cocaine and morphine on the black market and in pharmacies is extracted from coca leaves and opium poppies.

Extraction and purification of some plant drugs is long and complicated, requiring sophisticated techniques and equipment. In other cases, the process is so simple that unskilled people can do it in the kitchen. Black-market cocaine is usually made in primitive jungle factories; of course, it is likely to contain many impurities.

Whether natural drugs are manufactured by chemists or extracted from plants, they may be safer than drugs that nature never thought of, because natural drugs interact more smoothly with the body's own chemistry. Since their structures tend to be closer to those of endogenous drugs, the effects of natural drugs and endogenous drugs tend to be similar. As we have noted, however, it is important to distinguish natural drugs in the dilute form of crude plants from refined powders with much higher toxicity and abuse potential.

Semisynthetic Drugs

Pharmacologists often take refined natural drugs and change their chemical structure to vary their properties. A very simple change is to combine an insoluble drug from a plant with an acid to make a water-soluble salt. In this way the "freebase" form of cocaine, which is usually smoked because it will not dissolve, is turned into cocaine hydrochloride, a water-soluble compound that can be inhaled or injected.

A slightly more complicated transformation is the addition of chemical groups to a natural drug molecule to make it stronger. At the end of the nineteenth century, German chemists created aspirin by adding an acetic acid group to a natural pain-relieving chemical found in the bark of some willow trees. Native Americans drank willow-bark tea to treat headaches and rheumatism, but aspirin is a more powerful pain reliever than willow bark. (It is also much more toxic.) A similar addition of two acetic acid groups to morphine turns it into heroin, a similar but more potent drug. That is, it takes less heroin than morphine to produce the same effect.

These transformations of natural drugs result in new substances called semisynthetic drugs. Chemists like to make semisynthetic drugs because it is easier to play with an existing molecule than to start from scratch. Sometimes their experiments only intensify the action of the original compound, as in the examples of aspirin and heroin, while in other cases, the results are completely novel. LSD (lysergic acid diethylamide) is an example of a semisynthetic drug with novel properties. It was made from a natural chemical in a fungus called ergot that attacks grasses and grains, but the original chemical (lysergic acid) is toxic and has little psychoactivity.

The ability of chemists to create new drugs from natural compounds raises an old argument about whether human beings should tamper with nature. We think that people are meant to interact with the natural world and modify its creations. In fact, people can improve on nature. A fine example is the development of excellent varieties of fruits and vegetables from unimpressive wild species. The issue for us is whether the results of the manipulations are beneficial or harmful. Plant selection and breeding to enhance flavor and nutrition are clearly worthwhile. On the other hand, the production of square, hard, tasteless tomatoes to facilitate mass packing and shipping is inspired by greed rather than a desire to benefit humanity.

In the same way, when chemists tinker with natural drugs, they should attempt to maximize desirable qualities. Extreme potency is not necessarily desirable, because it often goes hand in hand with great toxicity. We pay a high price today for our rejection of natural medicines in favor of potent chemicals. The tendency of pharmacologists and doctors to regard more potent drugs as better drugs encourages the use of dangerous derivatives of plants, when often the milder, natural originals would do as well.

Synthetic Drugs

Wholly synthetic drugs are made from scratch in the laboratory and do not occur naturally. Valium, PCP (phencyclidine), and secobarbital (Seconal) are examples. It may be that synthetic drugs are the most dangerous of all and the hardest to form a good relationship with, but it is risky to make such sweeping judgments. Very recently, researchers discovered Valium receptors in the human brain, leading them to believe that the body must produce some internal analog to that completely synthetic tranquilizer. Did the chemists who created Valium in a laboratory hit upon that molecule only by chance? Has Valium become so popular because its effect resembles that of an endogenous substance? Or might Valium receptors have developed in the brain in response to use of the drug? It is interesting to speculate on these questions, even though science may never be able to answer them.

In the following pages we describe all the psychoactive drugs that people are likely to encounter, both those that are legal and those that are not. We discuss them category by category, explaining how they work and what their benefits and dangers are. In any category, such as stimulants, some drugs may be natural — in crude or refined form — some may be semisynthetic, and some totally synthetic. We do not dwell on these differences but encourage the reader to keep in mind that dilute, natural forms of substances are always safer and may give users the best chance to build stable relationships with the drugs that they take.

SUGGESTED READING

There is no good book on the different types of drugs discussed in this chapter or on the new discoveries about endogenous drugs.

Guide to Psychoactive Drugs by Richard Seymour and David E. Smith (New York: Harrington Park Press, 1987) is a good, readable reference book. See also *Uppers, Downers, All Arounders: Physical and Mental Effects of Psychoactive Drugs* by Darryl S. Inaba and William E. Cohen (Ashland, Oreg.: Cris Productions, 1997).

Buzzed: The Straight Facts About the Most Used and Abused Drugs from Alcohol to Ecstasy by Scott Swartzwelder et al. (New York: W. W. Norton, 1998) is a succinct and clear guide to the often overcomplicated subject of neurochemistry. The book is divided into twelve sections covering all types of drugs.

6. Stimulants

STIMULANTS ARE DRUGS that make people feel more alert and energetic by activating or exciting the nervous system. There are many stimulant drugs in current use; some are plants found in nature, others are chemicals made in the laboratory. These different drugs produce somewhat different effects, lasting for varying lengths of time, but all of them raise the energy level of the nervous system in roughly the same way.

The individual nerves in our bodies communicate with each other both electrically and chemically. A nerve impulse is an electric discharge that moves quickly along the fiber of a nerve cell. The fiber may end at a muscle, a gland, or another nerve cell, but there is always a tiny space between the end of the nerve fiber and the next cell. To bridge this gap, the nerve fiber releases small amounts of powerful chemicals called neurotransmitters that affect the next cell. Some neurotransmitters are strong stimulants that cause muscle cells to contract, gland cells to secrete, and other nerve cells to fire off electrical discharges. The most common stimulant neurotransmitter is a chemical called noradrenaline, or norepinephrine. This chemical is closely related to the hormone adrenaline (or epinephrine), which is produced by our adrenal glands. (*Adrenal* is a Latin word meaning "on the kidney," because

> Thank God for tea! What would the world do without tea? — how did it exist? I am glad I was not born before tea.
>
> — Sydney Smith (1771–1845), English clergyman, writer, and wit

the adrenal glands sit on top of the kidneys like little caps. *Epi-nephros* means the same thing in Greek. In America the Parke-Davis pharmaceutical company succeeded in registering Adrenalin as a trademark for its brand of adrenal hormone, which is why American scientists generally use the more cumbersome words *epinephrine* and *norepinephzine*. We prefer the Latin form.)

Stimulant drugs work by causing nerve fibers to release noradrenaline and other stimulating neurotransmitters. Although different stimulants bring about this release in different ways, the end result is always the same: the release of more stimulating neurotransmitters. So the stimulation that people feel when they take stimulant drugs is simply a result of the chemical energy of the body's going to work in the nervous system. The drug just makes the body expend this energy sooner and in greater quantity than it would ordinarily.

This release of chemical energy in the form of noradrenaline causes certain predictable changes in the mind and body. It makes a person feel wakeful, alert, and, often, happy. It makes the heart beat faster and may cause the blood pressure to rise. Because it produces changes in blood flow, the fingertips and tip of the nose may become cold. It gives a feeling of butterflies in the stomach and may cause a laxative effect.

Some of these changes are mediated by a branch of the nervous system called the sympathetic nervous system. The main function of the sympathetic nervous system is to respond to emergencies by preparing the body for fight or flight. It does so by shutting down nonessential functions and speeding up vital ones. The sympathetic nervous system relies on noradrenaline as its chemical messenger.

Noradrenaline acts in many of the same ways as adrenaline, the hormone secreted by the adrenal glands, also in response to emergencies. Experiences that cause the adrenals to secrete adrenaline into the bloodstream produce feelings very much like those of stimulant drugs. The rush of excitement during a roller coaster ride, for example, may feel a lot like the effect of a dose of amphetamine, and no doubt both these techniques are popular for the same reason — because they give people a sense of increased mental and physical energy and make them feel, temporarily at least, more alive.

In recent years, scientists have begun to find out many interesting things about biorhythms, the cycles by which our vital processes wax and wane. The most obvious daily biorhythm is that of sleeping and waking. Production of hormones and neurotransmitters has its own ups and downs, and these cycles probably explain why people feel naturally stimulated at certain times and naturally lethargic at others. A common pattern is to feel energetic and able to concentrate well in the morning but to become tired and mentally sluggish in the late afternoon.

One reason that stimulant drugs are popular is that they give us temporary control over the rhythms of wakefulness and the ups and downs of mood. If you have a mental task to do at 3 P.M., when your brain wants to rest, you can mobilize it to concentrate by taking a stimulant drug and thereby forcing your nervous system to release some of its stored-up chemical energy. Or if you have to drive a long distance at night when your whole nervous system is ready for sleep, you can stay awake by putting a stimulant into your body. Or if you are feeling depressed when you have to go out and meet important people, a stimulant might brighten your mood for a while.

Another reason that people like stimulants is that they suppress hunger, making it possible to think about something other than food and concentrate better on the task at hand. Not eating, moreover, tends to further increase one's energy and sense of alertness. The reason that stimulant drugs suppress hunger probably has to do with the preparation of the body for emergencies. In emergencies, all digestive functions become nonessential compared to such processes as blood circulation and speed of muscular response. Under stress, therefore, the body shifts energy away from the stomach and intestines to the brain, heart, and blood vessels.

Because the nerves and muscles receive more attention under

the effect of stimulants, these drugs may improve certain kinds of physical and mental performance for a time. They may enable people to concentrate longer and better or to perform physical work more efficiently and with greater endurance. This probably explains why these drugs are especially popular with students and athletes.

Of course, stimulants do not affect everyone in the same way; some people find the effects of these drugs unpleasant, just as some people find roller coaster rides unpleasant. Far from making everyone cheerful and alert, these drugs make many people anxious, jittery, and unable to sit still. Some people are so sensitive to stimulants that they cannot sleep at all, even twelve hours after taking a small dose. Others get such distressing symptoms as heart palpitations, diarrhea, and urinary frequency and urgency. Instead of automatically improving physical and mental performance, stimulants sometimes just make people do poor work faster. There are famous (probably apocryphal) stories of college students who, under the influence of amphetamines, wrote what they imagined to be brilliant final exams, only to find later that they had written the same line over and over or scribbled the whole exam on one illegible page.

Still, at first glance, stimulants sound attractive: they can make you feel alert, happy, wakeful, energetic, strong, and resistant to hunger, boredom, and fatigue. But one of life's basic rules is that you never get something for nothing (or, there's no such thing as a free lunch), and stimulants are no exception to this rule.

The most serious problems with stimulant drugs result from the way they work. For, instead of miraculously delivering free gifts of cosmic energy, stimulants merely force the body to give up some of its own energy reserves. So, when the effect of a stimulant wears off, the body is left with less energy than usual and must replenish its supplies.

People experience this depletion of energy as a "down" or "low" state, marked by the very same feelings that they take stimulants to avoid, namely, sleepiness, lethargy, laziness, mental fatigue, and depression. The price that you pay for the good feeling that a stimulant gives you is a not-so-good feeling when the stimulant wears off.

If you are willing to pay this price and let your body recharge itself, there is nothing wrong with using stimulants now and then. The trouble is that many people are not willing to let their bodies readjust; they want to feel good again right away, so they take another dose of the drug. It's very easy to fall into a pattern of using stimulants all the time in order to avoid the down feeling that follows the initial up.

Unfortunately, when stimulants are used in this way, they quickly produce dependence. People who regularly take stimulants find that they cannot function normally without them. They need them just to open their eyes in the morning, move their bowels, work, or do any of the tasks of everyday life. Without stimulants these people just don't feel like doing much of anything.

Kinds of Stimulants

Coffee and Other Caffeine-Containing Plants

Caffeine, the most popular natural stimulant, is found in a number of plants throughout the world. The drug was first isolated from coffee in 1821 and was named for that plant, but the effects of coffee and caffeine differ. In many ways, coffee seems to be more powerful than refined caffeine or other caffeine-containing plants.

A shrubby tree native to Ethiopia, coffee is now cultivated in many tropical countries throughout the world. Each of its bright red fruits, called cherries, contains two seeds, or beans. The raw beans are gray-green and odorless, but when roasted they turn dark brown and develop their characteristic aroma and flavor. Legend has it that coffee was first discovered long ago by Ethiopian nomads who noticed that their domestic animals became frisky

> In the morning, I drink two cups of coffee. If I don't, I feel irritable. If I drink three cups, I get a little speedy, but with two I feel just about right.
>
> — thirty-nine-year-old man, college administrator

after eating the fruit of the trees. When people tried eating the seeds, they got frisky too, and eventually they learned to make a flavorful drink from the roasted seeds.

More than a thousand years ago, groups of Muslims in the Middle East began using coffee in religious rituals and ceremonies. Groups of men would meet one night a week, drink large amounts of coffee, and stay up all night praying and chanting. These mystics confined their use of coffee to occasional ceremonies, but as coffee became more widely known, other people began to use it, not for religious reasons but just because they liked its stimulant effect. When people started to drink coffee every day in large amounts, many of them found that they couldn't stop.

When coffee first came to Europe in the seventeenth century, it stirred up great opposition as a new and unapproved drug. Authorities tried to prohibit its use, but of course their efforts were to no avail; coffee soon established itself there and all over the world. Coffee houses sprang up in all European cities, and whole populations became dependent on the drug almost overnight. Johann Sebastian Bach is rumored to have been a coffee addict. He extolled the virtues of the new drink in his famous Coffee Cantata. The French writer Honoré de Balzac could not work without coffee. He drank larger and larger amounts of a brew that was so strong that it looked like thick soup; then he complained of the stomach cramps that coffee gave him.

Today, coffee is a thoroughly approved drug — so approved, in fact, that many people who drink it regularly are surprised to learn

> Far beyond all other pleasures, rarer than jewels or trea-
> sures, sweeter than grape from the vine. Yes! Yes! Greatest
> of pleasures! Coffee, coffee, how I love its flavor, and if
> you would win my favor, yes! Yes! let me have coffee, let
> me have my coffee strong.
>
> — from the Coffee Cantata, by Johann Sebastian Bach (1685–1750)

that it is a drug at all, let alone a powerful drug that can cause dependence and illness.

The truth is that coffee is a strong stimulant, one that is hard on
certain parts of the body. It is irritating to the stomach, for example, and many people who drink a lot of it have indigestion most of
the time. (In the United States, where people regularly consume
coffee in large quantities, there are nearly as many brands of antacids as there are brands of coffee.) It is irritating to the bladder,
too, especially in women, and is a frequent cause of urinary complaints. Coffee also makes many people shaky by upsetting the
delicate balance between nerves and muscles. It is a common
cause of headaches, heart palpitations, anxiety, and insomnia.

Today, dependence on coffee is very common in Western society. Many regular users cannot think clearly in the morning until
they have had their first cup. Without it, they can't concentrate,
move their bowels, or do their work. Also, they suffer real withdrawal symptoms if they stop using coffee suddenly. The withdrawal reaction begins twenty-four to thirty-six hours after the last
dose. Symptoms are lethargy, irritability, and a distinctive throbbing (vascular) headache that is often severe. Nausea and vomiting may occur. These symptoms will last from thirty-six to sev-
enty-two hours. They disappear rapidly if the user takes caffeine in
any form. Such problems all come from using coffee so frequently
that the body never gets a chance to replenish its stores of chemical energy and comes to rely more and more on the external drug.

Coffee and caffeine have been suspected of causing birth defects. So far, the evidence is not conclusive, but pregnant women should remember that coffee and caffeine are drugs and that they should not consume them in large amounts. Coffee and caffeine may also raise serum cholesterol, increasing the risk of heart attack. The evidence for this effect remains contradictory. On the other hand, coffee may offer protection from pancreatic cancer, a rare and deadly disease.

Note that decaffeinated coffee is not inert. In addition to small amounts of caffeine (enough to stimulate sensitive individuals), it contains other active substances from the coffee bean that can be irritating to the nervous, gastrointestinal, cardiovascular, and urinary systems. This is true of water-processed decaf as well as the less safe solvent-extracted brands, which may contain residues of toxic chemicals.

Other caffeine beverages don't seem to be as powerful or as toxic as coffee — even though they may contain as much caffeine or equivalent drugs. Tea is not nearly so irritating to the body as coffee, and cases of dependence on tea are less common in our society. Of course, tea is a stimulant, and if you drink it in large amounts or make it strong enough, you can get powerful effects, including jitteriness and insomnia. In England, tea drinking has been a national pastime and habit since the early seventeenth century, when it was introduced from Asia. Tea addiction is not uncommon in England, Ireland, and Asia. Japanese people drink green tea throughout the day. In addition, they conduct tea ceremonies, elaborate rituals built around the consumption of *matcha,*

> We had a kettle; we let it leak.
> Our not repairing it made it worse.
> We haven't had any tea for a week . . .
> The bottom is out of the Universe.
>
> — "Natural Theology," by Rudyard Kipling (1865–1936)

a special powdered green tea that is whipped with water into a bitter, frothy beverage. This strong form of tea was developed in Zen Buddhist monasteries to help monks stay awake during long hours of meditation.

A great deal of recent medical research has documented the health benefits of tea, especially green tea, which is a rich source of antioxidants that may lower cholesterol and help prevent cancer and other chronic diseases. The main antioxidant in tea is EGCG (epigallocatechin gallate). It is highest in the least processed forms of tea, such as Chinese white tea and Japanese green, lower in leaves that have been oxidized to change their color and flavor, like oolong and black tea. Another interesting compound in tea is L-theanine, which causes "alert relaxation." (It is now available as a dietary supplement.) This compound may modify the effect of caffeine, which is why most people find even strong tea to be less "jangling" than coffee.

Cola is a caffeine-containing seed, or nut, from a tropical tree, the cola tree. In some African countries, cola nuts are so valuable that they are used as money. The nuts have a bitter, aromatic taste, and people chew them for their stimulating effect. Bottled cola drinks have very little cola nut in them and do not taste like cola nuts at all. Though they do contain caffeine, it is usually synthetic caffeine or caffeine extracted from coffee or tea. These soft drinks are also drugs, and people can become dependent on them, as with coffee. Also, they contain a lot of sugar.

The combination of sugar and caffeine seems to be especially habit-forming. Many people drink enormous amounts of cola, and although they may think that they are merely quenching their thirst, they are also consuming calories and enough sugar to damage their teeth (and upset their metabolism), not to mention large doses of caffeine. (Diet colas eliminate the sugar but not the caffeine.) Like other stimulants, cola drinks are not unhealthy if used in moderation; people who like them should just be aware of their nature and their potential for abuse. Parents especially should remember that so-called soft drinks are actually drugs that can affect

the health and mood of their children. (The popularity of stimulating cola drinks has led manufacturers to add caffeine to some
other flavors of carbonated beverages. Drinks so fortified must list
caffeine as an ingredient. If you do not want to take drugs with
your soda, you should make a habit of reading the information on
bottles and cans.)

In other parts of the world, people use a number of less well-
known caffeine plants. The national drink of Brazil is *guaraná*
(pronounced gwah-rah-NAH), made from the seeds of a jungle
shrub. It contains more caffeine than coffee and is often made
into sweet carbonated drinks. Tablets of *guaraná* powder have appeared in health food stores in the United States under such
brand names as ZOOM and ZING, and more recently many
brands of *guaraná*-based energy drinks have joined the tablets; the
drinks are marketed as new organic stimulants from the Amazon
rain forest.

In Argentina, the most popular caffeine drink is maté (pronounced mah-TAY), which is made from the leaves of a holly
plant. Some kinds of maté taste like smoky tea. Maté leaves can be
bought in health food stores and tea shops and are ingredients in
some herbal tea mixtures, such as Celestial Seasonings' Morning
Thunder. Packages of maté sometimes misrepresent the product
as a caffeine-free herbal tea.

One of the most famous sources of caffeine is chocolate, also
made from the seeds of a tropical tree. (The tree is called cacao
[pronounced cah-COW], and its seeds are cacao beans, or cocoa
beans. The fat in them is cocoa butter. White chocolate is just cocoa butter mixed with sugar. The roasted ground-up beans, with
most of the fat removed, are cocoa. Regular chocolate is made by
adding extra fat to roasted ground-up beans.) Chocolate, which
contains a lot of fat and is very bitter, must be mixed with sugar to
make it palatable. Chocolate, too, contains a stimulating drug, and
cases of chocolate dependence are easy to find. You probably know
a few "chocoholics." People who regularly consume chocolate or
go on chocolate-eating binges may not realize that they are in-

> Five years ago, hoping to kick a chocolate habit that was significantly affecting my life, I enrolled in a program at the Shick Center for the Control of Smoking, Alcoholism, and Overeating, in Los Angeles. I was then thirty-three. I could not remember the last time I had managed to get through a whole day without eating chocolate in one form or another, usually in quantities most people would regard as excessive, if not appalling . . . Frankly, I am mystified by what happened and to this day cannot explain it. Being addicted to chocolate was so much a part of my definition of myself that it constantly amazes me to think that I am now free of it.
>
> — thirty-eight-year-old woman, social worker

volved with a drug, but their consumption usually follows the same sort of pattern as with coffee, tea, and cola drinks.

Chocolate contains only a small amount of caffeine but has a lot of theobromine, a close relative with similar effects. By itself, theobromine cannot account for all aspects of chocolate addiction, because chocolate addiction looks different from other forms of stimulant dependence. Most chocoholics are women, and many of them crave chocolate most intensely just before their menstrual periods. Women who develop an addictive relationship with chocolate usually eat it in cyclic binges rather than continually and often say that it acts on them like an instant antidepressant. As there is no reason to think that theobromine affects men and women differently, other components of chocolate must be involved. Very little research has been done on chocolate, so no one knows for sure.

Cacao was known to the ancient Aztecs, who considered it a sacred plant and used it in religious rituals. Dark chocolate is a rich source of health-protective antioxidants, like green tea and red wine. It has heart-protective effects and may actually help lower cholesterol. In moderation, chocolate is a pleasant and interesting addition to the diet, but overuse may not be wise, especially since the combination of sugar, fat, and drugs can be so habit-forming. People who tend to gain weight easily should be especially careful about their intake of chocolate.

Coca and Cocaine

Coca, a shrub native to the hot, humid valleys of the eastern slopes of the Andes, has been cultivated by the Indians of South America for thousands of years. Today, the plant is legal in Peru and Bolivia, where millions of Indians still chew coca leaves every day as a stimulant and medicine. (Coca, by the way, is not related to cocoa.)

Coca contains fourteen drugs, the most important of which is cocaine. The other drugs are present in smaller amounts and seem to modify the stimulating effect of the cocaine. In addition, coca leaves contain many vitamins and minerals that are probably important in the diets of Indians who use the leaves. There are several varieties of coca: some taste like green tea, some like wintergreen. Coca users put dried leaves in their mouth and work them into a large wad. They suck on this wad for thirty minutes or so, swallowing the juices and then spitting out the residue. To get an effect from coca, the user must add a tiny amount of some alkali, such as lime (the powdered mineral) or ashes, to the wad of leaves.

After a few minutes of chewing coca, the user's mouth and tongue become numb; then people begin to experience the usual effects of a stimulant. Unlike coffee, coca soothes the stomach and doesn't produce jitteriness. It may also be more powerful than caffeine in producing a good mood.

In the late 1800s, coca became very popular in Europe and America in the form of tonics and wines. Coca-Cola began as one

> Had drugs been decriminalized seventeen years ago, crack
> would never have been invented. It was invented because
> the high cost of illegal drugs made it profitable to provide a
> cheaper version.
>
> — economist Milton Friedman, writing in the *Wall Street Journal*,
>   September 7, 1989

of these early preparations. At the same time, scientists isolated cocaine from the leaves and made it available to doctors in the form of a pure white powder. As the first local anesthetic, cocaine revolutionized surgery, especially eye operations, which had always been terribly painful and difficult. In the 1880s, doctors began to prescribe cocaine for all sorts of medical problems, including dependence on opiates and alcohol. It soon became apparent that this kind of treatment was not a good idea, because many patients suffered ill effects from cocaine, and many became dependent on it. So, in the early 1900s, laws were passed to prevent the widespread use of coca and cocaine. The Coca-Cola Company took cocaine out of its drink (it still contains a drug-free extract of the leaves as a flavor). Other coca products swiftly disappeared from the shelves of drugstores. Safer local anesthetics were invented in laboratories, and today doctors use cocaine only for certain operations in the eye, nose, throat, and mouth.

In the hundred years since Congress restricted the use of coca, a huge black market has developed to supply cocaine to the many people who like the feeling that it gives. All illegal cocaine comes from leaves grown and processed in South America. It is always cut (diluted) with various substances before reaching consumers here. Most people snort cocaine, that is, they snuff the powder up their noses. Used in this way, the stimulant effects come on very fast, are very intense, and are very short-lived. Some people shoot cocaine, that is, inject it intravenously, which gives even faster, more intense, and shorter effects (see Chapter 12 for the health problems related to intravenous drug use), and some people use water pipes to smoke a special form of cocaine called freebase. Crack cocaine is a newer, smokable form of the drug marketed as small pellets. It first appeared in the mid-1980s, and crack use quickly reached epidemic proportions in cities throughout America. Smoking puts cocaine into the bloodstream even faster than intravenous injection and gives similar effects — very intense and very brief. Few people take cocaine by mouth, even though it works and is actually much safer that way.

Coca and cocaine are very different, and the difference shows how it is easier to form good relationships with natural drugs than with isolated and refined ones.

Coca leaves contain low concentrations of cocaine (usually only 0.5 percent), in combination with other drugs that modify its effects in a good way; they also contain valuable nutrients. The cocaine is highly diluted by inactive leaf material. What's more, getting stimulation from coca takes work: you have to chew a mouthful of leaves for half an hour. In this natural form, small amounts of cocaine enter the bloodstream slowly through the mouth and stomach.

Relatively pure street cocaine may contain 60 percent of the drug, which, when it is put directly into the nose, lungs, or veins, enters the bloodstream all at once. The stimulation, or "rush," is therefore very intense, but it lasts only a short time, usually disappearing within fifteen to thirty minutes. Then the user may crash, feeling tired, sluggish, unhappy. Because cocaine can make people feel so good for so short a time and not so good immediately thereafter, users tend to go on using it, trying to get back the good feeling. Many people can't leave this drug alone if they have it, even though all they get from it after a while is the unpleasant effects characteristic of all stimulants used in excess: anxiety, insomnia, and general feelings of discomfort. Besides, snorting too much powder cocaine irritates the nose, while smoking crack may be bad for the lungs and is even more likely to lead to overuse and a stubborn habit.

Indians in South America, on the other hand, rarely have any problems with coca leaf. They can take it or leave it, continue to get good effects from it over time, and use the stimulation to help them work or socialize. They also use it as a medicine for a variety of illnesses, especially digestive ones. Among South American Indians, there is little abuse of coca leaf.

Use and abuse of cocaine have skyrocketed in recent years, provoking much public alarm. Sensational news stories about crack, with graphic descriptions of inner-city crack houses and impaired "crack babies" born to addicted mothers, led directly to escalation of the current war on drugs. For drug warriors, crack became the new devil drug, so dangerous as to justify the most repressive measures.

In their enthusiasm to fight cocaine these crusaders often exaggerated its dangers, at least its physical toxicity. Both powder and crack cocaine can increase the workload of the heart and cause irregular heartbeats, but death from cocaine is rare, and the body has a great capacity to metabolize and eliminate the drug from its system. Actually, what drug education should emphasize are the psychological and social dangers of cocaine.

First of all, the addictiveness of this stimulant is great. (Smoking crack is as addictive as smoking cigarettes.) Cocaine addiction almost always interferes with social and economic functioning, since addicts often alienate their family and friends, lose their jobs, and spend phenomenal amounts of money on their habits ($15,000 a year and more). They become paranoid, isolated, and depressed, unable to stop thinking about their next dose. Treatment of this addictive behavior is difficult, time-consuming, and costly.

Occasional snorting of powder cocaine in social situations is probably not harmful for most people, but everyone should be aware that the possibility of using this drug to excess is very real and that excessive cocaine use can wreck a person's life. It is even more difficult to limit the intake of crack cocaine to levels compatible with good physical and emotional health.

Once the drug of choice of yuppies, socialites, and dot-com millionaires, cocaine has now diffused through much of American society, although it has been replaced in some communities by methamphetamine, which is cheaper and gives longer-lasting stimulation. Nevertheless, the production of coca in Peru and Bolivia and the refining of leaves into cocaine in Colombia continue unabated, as does the American effort to eradicate the plant.

It seems a shame that the laws and policies on drugs in our society have led to the disappearance of coca, along with knowledge of its uses and benefits. At the same time, by outlawing something that many people want, legislators have made it profitable to smuggle the concentrated drug and so have encouraged the growth of a vast black market in cocaine. The American-led war against the cocaine trade has caused incalculable social, political, economic, and ecological devastation in the producing countries of South America.

Amphetamines and Related Drugs

Amphetamines are synthetic stimulants that were invented in Germany in the 1930s. Their chemical structures resemble those of adrenaline and noradrenaline, the body's own stimulants. The effects of amphetamines resemble those of cocaine but are much longer lasting. A single oral dose of amphetamine usually stimulates the body for at least four hours.

Amphetamines are more toxic than cocaine and, when abused, cause worse problems. The body has a great capacity to metabolize and eliminate cocaine: the liver can detoxify a lethal dose of cocaine every thirty minutes. It cannot handle amphetamines as efficiently. At the same time, people can establish a stable relationship with amphetamines more easily than they can with cocaine, probably because the intensely pleasurable but very short effect of cocaine is more seductive and invites repetitive dosing.

For many years after the invention of amphetamines, they were tolerated and their use was even encouraged by authorities. Soldiers in World War II received rations of amphetamines to make

> I decided to try and make up for lost time by staying up all night to study for my European history exam, but by midnight the text was blurring before my eyes . . . An upperclassman took pity on me and offered me a green-and-white capsule along with the promise that my drowsiness would be cured by taking it. I took it without a second thought and within half an hour or so found myself studying like mad. Not only was I completely engrossed in European history, I felt exhilarated; I was actually enjoying myself . . . I got an A on my history exam — as I was sure I had — and have been involved, to some extent, with amphetamines ever since.
>
> — forty-two-year-old woman, writer

them march longer and fight better. The governments of several countries, among them the Soviet Union, experimented with giving amphetamines to factory workers, hoping to make them more productive (which, in the long run, they failed to do). Doctors in this country have prescribed them in great quantity for even more questionable reasons.

In the 1950s and 1960s, the U.S. pharmaceutical industry manufactured enormous quantities of amphetamines (many of which turned up on the black market). The companies urged doctors to prescribe their products for depressed housewives and people with weight problems.

There are a number of different amphetamines, but all have the same basic effect. Plain amphetamine (Benzedrine) was the first to become popular. Dextroamphetamine (Dexedrine) and methamphetamine (Methedrine) are effective in lower doses but otherwise are similar to the parent compound. A few other drugs — methylphenidate (Ritalin), for example — resemble amphetamines in effect, even though they have a different chemical structure. And a new class of "wakefulness promoting agents" has just appeared; the first on the market is modafinil (Provigil). Originally developed to keep military personnel awake while on duty, it is now used to treat narcolepsy, a medical condition marked by excessive sleepiness. A few users of amphetamines tell us that they would use modafinil only if they couldn't get their preferred stimulants.

Today, we know that regular use of amphetamines, especially by people who are neurotic, depressed, or fat, is not a good idea. Not only do the drugs fail to help their problems, they often complicate matters by creating another kind of dependence. Since the 1970s most cases of amphetamine abuse have involved legally manufactured and prescribed drugs. At about the same time, criticism of the promotional practices of pharmaceutical companies and of the prescribing practices of physicians brought about severe restrictions on the medical use of these compounds. Today, amphetamines can be prescribed for only a few conditions.

One of the more controversial uses still permitted is the control of attention deficit hyperactivity disorder (ADHD) in children. For reasons that scientists do not yet understand, amphetamines (and other stimulants) have a calming effect on many children. Unfortunately, the diagnosis of ADHD often is applied to children who simply misbehave or don't pay attention in school. Giving them amphetamines not only fails to get to the root of the problem, it introduces young people to powerful drugs and encourages among adults the false notion that all of life's problems can be solved by taking pills. Stimulants can be life changing for some children with ADHD, but it cannot be good for so many young people to be on these drugs. One popular drug for ADHD is Adderall, a combination of dextroamphetamine and methamphetamine. Extra-long-acting forms of these stimulants are now popular with parents and doctors. But the intense appetite suppression that they cause can actually interfere with nutrition and growth in young children.

Given the restrictions on the legal supplies and uses of amphetamines, black markets in them grew, and, as so often happens, this change promoted abuse. In the days of legal pills, most users took them by mouth. Today, many people snort powdered amphetamines like cocaine, smoke them like crack, and even inject them intravenously.

Intravenous use of amphetamines first appeared in the late 1960s. Young "speed freaks" who fell into this pattern of use experienced very bad effects on their bodies and minds. After only a few weeks, they became emaciated and generally unhealthy; they stayed up for days on end, then "crashed" into a stupor. They became jumpy, paranoid, and even psychotic. Members of the drug subculture itself recognized the dangers of shooting amphetamines and warned people about it with the phrase "speed kills."

But the most noteworthy change in the distribution and use of amphetamines has been the explosive popularity of methamphetamine, known as "meth" or "crank." The crystalline, smokable form of it is called "ice" or "crystal." Heavy ice smokers go on binges that can last for days, a practice known as "tweaking" or "amping." Crystal meth is now the illegal drug of choice in much of rural America, its use rampant in economically depressed farm communities of the Midwest and West. A great increase in property crime has followed in the wake of this epidemic. Smoking crystal meth is as hazardous as injecting it.

It is easy to make methamphetamine from such ingredients as agricultural fertilizer, and large numbers of meth labs have appeared all over the country, especially in less populated areas, where the strong odors resulting from cooking the drug are less likely to draw attention. It is not uncommon to hear of disastrous accidents during meth production — explosions and serious injuries. Once an area has been used as a meth lab, it is an environmental hazard, very costly to clean up.

Note that many people are able to use amphetamines without problems, especially if they take them orally, moderately, and purposefully. For example, some college students use them to study for or take exams. Some writers take them to work. Truckers and other drivers sometimes take them for long-distance travel on highways, especially at night. Athletes, such as football players, sometimes use them to play big games. Actors and dancers take them occasionally to perform. Used in this way, amphetamines do not usually cause physical harm, especially if people rest afterward. Problems arise when people take amphetamines all the time, just because they like the feeling of stimulation, especially if they snort, smoke, or shoot amphetamines.

"Look-alike" Drugs

As the regulation of medical prescription of amphetamines tightened up, a flood of bogus products appeared. Called look-alikes, they are tablets and capsules that are made to look like pharmaceutical amphetamines but that contain no controlled substances. Some are legally manufactured for over-the-counter sale in drug and health food stores; others appear in head shops or are sold by mail order or on the Internet or street.

Look-alikes contain caffeine, ephedrine, phenylpropanolamine, or synephrine, either singly or in combination. Ephedrine is a natural stimulant with a chemical structure that resembles adrenaline, but ephedrine produces more anxiety and less euphoria than amphetamines. It occurs in a desert shrub and has been used as a treatment for asthma (see page 63). Phenylpropanolamine (PPA) is a synthetic drug that once was added to many cold remedies as a nasal decongestant. Not long ago it was also an ingredient in a number of over-the-counter diet pills. Now that PPA and ephedrine are banned, manufacturers have turned to synephrine, which is obtained from bitter orange. Look for a ban on it in the near future.

Look-alike drugs have received much bad publicity. They are accused of killing some people by causing strokes and disturbances of their heartbeat. There is no hard evidence to support this, but people with high blood pressure or a history of heart irregularities should be wary of them (as they should be of all stimulants).

Several years ago, I fell madly in love with an ex-smoker, a man who, though broad-minded in other respects, was a fanatic on the subject of cigarettes . . . I had always thought I'd be able to kick my addiction to cigarettes for someone I loved. That assumption turned out to be wrong. In the end, when forced to choose between love and cigarettes, I chose cigarettes. It was that simple. I did make one resolution at the time, which I have stuck to ever since. It was that I would never again become involved with a man who does not smoke cigarettes.

— forty-one-year-old woman, teacher

Tobacco and Nicotine

Tobacco is one of the most powerful stimulant plants known, and nicotine — its active principle — is one of the most toxic of all drugs. An average cigar contains enough nicotine to kill several people.

When tobacco is smoked, burning it destroys most of the nicotine. (To kill people with a cigar, you'd have to soak the cigar in water till it turned dark, then make people drink the liquid.) Nicotine is so strong and dangerous that the body quickly develops tolerance for it to protect itself. If someone begins smoking regularly, tolerance for the poisonous effects of nicotine develops in a matter of hours (as compared to days or weeks for heroin and months for alcohol).

In the form of cigarettes, tobacco is one of the most addictive drugs known, equivalent to crack cocaine and ice. It is harder to break the habit of smoking cigarettes than it is to stop using heroin or alcohol. Moreover, many people learn to use alcohol and heroin in nonaddictive ways, whereas very few cigarette smokers can avoid becoming addicts. Occasionally, you will meet someone who smokes two or three cigarettes a day or even two or three a week, but such people are rare. Interestingly, these occasional users get high from smoking and like the effect, while most addicted smokers do not experience major changes in consciousness.

Smoke from cigarettes inhaled deeply delivers concentrated nicotine to vital brain centers within a few seconds — faster than heroin reaches the brain when it is injected into a vein in the arm. This probably explains why smoking cigarettes is so addictive.

Treatment of tobacco addiction is very difficult. Doctors frequently prescribe substitute forms of nicotine, such as chewing gum and skin patches, to help addicts through the physical withdrawal, but these methods often fail to curb the psychological craving for cigarettes.

Doctors know also that regular cigarette smoking is a leading cause of serious disease of the lungs, heart, and blood vessels. This does not mean that everyone who smokes will necessarily get lung cancer. Some people smoke heavily all their lives and show no ill effects, probably because they have healthy lungs and strong constitutions to begin with. Others are not so lucky.

Pipes and cigars are less hazardous than cigarettes because smoke from them is harsher, discouraging deep inhalation. Many smokers of pipes and cigars do not inhale at all and so completely avoid the risk of lung disease. In addition, since pipes and cigars don't deliver rapid pulses of nicotine to the brain, pipe and cigar smokers are less likely than cigarette smokers to become addicted to tobacco so strongly or so fast. Pipes and cigars are not without risk, however. They still put nicotine into the body, affecting the heart and circulation, and increase the risk of cancer of the lips, mouth, and throat.

Another health hazard of tobacco is secondhand smoke. If you live or work with smokers, you can inhale the equivalent of smoking one-half to one pack of cigarettes a day, raising your risk of tobacco-associated disease. (The smoke coming off the lighted end of a cigarette actually contains more toxins than smoke inhaled through the other end, which has been filtered through a mat of tobacco.)

Some tobacco users take the drug without burning it. Tobacco chewers place wads of it in their mouth, letting the nicotine diffuse into their system through blood vessels in their tongue and cheeks. Others use snuff (finely powdered tobacco) by inhaling it or putting pinches of it in their mouth. Many Amazonian Indians cook tobacco and water to form a paste that they rub on their gums.

All of these preparations provide strong stimulation in the form of high doses of nicotine — higher than cigarettes, pipes, and cigars — because burning destroys so much of the nicotine in tobacco. Nevertheless, chewing tobacco or taking snuff is less addicting than smoking because it puts nicotine into the blood and brain much less directly.

Most people who use snuff or chewing tobacco for the first time dislike it. These products burn the mouth or nose, taste terrible, cause intense salivation and sneezing, and often produce rapid dizziness and nausea. With repeated trials, however, users grow tolerant of the worst effects and come to like the sensations in their mouth and nose. Tobacco companies now sell snuff as "smokeless tobacco," some of it with mint and fruit flavoring to make it more acceptable to novices. The companies promote it as a new and pleasant way to use the drug, even in nonsmoking areas. Smokeless tobaccos have recently become popular among teen-agers, probably because it is easier to use the drug without detection. An unquestionable plus for snuff users and tobacco chewers is that they do not pollute the air with smoke and expose nonusers to nicotine and other irritants.

Despite growing awareness of its toxicity and addictiveness, tobacco remains an accepted drug in our society. Its use is even encouraged by extensive advertising that makes smokers seem mature and sexually appealing. Our government actively supports the tobacco industry with public funds. Certainly, this is an example of how our division of drugs into good and evil is not at all rational.

New World natives used tobacco in religious and magical rituals thousands of years ago, and some South American Indians still use strong tobacco as a consciousness-altering drug today. On special occasions, they build giant cigars that the men take turns inhaling. They quickly become very intoxicated. Because they do not use tobacco except on special occasions, they have no tolerance for its effects and so get very high. In North America today, all Indian medicine men and women use tobacco ceremonially; they believe that tobacco smoke carries their prayers to the spirit world. When the Spanish discovered America, they observed Indians using tobacco and began using it themselves.

In the 1500s, Europeans also used tobacco to alter consciousness. It was a scarce and precious substance from the New World, and people smoked it occasionally, inhaling as deeply as they could and holding the smoke in their lungs to maximize the effect. Early tobacco was so harsh that people could not do this often enough to develop rapid tolerance and addiction. Still, authorities at the time were very upset at what they considered to be a new form of evil and tried their best to prohibit tobacco use. In many countries, the penalty for people caught possessing tobacco was death.

Needless to say, these measures did not work, as criminal penalties for drug use never do. Tobacco supplies grew, and more people began smoking more and more regularly. As tobacco became increasingly common, it lost its special significance, and its users, instead of getting high on it once in a while, became addicts who needed it just to feel normal. Governments then began to see in tobacco a new source of revenue, which they depend on to this day. The development of milder tobaccos, which could be inhaled deeply and often, gave birth to cigarette addiction as we know it today and with it the rise of the modern tobacco industry. Throughout the first half of the twentieth century, authorities encouraged the use of tobacco on the grounds that it promoted concentration and relaxation. In movies of the 1930s and 1940s, all the characters smoke incessantly. During World War II, cigarettes were standard issue in the rations for American soldiers, and as late as the 1950s, doctors appeared in cigarette ads promoting particular brands as "soothing to the throat."

Toward the end of the twentieth century, society's views on tobacco began to change. Smoking became unfashionable as a result of persistent educational efforts, nonsmokers began to demand and get smoke-free environments, and smokers became second-class citizens. Smoking is now banned on airplanes and buses and in airports, as well as many restaurants and bars. Workplace smoking has been virtually eradicated. A large number of cities and towns have banned smoking in all public places. Norway has done it for the whole country, with other European countries considering similar legislation.

In 1998, Mississippi became the first state to instigate litigation against the four largest cigarette-producing companies (collectively known as Big Tobacco), seeking compensation for tobacco-related health care costs. Florida, Minnesota, and Texas soon followed suit. The states settled their lawsuits for a combined total of $40 billion. The remaining states and the District of Columbia later settled a major class action lawsuit against Big Tobacco for $206 billion.

There is legitimate reason for the concern about the health effects of tobacco smoking. A recent British government study of adolescents shows that a youngster who smokes more than *one* cigarette has only a 15 percent chance of remaining a nonsmoker. If you are thinking about experimenting with tobacco, especially in the form of cigarettes, consider the fact that most experimenters fall into this trap and become addicts before they know it.

Four Exotic Stimulant Plants

Betel. The betel nut is the spicy-tasting seed of a tropical palm tree. In Asia, millions of people chew it daily, combining it with a pinch of lime (the alkaline mineral, not the fruit) and wrapping it in a fresh leaf of another plant called the betel pepper. This combination produces a great deal of red juice, which betel chewers spit out. In India, this mixture is called *pan* and is often livened up with spices like clove and sugar and enjoyed as an after-dinner digestive aid. Betel nut contains a drug called arecoline, a stimulant comparable to caffeine. Betel chewing is a habit that is similar to the habits of chewing gum and drinking coffee or cola drinks in industrialized societies. Betel juice stains teeth black over time. Heavy use may increase the risk of oral cancers.

Qat (khat, chat, miraa). Qat is a popular stimulant in a wide area of east Africa and the Middle East. It is a shrubby tree whose fresh leaves and young twigs are eaten for their stimulating effect. The leaves lose their power when they dry out. Qat contains many active chemicals, some of which resemble amphetamines in their structure. Unlike coca, the leaves of qat, which have a bitter, astringent taste, are usually swallowed. Truck drivers in Kenya are big users of this plant. (It is called *miraa* there.) Ethiopia is a major producing country. In fact, Ethiopian Airlines was formed to deliver fresh qat to Yemen, a country with many consumers but no production, because it is a desert. In the United States, qat is sometimes sold under the table at Ethiopian restaurants.

Yohimbe. Yohimbe, the bark of an African tree with a bitter, spicy taste, contains a drug called yohimbine that is used in a few prescription medicines to treat sexual impotence in men. Yohimbe bark is available at some herb stores and can be brewed into a stimulating tea. It is supposed to be an aphrodisiac, and some users say that it causes tingling feelings along the spine.

Ephedra. Ephedras are leafless bushes that grow in deserts throughout the world. They are related to pine trees and bear tiny cones. Several species contain the drug ephedrine, a stimulant and a remedy for asthma. American ephedra, found throughout the western United States, is known as Mormon tea because early Mormon settlers used it instead of caffeine beverages, which are prohibited by their religion. Until recently, herb stores sold both

American ephedra and the much stronger Chinese type. The dry stems are boiled with water to make a pleasant-tasting tea that can be very stimulating. Chinese ephedra and ephedrine were common ingredients of herbal uppers sold in health food stores for weight loss and energy. Manufacturers have often packed these products with high doses of these herbs and added caffeine for good measure. Adverse reactions, including a few deaths, were common in people who took these products. Sensational publicity about the dangers of ephedra and ephedrine prompted Congress to ban them in 2004. Ephedra will still be allowed in Chinese herbal medical formulas.

Over-the-Counter (OTC) Drugs

Many cold remedies and other over-the-counter preparations contain caffeine to offset the drowsiness caused by antihistamines. (See pages 173–75 for a description of the effects of antihistamines.) Another stimulant in these products is pseudoephedrine, used as a nasal decongestant. Also look for synephrine, sometimes concealed as "bitter orange extract."

Some Rules for Using Stimulants Safely

Because stimulants are so common, most people will use one or another at some time. If you become involved with stimulants, here are some rules that will help you stay in a good relationship with them.

1. *Limit* your *frequency of use.* All trouble with stimulants arises from using them too often. If you like the feeling a stimulant gives, it is all too easy to let your frequency of use creep up. Set limits! For example, never take a stimulant two days in a row.
2. *Use stimulants purposefully.* Taking these drugs just to feel good will not help you limit your use. If you are going to take a stimulant, you should use the stimulation for something — a physical or mental task, for instance. One side benefit of such

purposeful use is that the satisfaction of accomplishment will offset the letdown when the drug wears off.

3. *Do not take stimulants to help you perform ordinary functions.* You should be able to get up in the morning, move your bowels, and make it through the afternoon without drugs. If you cannot, you should change your patterns of diet, sleep, and exercise. Relying on stimulants for everyday activity leads to too-frequent use and dependence.

4. *Take stimulants by mouth.* Putting these drugs more directly into the bloodstream (as by snorting, smoking, or shooting) accentuates the letdown that follows the high and encourages frequent administration. It also increases the harmful effects on the body.

5. *Take dilute forms of stimulants rather than concentrated ones.* The more dilute the preparation of a stimulant, the easier it is for the body to adjust to it and the more gentle the letdown at the end. Preparations of plants such as coffee and tea are naturally more dilute than refined or synthetic drugs and are easier to stay in good relationships with.

6. *Maintain good habits of nutrition, rest, and exercise.* Remember that stimulants force your body to give up its stores of chemical energy. Whenever you use stimulants, especially if you take them with any regularity, it is important to let your body recharge itself. The healthier you are, the less you will feel that you need outside stimulation.

7. *Do not combine stimulants with depressants or other drugs.* Combinations of drugs always complicate matters. Some people can't sleep at night because they take too many stimulants during the day. So they take depressants at night. Then they can't get moving in the morning and have to take more stimulants. This pattern of drug-taking quickly leads to trouble.

8. *Avoid look-alike drugs.* They have nothing to recommend them.

It should not be difficult to use stimulants wisely and stay in good relationships with them. They are not the answer to the ups and downs of life, and taking them to try to avoid the downs only leads to problems. Nor do they give anything for nothing. Users pay later for any energy and good feeling that stimulants give them. If you remain aware of what stimulants are and how they work, you will be able to avoid the trap of becoming dependent on them.

SUGGESTED READING

Coffee and tea are the subjects of *The Book of Coffee and Tea* by Meri Shardin (second revised edition; New York: St. Martin's Press, 1996). A classic book on the colorful history of coffee and human beings is *Coffee: The Epic of a Commodity* by Heinrich Eduard Jacob and Kynn Alley (Springfield, N.J.: Burford Books, 1999). The most famous work on tea is Kakuzo Okakura's *The Book of Tea* (Boston: Charles E. Tuttle, 1956), first published in 1906. About much more than tea, it is an elegant treatise on Japanese culture and philosophy written to help dispel Western misconceptions about Japan. A more recent work on the same subject is *Tea: The Eyelids of Bodhidhaima* by Eelco Hesse (Berkeley, Calif.: And/Or Press, 1982). An interesting book on the origins and development of Coca-Cola is *For God, Country, and Coca-Cola: The Definitive History of the Great American Soft Drink and the Company That Makes It* by Mark Pendergrast (second edition; New York: Basic Books, 2000). Chocolate devotees may be interested in a book by Sandra Boynton called *Chocolate: The Consuming Passion* (New York: Workman, 1982), a profile and ardent defense of that substance by a self-proclaimed chocoholic. See also Allen M. Young's *The Chocolate Tree: A Natural History of Cacao* (Washington, D.C.: Smithsonian Institution Press, 1994), a detailed examination of the source of chocolate.

Many books on coca and cocaine are available. Here is a selection of the best:

W. Golden Mortimer's *History of Coca: Divine Plant of the Incas* (Corvallis, Oreg.: University Press of the Pacific, 2000) was first published in 1901. It is a long description of Incan civilization, Peru, and coca and contains valuable information. An excellent book on the origins and history of cocaine is *Cocaine: Global Histories*, edited by Paul Gootenberg (New York: Routledge, 1999). Dominic Streatfield's *Co-*

caine: An Unauthorized Biography (New York: Picador USA, 2003) is a well-researched, humorous narrative on the subject, with accounts of the author's visits to crack houses, maximum security prisons, and the South American rain forest. In *Cocaine: From Medical Marvel to Modern Menace in the United States, 1884–1920* (Baltimore: Johns Hopkins University Press, 2000), Joseph F. Spillane investigates lesser-known facets of the drug's history, including the role of American business in helping to create interest in it.

For firsthand accounts of cocaine abuse, see *Cocaine Changes: The Experience of Using and Quitting* by Dan Waldorf (Philadelphia: Temple University Press, 1991). The book includes over two hundred interviews with heavy cocaine users and concludes that the national hysteria over the drug is largely unfounded. The horrors of crack houses are recounted in *Crackhouse: Notes from the End of the Line* (New York: Perseus, 1992) by Terry Williams and Terence T. Williams. *The Seven Per Cent Solution* by Nicholas Meyer (New York: Dutton, 1974) is a novel that concerns Sherlock Holmes's cocaine habit. It was made into a popular movie. The problems and perils of freebasing cocaine are brilliantly depicted by comedian Richard Pryor in his movie *Richard Pryor: Live on the Sunset Strip*. Pryor's real-life habit of freebasing cocaine resulted in a near-fatal accident. An excellent movie about the cocaine trade is *Blow*.

Despite their widespread use, amphetamines have attracted far less attention from writers than cocaine. All of the best books are out of print. The best of all, *Synthetic Panics: The Symbolic Politics of Designer Drugs* by Philip Jenkins (New York: New York University Press, 1999), is readily available on the Internet. For a firsthand account of methamphetamine abuse, see *Meth=Sorcery: Know the Truth* by Steve Box (Above All Distributing, 2000).

Recent years have finally seen the appearance of a few good books on tobacco. *Regulating Tobacco: Premises and Policy Options* (New York: Oxford University Press, 2001), edited by Robert L. Rabin and Stephen D. Sugarman, is an excellent collection of essays on strategies that have influenced tobacco use. An interesting and surprising account of the antismoking movement is *For Your Own Good: The Anti-Smoking Crusade and the Tyranny of Public Health* by Jay S. Cohen (New York: Tarcher/Putnam, 2001). John Barth's novel *The Sot-Weed Factor* (New

York: Bantam, 1969) revolves around tobacco. Probably, the best account of cigarette addiction occurs in a comic novel by Italo Svevo, *Further Confessions of Zeno* (Berkeley: University of California Press, 1969). The author describes the endless tricks and self-deceptions used by a cigarette addict, as well as the low probability of cure.

The best book available on qat is John G. Kennedy's *The Flower of Paradise: The Institutionalized Use of the Drug Qat in North Yemen* (Boston: D. Reidel, 1987).

7. Depressants

DEPRESSANTS ARE DRUGS that lower the energy level of the nervous system, reducing sensitivity to outside stimulation and, in high doses, inducing sleep. Many depressants are used medically and socially, and many are consumed illegally. In fact, depressants include some of the most popular drugs that affect mood.

At first glance, it may seem odd that people would want to take substances in order to depress their nervous systems. Who wants to feel groggy and depressed? Actually, depressants make people sleepy and stuporous only in high doses; in lower doses, they often make people relaxed and happy. Alcohol is a good example. One or two drinks can make people feel cheerful, alert, and more alive, while three or four can make them drunk, with obvious symptoms of reduced brain function.

Scientists don't really know why low doses of depressants make people feel stimulated. One theory is that the first parts of the brain to be depressed are inhibitory centers that normally act to dampen mood. As the dose is increased, more and more parts of the nervous system are slowed down. Very high doses of depressants can cause coma, in which all consciousness is lost; a person in a coma is insensible to all stimulation — even loud noise and intense pain. Still higher doses of these drugs can shut down the most vital centers in the brain, such as the one that controls respiration, resulting in a quick death from lack of oxygen.

Depressant drugs are more dangerous than stimulants because overdoses of depressants are apt to kill people by interfering with vital brain centers. Also, depressants produce a wider variety of effects, from relaxation and euphoria in low doses to unresponsive coma in very high doses.

Depressants include several distinct categories of drugs, each with its own benefits and dangers.

Sedative-Hypnotics

This large category of depressants comprises alcohol, "sleeping pills," and antianxiety drugs. In low doses, these drugs promote relaxation and restfulness (sedation), especially in the daytime. Larger doses, especially at night, induce sleep (the word *hypnosis* comes from the name of the Greek god of sleep). The term *sedative-hypnotic* refers to this double action.

Alcohol (Ethyl Alcohol, Ethanol)

Alcohol is the most popular psychoactive drug in the world, used every day by many millions of people. Probably, it is also the oldest drug known to human beings, because it is easy to discover that fruits and juices, left to stand in a warm place, soon ferment into an alcoholic mixture. Alcohol is so commonplace and its effects, both good and bad, are so well known that they need little description. Anyone who has felt the pleasant stimulation of a glass of wine knows the beneficial side of this drug. Anyone who has interacted with a drunk person knows how powerful and unpleasant alcohol can be in overdose. Anyone who has lived with an alcoholic can attest to the horrors of alcohol addiction.

Production of ethyl alcohol depends upon yeast, which feeds on sugar, making alcohol and carbon dioxide as by-products. Yeasts are simple one-celled forms of life found everywhere — in the air and on the skins of many fruits, especially grapes. To grow and multiply, yeast cells need water, sugar, and warmth. They keep on growing until they use up all the sugar or until the rising concentration of alcohol kills them. Alcohol is a poison as well as a drug; in high enough doses, it kills living things, including the yeasts that make it.

Natural sources of sugar available to primitive people were fruit and honey, both of which can be made into wine with a maximum alcohol content of about 12 percent. Starch is also a potential source of alcohol, but enzymes must convert starch to sugar before yeast can digest it. There are enzymes in saliva that can accomplish this, and one of the earliest kinds of beer was made by natives in tropical America who learned to chew corn to a pulp, spit it into clay pots, mix it with water, and let it ferment. Sprouting grains also produce usable enzymes; in standard beer making, sprouted barley (malt) is used to convert the starch of grains to sugar so that yeast can grow and produce alcohol. The alcohol content of beer is usually less than half that of wine. Beer is also more nutritious than wine because it has a lot of calories in the form of carbohydrates.

Distilled alcohol is a relatively new product, only a few hundred years old: brandy was the first distilled liquor made; it was obtained by heating wine and then cooling and condensing the vapors in another container. This process increases the alcohol content dramatically: from 12 percent up to 40 or 50 percent. The original idea of distillers was to concentrate wine so that its volume would be smaller, to make it easier to ship it in barrels overseas. At the end of the voyage, the brandy was to be diluted with water for an alcohol content of 12 percent. What happened, of course, was that when people got their hands on what was in the barrels, no one waited to add water. Suddenly, a new and powerful form of alcohol flooded the world.

Our society now manufactures and consumes many distilled liquors. Scotch and bourbon whiskeys are made from beerlike preparations of grain. Rum is distilled from fermented molasses; vodka is just diluted ethyl alcohol (so is gin, with flavor added), also usually distilled from grain. Because of their much higher alcohol content, these hard liquors are stronger and more intoxicating than fermented drinks.

From earliest times, people probably used beer and wine much as we use them today: as social and recreational drugs, to dispel

> I like alcohol. It is a powerful drug and, God knows, for some people a hellish one, but if used carefully it can give great pleasure. After a long, hard day, the splendid warm glow that strong drink provides is one of my favorite feelings; it starts in the pit of my stomach, then spreads to my limbs and brain. I know that alcohol is a depressant, but it acts and feels like a gentle relaxant — of the spirit as well as of the physical body. Just notice the increased vivacity and noise level at a cocktail party after a drink has been served to see how alcohol can put people at ease emotionally.
>
> — sixty-two-year-old man, psychoanalyst

worry and anxiety, to feel high, and as a change from the dull routines of work. Our early ancestors probably also noticed that the effects of alcohol were variable and related to the dose, and that some people became dependent on alcohol.

Alcohol is absorbed very quickly from the digestive system, enters the bloodstream, and reaches the brain, where it causes its effects on mood and behavior. The body has to work hard to eliminate alcohol; it burns some of it as fuel and excretes some unchanged in the breath and urine. The burden of metabolizing alcohol falls especially on the liver.

The effects of alcohol are directly related to how much of it is in the blood at any time. Low concentrations, particularly at the beginning of drinking, cause alertness, a good mood, feelings of energy, warmth, and confidence, and the dissipation of anxiety and inhibition. Most people find these changes pleasant.

It is important to note, however, that some of the sensations produced by low doses of alcohol — especially the sense of confidence — may be false. Unlike stimulants, alcohol and other depressants slow the functioning of the nervous system, including reflexes, reaction time, and efficiency of muscular response. Although people often feel that they are performing better after a few drinks, scientific tests show otherwise. This is one source of danger in using depressant drugs to feel good: the false sense of confidence can lead people to take unwarranted risks, such as driving a car while the imbiber is in a condition that favors disaster.

Similarly, the sense of warmth produced by drinking is deceptive. It is due to increased blood flow to the skin, which allows more heat to radiate to the outside of the body. In fact, inner body temperature is dropping even as the sensation of warmth increases, so that people who dress inadequately for cold weather and drink in order to feel warm may fall victim to hypothermia.

Another example of the deceptive nature of alcohol is its sexual effect. Many people who drink to enhance sex claim that alcohol increases desire, removes inhibitions, and promotes relaxation. In men, however, the depression of the nervous system by alcohol can prevent erection and drastically interfere with sexual performance. Writers as far back as Shakespeare have noted this property of alcohol. In act 2, scene 3, of *Macbeth*, the following exchange occurs between Macduff and a porter in Macbeth's castle:

MACDUFF: What three things does drink especially provoke?
PORTER: Marry, sir, nose painting, sleep, and urine. Lechery, sir, it provokes, and unprovokes; it provokes the desire, but it takes away the performance.

People who drink should be aware that their subjective impressions while under the influence of alcohol may not correspond to reality.

Further, it is clear that, as with any psychoactive drug, the pleasant feelings that alcohol can provide depend as much on set and setting as on pharmacological action. The same amount of wine that makes someone pleasantly high at a party may make a depressed person in a lonely room even more depressed.

The concentration of alcohol in the bloodstream is determined by several factors: first, by the concentration of alcohol in the drink; second, by the rate of drinking; third, by the presence or absence of food in the stomach; and fourth, by the rate at which the body can metabolize and eliminate alcohol.

The stronger the drink, the faster the blood alcohol level will rise and the sooner a person will get drunk. Gulping down cocktails and drinking wine like water are good ways to speed through the more pleasant, early effects of alcohol intoxication and go right to the less desirable ones.

Food in the stomach, especially milk, slows down absorption of alcohol into the blood. Therefore, drinking on an empty stomach can result in faster and more intense drunkenness. Eating before and during drinking moderates the intensity of alcohol's effects.

Finally, some people metabolize alcohol more rapidly than others and so can handle larger doses. This may be genetically determined; if so, some people could inherit a tendency to become alcoholic. People who drink alcohol regularly metabolize it faster than people who do not, and regular drinkers won't be affected by doses that nondrinkers would certainly feel. This is tolerance, and it develops quickly for alcohol and other sedative-hypnotics. Alcoholics show very high tolerance for the drug; they can even survive doses of alcohol that would kill nondrinkers. Other people may have lower than normal abilities to metabolize alcohol. Some Japanese, for example, have an inborn biochemical quirk that causes them to get drunk on doses of wine or liquor that would hardly affect most Americans or Europeans.

As alcohol increases in the bloodstream, it depresses more and more of the nervous system, producing the familiar symptoms of drunkenness: slurred speech, incoordination, insensitivity to pain, and inappropriate behavior. People become drunk in very different ways, depending on their personalities, their mood at the time, and the social setting. Some people become boisterous and obnoxious; others become overly friendly, confiding the most intimate details of their lives to perfect strangers. Some people get belligerent, even violent, while others become gloomy, tearful, and self-pitying.

Drunkenness is a serious problem throughout the world, accounting for many accidents, acts of violence, injuries, and deaths. Many traffic accidents are directly related to alcohol intoxication, as are many murders. It isn't uncommon for drunk people to kill friends or relatives and have no memory of these events the next day, a consequence of alcohol's depressant effect on parts of the brain responsible for reason, thought, and memory.

Most people who get drunk eventually fall into stuporous sleep. When they wake up, they are hung over, with such symptoms as sour stomach, headache, weakness, shakiness, depression, and inability to concentrate, work, or think clearly. These symptoms reflect the toxic effects of alcohol on the body and are very uncomfortable. Alcohol is strongly diuretic — that is, it increases the flow of urine, causing the body to lose water. A night of hard drinking can result in serious dehydration if the drinker does not replace the lost water, and this condition may contribute to the discomfort of the next day's hangover.

Because additional alcohol ("the hair of the dog that bit you") makes a hung-over person feel better in the short run, excessive drinking can lead to further drinking and start people on the path to dependence.

Dependence on alcohol is a true addiction, marked by extreme craving for the drug, tolerance, and withdrawal. The craving for alcohol among alcoholics is legendary and has been the subject of many books and films (see pages 107–108). Recovering alcoholics tell frightening stories of the lengths to which they went to obtain their drug when deprived and of squandering all of their money on drink. Withdrawal from alcohol is a major medical crisis. Some of its worst forms, such as delirium tremens (the DTs), can be fatal and are more serious than withdrawal from narcotics.

Moreover, because alcohol is such a strong and toxic drug, prolonged regular use can cause tremendous physical damage. Cirrhosis of the liver, in which normal liver cells are replaced by use-less scar tissue, is a direct and common result of overuse of alcohol and leads to many distressing symptoms, among them, loss of sexual potency and inability to digest food. The other or-gans that bear the brunt of alcohol's poisonous effect are the brain and the peripheral nervous system. Alcoholics develop shakes, amnesia, and loss of intellect, which may reflect permanent dam-age to nerves. The list of medical problems associated with exces-sive drinking is much too long to reproduce here. It includes ad-verse effects on unborn babies of alcoholic women (fetal alcohol syndrome) and increased susceptibility to such infectious diseases as pneumonia and tuberculosis. Hospitals around the world are filled with chronic medical patients whose bodies are ravaged by alcohol.

Alcoholism is also one of the most stubborn forms of drug ad-diction, very resistant to treatment. Many doctors who work with alcoholics admit that they have little success with them. The only groups that seem to be able to help are Alcoholics Anonymous, which depends on an almost religious adherence to a group ethic, and the Native American Church, which uses peyote in religious rituals and vigorously crusades against drinking among American Indians (see pages 123–24).

Not all regular drinkers become alcoholics. In fact, most regular drinkers are not addicted. Some people may inherit a tendency to become addicted because of peculiarities in their biochemistry or metabolism. Children of alcoholics are more likely to grow up to be alcoholics, but so are the children of two teetotalers. That sug-gests that a childhood lack of good role models for healthy drink-ing may also be an important factor.

One of the clearest signs of alcoholism is repeated drinking to get drunk. Alcoholics cannot limit their intake to a social drink or two; they invariably go much further. But drunkenness isn't much fun, either at the time or the following day. Why, then, do so many people consume overdoses of alcohol?

> Although I kept trying to use alcohol moderately, whenever I'd set out to get high on it, I would always keep on drinking till I got drunk, no matter how many resolutions I made not to . . . I've tried various drugs since those days and don't think anything comes close to alcohol in terms of raw strength and potential for trouble. I couldn't learn to control it well, and I see many people around me who have the same problem.
>
> — thirty-seven-year-old man, college professor

This question points up the main problem with alcohol. As noted earlier, most people like the early effects of the drug, which resemble those of stimulants, but taking more of it dramatically changes the quality of the effects. It isn't easy for people to learn how to stay within the dose range that makes them feel good; it is very easy to cross into the zone of unpleasant effects and regret it. Young people beginning to drink should recognize that this is a problem that they will have to deal with by acquiring experience. Many people — if they are metabolically normal, come from supportive families, and don't have serious psychological problems — learn how to control their intake of alcohol and keep from sliding into the trouble zone, but others do not.

Alcohol is one of the most difficult drugs to control because it is so strong and because the dose-related difference in its effects is so great. Used intelligently, alcohol can relieve stress. Some people even claim that alcohol promotes health. For example, some medical studies suggest that moderate drinking decreases the risk of heart attacks by reducing the clotting tendency of the blood and by improving the metabolizing of cholesterol. Wine lovers say that drinking wine with meals aids digestion. Some physicians think that old people benefit from alcohol in small amounts. These claims may be true. Unfortunately, some people cannot learn to drink moderately. Recovering alcoholics, for example, usually become drunks again very quickly if they try to drink socially.

There is no question that alcohol is the most toxic of all the drugs discussed in this book. Yet our own society has made alcohol its social drug of choice. It is widely available in many attractive forms, extensively advertised, and used to the point that it is hard to avoid. In certain groups, liquor is so much the required social lubricant that nondrinkers feel uncomfortable and out of place. Alcohol comes into people's lives at every turn. Friends give each other bottles of liquor as holiday gifts. Airlines sell drinks in flight and placate passengers with free drinks if planes are delayed unduly. Billboards and magazines everywhere extol the pleasures of drinking. Everyone in our society must learn to come to terms with this powerful drug.

Unless you are a Muslim or a Mormon or belong to some other group that prohibits its use altogether, you will have to learn how to refuse alcohol if you don't want to drink or how to drink it intelligently and not let your use get out of control.

Some Suggestions for Using Alcohol Wisely

1. Define what benefits you want from alcohol. Remember that alcohol is attractive because it can make people feel temporarily better, both physically and mentally. You can enjoy these good effects if you learn to use the drug carefully and purposefully. If you feel feverish and achy from flu, going to bed and taking a small drink may be a good remedy. If you walk into a party and feel awkward, anxious, and inhibited, a little alcohol may help you get into the swing of things.

2. It is good to make rules about when and where *not* to drink. For example, a person who uses alcohol to relax after a hard day shouldn't drink at the end of an easy one or before a day is done. No one should drink and drive.

3. Rules about times, places, and situations that are appropriate

for drinking help control the tendency of alcohol to get out of hand. You might decide to drink with friends but not by yourself, on weekends and holidays but not during the week, after sunset but not during the day.

4. Learn to regulate the amount of alcohol in your bloodstream. Once it's there, only time can get it out. You can control the rate of absorption of alcohol into your blood by drinking dilute forms of it rather than concentrated ones (for example, by adding water to wine and mixers to hard liquor). You can also make sure that you have food in your stomach before and during drinking. You can practice consuming alcoholic drinks slowly. Finally, you can practice saying no to more drinks when you've had enough.

5. Whenever you consume alcohol heavily, remember to drink plenty of plain water to offset fluid losses from increased urination. By doing so, you may moderate the next day's hangover.

6. Don't spend time with people who drink to excess or encourage you to drink more than you want.

7. Be careful about falling into patterns of regular drinking to deal with ongoing emotional problems, such as anxiety or depression. Alcohol may mask the symptoms temporarily, but it cannot solve the problems, and this kind of use is more likely to lead to dependence.

8. Adolescence, with its confusions, peer pressures, and tendency toward rebellion, is a time when unhealthy patterns of drug use can develop that may persist into later life and be very hard to break. Young people may think that they aren't as susceptible to dependence on alcohol as adults, but the evidence contradicts this view. Alcohol is a difficult drug to control at any age, and alcoholism doesn't appear overnight. It is the result of unwise drinking over time, beginning with the earliest experience with the drug.

9. Alcohol contains calories. If you are trying to lose weight, watch your intake.

10. The best way to protect yourself from the harmful effects of alcohol is not to drink it every day.
11. If you drink regularly, make sure that you maintain good habits of rest, exercise, and nutrition. In particular, take supplemental vitamin B-1 (thiamine), 100 milligrams a day on days that you drink. Alcohol selectively destroys this vitamin. Also, take milk thistle, a nontoxic herb that protects liver cells from chemical damage.
12. If you begin to suspect that you have problems with drinking, or if people who know you think that you do, seek help from professionals. It is difficult or impossible to deal with problem drinking without outside help.

Barbiturates and Other Sleeping Pills ("Downers")

This class of sedative-hypnotic drugs — loosely known as sleeping pills, or downers — has been around for some time. They are manufactured both legally and illegally and are widely used. Medical doctors prescribe these substances in low doses to calm people during the day and in higher doses to help them sleep at night. There are millions of people who take sleeping pills every night and can't fall asleep without them. Millions of others take downers for nonmedical reasons: to get high, to feel good, or to party.

Barbituric acid was discovered in 1864. Since then, a number of derivatives of it have been introduced. They are all known as barbiturates and are the most important drugs in this class. The first barbiturate sleeping drug, called barbital, appeared in 1903. The second, called phenobarbital, appeared in 1912. Hundreds of barbiturates are now known, and many are in use today.

Some of the barbiturates are slowly metabolized and eliminated by the kidneys. Barbital and phenobarbital are in this group and are known as long-acting barbiturates because their effects last twelve to twenty-four hours. They are used as daytime sedatives more than as nighttime hypnotics, and since they don't produce much euphoria or stimulation, few people take them to get high.

Another group of barbiturates is more rapidly metabolized by the liver. Their effects last six or seven hours, and they are called short acting. They include amobarbital (Amytal), pentobarbital (Nembutal), hexobarbital (Sombulex), and secobarbital (Seconal). These drugs behave very much like alcohol, giving pleasant feelings in low doses, especially as they begin to take effect. Therefore, some people seek them out to change the way they feel, and there is no shortage of these drugs on the black market.

Finally, there are very short-acting barbiturates that produce almost immediate unconsciousness when injected intravenously. Thiopental (Pentothal) is the main example; dentists and doctors use it as an anesthetic for surgical operations. Since it wipes out awareness quickly and leaves no memory of the experience, no one takes it for fun.

When people talk about taking downers, they usually mean the short-acting barbiturates or a few similar drugs that we will discuss later. All of these substances are like alcohol, and most of the statements in the alcohol section apply to downers as well (see pages 72–78). Sleeping pills can make people feel and look drunk, leave users with hangovers, kill when taken in overdose by knocking out the respiratory center of the brain, and produce stubborn addiction with dangerous withdrawal syndromes, marked in some cases by convulsions and death.

Since the similarities between downers and alcohol are so numerous, it might be easier to talk about how they differ.

Unlike alcohol, sleeping pills are noncaloric; the body cannot burn them as fuel but must metabolize them in other ways. They are also not as toxic as alcohol over time and don't cause the kind of liver disease and other medical damage so common in alcoholics. Tolerance for downers occurs, as with alcohol, but there is an important and curious difference. As people use downers regularly, tolerance for the effects on mood develops faster than tolerance for the lethal dose. For this reason, people run a greater risk of accidentally killing themselves with downers. For example, people who get into the habit of taking sleeping pills every night to fall asleep might start out with one a night, progress to two, then

> The barbiturate addict presents a shocking spectacle. He
> cannot coordinate, he staggers, falls off bar stools, goes to
> sleep in the middle of a sentence, drops food out of his
> mouth. He is confused, quarrelsome, and stupid. And
> he almost always uses other drugs, anything he can lay
> his hands on: alcohol, benzedrine, opiates, marijuana.
> Barbiturate users are looked down on in addict society:
> "Goof-ball bums. They got no class to them." . . . It seems
> to me that barbiturates cause the worst possible form of
> addiction, unsightly, deteriorating, difficult to treat.
>
> — **William S. Burroughs, from his novel *Naked Lunch* (1959)**

graduate to four to get the same effect. One night the dose that they need to fall asleep might also be the dose that stops their breathing.

Because their depressant effects are additive, combining alcohol and downers is especially dangerous. A dose of alcohol that a person is used to, combined with a dose of a downer that would be all right by itself, may lead to coma and death. Many people have died because they were ignorant of this fact.

As with alcohol, the effects of downers on mood are extremely variable, depending on individual personality, expectation, and setting. Some people who take sleeping pills feel nothing but sleepiness. Others fight off the sleepiness and say that they feel high. A dose of Seconal taken at a wild party might inspire violent excitement, whereas a person taking the same dose in a quiet room might be overcome with lethargy. Some medical patients have strange reactions to prescribed downers, becoming anxious and agitated instead of calm. Old people are likely to become intoxicated on ordinary doses, as are people with liver or kidney disease.

Most people take these drugs by mouth, but injectable forms are available. In hospitals, hypnotic doses of Nembutal are often

given by intramuscular injection, especially to patients who cannot take medicine by mouth. On the street, some users inject barbiturates intravenously (sometimes crushing and dissolving oral
preparations), a practice that greatly increases their toxicity.

Other users like to combine downers and stimulants, claiming
that the combined effect is more pleasant than either drug by
itself. A few such combinations are even made legally for medical use. One example, Dexamyl, is a mixture of amobarbital and
dextroamphetamine (Dexedrinc). Supposedly, the barbiturate
counteracts any tendency of the amphetamine to cause anxiety or
jitteriness, while the amphetamine reinforces the potential of the
barbiturate to produce euphoria. Similarly, people who use a lot of
cocaine say that drinking alcohol at the same time reduces the unpleasant side effects of that drug, while the cocaine keeps them
from getting drunk and minimizes hangovers. Although these
combinations probably do no harm when used occasionally, they
may have a higher potential for abuse than their components
would if used separately, because their combination makes it easier to take larger quantities of the drugs.

Dependence on barbiturates can occur in both medical patients
and street users. Doctors write vast numbers of prescriptions for
sleeping pills, and many people fall into the habit of taking them
every night. Certainly, it is appropriate to take these drugs when
insomnia is temporary and due to a specific, identifiable cause.
For instance, the death of a close friend or relative, the breakup of
a family, the loss of a job, or even moving may produce serious
disturbances of sleep, and sleeping pills may help during the crisis. Some people take these drugs to help them sleep on long
plane flights, during other kinds of travel, after periods of intense
work or stress, and when working shifts. There is no harm in taking sleeping pills a few nights in a row in such situations.

Problems arise when people take them every night over a long
time. Persistent insomnia is always a symptom of other trouble,
either physical or emotional. Sleeping pills treat only the symptom. Moreover, the sleep induced by downers is not the same as

There is no question that Quaalude can be dangerous when used irresponsibly or that it can be addicting. As a recreational drug, taken on occasion in a responsible manner, it seems to me safe and interesting and gives me an experience different from anything else.

— thirty-six-year-old man, drug counselor

natural sleep. It doesn't provide as much dreaming time, for one thing, and is likely to be followed by a hangover. Because drug-induced sleep may not supply all the needs of body and mind, over time it may aggravate an underlying problem. Although many people take sleeping pills regularly for years without having to increase the dose or suffering any obvious difficulties, this kind of usage is a form of drug dependence.

Taking downers as a means of dealing with feelings of depression or low self-esteem is probably the riskiest way of using them. Like alcohol, these drugs may mask the symptoms temporarily, but over time they often increase anxiety and depression, encouraging further drug-taking in a downward spiral that can end in suicide.

As we noted earlier, there are a number of nonbarbiturate downers, the most popular of which once was methaqualone, marketed under such brand names as Quaalude, Sopor, and Mandrax. Its effects are equivalent to those of the barbiturates, although on its own it is less likely to depress the respiratory center in overdose. Still, deaths have occurred as a result of combining alcohol and methaqualone. Street users talk about "luding out" — that is, taking Quaaludes and wine to produce a numb, euphoric state. Quaalude has gained a street reputation as a sex enhancer and party drug. Like all downers, it can lower inhibitions and reduce anxiety in the same way as alcohol. But also like alcohol, it will interfere with sexual performance in males and may make it more

DEPRESSANTS

difficult for women to experience orgasm. Real Quaalude is seldom available today, but look-alike tablets containing no methaqualone are commonly sold to gullible buyers on the black market.

Another downer, chloral hydrate, is the oldest sleeping drug still in medical use. Although rare today, abuse of it was not uncommon in the last century. Slipped into alcoholic drinks, it was the notorious "Mickey Finn," or "knockout drops," used to drug unsuspecting people into unconsciousness in order to rob or kidnap them.

Still other nonbarbiturate downers include glutethimide (Doriden), methyprylon (Noludar), ethchlorvynol (Placidyl), and paraldehyde. All of these drugs are used in medicine as hypnotics. They sometimes find their way to the black market, where users of illegal downers buy them. The benefits and dangers of these downers are the same as those of the barbiturates.

The most popular downer today is zolpidem (Ambien), widely prescribed as a sleeping pill and chemically different from the other drugs discussed here. Its manufacturer advertises it aggressively as safe and effective for regular use, but we think that it has all the drawbacks of other downers. It is addictive, does not reproduce natural sleep, and can be abused. (Users crush and snort the pills or cook them for injection.)

Suggestions for Using Downers Safely

1. Take sleeping pills by mouth in doses no higher than those recommended by doctors, pharmacists, or manufacturers. (Often, lower doses will do.)
2. Don't drive or operate machinery while under the influence of these drugs. Like alcohol, they impair judgment, coordination, and reflexes.
3. Exercise extreme caution about using downers in combination with alcohol or other depressant drugs.
4. Don't fall into the habit of relying on downers for sleep. Insomnia can usually be overcome by improving health; getting more exercise; cutting down on intake of stimulants, includ-

ing caffeine and tobacco; taking warm baths before bed; and by many other means not involving drugs.

5. Be wary of relying on these drugs to get you out of bad moods.
6. Don't take downers regularly in combination with stimulants.
7. Don't take downers if you are ill, especially if you have any liver or kidney problems, unless they are prescribed for you by a doctor who is aware of your medical problems.
8. If you find yourself becoming dependent on downers, with tolerance or the development of any unusual physical or mental symptoms, seek professional help.

Antianxiety Drugs

The third and last class of sedative-hypnotics consists of relatively new drugs, products of the modern pharmaceutical industry. Dating only to the mid-1950s, these drugs used to be called minor tranquilizers, terminology that is misleading. The word *minor* was supposed to distinguish these drugs from the "major" tranquilizers — compounds such as chlorpromazine (Thorazine), which is used to manage psychotic patients (see pages 170–71). Actually, these two kinds of tranquilizers are chemically and pharmacologically unrelated. Minor tranquilizers are not, as their name implies, mild drugs. There is nothing minor about their effects, the problems that they can cause, or their potential for abuse. Since their invention, the minor tranquilizers have achieved enormous popularity in medicine. Doctors have written millions upon millions of prescriptions for them, and pharmaceutical companies have made billions of dollars by promoting and selling them as antianxiety agents. In fact, these drugs have been among the most widely prescribed drugs in the world.

The first minor tranquilizer to be released to the world was meprobamate; it appeared in 1954 under the brand name Miltown (it was also marketed later as Equanil), and soon after its appearance, people were holding Miltown parties — taking the drug socially and recreationally, just to get high.

The most popular minor tranquilizers appeared in the 1960s

— a family of drugs called benzodiazepines. Some of the most famous are chlordiazepoxide (Librium), diazepam (Valium), triazolam (Halcion), alprazolam (Xanax), lorazepam (Ativan), temazepam (Restoril), and clonazepam (Klonopin). The manufacturer of Librium and Valium, once a small company selling vitamins and antacids, became one of the most powerful pharmaceutical corporations in the world.

The pharmaceutical industry has tried hard to convince doctors and patients that these chemicals are revolutionary drugs that specifically reduce anxiety, making people calm and relaxed. In fact, the benzodiazepines are just another variation on the theme of alcohol and other sedative-hypnotics, with the same tendency to produce adverse effects and dependence.

Compared with barbiturates, antianxiety drugs are safer in overdose and somewhat less dangerous in combination with alcohol. Also, the benzodiazepines are useful in relaxing tense muscles. As daytime sedatives, they produce less drowsiness than barbiturates, but they can still make driving dangerous and interfere with other motor skills, as well as with memory and clear thinking. As nighttime hypnotics, they induce sleep and may be preferable to barbiturates if anxiety or muscle tension is present or if the patient needs a sleeping pill for more than a few nights in a row. Again, however, they do not reproduce natural sleep.

Street users of benzodiazepines take them for the same reasons that they take illegal downers: to improve mood, reduce anxiety and inhibitions, and promote social interaction.

Abuse of the minor tranquilizers, particularly of Miltown, Librium, and Valium, began in the 1950s and was the direct result of irresponsible marketing and prescribing practices. In promoting these drugs, the manufacturers portrayed stresses of everyday life as diseases. For example, ads in medical journals recommended Librium for the college student whose "newly stimulated intellectual curiosity may make her more sensitive to and apprehensive about unstable national and world conditions" (in other words, if the news freaks you out, pop a Librium). Other ads suggested giving tranquilizers to harried mothers and bored housewives, to "the woman who can't get along with her new daughter-in-law," and to "the newcomer in town who can't make friends."

Critics of this kind of salesmanship pointed out that women were targets far more often than men. Just as pharmaceutical companies encouraged doctors to prescribe amphetamines to depressed housewives in the 1960s, they have urged doctors to give benzodiazepines to anxious women. Increasing opposition to these practices has curtailed them to some extent.

A newer drug of this class deserves special comment. Flunitrazepam (Rohypnol) is not approved in the United States but is marketed in the rest of the world as a remedy for insomnia and as a pre-anesthetic medication for patients undergoing surgery. It is much more potent than Valium, lasts longer (eight hours or more), and has become widely available on the black market under the name "roofies." Most users take it with other drugs. For example, they use it to enhance the high of low-quality heroin or to come down off crack cocaine. Most often, people mix it with alcohol, a potentially dangerous combination that can cause disorientation, amnesia, respiratory depression, and death. Rohypnol has gained notoriety as a "date rape" drug, when women unknowingly consume alcoholic beverages spiked with it. Some wake up naked in unfamiliar surroundings with no memory of what happened to them, and some have been sexually assaulted.

Using tranquilizers to deal with everyday difficulties causes the same problem associated with all depressant drugs: long-term dependence of a particularly stubborn kind. It is *very* difficult to wean people off benzodiazepines, since the withdrawal is unpleasant and dangerous. (Abrupt cessation can cause seizures and respiratory arrest.) Even though the health consequences of dependence on antianxiety drugs may be less severe than those of dependence on alcohol, the result is the same. There is no treatment of the underlying causes of anxiety, merely the creation of a legal drug habit.

The maker of Valium and Librium at one time pushed the idea

of using these drugs to treat alcoholics, and many doctors followed their advice. When the alcoholics drank less, the doctors imagined that they had achieved something, but all they had really done was to substitute one sedative-hypnotic for another. (One expert on alcoholism has called Valium "whiskey in a pill.")

Throughout history, doctors have relied on mood-altering drugs to deal with difficult patients. Psychoactive drugs change the way that people feel, satisfy patients' desire for medicine, and make doctors feel that they have been useful — or at least make the patients go away. A hundred years ago, opium and alcohol were the mainstays of medical treatment, along with cannabis (marijuana). At the turn of the twentieth century, doctors doled out cocaine for all sorts of complaints. Today, the benzodiazepines are some of the most widely consumed drugs. Certainly, they have their place in medicine, but prescribing them for weeks or months at a time to people who are anxious, depressed, or unable to sleep is symptomatic treatment of the worst sort.

Suggestions for Avoiding Trouble with Tranquilizers

1. Be aware that these drugs are strong depressants, similar in effect to alcohol, and can cause unpleasant reactions and dependence.
2. All of the cautions about downers apply to the minor tranquilizers as well.
3. If you take these drugs, whether by medical prescription or for fun, don't use them every day. Take them intermittently or occasionally to avoid falling into a pattern of habitual use.

GHB (Gammahydroxybutyrate)

GHB is an endogenous downer, made in small amounts in the brain as a metabolite of the sedative neurotransmitter GABA. In studies that go back to 1960, scientists have found it to be a safe inducer of sleep that does not cause tolerance or addiction. In the early 1990s, synthetic GHB became popular among body builders because it stimulates the pituitary gland to release growth hormone, which can help convert fat to muscle. The drug was unregulated, and manufacturers sold it through mail-order catalogs and to health food stores, where it was often described as a nutrient rather than a drug.

A teaspoon of GHB powder (about 2.5 grams), dissolved in warm water and taken on an empty stomach, produces within fifteen minutes a dramatic effect akin to alcohol or methaqualone intoxication. Most people find the effect pleasant, but in some individuals, especially with higher doses, GHB can cause nausea and marked incoordination, along with "hypersomnolence" (a kind of temporary stupor, in which people can stop breathing for periods). When GHB is combined with alcohol, adverse effects are more likely.

Unlike most psychoactive drugs and certainly most depressants, GHB increases rather than suppresses dreaming, and the sleep that it induces closely resembles natural sleep. It does not pose the risks of other drugs in this class, but users should be aware of the potential dangers of overdose, especially in situations that require full alertness, such as driving.

The Food and Drug Administration (FDA) has declared GHB to be a prescription drug and has halted distribution of it through the mail and through health food stores. The Drug Enforcement Administration has made it a controlled substance. In response, black-market manufacture of it has increased.

General Anesthetics

General anesthetics are powerful depressants used in surgery to make people insensible to pain. General anesthetics are gases or volatile liquids administered by inhalation through a mask placed over the face or tubes in the throat. Most are never seen outside operating rooms, but a few have been popular recreational drugs in the past, and one — nitrous oxide, or laughing gas — is still in common nonmedical use.

When inhaled, general anesthetics enter the blood very rapidly, depressing brain function within seconds. The stronger ones quickly produce complete unconsciousness, a state that lasts as long as the drug is administered and for a short time afterward. Like all depressants, general anesthetics can kill by shutting down the respiratory center and other vital functions. During surgery, therefore, a specially trained doctor or technician must monitor the administration of the drugs and the moment-to-moment condition of the patient.

In low doses, general anesthetics produce changes in consciousness similar to alcohol and sedative-hypnotics, and for many years people have experimented with general anesthetics to get high and to explore their minds.

Chloroform is one of the oldest drugs in this group. Since it is very toxic, it is no longer used. Years ago, people sometimes sniffed the fumes of liquid chloroform or swallowed small amounts in order to experience what disapproving critics called a "cheap drunk."

The era of surgical anesthesia began in 1846, when a dentist in Boston demonstrated that ether could safely render patients insensible to the pain of operations. Today, ether (or, more correctly, diethyl ether) is still widely used to induce unconsciousness before surgery. Ether is a volatile liquid, easily administered to people through breathing masks. It has a strong chemical smell, and its main disadvantage is that its fumes make an extremely explosive mixture with air. Great care must be taken when ether is in use to prevent violent explosions from accidental sparks or flames. Another disadvantage of ether is that overdoses of it rapidly put people into deep comas and stop their respiration.

Before 1846, surgery was horribly painful; patients had to be tied down, and their screams could be heard far from the operating room. The discovery of ether anesthesia revolutionized surgery. Even before this event — as long ago as 1800 — ether was a well-known curiosity; many people played with it just to experience its unusual effects on consciousness.

Ether parties were popular throughout the 1800s. People would gather for the express purpose of sniffing the fumes or drinking tiny doses of the liquid. When the drug was used in this way, its effects came on in a few minutes and ended within a half-hour. As might be expected, the reactions were highly variable, just as with alcohol. But although there are reports of a few "ether addicts" from this period, most people probably tried the drug only once or twice out of curiosity. A few writers of the time claimed that ether gave them profound insights into the nature of reality and even mystical revelations. (An 1874 book by the American physician Benjamin Paul Blood was titled *The Anesthetic Revelation and the Gist of Philosophy*.) Occasionally, people still experiment with ether, but if they like the effect that it gives, they tend to look for other drugs that are less toxic, don't smell as bad, and won't blow up so easily.

Nitrous oxide is such a drug. A gas with only a faint odor, it is relatively nontoxic and also nonflammable — although it will support combustion the way oxygen does and should be kept away from flames. Discovered in the late 1700s, nitrous oxide was quickly found to produce interesting changes in consciousness, as well as insensitivity to pain. Oddly enough, no one thought to use it in surgery until after the demonstration of ether anesthesia.

Nitrous oxide is a weaker drug than ether and the other general anesthetics; it does not produce complete loss of consciousness or anesthesia deep enough for major surgery. Nor is it so strong as to stop respiration. It is often used by itself in dentistry and minor surgery. In addition, many hospital anesthesiologists like to begin an operation by having the patient breathe nitrous oxide, then shift to ether and stronger drugs when the patient becomes totally relaxed and semiconscious.

People have been experimenting with nitrous oxide as a curiosity for the past two hundred years. Its effects, which come on within seconds, last as long as the gas is breathed, then disappear suddenly when it is stopped. Artists, writers, and philosophers have breathed nitrous oxide over and over in pursuit of elusive insights — revelations that seem overpowering under the influence of the gas but that evaporate as soon as normal consciousness returns. When the English poet laureate Robert Southey tried the gas at a nitrous oxide party in London in the 1790s, he commented afterward that the atmosphere of the highest of all possible heavens was no doubt composed of nitrous oxide.

On the other hand, many others have used nitrous oxide for less spiritual ends, especially to get hilariously intoxicated. The name "laughing gas" comes from a time when traveling medicine shows and carnivals would invite the public to pay a small price for a minute's worth of nitrous oxide. In these rowdy settings, the gas commonly produced silliness and uncontrollable laughter. Often, the laughers would stop in sudden confusion when the effect of the drug came to its abrupt end.

Today, nitrous oxide is available in many dentists' offices. Aware that people like to get high on it, some dentists give nitrous oxide even for routine procedures such as cleaning teeth. A fair number of tanks of the gas regularly disappear from hospitals and medical supply houses to find their way into the homes of recreational users. Many more people obtain smaller cylinders of the gas from restaurant suppliers, who use it to pressurize instant whipped cream cans. Some people even buy cans of instant whipped cream and attempt to get the gas out of the cans without the cream. Balloons of nitrous oxide are sold at some rock concerts.

Physicians and dentists have long considered nitrous oxide to be a safe pharmacological agent. Nevertheless, there is some evidence that excessive or prolonged use of it can damage the bone marrow and nervous system by interfering with the action of vitamin B-12. Moreover, its use in nonmedical settings presents several hazards that users should keep in mind. Breathing it directly from pressurized tanks is dangerous for two reasons. First, gas flowing from such tanks is very cold — cold enough to cause frostbite to noses, lips, and (most serious) vocal cords. Because users are anesthetized, they may be unaware of such injuries until it is too late. Second, because nitrous oxide does not support life, it should be mixed with oxygen if it is to be breathed for more than a few minutes. People throwing private parties that feature nitrous oxide seldom supply oxygen tanks, and people have died of asphyxiation by breathing straight nitrous oxide through a face mask. One way to avoid these dangers is to fill balloons with nitrous oxide from a tank and inhale it from the balloons.

Further, nitrous oxide rapidly leads to complete loss of motor control, and anyone who breathes it while standing will soon reel about and fall down. Therefore, the only truly safe positions for trying the gas are sitting and lying down. Serious injuries have resulted when people inhale laughing gas while standing in front of an open window, driving a car, or operating machinery. Others have been badly hurt by accidentally pulling a heavy tank of nitrous oxide over onto themselves while intoxicated.

People who breathe nitrous oxide for more than a few minutes at a time may experience nausea, especially if they have just eaten. They may also feel hung over for some time after. Addiction to nitrous oxide is a real possibility. Addicts may suffer serious mood and personality changes in addition to the bone marrow and nervous system damage already mentioned.

Warnings About Nitrous Oxide

1. Never breathe nitrous oxide directly from a pressurized tank.
2. Never breathe nitrous oxide for more than a few minutes at a time.
3. Do not use nitrous oxide regularly over long periods of time.
4. Never breathe nitrous oxide while standing up or while doing anything that requires normal motor coordination.

Narcotics

The word *narcotic* comes from a Greek word meaning "stupor." Stupor is a state of reduced sensibility that has given rise to our familiar adjective *stupid*. Narcotics are drugs that can produce stupors by depressing brain function, but their depressant action is different from that of sedative-hypnotics or general anesthetics.

The parent of all narcotic drugs is opium, a dark gummy solid made from the opium poppy. Opium poppies are striking flowers, probably native to southern Europe and western Asia but now cultivated all over the world. As the flowers wither, the green pods, which contain many tiny seeds, begin to ripen and swell. If the pods are allowed to ripen fully, they turn brown and dry, whereupon the edible seeds can be gathered for use in cooking. While still unripe, the pods contain a milky juice that can be collected by letting it ooze from knife cuts. When dried, this juice is crude opium.

One of the oldest of all drugs, opium was used in prehistoric times; the ancient Greeks recognized its pain-relieving properties. Throughout history, opium has been an important item of commerce, and in some periods, it was the most widely used medical drug.

Opium can be taken by mouth or it can be smoked, but since smoking was unknown in Europe and Asia until Columbus brought news of it from the New World, opium smoking did not exist before 1492. Although the Chinese had used opium for centuries, widespread opium addiction did not occur in China until the early 1700s, when Portuguese sailors introduced the practice of mixing it with tobacco and smoking it. Many oral preparations of opium were made in the past. Two that survive into our own times are paregoric, a dilute tincture of opium combined with camphor, and deodorized tincture of opium, formerly known as laudanum, which is more concentrated.

Crude opium tastes very bitter and contains more than twenty different drugs, of which the most important is morphine. Named for Morpheus, the Greek god of dreams, morphine was isolated from opium in 1803 by a German pharmacist — an event that marked the beginning of the modern era of drug treatment, because it was the first time that an active principle was extracted from a drug plant. Morphine is prepared as a soluble white powder that can be mixed with water and injected into the body. Given by injection, it is a far more powerful and dangerous drug than when taken by mouth. Injection of drugs is relatively recent, dating only to the invention of the hypodermic syringe in 1853. Interestingly, the world's first morphine addict was the wife of the man who came up with that device.

Codeine (methylmorphine) is another natural constituent of opium. More active by mouth than other narcotics, it is a weaker pain reliever than morphine, and doctors frequently prescribe it today to treat moderate pain.

In the late 1800s, chemists began to experiment with variations on molecules of morphine and other compounds of opium. One of the drugs that they produced was heroin, a simple derivative of morphine first made available in 1898. Heroin (diacetylmorphine) is more potent than morphine — that is, it produces the same effect in smaller doses — but otherwise the two are very similar. In fact, the body promptly reconverts heroin to morphine. First marketed as a safe cough suppressant, heroin was declared to be nonaddictive, a claim that many users did not discover to be false until it was too late.

Drugs derived from morphine and other opium compounds are called opiates. Today, many hundreds of opiates are known; some are semisynthetic derivatives, like heroin, and others are purely synthetic, like Demerol. In general, all of the opiates produce similar effects. They differ from each other in potency, duration of action, how active they are by mouth, and how much mood change they cause relative to their physical effects. Opiates that are more potent, shorter acting, and more active by injection lend themselves more easily to abuse.

The main effects of opium and its derivatives are on the brain and the bowel. In the brain, these drugs cause relief of pain, suppression of the cough center, stimulation of the vomiting center, relaxation, and drowsiness. They may also cause mental clouding and inability to concentrate. Although they may induce sleep, they do not do so as reliably as the sedative-hypnotics. Some people become anxious, restless, and wakeful after taking opiates; others fall into a kind of twilight sleep marked by vivid dreams. Opium and opiates cause the pupils to contract, sometimes to tiny pinpoints; they also cause nausea and sweating, which can be profuse and uncomfortable. Larger doses often produce vomiting and depression of breathing. High doses of opiates, especially by injection, can cause death by stopping respiration, just like other strong depressants.

Because narcotics paralyze intestinal muscles, doctors prescribe them to treat diarrhea, particularly when it is accompanied by painful cramps. Regular use of opiates commonly results in chronic constipation.

In medicine today, narcotics are the main drugs used to treat severe pain. They are also prescribed to control bad coughs. In proper doses, when they are really needed, opiates are safe and extremely effective. Anyone who has experienced the rapid relief of terrible pain by narcotics knows what a blessing they can be. By allowing sick and injured people to take their mind off pain, to feel better, to relax and rest, narcotics can also indirectly promote healing. Opium and its derivatives have earned a secure place in treatment over many years of medical experience.

Yet narcotics have generated more fear and argument than any other class of drugs. The reason, of course, is their potential to cause addiction, a problem that was probably recognized even by ancient peoples when the only form available was crude opium, from poppies.

Narcotics addiction provides the classic model of drug dependence, and many of our current notions of drug abuse are based on it. For example, the fundamental principle that addiction consists of three features — craving for the drug, tolerance, and withdrawal — developed from observations of opiate addicts. Many popular beliefs about narcotics are untrue, however, and the whole subject is highly contaminated by prejudice and emotion.

There is no question that dependence on narcotics can develop quickly with repeated administration. When medical patients re-

> Laudanum gave me repose, not sleep; but you, I believe,
> know how divine that repose is, what a spot of enchant-
> ment, a green spot of fountains and flowers and trees in
> the very heart of a waste of sands!
>
> — Samuel Taylor Coleridge (1772–1834), from a 1798 letter
>   to George H. Coleridge

ceive morphine by injection every four hours, some degree of dependence can occur in as few as twenty-four hours. If the drug is
stopped even after a short period of use, mild withdrawal symptoms may occur — including sweating, nausea, weakness, headache, restlessness, and increased sensitivity to pain.

Tolerance for narcotics also develops rapidly and can reach
striking levels. The usual pain-relieving dose of tincture of opium
(laudanum) is twenty drops in a glass of water, repeated every four
to six hours if necessary. In England in the early 1800s, a number
of writers and artists were laudanum addicts with phenomenal
habits. The poet Samuel Taylor Coleridge, for example, consumed
as much as two *quarts* of laudanum a week. Thomas De Quincey,
best known for his *Confessions of an English Opium Eater,* took up
to eight thousand drops a day. Such doses would certainly kill people who have not built up their tolerance.

There is an important difference between tolerance for narcotics and tolerance for sedative-hypnotics. As we noted earlier, tolerance for the active dose of some sedative-hypnotics develops more
rapidly than does tolerance for the lethal dose, a process that can
— and does — result in fatal accidents. This is not the case with
narcotics, however, which makes them safer drugs. Heroin addicts occasionally die of overdoses, but such deaths result from
poor quality control in street supplies of the drug rather than from
the properties of heroin itself. (For example, an addict used to a
certain dose of impure street heroin may buy a packet of the drug

that, by accident, hasn't been cut as much as usual; injecting what he thinks is the right dose, he can unwittingly take too much.)

Withdrawal from narcotics is also less hazardous than withdrawal from sedative-hypnotics. Alcohol, downers, and the minor tranquilizers can produce violent withdrawal, marked by convulsions and, sometimes, death. Narcotic withdrawal can be intensely unpleasant, but it is not life threatening.

Also, the physical consequences of long-term narcotics use are minor compared with those of alcohol. People can take opium and opiates every day for years and remain in good health, provided they maintain good habits of hygiene and nutrition. There are many documented cases of opium and morphine addicts who, despite a heavy lifelong habit, survived to a ripe old age, remaining healthy to the end. Thomas De Quincey, for instance, who started taking laudanum for a toothache as a college student, died at seventy-four, still an addict. The worst medical effect of regular opiate use is severe and chronic constipation, which can be distressing but hardly compares to the cirrhosis of the liver and degeneration of the nervous system so commonly seen in chronic alcoholics.

Some addicts even claim that opiates help them to resist disease. Many heroin users say that they don't get colds or other respiratory infections as long as they take their drug. Since the symptoms of heroin withdrawal resemble those of a respiratory flu, it is possible that the drug somehow suppresses this kind of reaction. No one has investigated this claim of addicts; it would make an interesting subject of research.

The strong craving that characterizes opiate addiction has inspired many critics of narcotics to suggest that they destroy the will and moral sense, turning normal people into fiends and degenerates. Actually, cravings for opiates are no different from cravings for alcohol among alcoholics, and they are less strong than cravings for cigarettes, because nicotine is a more addictive drug.

The antisocial behavior of some opiate addicts seems more a function of personality, cultural background, expectation, and set-

> Junk is not a kick. It is a way of life.
>
> — William S. Burroughs, from his novel *Junky* (1953)

ting than of the drugs. Medical patients who become addicted to morphine in a hospital setting usually do not conform to stereotypes of addicts. They often have little difficulty separating themselves from narcotics once they are better and leave the hospital setting. People who can afford to support an opiate habit legally often lead normal lives while also being addicted. There are numerous cases on record of doctors and nurses who were opiate addicts yet seemed outwardly normal and fulfilled their professional and social responsibilities.

Apparently, a crucial difference exists between people who become addicted by chance or through medical circumstance and those who seek out opiates as a means of dealing with life's everyday difficulties. As with other depressants, serious dependence is most likely to develop when people use the drugs to screen out feelings of anxiety, depression, or boredom. Narcotics may be particularly seductive because they insulate people from discomfort and pain, seem to make time pass more rapidly, and create an inner world of security and comfort into which users can temporarily retreat from reality and its demands.

In the twenty-first century, heroin addiction is at epidemic levels worldwide. Thanks in no small part to America's "war on drugs," the world's supply of raw opium — already at record highs — is now expected to double every five years. The opium poppy grows well all over the world, but harvesting opium is very labor intensive. In countries with large pools of laborers willing to work for brief periods at low pay, no crop is more profitable than poppies. Converting raw gummy black opium into white powder heroin is also easier than you might think, much simpler than distilling alcohol, for example. It does not take much trouble or equipment to set up a heroin factory or to move it to another location if necessary. International heroin trafficking is a multibillion-dollar-a-year, mafia-controlled global system with supply routes connecting third-world producers with first-world consumers.

Heroin addiction condemns many people, especially the young, to unproductive lives of great hardship and cost to themselves and society and is rightly a cause for serious concern. It is not only the downtrodden poor of urban ghettos who become heroin addicts but the children of all social and economic classes and many of their parents as well. In opium-producing countries, populations of heroin addicts are steadily rising and contributing to the spread of serious communicable diseases like AIDS (acquired immune deficiency syndrome) and viral hepatitis.

When ordinary people look at heroin addicts, what they mostly see are victims of grinding social forces. Visible addicts tend to be in trouble, involved with crime, in poor health, purposeless, psychologically damaged, unhappy, and unable to get out of their grim predicament. Many of these conditions are more the result of society's blunders in trying to control the abuse of drugs than of heroin itself.

Heroin is often portrayed as the very worst of all possible drugs, a "devil drug," always productive of evil and somehow especially dangerous. In reality, it isn't very different from morphine, an accepted medical drug. Heroin is strictly illegal in the United States; even doctors cannot obtain it to use on patients. It is legal in England, however, where doctors do use it, sometimes with good results. Because it is more potent than morphine, it is sometimes a better pain reliever in small doses for people who are too sensitive to the nauseating effect of morphine.

By making heroin illegal, a society ensures that its heroin addicts will all be criminals. It is clear that drug laws have done nothing to discourage people from becoming addicts. There are more addicts than ever, and the kinds of addiction are worse than before those laws were passed.

The prohibition of opiates has spawned an ugly criminal underworld, given rise to powerful drug warlords, and led to the widespread corruption of public officials. Campaigns to stamp out heroin, while popular with politicians, have invariably had the opposite of their intended effect, ultimately causing more heroin to enter the world market, not less. And because people are so susceptible to opiate addiction, when the supply of heroin increases, so does demand for the drug.

Since the mid-1990s, opium production has reached unprecedented levels in southeast and southwest Asia, and opium farming has extended into new areas in central Asia and Latin America. This explosive growth has caused the street price of the drug to plummet. In the mid-1990s, the street price for a gram of highly adulterated material was about $1,000. Today users pay $70 to $100 for a gram of heroin that may be 80 percent pure.

Because heroin is so abundant and cheap, new users tend to snort or smoke the drug, rather than inject it into a muscle or vein, which is more cost efficient. Heroin's reputation, long tainted by its association with the hypodermic needle, is beginning to change, especially among young people. They perceive heroin not as a dangerous and unsavory "ghetto drug" but rather as a chic, leading-edge intoxicant, and the taking of it has become something of a fashion statement. Although avoiding the needle, this group is ingesting large quantities of high-purity heroin and progressing rapidly toward addiction.

The aspects of addiction that are attributable directly to heroin have to do with the high potency of the drug, its short duration of action, and the tendency for people to use it intravenously. (The health problems associated with intravenous drug use are discussed in Chapter 12.) Heroin can be smoked (mixed with tobacco or marijuana), snuffed up the nose, or injected under the skin, into a muscle, or into a vein. By any of these routes, it is much more powerful than by mouth. Oddly enough, most people who try heroin for the first time, by whatever route, don't find it pleasant; more often than not, they experience little besides nausea, sweating, and a general feeling of discomfort. After a few doses, however — particularly when it is injected directly into the blood-

> There's nothing like a heroin rush. I started shooting heroin when I was fourteen. It's just the most intense, wonderful feeling. I was always interested in getting high. One of my favorite ways when I was little was rolling down big hills. I did it over and over. Heroin has caused me a lot of problems. I'm scared of withdrawal, but I know I have to do it. I'm also interested in meditation and things like that, but I worry that I will always be tempted to feel the heroin rush again, because nothing else I've tried comes close to it.
>
> — seventeen-year-old woman, patient in a private addiction treatment center

stream — some people experience an intense "rush" of good feeling that lasts for a few minutes, and then they become drowsy.

To hear heroin addicts talk about the intensity of this rush is both fascinating and frightening. Some say that it is the most pleasurable sensation that they have ever felt, much more powerful than orgasm. Users who get this experience from mainlining heroin — not all do — find it hard to appreciate other kinds of highs, especially nondrug highs, which tend to be more subtle. The power of the heroin rush to make people uninterested in other experiences and totally committed to heroin is so overwhelming as to be an argument against ever trying the drug at all. One junkie expressed this sentiment in a much-quoted line: "It's so good, don't even try it once."

Nonintravenous heroin doesn't give nearly as intense a rush and so is less addicting. People who snort heroin can do so off and on for long periods of time without becoming strongly addicted. Even people who inject it subcutaneously ("skin-popping") can sometimes avoid full-blown dependence, because they are able to confine their use of the drug to occasional sprees. There is no question that some users can mainline heroin only once in a while, usually shooting the drug only in certain situations — to reduce anxiety in personal relationships, for example, or to feel good at weekend parties. In street jargon, this sort of occasional use of heroin is known as "chipping," and it seems that some lucky individuals remain successful chippers over months and even years. Unfortunately, a high percentage of chippers eventually go on to become addicted, so the practice is risky. Most junkies began as chippers, and many never thought that they would become addicts.

Once physical dependence develops, the need to avoid withdrawal becomes a powerful motive for taking more of the drug. Three to eight hours after her last dose, a heroin addict will begin to feel sick, and unless she takes another fix, these feelings will grow more and more intense.

Although heroin remains the most popular street opiate, many people have been discovering another poppy derivative — oxycodone. A semisynthetic opiate, oxycodone once was best known in combination forms: blended with aspirin as Percodan and with acetaminophen as Percocet, both widely prescribed drugs for pain. In 1995, the FDA approved Oxycontin, a more potent, time-release version of oxycodone. Aggressive marketing quickly made Oxycontin a blockbuster drug, and it soon became immensely popular with heroin addicts, who found that snorting the crushed pills delivered the full twelve-hour dose all at once. Since the late 1990s, Oxycontin has been rampant in areas where prescription drug abuse is common, such as working-class communities and Appalachia. In that region, it is known as "hillbilly heroin."

It is too bad that whole opium has disappeared from our society. When eaten, it is a much safer drug — less concentrated, longer acting, and easier to form a stable relationship with than other forms. Because it is a gummy solid, it cannot be injected directly into the bloodstream, and though people can certainly become addicted to it — as they did in England and America in the 1800s — the risk is much lower. Taking opium orally doesn't give a rush, and high doses cause unpleasant nausea, encouraging users to moderate their intake. Smoking opium puts drugs into the blood and brain more directly and has a higher potential for abuse.

Many junkies are as addicted to giving themselves intravenous injections as they are to the effects of heroin. Some addicts experiment with shooting other drugs, and some combine other drugs with their heroin. For instance, some addicts mix heroin and cocaine into a "speedball" that gives an intense euphoric effect. Of course, this practice is dangerous, much more so than combinations of stimulants and depressants taken by mouth.

Treatments of narcotics addiction are not very satisfactory. The physical component of an opiate habit can be broken fairly easily by withdrawing people gradually and treating symptoms as they develop. As with cigarette addiction, however, the relapse rate is very high, and junkies often go back to being junkies even after being drug-free for months or years.

Heroin maintenance — that is, supplying addicts with pure, legal heroin in some sort of supervised setting — has been proposed as a possible treatment, but our society, unwilling to abandon its prohibitionist mentality, has been unwilling to try it, even as an experiment. Instead, it has supported maintenance with methadone, a synthetic opiate that is active by mouth and has a long duration of effect. Oral methadone is an addicting narcotic but gives little euphoria. It does block the effect of heroin, however, and so may reduce a junkie's motivation to shoot heroin. Some addicts sign into methadone programs only to take a break from the street scene; after a time, they go right back to their old ways. Other addicts, if they are highly motivated, can use methadone programs to help them break their heroin habit once and for all.

The main advantage of methadone maintenance is that it is better than leading a criminal life. The real problem with it is that it doesn't go to the root of addiction. Nor does it show heroin users how to get high in more natural, less restricting ways. It offers

> The first opiate I ever took was codeine . . . It made me feel
> right for the first time in my life . . . I never felt right from as
> far back as I can remember, and I was always trying differ-
> ent ways to change how I felt. I used lots of drugs, but
> none of them really did it for me. Codeine was a revelation,
> and I've been an opiate user ever since . . . Opiates have
> caused me lots of trouble, but what they do for my head is
> worth it.
>
> — **thirty-four-year-old woman, rock singer**

them no help with the problems that led them to abuse heroin in
the first place. All it does is substitute one narcotic for another; the
addict remains an addict, albeit in a less destructive way.

(A new semisynthetic opiate called buprenorphine has recently
gained attention as a treatment for heroin addiction. It blocks the
high of heroin and can be given at higher doses than other opiates
without suppressing breathing. The FDA approved buprenorphine in 2002. An advantage for addicts is that they can get this
drug directly from doctors rather than only from special clinics.)

No matter how you look at it, heroin addiction limits your personal freedom. Like cigarette addicts, junkies cannot go anywhere
or do anything without thinking about where their next fix is coming from. Unlike a cigarette addict, they cannot buy their drug for
a reasonable price at the corner store, and they will become really
sick if they cannot get it.

Nowadays, heroin use is becoming more and more common —
invading affluent and respectable segments of society. In some
circles, it is fashionable to try heroin or use it occasionally, particularly by means of "chasing the dragon," the practice of heating the
drug on tinfoil and inhaling the vapors. Though the medical dangers of heroin have certainly been exaggerated, the risk of addiction is real.

If you do not try heroin, you will not use it. If you do not use it, you will never become addicted.

Many questions about opiate addiction remain unanswered. How much of it is biochemical and how much is psychological? Opiate molecules interact with special receptor sites on nerve cells in the brain. Might addiction be the result of suppression of the brain's own opiate-like molecules, the endorphins? Why do some people who try opiates find them so compelling that they go on to become addicts while others do not? Is this a matter of differences in brain chemistry or differences in personality? Unfortunately, the answers are still eluding scientists.

Given these uncertainties, it is impossible to say who is at greatest risk of addiction and who is not. There is no assurance that you will not become an addict once you start using opiates regularly, and there is no way to take the drugs *and* protect yourself from that possibility. Furthermore, once addiction develops, there is no reliable method of breaking it.

Precautions About Narcotics

1. Opium and its derivatives are powerful drugs that should be reserved for treating severe physical pain and discomfort.
2. Taking narcotics to reduce anxiety or depression, or just to feel good in the absence of physical pain, can easily lead to habitual use and addiction.
3. Never inject a narcotic into your body for nonmedical purposes.
4. If you ever try a narcotic intravenously and feel overwhelming pleasure, *never repeat it.*
5. If you begin to use narcotics regularly, by any method, and think that you can avoid going on to intravenous use and addiction, remember: most junkies thought that, too.

SUGGESTED READING

Drinking Occasions: Comparative Perspectives on Alcohol and Culture by Dwight B. Heath (Philadelphia: Brunner/Mazel, 2000) is an excellent look at different approaches to alcohol use around the world. Evelyn Waugh's *Brideshead Revisited* (Boston: Back Bay Books, 1999) describes the evolution of an English alcoholic. For a view of the use and abuse of alcohol on this side of the Atlantic, see *The Alcohol Republic: An American Tradition* by W. J. Rorabaugh (New York: Oxford University Press, 1979). Andrew Barr examines Americans' drinking habits in *Drink: A Social History of America* (New York: Carroll & Graf, 1999).

Several excellent films dramatize the problem of alcoholism. One classic is *The Lost Weekend*, about an alcoholic writer played by Ray Milland. *Days of Wine and Roses*, starring Jack Lemmon and Lee Remick, is an agonizing portrait of a pair of alcoholics whose lives are destroyed by drinking. An equally moving account of a person ravaged by alcohol (and other drugs) is *The Rose*, based on the life of the late rock singer Janis Joplin. *Only When I Laugh*, starring Marsha Mason as an alcoholic mother, takes a somewhat more humorous view of the problem drinker.

A novel in which downers figure prominently is Jacqueline Susann's *Valley of the Dolls* (New York: Bantam, 1967), which was also made into a movie. The minor tranquilizers and their manufacturers are strongly criticized in *The Tranquilizing of America: Pill Popping and the American Way of Life* by Richard Hughes and Robert Brewin (New York: Harcourt Brace Jovanovich, 1979, now out of print). One woman's personal story of addiction to Valium is told in *I'm Dancing as Fast as I Can* by Barbara Gordon (New York: Harper & Row, 1979).

A short but entertaining and informative book on nitrous oxide is *Laughing Gas (Nitrous Oxide)*, edited by Michael Sheldin and David Wallechinsky, with Saunie Salyer (revised edition; Berkeley, Calif.: And/Or Press, 1992).

The history of opium since ancient times is presented in *Flowers in the Blood: The Story of Opium* by Dean Latimer and Jeff Goldberg (New York: Franklin Watts, 1981). An excellent look at the history of opium in the United States is *Dark Paradise: A History of Opiate Addiction in America* by David T. Courtwright (Cambridge, Mass.: Harvard University Press, 2001). For a portrait of opium smoking in nineteenth-century China, see *The Fall of the God of Money* by Keith McMahon (Lanham, Md.: Rowman and Littlefield, 2002). Thomas De Quincey's

Confessions of an English Opium Eater, first published in 1821, is available in a modern edition (New York: Penguin, 1971). *The Opium Eater: A Life of Thomas De Quincey* by Grevel Lindop (Mineola, N.Y.: Dover, 1995) is a fascinating biography of the man who became world famous at the age of thirty-six, when his *Confessions* appeared. A number of novels concern opium, among them Charles Dickens's last work, *The Mystery of Edwin Drood,* written in 1870 and concluded by Leon Garfield (reissue edition; Oxford: Clarendon, 1987), and Wilkie Collins's classic from 1873, *The Moonstone* (reprint edition; New York: Dover, 2002). Louisa May Alcott wrote a short story about opium, "A Marble Woman: *or,* The Mysterious Model," collected in *Plots and Counterplots: More Unknown Thrillers of Louisa May Alcott,* edited by Madeleine Stem (New York: William Morrow, 1976). Barbara Hodgson's good book about laudanum is *The Arms of Morpheus: The Tragic History of Laudanum, Morphine, and Patent Medicines* (Buffalo, N.Y.: Firefly Books, 2001).

In *Heroin Century* (New York: Routledge, 2002), Tom Carnwath and Ian Smith elegantly present the sociological, medical, and historical facts about heroin. An excellent book on the history of that drug is *One Hundred Years of Heroin* by David F. Musto (Westport, Conn.: Auburn House, 2002). For treatment of heroin addiction, see the Drug Policy Alliance (www.drugpolicy.org/homepage.cfm) (last accessed April 2004) booklet *About Methadone* (New York: Drug Policy Alliance, 2003). The Drug Policy Alliance is the leading organization working to end the war on drugs. Another good book about treatment is *Methadone Maintenance Treatment and Other Opioid Replacement Therapies* by Jeff Ward, Richard P Mattick, and Wayne Hall (Amsterdam: Harwood Academic, 1998). A book that humanizes the perceptions of heroin addicts in modern times is *Tragic Magic: The Life and Crimes of a Heroin Addict* by Stuart L. Hills and Ron Santiago (Chicago: Nelson-Hall, 1992). Another interesting look at the drug is found in *The Politics of Heroin: CIA Complicity in the Global Drug Trade* by Alfred W. McCoy (Chicago: Lawrence Hill, 2003). Finally, see Edward J. Epstein's *Agency of Fear* (New York: Putnam, 1977), which details the dirty politics behind the Nixon administration's war on heroin and heroin addicts.

A number of creative writers have left us autobiographical records of their involvement with opium and opiates. One of the best is *Opium:*

The Illustrated Diary of His Cure by the French artist, writer, and film-maker Jean Cocteau and translated by Margaret Crosland and Sinclair Road (Dufour Editions, 1990). Another is *Junky* by William S. Burroughs (New York: Penguin USA, 2003), which was first published in 1953 under the pseudonym William Lee. Ann Marlowe's memoir, *How to Stop Time: Heroin from A to Z* (New York: Basic Books, 1999), examines heroin addiction in the context of modern times. Aleister Crowley's *Diary of a Drug Fiend* (New York: Red Wheel/Weiser, June 1977) is an autobiographical novel about two English aristocrats addicted to heroin and cocaine. Alexander Trocchi's novel *Cain's Book* (reprint edition; New York: Grove Press, 1992) is a vivid picture of the often nightmarish world of the addict. *Heavier Than Heaven: A Biography of Kurt Cobain* by Charles Cross (New York: Hyperion, 2001) recounts the late rock star's struggles with heroin. One of the best-known novels about heroin addiction is Nelson Algren's *The Man with the Golden Arm* from 1949 (Seven Stories Press, 1999); it was made into a popular movie starring Frank Sinatra. Eugene O'Neill's play *Long Day's Journey into Night*, also made into a movie, is a harrowing account of his mother's addiction to morphine. Two recent films about the lives of heroin addicts are *Trainspotting*, based on the novel by Irvine Welsh, and *Permanent Midnight*, based on Jerry Stahl's memoir.

8. Psychedelics, or Hallucinogens

THE PLANTS AND CHEMICALS discussed in this chapter are some of the most colorful and controversial of all drugs. Some users have recommended them enthusiastically, claiming they are keys to understanding our minds and the origins of religious feelings. Many nonusers are fearful of them, regarding them as dangerous agents capable of driving people to insanity and suicide.

So heated is the debate over whether these drugs are good or evil that it's hard even to find a neutral name for them. When they first came to the attention of scientists in Europe and America in the 1950s, they were called *psychotomimetics,* based on the belief that they made people temporarily insane. (Psychiatrists now recognize that psychosis and the states induced by these drugs are very different.)

Many of the subjects who volunteered for the early research with these chemicals liked their effects very much. Unlike the doctors studying the drugs, the subjects thought of these drugs in positive ways and frequently wanted to repeat the experiences with friends outside the laboratory. As this group of devotees grew in number, they sought a more favorable name for the substances and came up with *psychedelics,* a word coined from Greek roots meaning "mind manifesting." The implication is that psychedelic drugs can develop the unused potential of the human mind.

At about the same time, the medical profession was using the term *hallucinogens* for the same compounds, meaning "causers of hallucinations." Since hallucinations are common symptoms of schizophrenia, this term carries the suggestion that the drug state is abnormal and unhealthy. The battle over names goes on. Recently, proponents have pushed for adoption of the term *entheogen,* meaning "creating God within." We will stick to *psychedelics* and *hallucinogens* and use the two interchangeably.

The substances in this class probably have the lowest potential for abuse of any psychoactive drugs. In purely medical terms, they may be the safest of all known drugs. Even in huge overdose, psychedelics do not kill, and some people take them frequently all their lives without suffering physical damage or dependence. In the right hands, they can bring about dramatic cures of both physical and mental illnesses. Yet these same drugs can cause the most frightening experiences imaginable, leaving long-lasting psychological scars.

Primitive people discovered hallucinogenic plants and began using them long before recorded history. Though many such plants exist, most are concentrated in North and South America, with heaviest use occurring among Indians of Mexico and Colombia. Very few natural psychedelics are native to the Old World, and there is little traditional use of them there. The main Old World psychedelic is a plant called iboga, whose root is made into a drink consumed in religious rituals by a few tribes of west Africa.

By contrast, hundreds of tribes of New World Indians use dozens of different hallucinogenic plants in tropical areas of North and South America. Among these people, the use of hallucinogens is tied to native practices of magic, medicine, and religion, particularly to the primitive religion called shamanism. In shamanism, specially trained individuals called shamans attempt to control the forces of good and evil within the tribal community by acting as a liaison for the human world and the spirit world. To contact the spirit world, shamans put themselves in an altered state of consciousness, often by consuming hallucinogenic plants. Shamans (or medicine men) also take psychedelics to see visions, and they use the visions to locate missing persons or lost objects and to diagnose illness. They often treat illness by administering psychedelics to sick people. In certain tribes, many people consume the plants at the same time in group vision-seeking rituals.

Most hallucinogenic plants taste bitter and cause nausea, vomiting, or other unpleasant physical symptoms at the onset of their effects. Then they induce unusual states of consciousness, altered perceptions, and fantastic visions that users see when their eyes are closed. However, visions and other sensory changes seem to come from taking these plants in particular ways and are by no means invariable occurrences. Indians who believe in the importance of visions and who eat hallucinogenic plants at night in front of a fire while chanting and praying under the direction of skilled shamans are much more likely to have visions than non-Indians who eat the same plants for purely recreational purposes. In fact, the mental effects of psychedelics are completely dependent on set and setting — on who takes them and why, where, and how.

Physical effects are more constant, because all of the hallucinogenic drugs have some common pharmacological actions. All of them are strong stimulants, for instance, causing increased brain activity and wakefulness. And they all stimulate the sympathetic nervous system, usually causing widely dilated eyes, a sensation of butterflies in the stomach, and feelings of cold in the extremities. The various psychedelics differ mainly in their duration of action and how fast their effects come on.

These substances fall into two broad chemical families. The first, called indoles, contain a molecular structure known as the indole ring and are related to hormones made in the brain by the pineal gland. The drugs in the second family lack the indole ring; instead, they closely resemble molecules of adrenaline and the amphetamines.

Indole Hallucinogens

LSD (Lysergic Acid Diethylamide, Acid, LSD-25)

LSD is the most famous of the psychedelics, probably the one that has been tried by the most people. It is a semisynthetic drug, not found in nature. A Swiss chemist, Albert Hofmann, first made it in a laboratory in 1938 from lysergic acid, a chemical in ergot, the fungus that attacks cereal grains, especially rye. At the time, he was interested in developing medical drugs from compounds in ergot. In 1943, Hofmann accidentally consumed some LSD and so discovered its psychoactivity. Beginning in the late 1940s, the Swiss pharmaceutical company he worked for supplied LSD as a research drug to doctors and hospitals throughout the world.

LSD is one of the most potent drugs known, producing its effects in doses as small as 25 micrograms. (A microgram is one millionth of a gram, and there are 28 grams in an ounce. An average postage stamp weighs about 60,000 micrograms.) An LSD trip lasts ten to twelve hours.

Throughout the 1950s, LSD remained mostly in the hands of researchers, especially psychiatrists. But many people who tried the drug found it so interesting that they publicized its effects and began taking it on their own. At first, most of the LSD in circulation was pure pharmaceutical material from the Swiss laboratory that originally made it. In the 1960s, when the psychedelic movement started in Europe and America, black-market LSD began to appear.

For the most part, people who took LSD in the early days had positive trips. They talked about experiencing powerful feelings of love, mystical oneness with all things, union with God, and a deeper understanding of themselves. Some described vivid sensory changes, such as seeing flowers breathe, objects shimmer with energy, and mosaic patterns appear on all surfaces. Such descriptions made other people, especially young people, eager to try the drug for themselves.

From the very first, however, it was apparent that not everyone who takes LSD has a good time. Some people had bad trips: they became anxious and panicky, afraid they were losing their minds and would be unable to return to ordinary reality. They almost always did return, when the drug wore off twelve hours later, but some of them remained depressed and anxious for days afterward, and a few had lasting psychological problems.

When people are panicked, they often behave in violent and irrational ways. In the 1960s, some bad trips on LSD may have led to accidents and suicides. Even though these cases were exceptional, the media seized on them and made it seem as if LSD were a new drug menace that threatened to turn teen-agers into lunatics.

Bad trips are more likely to occur when people take LSD in inappropriate settings, especially if they have never taken it before and if they take high doses. Throughout the 1960s, black-market LSD was unreliable, sometimes contaminated with other drugs, and since not many people were familiar with the effects of LSD, bad trips were common. By the 1970s, bad trips were rare, not because fewer people were taking the drug but because people had learned how to use it intelligently. They took reasonable doses in good settings (such as a familiar room or a peaceful field in the country), with friends who knew what to expect.

Street LSD comes in a bewildering array of forms, from small tablets of all colors and tiny transparent gelatin chips ("windowpane") to pieces of paper soaked in a solution of the drug or stamped with ink designs containing it. The windowpane and paper forms are likely to be the purest, since they are too small to contain contaminants.

Despite loud arguments and much bad publicity about the medical dangers of LSD in the 1970s, there is no evidence that it damages chromosomes, injures the brain, or causes any other physical harm. (Like other ergot derivatives, LSD causes contractions of the uterus. Pregnant women should not take it.)

Morning-Glory Seeds

The closest substance to LSD that occurs in nature is a chemical called ergine, or lysergic acid amide, found in the seeds of certain morning-glories. Indians in southern Mexico were eating morning-glory seeds for ritual purposes before the Spanish arrived, and some still use them today.

Not all the varieties of morning-glories available from seed companies are psychoactive. Of those that are, the best known are Heavenly Blue (with large blue flowers), Pearly Gates (white), Wedding Bells (pink), and Flying Saucers (blue with white stripes).

Because the concentration of LSD-like activity in the seeds of these plants is low, it takes a great many to produce a noticeable psychedelic effect, even up to several hundred, or a whole cupful. The seeds, which have hard, indigestible coats, must be cracked or ground up to release the drug. Also, they are mildly toxic, frequently causing nausea, vomiting, and other uncomfortable side effects. For these reasons, they are not popular; even the Mexican Indians who use morning-glory seeds regard them as a back-up psychedelic, taking them only when they can't get the hallucinogenic mushrooms that they prefer.

One species of morning-glory that is stronger than others is the Hawaiian Baby Woodrose, a creeping plant that covers many Hawaiian beaches and whose flowers are often dried and sold by florists. A dozen of the large, hard seeds will produce a strong intoxication, but they, too, frequently make people feel sick.

Devotees of psychedelics say that morning-glory seeds are definitely second rate, producing too much discomfort relative to the effects that they like. Another problem is that many commercial morning-glory seeds are now dipped in poisons to discourage people from eating them — sometimes without any caution to the buyer.

Mushrooms (Magic Mushrooms, Psilocybin)

Mushrooms are the most important natural psychedelics of southern Mexico, used in ceremonies so sacred that Indians carefully concealed them from Europeans until the twentieth century. It wasn't until the 1950s that descriptions of Mexican mushrooms came to the attention of the world. Soon after, botanists began to identify the mushrooms in use, and chemists found that their psychoactive properties came from psilocybin, an indole hallucinogen similar to LSD but with a shorter duration of action: four to six hours.

Mexican mushroom ceremonies are conducted by shamans,

usually women, and are held for purposes of treating illness, solving problems, foreseeing the future in visions, and putting people in contact with the supernatural world. They take place at night, by candlelight, and today are curious blends of shamanism and Roman Catholic ritual.

For some years, scientists believed that mushrooms containing psilocybin grew only in southern Mexico, and during the late 1960s and early 1970s thousands of people, mostly from Europe and North America, traveled there to take magic mushrooms in remote Indian villages. For a time, several Swiss pharmaceutical companies manufactured pure psilocybin, supplying it to researchers. As with LSD, some of this material eventually found its way to the street, but underground chemists never manufactured it because the synthesis is too costly.

As natural substances with a reputation for producing interesting experiences and fewer bad trips than LSD, magic mushrooms have been in great demand on the black market. For a long time, they were unavailable, though unscrupulous dealers often sold ordinary supermarket mushrooms laced with LSD and other drugs at high prices to unsuspecting customers.

Since the late 1970s, this situation has changed. In the first place, psilocybin mushrooms have been found in great numbers in many parts of the world. One of the principal species, called *Psilocybe cubensis,* is a large mushroom that grows in cow pastures in warm climates. It occurs in southeast Asia, in Central and South America, all along the Gulf Coast of the United States, and in many southeastern states. More than a dozen species of psychoactive mushrooms grow in the fields and woods of the Pacific Northwest. Some grow in Europe as well. In certain areas, the mushrooms are so abundant that collectors can easily gather enough for sale as well as for their own use.

Needless to say, collecting wild mushrooms of any sort requires knowledge and practice, because some mushrooms are very poisonous. No one should attempt to pick magic mushrooms without knowing how to recognize them.

Psilocybin mushrooms can also be cultivated. Although growing mushrooms from spores is much harder than growing green plants from seeds, many people have mastered the technique. *Psilocybe cubensis* is the easiest variety to grow; in recent years, kits that include spores of the mushrooms have been widely sold through the mail and in stores. Since the spores didn't contain psilocybin, they weren't illegal. Taking advantage of this loophole in the law, thousands of people have produced and distributed magic mushrooms. Real, unadulterated mushrooms are now obtainable on the black market.

Both wild and cultivated mushrooms vary greatly in potency. One medium-sized mushroom of a potent strain may give the same effect as twenty of a mild strain. It is important, therefore, to get advice on potency and dosage before eating mushrooms in order to avoid unpleasant effects from too-high doses.

Many wild mushrooms are hard to digest raw, and some are mildly toxic until they are cooked. Psychedelic mushrooms may taste better and are less likely to cause discomfort if they are dried or lightly cooked before being eaten. Still, mushrooms are generally easier to take than the other hallucinogenic plants. One reason that people prefer mushrooms to other psychedelics is their ease of consumption. Another is that the effects are shorter, usually ending after six hours, and therefore are less demanding on the body. People usually feel sluggish the day after taking LSD or other long-acting psychedelics. This is less common with mushrooms. (*Amanita muscaria*, the bright-red fly agaric [mushroom] with white dots on the cap, is not a true hallucinogen. It is discussed in Chapter 10, along with other deliriant drugs.)

Ibogaine

Ibogaine is the active principle of the African hallucinogenic plant iboga. Though the iboga root is almost unknown outside Africa, the pure drug can be made synthetically and sometimes appears on the black market. It is a long-acting psychedelic resembling LSD in effect, but it is an even stronger stimulant. Africans who drink iboga in all-night ceremonies that include vigorous dancing may stay up the next day and night until the stimulation wears off. Eventually, they fall into a deep sleep.

Recently, ibogaine has been in the news as a potential new treatment for opiate addiction. After several heroin addicts discovered that a single ibogaine session eliminated their cravings for narcotics, scientists began to study this exotic drug in animals. Early reports suggest that it may work, but much more research is needed before ibogaine becomes an accepted treatment for addiction.

DMT (Dimethyltryptamine) and 5-MeO-DMT (5-Methoxydimethyltryptamine)

DMT is the drug responsible for the hallucinogenic properties of several plants used by South American Indians. It is a simple chemical closely resembling certain hormones made in the brain, and it is likely that the brain also produces DMT itself. DMT may be our own endogenous psychedelic. It is a compound easily made in laboratories; in the 1960s, synthetic DMT was sold in quantity on the black market.

DMT is peculiar among the psychedelics in that it cannot be taken by mouth; an enzyme in the stomach breaks it down before it can enter the bloodstream. Indians who use DMT-containing plants often prepare them as powdered snuffs. Users of the isolated, black-market chemical either smoke it or, less frequently, inject it intramuscularly.

A typical DMT snuff of South America is yopo, used by tribes of the Amazonian forests. It is made from the resin of a huge jungle tree, cooked down, dried, and pounded into a fine powder that the men blow forcefully into each other's noses through a long tube. Taken in this way, yopo causes a very intense intoxication within seconds but lasts only thirty minutes or less. While under its influence, Indians dance, sing, and see visions of gods and spirits.

Black-market DMT is usually a brown solid that smells like mothballs; users place tiny bits of it in the end of a joint made with marijuana, mint, or oregano in order to smoke the DMT. Sometimes a single inhalation of such a joint will be sufficient to initiate a five- to ten-minute trip of remarkable intensity. The effect may begin before the smoker can remove the joint from her or his lips and usually reaches its peak within the first minute. Some users, overwhelmed by visual hallucinations, lose all awareness of their surroundings. Fans of DMT say that it gives an ultimate psychedelic rush; needless to say, this experience can be quite frightening to someone unprepared for it.

After fifteen minutes, the strong effects subside, and after thirty minutes users again feel normal. Because of its short duration of action, DMT is known as the businessman's trip.

A close chemical relative of DMT is 5-MeO-DMT. It gives an equally powerful rush when smoked, but instead of visual hallucinations, the smoker experiences complete dissolution of reality. Some users describe this trip as "a rocket ship into the void." DMT and 5-MeO-DMT usually occur together in the plant sources of South American snuffs, but although synthetic 5-MeO-DMT has been readily available in North America, it has far fewer fans than its chemical cousin. The reason is that 5-MeO-DMT is often more frightening than delightful.

Nonetheless, a new natural source of this drug was discovered in the mid-1980s and has piqued the interest of many psychedelic explorers. The Sonoran Desert toad, a huge toad found in southern Arizona, produces large amounts of 5-MeO-DMT in its venom glands. These can be milked without harming the toad, and the venom can be dried and smoked. Users say the experience is gentler than smoking the synthetic drug.

Articles in tabloid newspapers have sensationalized this story, reporting inaccurately that people are licking toads to get high. Licking toads is dangerous. Only the Sonoran Desert toad's venom is psychoactive (other species are purely toxic), but it can cause serious poisoning if it gets in the eyes or mouth. Apparently, smoking destroys most of the toxic constituents while sparing the 5-MeO-DMT.

The dramatic effects of DMT and 5-MeO-DMT are good examples of the correlation between route of administration, duration of action, and intensity of effect. Short-acting drugs, introduced directly into the bloodstream by smoking or injection, tend to give rushes. Some people are especially fascinated by drug rushes, and, as we noted in the section on narcotics (pages 94–107), the pursuit of a rush can be the basis of addictive use.

That addiction to DMT and 5-MeO-DMT is unknown is due in part to the rapid development of tolerance for their interesting effects. When smoked regularly, they soon become ineffective. Another reason is the "high impact" of these experiences; they cannot easily be integrated into daily life in the way that highs of alcohol, marijuana, and cocaine can be.

All of the psychedelics share these characteristics. The body develops rapid tolerance for them, so that if you try to take them often, you do not get the results you want. Even people who really like these drugs don't take them every day, and most users save them for special occasions.

Ayahuasca (Yagé, Caapi)

Ayahuasca is a strong psychedelic drink made from a woody vine of the Amazon forests. Indians pound lengths of the vine with stones, then cook them in water for several hours, sometimes adding other plants to heighten the effect. They use the drink in all-night vision-seeking rituals with shamans or in large tribal ceremonies, such as coming-of-age rites for adolescent boys. The plant owes most of its activity to harmine, a drug rarely seen on the black market. Ayahuasca first causes intense vomiting and diarrhea and then a more relaxed and dreamy state than that produced by LSD; it lasts from six to ten hours. Indians say the spirit of the vine enters their bodies and makes them see visions of jungles and jungle animals, especially jaguars. Also, the drug is supposed to enable the Indians to see the future and communicate telepathically over great distances. Seeing visions while on ayahuasca, as with other psychedelics, depends very much on set and setting.

Curiously enough, the plant most commonly added to ayahuasca in making the drink is a leaf containing DMT. Indians say the addition makes for better and brighter visions. When scientists first learned of this practice, they dismissed it as useless on the ground that DMT is destroyed in the stomach. Further research has now shown that harmine inactivates the enzyme that destroys DMT. Combined with ayahuasca, therefore, DMT becomes orally active, and in this form it is a longer-acting, less intense drug that doesn't produce a rush.

How did Indians discover this remarkable combination of plants? Anthropologists and botanists say that the Indians did so by trial and error. Given the number of plants in the Amazonian jungles, that would mean a great deal of trial and error. The Indians themselves say they were inspired by visions — that the spirit of ayahuasca showed them the other leaves and the method of cooking the two together.

In recent years, religious groups using ayahuasca as a sacrament have proliferated in Brazil. Two of them — Santo Daimé and the União do Vegetal, or UDV — have attracted thousands of converts and remarkably little interference from Brazilian authorities. In both organizations, participants consume ayahuasca in groups, sing, dance, and commune with nature and the spirit world. Medical studies of members have found them to be physically and emotionally healthy. The UDV and Santa Daimé both report miraculous healings among participants. Missionaries from these organizations have brought the ceremonies and the psychedelic beverage to North America. At the same time, shamans, some imported from Peru and Colombia, others homegrown, have been conducting ayahuasca ceremonies for curious Americans, making this once unobtainable psychedelic plant quite easy to access. It has become extremely popular among intellectuals and seekers.

Hallucinogens Related to Adrenaline and Amphetamines

Indole hallucinogens make people feel high very rapidly. Typically, their effects begin in twenty to forty minutes and reach a

My first vivid show of mescal colour effects came quickly. I saw the stars, and then, of a sudden, here and there delicate floating films of colour — usually delightful neutral purples and pinks. These came and went — now here, now there. Then an abrupt rush of countless points of white light swept across the field of view, as if the unseen millions of the Milky Way were to flow a sparkling river before the eye. In a minute this was over and the field was dark. Then I began to see zigzag lines of very bright colours.

— from an essay by Dr. S. Weir Mitchell (1829–1914), an American physician and novelist who drank an extract of peyote in 1896

peak within the first hour or two. The drugs in this second family of psychedelics may also be felt quickly, but their onset is more gradual, reaching a peak after several hours. Some users find them less "electric" than LSD and its relatives, although in high doses the adrenaline relatives are more toxic than the indoles.

Peyote and Mescaline

Peyote is a small, spineless cactus with white, hairy tufts; it is native to the Rio Grande Valley in southern Texas and north-central Mexico. The tops of the cactus, cut off at ground level, dry into peyote "buttons" that retain their potency for a long time.

Some Indians in Mexico have used peyote since before recorded history, making long pilgrimages to the desert to collect it, then eating it in elaborate ceremonies. When the Spanish conquered Mexico, the Roman Catholic Church tried to stamp out peyote use, calling it sinful and diabolic, but to no avail. In the late 1800s, the use of peyote spread northward to Indians in the United States, who invented new rituals around it. As it moved north, peyote became even more popular; Indians of the midwestern plains organized a new religion based on it and helped spread its use all the way to Canada.

Not surprisingly, the explosion of this psychedelic movement among Indians generated intense opposition by non-Indians. Churches and government agencies charged that peyote made Indians crazy and violent; stories circulated of Indian men who, upon eating the cactus, axed helpless victims to death, while Indian women under its influence supposedly ripped off their clothes in a sexual frenzy. The similarity of the early peyote stories to those told about other psychoactive drugs is striking. (If there were high-rise tipis, newspapers would doubtless have reported peyote-crazed Indians jumping out of them, thinking they could fly.) The very same charges have been made about LSD, marijuana, heroin, cocaine, and PCP. Rarely have they had any basis in fact.

In response to official efforts to suppress the use of peyote, Indians organized formal churches and fought in court for their right to eat the cactus. The Native American Church began in this way. Eventually, it won its court battles and now boasts hundreds of thousands of members throughout North America. Indians have used peyote legally in Native American Church ceremonies, although most states have prohibited non-Indians from participating. However, this situation could change; a 1990 Supreme Court decision regarding the church declared that guarantees of religious freedom did not extend to the use of illegal drugs.

Native American Church "meetings" begin after dark, often in a tipi. The meetings take place around a fire, last all night, and include a great deal of singing, chanting, and praying, all coordinated by a leader, or "road man." Peyote is eaten throughout the night, and participants ask the spirit of the cactus to help make them better people, better able to deal with their problems. Sometimes the ritual includes elements of Christian worship. Church members tell many stories of illnesses cured as a result of peyote meetings, as well as cures of alcoholism, an addiction notoriously resistant to treatment by conventional means.

Peyote has a nauseating, bitter taste that is not soon forgotten. People who try it for the first time often find it hard to swallow, and it commonly causes vomiting. After an hour or two, the discomfort usually passes. Indians say that with repeated use, especially in religious ceremonies, nausea and vomiting do not occur. A typical dose of peyote is six to twelve buttons. Some users boil them in water to make a tea, and some non-Indians even take the tea as an enema in order to avoid the bad taste and effects on the stomach.

A persistent myth in the drug subculture is that the white hairs in the center of a peyote button contain strychnine, which is supposed to account for the sickness. In fact, there is no strychnine in peyote (or any other hallucinogenic plant), and the hairs are just cellulose, probably indigestible but certainly not poisonous. Peyote is bitter and causes nausea because it has a lot of drugs in it — more than forty separate compounds. Chief among these is mescaline, which accounts for much of the hallucinogenic effect.

Mescaline was isolated from peyote in the late 1890s. It is the only naturally occurring psychedelic in this family of adrenaline-related drugs. Throughout the twentieth century, a few artists, philosophers, and psychologists experimented with it on themselves, but there was no general demand for it until the psychedelic revolution of the 1960s. Then black-market mescaline began to appear. However, since the drug commands a higher price than LSD, many dealers sold LSD as mescaline. Real mescaline comes as long, needlelike white crystals; half a gram is the usual dose. The pure drug may cause initial nausea, though not as frequently as peyote. Its effects last up to twelve hours and generally resemble those of the whole cactus.

STP (DOM)

STP is a synthetic drug closely resembling mescaline in its chemical structure. It produces a twelve-hour intoxication with strong stimulation and may be less euphoric than mescaline. In the late 1960s, it was blamed for an epidemic of bad trips lasting many hours. The problem was overdose; some black-market tablets contained twenty times the recommended amount. This episode left STP with such a bad reputation that few people seek it out.

MDA (Methylenedioxyamphetamine)

Chemical variations of the amphetamine molecule have resulted in a number of synthetic psychedelics in this family. MDA is the oldest and best known, first made in Germany in 1910 but not discovered to be psychoactive until much later. In doses of 100 to 150 milligrams, it produces a feeling of physical and mental well-being. In the drug subculture, MDA is known as the "love drug" because it's supposed to inspire loving feelings in groups of people. Unlike mescaline, it rarely changes visual perceptions. Although it is a strong stimulant, chemically related to amphetamine, people who take it say that it calms them and promotes relaxation. Some users say it makes them more coordinated, more energetic, and better at physical activities. People often feel sluggish and drained of energy the day after taking MDA, and high doses can cause unpleasant muscular tension, especially in the face and jaw.

MDMA (Methylenedioxymethamphetamine, Ecstasy)

A newer drug, MDMA (usually called ecstasy, formerly known as XTC, MDM, and Adam), gives the same general effect as MDA but lasts four to six hours instead of ten to twelve. Because of its shorter duration of action, it is gentler on the body, with less day-after fatigue. Ecstasy has become one of the most popular recreational drugs in the world.

Taken by mouth in a reasonable dose (125 milligrams) and in a good setting, MDMA rarely causes bad trips. It has gained a strong reputation as an enhancer of empathy between people and an aid to psychotherapy and counseling. In other circles, it gained an equally strong reputation as a party or club drug, used especially in settings that featured "acid house" music and wild dancing. The acid house phenomenon grew quickly in Europe (particularly in the Netherlands and the United Kingdom) and in some American cities. It was then supplanted by the "rave," featuring synthesized music and light shows. Raves happened all over the world, from Israel to China, with millions of young people attending them and taking ecstasy as part of the experience. MDMA has also become very popular in the gay community and in gay bars.

For a number of years after its introduction, MDMA was an uncontrolled substance. It became illegal when government scientists charged that it caused permanent damage to certain nerve cells in the brain. Research has failed to support this idea, but the drug remains illegal, and strange stories circulate about it. One is that it causes the spinal cord to liquefy.

There is no truth to these stories, but both MDA and MDMA can cause bad reactions at high doses. Some people snort them or (rarely) inject them intravenously, intensifying their action and potential for harm. Combining these drugs with alcohol or other depressants also increases the possibility of adverse effects. As sexual drugs, both compounds enhance the pleasure of touching, but they interfere with erection in men and with orgasm in both men and women. A few cases of dependence on MDMA have been reported; they resemble cases of amphetamine dependence.

Some users risk hyperthermia (overheating) from taking MDMA in hot, poorly ventilated clubs, engaging in intense dancing, and not drinking enough water. The drug does not cause hyperthermia; overexertion and dehydration in hot rooms do.

There is some evidence that the popularity of MDMA has begun to wane. Its enthusiasts say that no other drug gives quite the same experience, and some physicians and psychotherapists are still trying to convince the government that it should be made available for both research and treatment. The most common complaint about it from long-time users is that sensitivity to day-after fatigue seems to increase as people get older. Some people say they have sworn off the drug entirely because they feel so run-down after using it and find themselves more susceptible to colds, herpes outbreaks, and infections.

Designer Psychedelics

A number of other synthetic drugs exist in this series, with names like MMDA, TMA, PMA, 2CB, 2CT2, 2CT7, and so forth. Since they are custom-made by psychedelic chemists, writers often refer to them as "designer psychedelics." Most are pharmacological curiosities, rarely seen on the street. They differ from other drugs in this section and from each other in duration of action, euphoric potential, and tendency to affect visual perception.

2CB was first made in 1974 and is one of the more popular designer psychedelics. A close relative of mescaline, it produces a six-hour high that users say feels like a middle ground meeting of that drug and MDMA. That is, it gives the relaxed, centered, empathetic effect of ecstasy with more of the visceral stimulation and visual changes of mescaline. 2CB is quite potent; a typical dose is only 15 to 20 milligrams (an amount of white powder about the size of a match head). Some users snort the powder to get immediate effects. It is easy to take too much, and overdoses are unpleasant, commonly marked by nausea and incoordination. Unlike MDMA, 2CB causes minimal day-after fatigue.

A Psychedelic in a Class by Itself

Salvia divinorum is a Mexican sage with a long history of use by native peoples in the same region where magic mushrooms are used traditionally. In the past few years, it has become surprisingly popular in the United States, with living plants, dried leaves, and extracts all easy to obtain. The active principle is a substance called salvinorin-A; it is a potent inducer of visions but is unrelated to any of the other hallucinogenic drugs discussed in this chapter.

As a purified compound, salvinorin-A is active in microgram amounts, which makes it almost as potent as LSD. It can be vaporized and inhaled, but the effects can be overpowering and quite unpleasant if taken in this manner. It is much better taken by mouth or under the tongue. Better still is to smoke the leaves or soak them in water to make a tea. When smoked, *Salvia divinorum* produces effects that come on quickly, peak for five to twenty minutes, then subside. Oral preparations take effect more slowly and last longer, up to three hours.

Experiences vary from subtle alterations of consciousness to full-blown psychedelic trips. At moderate to high doses, users report profound peace, feelings of connection with the universe, vivid imagery, dramatic time distortion, encounters with beings, and travel to other places, times, and dimensions.

Scientists have no clue how *Salvia divinorum* and salvinorin-A work in the brain. The substances appear to be safe, but we have no data on long-term or repeated use. At this writing, only Denmark and Australia have laws against this exotic psychedelic.

Benefits and Risks of Psychedelic Drugs

Bad trips are the greatest danger of hallucinogenic drugs. Most bad trips are related to set and setting, but they also depend on dose and quality of the drug. Since legal sources of pure psychedelics do not exist, users are faced with the problem of not knowing what they are buying. All powders, pills, and capsules are suspect; only mushrooms and peyote buttons are likely to be genuine. Even good psychedelics can cause unpleasant effects if you take too much of them, and with street drugs it's not easy to determine how much is enough.

Psychedelics do not necessarily produce any particular mood or state of mind. They act as intensifiers of experience. If you take them when you are elated, they may make you super-elated. If you take them when you are depressed, they may make you super-depressed. If you take them with a friend you feel totally comfortable with, they may deepen your friendship. If you take them with someone you feel uncomfortable with, they may intensify that discomfort to an unbearable degree. Therefore, if you are going

You get out of the drug experience only what you put into it. The "Otherworld" from which you seek illumination is, after all, only your own psyche.

— Peter Furst, anthropologist, from his book *Flesh of the Gods* (1972)

to take these drugs, you must be extremely careful about when, where, and with whom you take them.

Because hallucinogens are strong stimulants that make people feel very different from normal, they cannot easily be combined with everyday activities. They demand that you set time aside from your routine. Their abuse potential may be low precisely because they make this demand. Other stimulants allow people to perform ordinary activities, but it is not appropriate to take psychedelics and expect to go about your business.

Some people who take psychedelics, especially LSD, later become worried about flashbacks — brief recurrences of psychedelic symptoms that may include visual changes and "spacy" feelings. Anxiety about these experiences is more the problem than the flashbacks themselves. Actually, many people who have never taken hallucinogenic drugs also have flashbacks or experiences very much like them, which may mean that these are normal events in the nervous system. The best treatment for flashbacks is reassuring the tripper that nothing is seriously wrong. As people worry less about their symptoms, they pay less attention to them, and soon the flashbacks themselves fade away.

The benefits that people have claimed from using psychedelics range from cures of mental and physical problems to increased appreciation of the beauty of nature to better understanding of themselves to just having a good time. Some medical doctors and psychologists have been able to cure patients of serious emotional disorders by means of psychedelic therapy. There is an extensive literature on the value of using these substances occasionally and intelligently (see the Suggested Reading at the end of this chapter).

Suggestions and Precautions for the Use of Hallucinogenic Drugs

1. Know your sources. Many fake and adulterated versions of psychedelics are sold on the street.
2. Do not attempt to pick wild psilocybin mushrooms without knowing what you are doing.
3. Cultivated psilocybin mushrooms vary greatly in potency. Get advice about dose before eating any.
4. Do not take psychedelics unless you are in good physical and psychological shape.
5. If you are trying one of the hallucinogenic drugs for the first time, take it with an experienced companion.
6. Take psychedelics only in a comfortable setting when you have no responsibilities for at least the next twelve hours.
7. Remember that you may feel tired and drained of energy the following day.
8. Do not take psychedelics on a full stomach; you are less likely to feel nausea or other discomfort if your stomach is relatively empty.
9. Do not combine psychedelics with other drugs. However, the interesting effects of psychedelics sometimes wear off while their stimulation continues. If you feel agitated, restless, and unable to sleep at the end of an experience with one of these drugs, it may be appropriate to take a hypnotic dose of a sleeping pill or minor tranquilizer.
10. Remember that hallucinogenic drugs can affect perception and thinking. Do not drive, operate machinery, or engage in hazardous activities while under their influence.
11. Take psychedelics by mouth. They are more likely to cause bad reactions by other routes of administration.

12. If you take MDMA in a club setting, be sure to drink plenty of water and get enough fresh air.

13. The best experiences with these drugs result from saving them for special occasions and the right circumstances. Taking psychedelics just because they are available is less likely to produce valuable results. Taking them to get yourself out of a bad mood may intensify that mood. Taking them frequently and carelessly reduces their potential to show you interesting aspects of yourself and the world around you.

SUGGESTED READING

Probably because they are so colorful and controversial, psychedelics are the subject of more books than most of the other categories of drugs. Many of the books are good.

In collaboration with Albert Hofmann, the discoverer of LSD, Richard Evans Schultes has written *Plants of the Gods: Origins of Hallucinogenic Use* (reprint edition; Rochester, Vt.: Inner Traditions International, 1992), a large and beautifully illustrated work on the world's psychedelic plants. Peter Stafford's *Psychedelics Encyclopedia* (third edition; Berkeley, Calif.: Ronin, 1992) covers the chemical psychedelics as well as plants and is filled with historical information, descriptions, pictures, and anecdotes. *PIHKAL: A Chemical Love Story* by Alexander Shulgin, Ann Shulgin, and David Nichols (Berkeley, Calif.: Transform Press, 1991) is an unusual autobiographical account by a renowned psychedelic chemist that includes detailed descriptions of many designer psychedelics related to mescaline and MDMA. *TIHKAL: The Continuation* is another book on psychedelics by Alexander and Ann Shulgin (Berkeley, Calif.: Transform Press, 1997).

A more comprehensive and scholarly work is *Psychedelic Drugs Reconsidered* by Lester Grinspoon and James B. Bakalar (third edition; New York: Bookworld Services, 1997); it contains a complete bibliography and discusses the uses of hallucinogens in psychotherapy.

Albert Hofmann, together with R. Gordon Wasson and Carl A. P. Ruck, wrote *The Road to Eleusis: Unveiling the Secret of the Mysteries* (reprint; New York: William Dailey Antiquarian, 1999), a fascinating speculation on the use of a psychedelic potion in ancient Greek religious rites. *Storming Heaven: LSD and the American Dream* by Jay Stevens (New York: Grove Press, 1998) is a fascinating account of the place of LSD in American culture. A good book on how LSD can influence creativity and imagination is *LSD, Spirituality, and the Creative Process* by Marlene Dobkin De Rios et al. (Rochester, Vt.: Park Street Press, 2003). See also *The Politics of Ecstasy* by Timothy Leary (Berkeley, Calif.: Ronin, 1990).

An excellent book on magic mushrooms is Paul Stamets's *Psilocybin Mushrooms of the World: An Identification Guide* (Berkeley, Calif.: Ten Speed Press, 1996); many of Stamets's other excellent books about mushrooms are available from www.fungi.com (last accessed April 2004). Terence McKenna's *Food of the Gods* (New York: Bantam, 1992) is an entertaining and articulate speculation on the influence of psilocybin on human evolution and the value of the psychedelic experience.

The best descriptions of the effects of ayahuasca appear in F. Bruce Lamb's *Wizard of the Upper Amazon: The Story of Manuel Córdova-Rios* (third edition; Berkeley, Calif.: North Atlantic Books, 1986). Other good books on the subject are *The Ayahuasca Reader: Encounters with the Amazon's Sacred Vine*, edited by Luis Eduardo Luna and Steven F. White (Santa Fe, N.Mex.: Synergetic Press, 2000), and *Ayahuasca: Human Consciousness and the Spirits of Nature* (New York: Thunder's Mouth Press, 1999), edited by Ralph Metzner et al.

Shabono by Florinda Donner (San Francisco: Harper, 1992) is the gripping story of a young American anthropologist who lived with a South American Indian tribe; the Indians value altered states of consciousness and use a DMT snuff. See also *DMT: The Spirit Molecule: A Doctor's Revolutionary Research into the Biology of Near Death and Mystical Experiences* by Rick Strassman, M.D. (Rochester, Vt.: Inner Traditions International, 2001).

The best recent work on peyote is Edward F. Anderson's *Peyote: The Divine Cactus* (second edition; Tucson: University of Arizona Press, 1996). For an analysis of the role of peyote in American Indian cultures by a historian who has studied the subject for fifty years, see Omer C. Stewart's *Peyote Religion: A History* (reprint; Norman: University of Oklahoma Press, 1993). Aldous Huxley provided many excellent writings on mescaline and other psychedelics. His most famous work on the subject is his 1954 essay *The Doors of Perception* (New York: Harper & Row, 1970).

Of the many recent writings on MDMA (ecstasy), the most important and complete book is *Ecstasy: The Complete Guide: A Comprehensive Look at the Risks and Benefits of MDMA* by Julie Holland, M.D. (Rochester, Vt.: Park Street Press, 2001).

For information on *Salvia divinorum*, see *Salvinorin: The Psychedelic Essence of Salvia Divinorum* by D. M. Turner (Tennessee: Panther Press, 1996).

Research information on psychedelics is available from MAPS, the Multidisciplinary Association for Psychedelic Studies, at www.maps .org (last accessed February 2004).

So far, the only movie to focus on the psychedelic experience in a positive way is *The Emerald Forest*. A more distorted picture is presented in *Altered States*. *Easy Rider* and *Midnight Cowboy* both have brief hallucinatory scenes. A visually interesting film about psychedelics is Terry Gilliam's *Fear and Loathing in Las Vegas*, based on the book of the same name by Hunter S. Thompson.

9. Marijuana

MARIJUANA is an ancient drug, used since prehistoric times in parts of the Old World. It is a product of the hemp plant, *Cannabis sativa,* a species that also provides a useful fiber, an edible seed, an oil, and a medicine. That is a lot for one plant to do, which explains why it has always been an important cultivated crop. Cannabis is probably native to central Asia. It tends to grow in waste places — along roadsides, in abandoned lots — around camps and settlements and has been associated with human beings for so long that it is unknown in a truly wild state.

The intoxicating properties of hemp reside in an aromatic, sticky resin exuded by the flowering tops, especially the tops of female plants. The strength of a preparation of hemp depends on the resin content; some strains produce a great deal of resin, others little. If whole plants are chopped up, leaves, stalks, and all, the resin-rich tops will be diluted by much inert material. Carefully cultivated female tops, gathered before the seeds form, are sticky to the touch with resin, highly aromatic, and very potent. The resin itself can be collected and pressed into cakes or lumps; that is hashish. Also, the resin can be extracted with solvents and concentrated into a thick, oily liquid called hash oil. Any of these preparations can be either smoked or eaten.

Marijuana is unique among the psychoactive drugs, in a class by itself. The chemicals it contains resemble no other drug molecules. Unlike most of the substances discussed in this book, marijuana molecules are insoluble in water but very soluble in oil. Therefore, they are absorbed unevenly when eaten, and they stay in the body for a long time because they accumulate in body fat. Marijuana is neither a stimulant nor a depressant but has some features of both. Many people regard it as a mild psychedelic, but its effects are different from those of the true hallucinogens, and it is not necessarily mild. Moreover, the abuse potential of marijuana is considerably higher than that of psychedelics, because it can be used frequently or continually in combination with everyday activities.

As a psychoactive drug, cannabis has a much longer history in other parts of the world than it does in Western countries. Europeans and Americans grew the plant exclusively for its fiber for many years, and even when tincture of cannabis was widely used in Western medicine in the 1800s, few people took it to get high or reported that they felt high when they did take it. The knowledge of how to smoke hemp was probably brought to Brazil by black slaves who used the plant in Africa; the practice traveled north to Mexico and, finally, reached the United States.

Marijuana smoking began in the United States after World War I. Introduced by Mexican migrant workers, it caught on first among black people in southern cities. Many of its early users were musicians. Over the years, it spread to other subgroups but was not associated with the white middle class until the 1960s, when it became a prominent symbol of the youth movement on college campuses. Since then, it has grown steadily more popular and today is the most widely used of all the illegal drugs. From the very first, marijuana — which is known by many slang names, including pot, grass, weed, and dope — provoked a great deal of contention, mostly as a result of its associations. It was the drug of minority races and deviant subcultures even before it got mixed up with hippies and revolutionaries. Despite its status as the most widely used illegal drug today, the dominant culture still views it as a dangerous drug, worse than alcohol and tobacco, likely to lead to heroin.

In this highly charged atmosphere, arguments about marijuana tend to be more political than factual. And because pharmacologists and medical doctors are just as caught up in the politics of marijuana as other people, it's difficult to get neutral information about the drug. Much marijuana research sets out to prove preconceived ideas, and much of it is not worth reading.

Politics aside, the effects of marijuana are hard to describe, because they are so variable — more so than those of other drugs. Some of this variation has to do with set and setting, but some is inherent in the drug.

People who smoke marijuana for the first time often feel nothing at all, even if they take high doses of strong pot. As with other psychoactive substances, people have to learn to associate changes of consciousness with the physical effects of the drug. Compared with other drugs, however, the physical effects of marijuana are not spectacular. It makes the heart beat somewhat faster, causes the mouth and eyes to become dry, and reddens the whites of the eyes. Of these, the most noticeable change is the dryness of the mouth. Only people who wear contact lenses are likely to notice the dryness of the eyes. Increased heart rate is easily ignored, although it can become the basis of a panic reaction in anxious first-time users, who may interpret it to mean that they are having a heart attack.

When people learn to get high on marijuana, their early experiences with it are often quite lively. Everything may strike them as funny, and all sensory experiences become novel and interesting. Listening to music, eating, and making love can become more than usually absorbing. Time seems long and drawn out. People sometimes have strange illusions, such as seeing a room expand or feeling as though their legs have become enormously long.

With repeated use, these remarkable effects tend to fade away. Regular users may find that pot makes them relaxed or more sociable without greatly affecting their perceptions or moods. Very heavy users usually feel little from the drug, often smoking it simply out of habit.

Bad reactions to marijuana are more likely when high doses of strong material are taken in bad settings, especially by inexperienced users. Most are simple panic reactions, easily treated with reassurance that everything will be all right as soon as the drug wears off. The effects of smoking marijuana usually diminish after an hour and disappear after two or three hours. Some people, if they have smoked a lot of pot, feel tired or "fuzzy" the next morning.

Some users find that marijuana stimulates them and keeps them awake at night; others use it to help them fall asleep. It makes some people depressed and irritable, and others groggy for several hours. Some kinds of pot may be more sedative than others. In recent years, stronger and stronger marijuana has become available, as breeders have selected strains for greater potency. Some of the most potent strains (like the "skunk weeds" from northern California and British Columbia) are as strong as hashish and can be disorienting to people who are not used to them.

Taken by mouth, rather than smoked, marijuana is a more powerful drug, slower to come on, with longer-lasting effects. Because the resin is insoluble in water, marijuana tea is not very effective. But the crude drug can be added to food, and the active principles are easily extracted in alcohol or fat. Although some users like to eat cannabis, most prefer to smoke it because it's less trouble, and the effect comes on very fast. The main problem with oral use is the risk of overdose. Since the stomach absorbs the drug unevenly, the right dosage is hard to estimate, and it's easy to take too much. Overdoses of cannabis are unpleasant, though not dangerous medically. They can make people extremely disoriented and delirious, as if suffering from a high fever, and are often followed by stupor and hangover. Perhaps because oral use requires more preparation and produces stronger effects, people who eat marijuana are less likely to become dependent on it than people who smoke it.

Whether they eat it or smoke it, users frequently combine marijuana with other drugs, such as alcohol, downers, stimulants, and even psychedelics. The effects of these combinations are not predictable, depending more on the individual than on the drugs. Because marijuana is not as powerful or as toxic as most of the other drugs, there is no special pharmacological danger in mixing it (as there is, say, in mixing alcohol with downers). Still, users should be aware that combinations that they are not used to may disagree with them and may produce unexpectedly strong effects.

The medical safety of marijuana is great. It does not kill people in overdose or produce other symptoms of obvious toxicity. Occasional use is no more of a health problem than the occasional use of alcohol.

Smoking marijuana regularly can, over time, significantly irritate the respiratory tract, causing chronic, dry coughs that resemble the coughs of some cigarette smokers. Further, marijuana smoke may contain more tars than tobacco smoke and can probably produce lung and bronchial disease in susceptible individuals. The risk depends on how much users smoke over how long a time. A few users avoid the irritation from smoke by consuming marijuana from a vaporizer, a device that heats the plant material but only to temperatures well below the point of combustion.

Aside from respiratory irritation, heavy marijuana use does not seem to cause other medical problems. Of course, warnings of the medical dangers of cannabis have been well publicized, with reports of everything from brain damage to injury to the immune and reproductive systems, but these are based on poor research, often conducted by passionate foes of the drug. Studies of populations that have smoked cannabis for many years do not reveal obvious illnesses that can be linked to marijuana.

Much has been made of the fact that tetrahydrocannabinol, or THC, the most active chemical in cannabis resin, accumulates in body fat, staying around for weeks after the last dose of marijuana is smoked. Although this is true, and it is very different from the pattern of quick elimination of water-soluble drugs, it is not a problem in itself. If THC were a very toxic drug, its persistence in body fat would be cause for concern, but THC and marijuana are less toxic than most of the drugs discussed in this book.

(Marijuana may be quite toxic if it is contaminated with para-

> I started dealing dope 'cause it was the only way I could afford to buy dope. Now I do it for the money.
>
> — sixteen-year-old man

quat, a very poisonous chemical herbicide used to kill unwanted plants. In 1975, American drug enforcement authorities began encouraging officials in Mexico to spray this poison from helicopters on the illegal marijuana fields of that country. The growers soon learned that if they harvested their pot immediately after it was sprayed, it would still look healthy and could be sold to dealers as usual. In this way, paraquat-contaminated Mexican marijuana began to find its way to users in the United States. The exact dangers of smoking paraquat are unclear, but it is certain that it cannot be good for you; the only question is how bad it is. Apparently, it can cause serious lung damage over time and may affect other organs as well. There is no easy way to spot paraquat on a sample of pot, but some drug testing labs can analyze for it. Although public outcry put an end to American support for the Mexican program, the drug enforcement authorities have continued to try to use paraquat on marijuana fields in other countries.)

Psychological problems related to regular use of marijuana are also controversial. Opponents of the drug charge that it interferes with memory and intellectual functioning and leads to an amotivational syndrome in which people lose their initiative and will to work. There is no question that young people who lack motivation often smoke a lot of pot and do very little else, but it is doubtful that marijuana made them that way. Heavy pot smoking is more likely to be a symptom of amotivation than a cause, and those same young people would probably be wasting their time in other ways or with other drugs if pot were not available.

As for its effects on memory and intellect, regular users often say that marijuana makes their minds fuzzy and can interfere

> If you can remember the sixties, you weren't there.
>
> — Robin Williams, actor

with memory. These effects disappear when people cut down on their use of the drug or stop using it altogether.

Dependence on marijuana certainly occurs and has become more common as use of the drug has increased. It does not exactly resemble dependence on any other psychoactive drug. At its worst, marijuana dependence consists of chain smoking, from the moment of getting up in the morning to the time of falling asleep — a pattern similar to that of many cigarette smokers. But dramatic withdrawal syndromes don't occur when people suddenly stop using marijuana, and craving for the drug is not nearly as intense as for tobacco, alcohol, or narcotics.

Tolerance for marijuana also occurs. Even the strongest varieties seem to lose their power if people smoke them day in and day out. This leads heavy users to keep searching for more potent pot so that they can feel stoned again. In fact, all they really need to do is cut back on their frequency of use; even a twenty-four-hour break from the routine of smoking all day long will allow a heavy user to become sensitive again to the psychoactive properties of marijuana.

Although dependence on marijuana has fewer physical components than dependence on more toxic drugs, it can still be very hard to break and very upsetting to people who find themselves caught up in it. Some heavy users are unable to stop smoking, even though they no longer get useful effects from pot and, in fact, get effects that they actively dislike, such as strong sedation and chronic coughs. There are now self-help groups modeled on Alcoholics Anonymous for people with unwanted marijuana habits.

Marijuana dependence can be sneaky in its development. It

Eventually, I became a daily pot smoker, sometimes starting in the morning. It was my main way of relating to other people. However, I started getting less and less effect from it that I liked. In fact, it began to make me groggy and sleepy most of the time and also gave me a cough. These unwelcome effects got worse and worse until I realized I would have to stop using pot. So I made a resolution to quit completely.

Well, it surprised me to find that wasn't so easy. It took me three years of trying before I really gave up smoking marijuana, even though I no longer got pleasant effects from it. I never realized how much of a habit I had and how hooked I was on it.

— forty-one-year-old man, lawyer

doesn't appear overnight like cigarette addiction, or in a matter of weeks like heroin addiction, but rather builds up over a long time. In most cases, people begin smoking pot only in special, usually social, situations. At first, because the drug causes such strong effects, they cannot imagine smoking it at other times. With increasing use, however, tolerance develops, and also people learn to adapt to being high. Soon they can perform normal activities while under the influence of marijuana. Users may then begin to smoke during the day, perhaps by themselves. With time, and unless precautions are taken, marijuana smoking can gradually pervade all their waking hours. At that point, the habit is not easy to break.

Even the heaviest usage of marijuana does not lead to heroin or any other drug. Many junkies smoked marijuana before they tried opiates, but few marijuana users take narcotics. Many junkies also drank alcohol heavily, sometimes at very young ages, before they discovered heroin, yet no one argues that alcohol leads to heroin.

> The danger is this: over fifty percent of these young addicts
> started on marijuana smoking. They started there and
> graduated to heroin; they took up the needle when the thrill
> of marijuana was gone.
>
> — Federal Narcotics Commissioner Harry Anslinger in testimony to
>   Congress in 1951

The reason, of course, is that alcohol enjoys general social approval, while marijuana is a "bad" drug and so invites false attributions of causality. Perhaps marijuana users are more likely than nonusers to try psychedelics and cocaine, because the distribution networks of these drugs overlap somewhat, but there is no quality of marijuana that induces its users to become consumers of other substances. The concept of marijuana as a "gateway drug" is nonsense.

Adaptation to marijuana enables users to learn to perform well under its influence. Unlike alcohol, it does not invariably depress reflexes and reaction times. People who aren't used to its effects will not be able to drive cars well or do any number of other routine tasks well while stoned. Even experienced users need time to practice a given task under the influence of marijuana in order to bring performance up to normal. Some users feel that marijuana helps them concentrate and enables them to work better, but even they have to learn to adapt to its effects. Most scientific tests show that marijuana impairs performance of all sorts. It is easy to come up with such results if you give marijuana to people who are not used to it, give it in much higher doses than they are used to, or give them hard tasks to perform, especially tasks that they have never done while stoned.

Many marijuana smokers drive cars, fly airplanes, ski, scuba dive, and engage in other hazardous activities after smoking. Many of them get away with it because they are experienced users with practice. This does not change the fact that marijuana can

> There have been a whole lot more people hurt on Astroturf than on grass.
>
> — Ken Kesey

drastically interfere with performance in some circumstances. Pot and driving may not be as bad a combination for everyone as drinking and driving, but it is certainly not a good one. For teen-agers who drive recklessly to begin with, it is especially dangerous.

Proponents of marijuana like to argue its merits, trying to per-suade others that it is really a beneficial drug. In fact, cannabis was used in medicine in the past, and many doctors today feel that it is still a valuable remedy for some ailments. Current federal laws prohibit all uses of marijuana, but synthetic THC is available (under the name Marinol), and many states have now legalized marijuana for specific therapeutic uses. Unfortunately, federal law takes precedence, and the federal government is waging an in-tense fight against medical marijuana.

Both THC and marijuana are good treatments for nausea and vomiting. Doctors have used them successfully with cancer pa-tients receiving chemotherapy, which involves very toxic drugs that often cause intense stomach upset. This effect was first dis-covered by teen-agers with leukemia who happened to be pot heads. Cannabis may also help asthma patients breathe easier, but if it is smoked, the smoke will probably make them worse. It also relaxes stiff muscles in a condition called spastic paralysis that re-sults from brain injuries and diseases such as multiple sclerosis. Finally, it stimulates appetite in wasting conditions that accom-pany serious chronic diseases like AIDS and cancer. Conventional medicine does not have good remedies for these conditions.

Although many patients prefer the effect of marijuana to that of pure THC, federal agencies won't permit doctors to prescribe the natural plant. Yet THC is not the same as whole marijuana and may not be as safe. Recently, several pharmaceutical companies

> I have multiple sclerosis. About three years after it was di-
> agnosed, I discovered marijuana. A friend told me it was
> relaxing. My main problem then, aside from partial blind-
> ness, was tenseness and tremors in my muscles. Pot cured
> it, and I've smoked regularly ever since, about four to five
> times a week. If I go without it for a week, the muscle trem-
> ors come back . . . Most people with MS have repeated
> attacks and keep losing body function. I'm convinced that
> pot has kept me in remission all these years.
>
> — forty-one-year-old man, part-time roofer

have come up with synthetic drugs related to THC and have tried to market them as antinausea remedies. In general, they are less effective and more toxic than marijuana. The most recent develop-ment, from the United Kingdom, is a liquid whole-marijuana preparation called Sativex, designed to be sprayed under the tongue. It should be vastly superior to Marinol.

Aside from specific uses for serious medical problems, many people find that pot relieves the symptoms of various mild ail-ments, from headaches to menstrual cramps. Probably, they use the marijuana to get high and use the high as a way of taking their mind off their discomfort. Taking your attention away from the symptoms of a minor ailment sometimes will allow it to subside. The less frequently you smoke marijuana, the more likely it is to work for you as a medicine.

Of course, the same principle applies to getting high from pot. The less frequently you use it, the better and more intense will be your experiences with it. The main danger of smoking marijuana is simply that it will get away from you, becoming more and more of a repetitive habit and less and less of a useful way of changing consciousness. The ease of integrating marijuana smoking with all activities, from parties to sports to watching television, favors habitual use. Also, tolerance for the interesting effects of the drug often encourages users to smoke more of it, when in fact they should be cutting down to increase their sensitivity. The absence of dramatic negative effects, such as a hangover, further encourages overuse. Unless you set rules for when and where you will smoke, you are likely to find yourself using pot more than you should — to the point where all the interesting and useful effects of the drug disappear and you are left with a stubborn, unproductive habit.

Some Suggestions About the Use of Marijuana

1. Marijuana is illegal. Being detected as a marijuana user (by urine screening or hair analysis, for example) can cost you your job and land you in a lot of trouble. Be aware of the dangers associated with acquiring an illegal drug. (See pages 204–205.)
2. Define what benefits you want from pot. Do not use it just because other people do or because it is available.
3. If you get effects that you like from marijuana, you will have to take precautions if you want to keep enjoying them.
4. Set limits on usage. For example, you may want to use pot only with certain friends, only on weekends, or only when you have no work to do. Such rules are necessary if you want to prevent your use from turning into a habit that gives you little satisfaction.
5. Remember that it can be dangerous to drive, operate machinery, or engage in hazardous activities under the influence of marijuana. The drug can cause illusions of time and space and always takes getting used to.
6. If you find the effects that you like from marijuana are becoming less intense or are disappearing altogether, *stop using it.* You can resume after a break and get them back. The trick is to keep frequency of use below the level where you become insensitive to marijuana's interesting effects on consciousness.

Odd as it may sound, less is more, and you can easily prove that to yourself.

7. If you find that the effects that you like are disappearing, the worst things you can do are smoke more or look for stronger pot. Those actions will just increase the problem.

8. Consider using marijuana by eating it in some form rather than smoking it. It is more trouble to take by mouth and the effects are different, but the risk of dependence is less. If you really prefer smoking, consider using a vaporizer.

9. Be careful about combining marijuana with other psychoactive drugs.

10. Be careful about set and setting, especially if you are trying marijuana for the first time.

11. Do not use marijuana on the job or at school. Most people would not drink alcohol in those situations, and just because it's easier to function on pot is no reason to use it. The more situations in which you allow yourself to smoke, the more likely you are to become dependent.

12. If you develop a cough or wheeze, or become more susceptible to chest colds, marijuana may be doing harm to your respiratory tract. Stop using it, cut down on use, or switch to eating it.

13. If you find that you are using marijuana more than you want to and are not getting useful effects from it, consider the possibility that it is controlling you more than you are controlling it. Try to do without it for a while. If you cannot, you may need outside help in breaking the habit.

14. If you have a medical condition that responds to marijuana, ask a doctor to write a letter supporting your use of it. In more and more places, local law-enforcement personnel will honor such letters, even if laws do not.

SUGGESTED READING

The best general history of marijuana is *Marihuana: The First Twelve Thousand Years* by Ernest L. Abel (London: Plenum, 1980). *Marijuana*

Botany by Robert Connell Clarke (second edition; Berkeley, Calif.: Ronin, 1992) is about the plant itself. It is lavishly illustrated. *Cannabis and Culture,* edited by Vera Rubin (The Hague, Netherlands: Mouton, 1975), is a fine collection of articles that looks at marijuana from various perspectives.

Marihuana Reconsidered by Lester Grinspoon, M.D. (second edition; Oakland, Calif.: Quick American Archives, 1994) is a comprehensive overview of the drug by a psychiatrist. *Cannabis and Cannabinoids: Pharmacology, Toxicology, and Therapeutic Potential,* edited by Franjo Grotenhermen, M.D., and Ethan Russo, M.D. (New York: Hawthorn Integrative Healing Press, 2002), is a comprehensive review of the pharmacology, botany, psychological effects, therapeutic potentials, and social and legal problems associated with both natural and synthetic cannabinoid compounds, with new and updated research from around the world.

The Marijuana Conviction: A History of Marijuana Prohibition in the United States by Richard J. Bonnie and Charles H. Whitebread (New York: Lindesmith Center, 1999) is a crisply written, scholarly history of marijuana in America. It discusses how the drug came to be classified as a dangerous narcotic and subjected to draconian laws.

Understanding Marijuana: A New Look at the Scientific Evidence by Mitch Earlywine (New York: Oxford University Press, 2002) is an excellent resource book and all-inclusive look at marijuana's history and pharmacology, its impact on thought and memory, the gateway effect, medical potentials, and law and policy.

In *The Emperor Wears No Clothes: The Authoritative Historical Record of the Cannabis Plant, Hemp Production, and How Marijuana Can Still Save the World* (Oakland, Calif.: Hemp Publishing, 1996), Jack Herer discusses how cannabis could provide the planet with an astonishing range of safe, nonpolluting products, from clothing to fuels.

Reefer Madness: Sex, Drugs, and Cheap Labor in the American Black Market by Eric Schlosser (New York: Mariner Books, 2003) is a highly detailed and comprehensive exploration of the causes and socioeconomic impact of the marijuana laws. It also looks at other facets of the underground economy in America. For a thoughtful historical analysis, see Jerome L. Himmelstein's *The Strange Career of Marihuana: Politics and the Ideology of Control in America* (Westport, Conn.: Greenwood, 1983).

Pot Planet: Adventures in Global Marijuana Culture by Brian Preston (New York: Grove Press, 2002) is an excellent firsthand account of a global trek to explore various marijuana cultures.

Louisa May Alcott wrote a short story about hashish in 1865 entitled "Perilous Play." A modern comic novel filled with references to marijuana is *The Fan Man* by William Kotzwinkle (reprint; New York: Vintage, 1994). Its hero, a delightful character named Horse Badorties, is never without pot. For a wonderful novel that tells the story of an eventful few months of growing marijuana in the backwoods of California, see T. Coraghessan Boyle's *Budding Prospects: A Pastoral* (reissue edition; New York: Viking, 1990).

Although teen-agers make up the bulk of the movie-going public, few films have capitalized on the popularity of marijuana among young people. Four older exceptions are *Up in Smoke* and *Nice Dreams* with Cheech and Chong; *The Harder They Come*, about marijuana in Jamaica in the 1970s; and Peter Fonda's classic from the 1960s, *Easy Rider*. An outrageous antimarijuana propaganda film from the 1930s, *Reefer Madness*, still plays on college campuses and in "art" movie houses, usually to the delight of mostly stoned audiences. Recent years have seen many poor marijuana movies, but two exceptions are *Dazed and Confused* and the documentary *Grass*, narrated by Woody Harrelson.

10. Solvents and Inhalants; Deliriants; PCP and Ketamine

THE DRUGS DESCRIBED in this chapter are a strange assortment of chemicals and plants that do not fit neatly into other categories. Some of them are more toxic than the substances discussed earlier, and, though all of them have their devoted fans, experienced users regard them as second-rate or substitute drugs, not worth taking unless preferred drugs are unavailable.

Organic Solvents

In chemistry, the word *organic* refers to compounds of carbon. Some of the simplest organic chemicals are clear, volatile liquids made by distilling petroleum. These liquids have many uses in industry. Some, like gasoline, make good fuels because they burn readily. Others, like benzene and toluene, dissolve grease and oil, making them useful as cleaning fluids and solvents.

The fumes of these organic solvents have strong chemical odors and make people feel lightheaded, hot, and dizzy. Cans and bottles of them usually carry warning labels about using them only with good ventilation. Many people dislike breathing solvent fumes, but some find it interesting and repeatedly sniff certain household products or gasoline to change their state of consciousness. Products containing organic solvents include some glues (rubber cement and model airplane glue), paint thinner, lighter fluid, and varnish, wax, and spot removers.

TAJAR: What made you want to smell gas, Bullet?

BULLET: Well, when you feel bad, you smell it and it makes you feel kind of hot and kind of drowsy, like you was floating through the air. It makes you feel sort of hot inside and different from the way you were before . . .

TAJAR: Bullet, how come so much gas was spilled on the cellar floor?

BULLET: Oh, I just wanted to get more on my rag. If you have a lot it makes you sort of dream. It gets all dark and you see shooting stars in it, and this time I saw big flies flying in it. They were big and green and had white wings.

— from an interview with a young gasoline sniffer, quoted in *Licit and Illicit Drugs*, by Edward M. Brecher and the editors of *Consumer Reports* (1972)

As psychoactive drugs, the organic solvents produce effects resembling low doses of general anesthetic, but they are more toxic and tend to cause dizziness, nausea, and other uncomfortable physical feelings. In high doses, they may induce visual hallucinations and vivid waking dreams. Some young people find that the effects are similar to the dizzy excitement that comes from spinning around. Since many children use spinning as a technique for changing their awareness, and since organic solvents are commonly found around the house, many children come to experiment with them. Often, these chemicals are a child's first introduction to consciousness-change by means of drugs.

Children who regularly sniff solvents develop tolerance for them. Although there is no physical withdrawal as with alcohol and narcotics, the sniffing habit can be very difficult to break. Just like grown-up drunks, solvent-sniffing children may spend most of their waking time in a stupor, unable to do their work or pay attention to what really matters.

Probably, some people have sniffed solvents occasionally over the years, just as some people have played with chloroform, ether, and nitrous oxide. For the most part, this use never attracted much notice. Beginning about 1959, however, newspapers in the United States began to focus attention on glue-sniffing as a new drug menace spreading among children in cities of the West and Midwest. A few children died from lack of oxygen by putting glue in plastic bags, then putting the bags over their heads. Seizing upon these cases, newspapers dramatized the hazards of glue-sniffing, making it seem extremely dangerous. Parents' groups and police officials then called for laws against it. The main effect of all this attention was to stimulate curiosity about glue-sniffing and cause a tremendous increase in the number of people doing it. At the beginning of the 1960s, gasoline sniffing was the most popular form of organic solvent use. Sniffing of other substances was rare and caused no concern. Then came a hysterical nation-wide crusade against glue-sniffing with scare stories in newspapers, legislative hearings, and, finally, arrest and imprisonment of some children. Only glue-sniffing received this kind of attention, and only glue-sniffing became enormously popular. Today, significant numbers of schoolchildren have tried or used glue in an attempt to get high.

All of the scare stories exaggerated the dangers of solvent inhalation, saying that it certainly led to brain, heart, and liver damage, destruction of the bone marrow, blindness, and death. There is medical evidence of harm from exposure to organic solvents, but most of it concerns factory workers who breathe the fumes all day long over months and years or rare individuals who drink the liquids. Young people who sniff solvents occasionally are not likely to develop these serious medical problems.

As with alcohol, anesthetics, and the other depressants, use of solvents can produce disorientation and impairment of judgment and coordination. Since these changes favor accidents, it would be silly to sniff solvent fumes while driving or doing anything else requiring good reflexes. Overdoses of fumes may lead to unconsciousness, and with complete lack of oxygen, death is a real possibility. Also, it is unwise to mix sniffing with drinking, both because that combination puts a great deal of stress on the liver and because it can depress respiration to a dangerous degree. In pregnant women, solvent fumes may raise the risk of birth defects. Fumes of some of the solvents can irritate the membranes of the nose.

Inhalation puts these chemicals into the blood and brain very fast, so the effects come on almost immediately. They usually last from fifteen minutes to half an hour after sniffing stops. Some people breathe fumes directly from the container; others put solvents or glue on a rag or in a paper bag. The practice is usually called "huffing" or "bagging."

The majority of huffers are between the ages of ten and seventeen, with children of certain ethnic groups predominating. The most common sniffers have been Hispanic males. Many Native American boys also sniff solvents — a source of great concern on many Indian reservations. African-American children, on the other hand, seem to prefer other drugs, and, until recently, few girls used solvents. No one knows why these differences exist, and today, with rising use of all drugs among young people, the older patterns may be changing.

Grown-ups tend to regard glue, gasoline, paint thinner, and the rest as cheap highs — easy to obtain and not very good. Among people who have tried many drugs, the organic solvents are always considered low class and second rate, much inferior to drugs such as alcohol and marijuana. The popularity of solvents among children reflects their easy availability and dramatic power to change consciousness fast rather than any really desirable qualities about them. When children grow up and discover other drugs that are less toxic and more useful, they generally stop playing around with solvents.

Aerosol Propellants

Until recently, most aerosol products contained types of fluorocarbons known by the brand name Freon. Freon, when inhaled, produces the same effects as the organic solvents and presents the same risks to the user. Because scientists now recognize that fluorocarbons damage the earth's atmosphere, manufacturers have switched to other propellants, usually simpler organic compounds that also cause changes in consciousness when people inhale them.

Inhaling aerosol propellants is a bit more complicated than inhaling solvents because the propellants come mixed with other substances. For example, when you press the button on a can of black spray paint, what comes out is a cloud of tiny droplets of black paint and gas. Inhaling black paint does not get you high and can make you very sick. Some users solve this problem by spraying the can into a bag or balloon so that the particles separate from the gas by adhering to the sides. Others turn the cans upside down so that only the propellant comes out, and still others inhale the sprays through cloth filters.

Nitrite Inhalants

Amyl Nitrite (Amys, Poppers, Snappers, Pearls, Aspirol, Vaporal)

Amyl nitrite is a simple chemical that has been used for more than a hundred years to relieve heart pain in people who suffer from coronary artery disease. Such people often feel severe chest pain when they exert themselves. If they breathe the fumes of amyl nitrite, the pain quickly disappears because the drug dilates arteries throughout the body, reducing the workload of the heart. Other effects are a sudden fall in blood pressure, a throbbing feeling in the head (or even a brief pounding headache), occasional dizziness and nausea, warmth and flushing of the skin, and a dramatically altered state of consciousness that reminds some people of fainting or going under general anesthesia.

Amyl nitrite is a clear, yellowish liquid with a strong chemical smell. It comes in inhalers and in cloth-covered glass capsules that can be crushed in the hand and sniffed. (They break with an audible "pop" — hence the common street name *poppers*.) Until 1960, amyl nitrite was a prescription drug. Although some people used it recreationally, most buyers were heart patients who carried it with them for medical purposes and did not think of it as a mind-changing substance. Then the Food and Drug Administration removed the prescription requirement, so that amyl nitrite became an over-the-counter drug, available to anyone.

During the 1960s, many users of street drugs experimented with amyl nitrite as a quick, legal high. It appealed especially to young people, to those who liked to sniff organic solvents, and to those who liked the highs of general anesthetics. In addition, poppers had a special reputation as an enhancer of sexual experience. Inhaled during a sexual act, the drug is supposed to intensify the experience and prolong and intensify orgasm. Although some heterosexual men and women use it in this way, male homosexuals have been the greatest fans of amyl nitrite. The effects of a single, deep inhalation last only for a few minutes and are often followed by less pleasant sensations, but gay men may pass the drug back and forth many times while having sex.

As recreational use of amyl nitrite spread, authorities opposed its unrestricted sale. Finally, in 1969, the Food and Drug Administration reimposed the prescription requirement, ending over-the-counter distribution. Today, however, it is still in wide use, especially in the gay community.

All nitrites are poisonous in excess, but amyl nitrite, when inhaled, breaks down easily and leaves the body very quickly. It is considered one of the safest drugs in medicine, and even people who inhale it frequently do not seem to suffer ill effects. Still, it is probably not wise to overdo it. The strong chemical odor of amyl nitrite is suggestive of materials that are hard on the body; it is possible that long-term use has physical consequences that doctors do not yet recognize. It should not be used at all by people with anemia, glaucoma, high blood pressure, or a recent head injury. Also, it may be harmful to pregnant women. Because the liquid drug can corrode the cornea, users should be careful to keep it away from their eyes.

Because amyl nitrite causes a sudden drop in blood pressure, it

I was first introduced to amyl nitrite during my senior year in college. The father of one of my friends had a heart condition for which he used the drug. He would amass huge numbers of poppers and give them out to anyone who wanted them . . . The effect was immediate. My arms and legs felt like liquid warmth, and at the same time, I got a pounding in my head . . . When I exhaled, my vision blurred, with small blue patches filling my field of vision.

— twenty-year-old man, medical student

can produce loss of coordination and fainting. It should not be inhaled in situations requiring muscular coordination or careful posture. Also, it should be used with good ventilation and never be put into closed containers, such as plastic bags, for continuous breathing. As with organic solvents, that method can lead to suffocation.

Butyl Nitrite and Isobutyl Nitrite (Locker Room, Rush)

Butyl nitrite and isobutyl nitrite are close chemical relatives of amyl nitrite that were not under any drug regulations for a long time. They used to be sold by mail order and over the counter in head shops. They came in small bottles or aerosol cans with labels identifying them as "liquid incense" or "room odorizer," but everyone who bought these products knew what they were for. Butyl nitrite and isobutyl nitrite are now banned. Their effects are the same as those of poppers.

Some Precautions About Organic Solvents and Inhalants

1. Organic solvents are highly flammable. Never use them near open flames or sparks.

2. People have died of asphyxiation by putting their heads in plastic bags containing small amounts of solvents.
3. Never sniff solvents while driving, operating machinery, or engaging in other hazardous activities requiring good reflexes, coordination, and attention.
4. If you sniff solvents, get plenty of fresh air afterward to flush the chemical out of your system.
5. Do not sniff solvents while drinking alcohol or using other depressants.
6. Do not sniff solvents if you have a history of liver disease.
7. Regular sniffing of solvents can become a stubborn drug habit, much like alcoholism. If you develop this pattern of use, you may need outside help to break it.
8. Remember that people who are most experienced with psychoactive drugs always say that highs from organic solvents are second rate.
9. Amyl, butyl, and isobutyl nitrite are less toxic than organic solvents and not as flammable. They should be used only with good ventilation and not breathed continuously.
10. Inhale nitrites only when you are in a comfortable sitting or lying position.
11. Be careful not to get liquid nitrites in your eyes.

Deliriants

Delirium is a state of mental disturbance marked by confusion and disorientation. People in delirium cannot think clearly and may not remember who they are, where they are, or what year it is. They may also hallucinate, seeing and hearing things that are not there. Usually, delirium is a temporary condition resulting from some disorder of the brain. For example, a high fever will cause delirium; when the fever comes down, the delirium ends. If you can remember the experience of a high fever as a young child, you know what delirium is.

Overdose of most psychoactive drugs will cause delirium because they are temporarily toxic to the brain. This kind of delirium is called a toxic psychosis because it is a malfunction of the brain that results from the presence of a toxin in the body. As the drug overdose is metabolized and eliminated, the toxic psychosis resolves. If delirium is very strong, people may not remember it clearly afterward, that is, they may have some degree of amnesia for the experience.

Depending on what causes the delirium, there may be physical effects as well, usually uncomfortable ones such as nausea, dizziness, headache, and prostration. The mental experiences are variable, too, and although many people find them unpleasant, some find them powerfully fascinating, more vivid than ordinary reality. Here is one man's description of a visual hallucination he had as a child during a high fever:

"I was standing on a cliff looking down at an ocean of cream. Somehow I knew that the cream was just about to curdle, and there was something absolutely horrible about that. But the tension just kept building and building. The ocean of cream was always just on the point of curdling, and the tension was unbearable. It is one of the most vivid memories of my childhood."

Some drugs, called deliriants, cause delirium at subtoxic doses. They come from chemicals found in a strange group of plants, some of which have been used for thousands of years to induce altered states of consciousness. Deliriants certainly do not appeal to all people, and some of them are dangerous. Nevertheless, they remain popular.

Nightshades (Jimsonweed, Datura, Belladonna, Henbane)

The nightshade family of plants includes some very popular foods: tomatoes, sweet and hot peppers, eggplant, and potatoes. It also includes tobacco and some poisonous plants that are infamous because of their association with crime, witchcraft, and black magic. Even their names are sinister: henbane, mandrake, and deadly nightshade, for example. Nightshades look scary, too.

They are rank, hairy plants with strange smells and peculiar flowers; some have dangerous fruit.

In North America, the main poisonous nightshades are two species of datura: *Datum stramonium,* or jimsonweed, in the East and *Datura meteloides,* or sacred datura, in the West. Sacred datura is so called because of its long involvement with Native American magic and religion.

All parts of these plants contain scopolamine, a drug that causes delirium and can be seriously poisonous in high doses. The lowest concentration of scopolamine is in the roots, making them the safest part of the plant to consume. The highest concentrations are in the seeds, making them the most dangerous. Roots, seeds, leaves, and flowers can all be eaten, smoked, brewed into teas, or even ground up in fat and rubbed on the skin. All of these methods put scopolamine into the bloodstream and cause intoxication.

The physical effects of scopolamine are very dramatic and often very uncomfortable. They include parched mouth and burning thirst; hot, dry skin and a feverish feeling; widely dilated eyes (making bright light painful); inability to focus the eyes at close distances; rapid heart rate; constipation; difficulty in urinating; and, in men, interference with ejaculation. These effects may last for twelve to forty-eight hours after a single dose of datura.

The mental effects are equally dramatic: restlessness, disorientation, and other symptoms of delirium, including vivid hallucinations that may seem so real that people lose all contact with ordinary reality. Because scopolamine usually leaves you with some amnesia, it is often hard to remember these hallucinations clearly when the drug wears off. Going into other worlds is fascinating, but the worlds that datura takes people to can be frightening, populated by monsters and devils and filled with violent, frenzied energy.

The ability of plants containing scopolamine to disconnect people from ordinary reality accounts for their popularity in certain circles. Criminals have used them for centuries in all parts of the world, slipping them to unsuspecting victims to make it easier to rob, rape, or kidnap them. Witches in medieval Europe used deadly nightshade (belladonna), henbane, and mandrake to have the experience of flying and to meet the devil in their visions. American Indian medicine men have used jimsonweed and sacred datura to initiate young men into the mysteries of the spirit world and to seek visions in group religious rituals.

Today, datura seems to appeal mostly to young people seeking strong intoxication. The plant is easily available in many places and is very powerful. It is in wide use as a recreational drug, often in combination with alcohol, among teen-agers on Indian reservations in the West. Drug crisis centers throughout the United States see frequent cases of bad trips on datura.

Although medical doctors consider datura very dangerous, it will probably not do physical harm to the average healthy person. The main danger of datura is accidental death or injury resulting from disorientation. For example, people intoxicated on this plant have drowned by stumbling into deep bodies of water, perhaps in an effort to quench the thirst and fever caused by scopolamine. Others, experiencing monsters chasing them, have taken serious falls.

Scopolamine is still used as a medical drug. Low doses can be applied to the skin in special patches to prevent motion sickness. Until recently, it also went into over-the-counter sleeping pills as well as some cold and allergy tablets to dry up a runny nose. Higher doses used to be given by injection to women in labor ("twilight sleep") to make them amnesic for the experience of childbirth, a practice that was not beneficial to either mother or baby because it produced a predictable, violent delirium. At one time, jimsonweed leaves were rolled into cigarettes for the treatment of asthma, and tincture of belladonna is still occasionally used to treat gastrointestinal spasms.

Amanita Mushrooms (Fly Agaric, Amanita muscaria; Panther Mushroom, Amanita pantherina)

Amanitas are a family of large, beautiful mushrooms that grow in many parts of the world. Some of them are deadly, the most poisonous of all wild mushrooms. Some are edible and delicious. Two are neither deadly nor edible as food but are used as psychoactive drugs.

Amanita muscaria, the fly agaric, is a big mushroom with white dots on a red or orange cap. (*Agaric* is an old word for mushroom; the name *fly* comes from an old practice of chopping this mushroom into a saucer of milk to attract and kill flies.) The fly agaric is often pictured in illustrations of fairy tales and cannot be mistaken for any other mushroom. Fly agarics growing in the eastern United States are yellow and not usually psychoactive. Those in the western states are red or orange; their pharmacological power correlates with cap color, the reddest mushrooms being strongest.

Amanita muscaria was the traditional intoxicant of a number of primitive tribes of Siberia — people who did not have access to other drugs but did have a shamanistic religion similar to that of many Native Americans. In the 1960s, news stories about the intoxicating effect of this mushroom led many young people in California and other western states to experiment with it as a new natural high.

People have consumed the fly agaric in many forms. The red peel of the cap, which is easily removed, can be dried and smoked. The whole mushroom can be eaten fresh, cooked, or dried, or it can be brewed into a tea and drunk. These different preparations may produce different results. Also, the mushrooms seem to vary greatly in strength and effect, depending on where and when they grow and what trees they grow around.

Moderate doses cause a dreamy intoxication that some people find pleasant, but there are often uncomfortable physical symptoms. High doses can produce delirious excitement and significant toxicity. The effect comes on within thirty minutes and lasts for four to eight hours.

The chemicals responsible are ibotenic acid and muscimol, substances that resemble GABA, one of the brain's own neurotransmitters. Higher doses of them are found in a close relative of *Amanita muscaria,* a brown mushroom with white dots called the panther mushroom, or *Amanita pantherina*. It grows in woods in the Pacific Northwest and other parts of the world, and in recent years many people have also experimented with it as a way of altering their consciousness.

Again, the panther's effects are very variable, so that it may be hard to estimate a manageable dose and easy to take too much. High doses of the panther can make people very sick for up to twelve hours, and a few eaters of it have injured themselves as a result of accidents while they were delirious.

It would be foolish to experiment with either of these mushrooms without good advice from someone experienced with them about exact dose and method of preparation.

Nutmeg and Mace

Nutmeg, the ground spice that goes into cookies, eggnog, and pumpkin pie, contains a drug called myristicin that may be converted in the body to one of the amphetamine-like psychedelics. Nutmeg is the seed of a tropical tree. The outer covering of this seed is ground into a similar spice, called mace, that often flavors cakes. Both nutmeg and mace have a long history of use as psychoactive drugs, especially by people who can't obtain better ones.

To get high on nutmeg or mace, you have to eat a lot of them:

> Someone told me you could get high by eating nutmeg. So one night I choked down a whole can, which was over an ounce. After three hours, I felt light and dreamy. It was a little like a light dose of pot. However, the next morning, I had a splitting headache, my heart was racing, and my mouth was really dry. I got dizzy whenever I managed to stand up. It lasted all day. I would never eat nutmeg again. I don't even like the taste of it in food anymore.
>
> — twenty-two-year-old man, carpenter

from a tablespoon up to a whole spice-can full. In that quantity, these spices taste awful. They are also fairly toxic and regularly leave people with a heavy hangover the next day. The effects are variable, ranging from mild feelings of floating to full-blown delirium. Most people who try nutmeg out of curiosity do not come back for a second try. Frequent users are usually found only in certain prisons or other situations where more desirable drugs are unobtainable.

Some Warnings About Deliriants

1. Delirium is an abnormal condition of the brain in which mental function is temporarily deranged. A delirious person doing anything other than lying still in a safe place is a good candidate for a serious accident.
2. Never take deliriant drugs by yourself. Make sure someone not under the influence of the drug is there to watch out for you.
3. If you must experiment with jimsonweed or other nightshades, use the root rather than leaves or seeds.
4. Do not experiment with *Amanita muscaria* or *Amanita pantherina* without good advice about dose and preparation from an experienced person in the area where the mushrooms grow. Smoking the dried colored peel of these mushrooms is the mildest way of taking them.
5. If you eat nutmeg or mace in an effort to get high, be prepared for a terrific hangover the next day.

PCP and Ketamine

The last two drugs in this chapter are strange synthetic compounds different from any other drugs. They are often called anesthetics, but unlike the general anesthetics discussed in Chapter 7, they are not depressants. In fact, they stimulate the vital functions of heartbeat and respiration, even though they produce some

mental effects resembling anesthesia. Other people call them psychedelics, but they are very different from those drugs, too.

PCP (Angel Dust, Peace Pill, Hog, Animal Tranquilizer, "THC," "Cannabinol")

PCP (phencyclidine) was invented in a pharmaceutical laboratory in the late 1950s and was introduced into clinical medicine in
the United States in 1963 under the trade name Sernyl. It was
marketed as a surgical anesthetic but did not make people unconscious in the same way as ether. Rather, it "dissociated" consciousness from the body so that patients were not bothered by surgical
procedures even though they retained some kind of awareness.
Enthusiasm about the medical value of PCP diminished when reports began to come in of unpleasant side effects in many patients. These reactions included strange mental states, such as
feelings of being out of the body, and visual disturbances that
some patients found frightening. In 1965, the drug was withdrawn from use for humans, but two years later it was reintro-
duced as a veterinary anesthetic under the name Sernylan. Animals
could not tell their veterinarians that they disliked the side effects.

Shortly thereafter, PCP appeared on the black market. It is a
cheap and easy drug to make, produces a strong intoxication, and
can be sold to unsuspecting buyers as other, more desirable drugs.
For instance, pills of PCP have often been sold as synthetic THC,
the chief component of marijuana. (In fact, synthetic THC is very
rare and expensive and is almost never available on the black market.) Supermarket mushrooms, treated with PCP alone or with
PCP and LSD, were sold as magic mushrooms throughout the late
1960s and early 1970s. PCP-LSD combinations have also been
sold as mescaline and psilocybin.

PCP comes as both pills and a powder. The powdered form,
called angel dust, can be sprinkled in a joint made of marijuana
or inactive herbs such as parsley, mint, and oregano, or it can be
dissolved in an organic solvent and sprayed on these materials.
When the solvent evaporates, it leaves an even residue of the drug.

Such joints are called dusters. Some people snort angel dust, and very few inject it. By any route, PCP produces distinctive effects. It causes decreased sensitivity to pain and a peculiar rubbery feeling in the legs with impaired coordination. It may also cause dizziness and nausea, flushing, sweating, and abnormal movements of the eyes.

The mental effects are very variable but often include a feeling of disconnection from the body and from external reality, apathy, disorganization of thinking, a drunklike state, and distortions of time and space perception. Overdoses can cause convulsions and coma. When it is smoked, PCP's effects come on within a few minutes, peak within five to thirty minutes, and last for four to six hours. Oral doses may last longer, and some people say they do not feel normal for up to twenty-four hours after a single oral dose.

Throughout the 1960s and early 1970s, most people who took PCP took it unwittingly, thinking that they were taking something else — mescaline, psilocybin, or some sort of supermarijuana. It came in all kinds of disguises. Few people took it for its own merits, and it had an unsavory reputation, often disparaged as an "animal tranquilizer."

In more recent years, however, PCP has become even more prevalent, and some people seek it out as their drug of choice. The PCP lovers who have received the most publicity are teen-agers from urban ghettos whose lives are filled with anger, frustration, and violence. Maybe they like the feeling of being cut off from the grim reality of their environment or from their own emotions. Because of heavy use of PCP by such persons, the drug has now gained a reputation for causing crime, violence, and insanity among young people. No doubt, some PCP-related murders have occurred, but newspapers, predictably, have blown the drug's association with violence out of all proportion, leading to legislative hearings and stiffer laws on PCP, as well as great hysteria about a new drug menace.

There does not seem to be anything about the pharmacology of PCP that automatically makes users become violent or commit

I've had very positive experiences with PCP, which is unusual, since everyone says it's a terrible drug . . . For years I have suffered lower back pains. Whenever I smoked PCP, I felt no pain and could even jog comfortably. Even after the drug wore off, I experienced no pain from physical activities . . . My thinking was often imaginative and lucid. I laughed a lot . . . I was taking it all the time, and people around me told me I was acting too crazily. So I stopped. Sometime I'd like to experiment with it again to explore those physical and mental powers it seems to release in me.

— thirty-six-year-old man, screenwriter

crime. Clearly, high doses can make people agitated and confused, but tendencies to criminal violence are inherent in certain people, not in certain drugs. PCP users who are not angry and violent to begin with do not become raving lunatics after smoking angel dust. The rash of scare stories about PCP seems to reflect society's need to have "devil drugs" more than it does the nature of PCP.

The main arguments against PCP are that its effects seem neither very interesting nor very productive for most people. Some users take it in ways that they find valuable — for example, as a social or party drug much like alcohol and downers — but many young persons take it just to get "messed up" or feel disconnected from reality. Also, the adulteration of other drugs with PCP is a deplorable practice, especially when these are sold or given to unsuspecting people.

Adverse reactions to PCP can include inability to talk or communicate, a blank stare and robotlike attitude, rigid muscles, confusion, agitation, and paranoid thinking. Heavy users sometimes develop problems with speech and memory that may last for some time after they stop taking the drug.

Ketamine (Ketalar, Ketaject, Super-K, Vitamin K)

Ketamine is a close relative of PCP, producing very similar effects. It is a legal prescription drug intended for use as an anesthetic. Ketamine comes in small bottles as a solution to be injected, either intravenously or intramuscularly.

Like PCP, ketamine produces an unusual kind of anesthesia, called a dissociative state, in which the patient's awareness becomes detached from the body and from external reality. Like PCP, ketamine has produced a number of bad reactions, since many patients become frightened when they find themselves in this unusual condition. So far, however, there has been no move to take ketamine off the market.

In recent years, a number of people have experimented with ketamine as a recreational drug, but they have been very different from PCP users, with the result that ketamine has a very different reputation and following from its notorious relative.

In the first place, all ketamine is manufactured legally. Since it is not a controlled substance, it is not closely watched, and supplies of it are easily diverted from hospitals and pharmacies into the hands of recreational users. Many of its fans are doctors who have introduced their friends, including nurses and other professionals, to the drug. Ketamine users tend to be better educated, older, wealthier, and much more experienced with drugs than most PCP users. They are able to take exact doses of pure material.

Because ketamine comes in an injectable form and because many of its users are medical personnel, it tends to be taken by injection, usually intramuscularly. Given in this way, it produces an altered state of consciousness that begins in a few minutes and lasts about half an hour. The feeling is one of dreamy, floating disconnection from external reality. Some ketamine enthusiasts like to take it while lying in a sensory isolation tank in an attempt to have an out-of-body experience.

The fact that ketamine remained an uncontrolled substance while PCP came to be seen as the chief devil drug of the 1980s is a good illustration of how the image of a drug is shaped by its users. Just as marijuana has never shaken off its association with deviants, minorities, and rebels, so PCP is now linked with an angry, violent, young segment of the population that is prone to commit crime. PCP does not cause crime, violence, or insanity any more than marijuana causes revolutions. The pharmacology of ketamine is practically the same as that of PCP, yet ketamine users (usually successful professionals) lie peacefully in dissociative states, causing no one any harm, and raising few alarms in society.

Unfortunately, many ketamine users do not realize that they can take the drug by safer routes than injection. Ketamine liquid can be evaporated to solid crystals that can be powdered and smoked, snorted, or swallowed, just like PCP. By the oral route, ketamine lasts longer, and the peak effect is less dramatic. By any route, high doses of ketamine can be as unpleasant as high doses of PCP.

Some Suggestions About PCP and Ketamine

1. Try to avoid taking PCP unintentionally. All street psychedelics in pill or powder form are suspect, as are funny-tasting joints that give a strange rush.
2. If you take PCP deliberately, avoid high doses.
3. As with other drugs, the oral route is safer. Smoking PCP gives a rapid, dramatic effect. Some users prefer to smoke it, because they know right away how high they are. If you take PCP by mouth, it is even more important to know the dose so that you don't get more intoxicated than you intend.
4. Do not take PCP with depressants or stimulants. The combined effects can be unpleasant and difficult to control.
5. Because PCP affects coordination, thought, and judgment, do

not do things under its influence that require those functions to be normal.

6. Because PCP can produce agitation, confusion, and difficulties in communication, it is not wise to take it in settings or with people that might add to those problems.

7. If you take PCP regularly and find you have trouble thinking clearly or remembering, cut down or stop taking it altogether.

8. If you meet people who want you to try ketamine, remember that it is essentially the same as PCP.

9. Remember also that ketamine can be taken by mouth and does not have to be injected.

SUGGESTED READING

Very few good books on solvent abuse are in print, and most of the available literature is aimed at a younger audience than our readers. A good book on the dangers of inhalants for teen-agers is *Need to Know: Solvent Abuse* by Sean Connolly (Portsmouth, N.H.: Heinemann Educational, 2002). A good Web site for information on solvents (and many other drugs) is The Vault of Erowid, www.erowid.org (last accessed April 2004).

For information on nightshade plants, see *The Fascinating World of the Nightshades: Tobacco, Mandrake, Potato, Tomato, Pepper, Eggplant, Etc.* by Charles Bixler Heiser (Mineola, N.Y.: Dover, 1987). The book discusses the edible nightshades and tobacco as well as the deliriant members of the family. For more on other psychoactive herbs, see *Legal Highs: A Concise Encyclopedia of Legal Herbs & Chemicals with Psychoactive Properties* by Adam Gottlieb (Berkeley, Calif.: Ronin, 1991).

Jonathan Ott includes *Amanita muscaria* and *Amanita pantherina* in his *Hallucinogenic Plants of North America* (reprint; New York: Bantam, 1993). In *Mushrooms and Mankind: The Impact of Mushrooms on Human Consciousness and Religion* (Escondido, Calif.: Book Tree, 2000), James Arthur tries to link many of the world's religions with Amanita cults.

A good book about ketamine is *Ketamine: Dreams and Realities* by Karl Jansen, M.D. (Sarasota, Fla.: Multidisciplinary Association for Psychedelic Studies (MAPS), 2001).

11. Medical Drugs; Herbal Remedies; Smart Drugs

A GREAT MANY psychoactive drugs are sold legally: as prescription medicines used by doctors, as over-the-counter remedies stocked in drugstores, and as herbal products available in many health food stores. Patients and consumers are often unaware of the effects of these substances. We review the more common ones in this chapter.

Psychiatric Drugs

Psychiatrists now rely heavily on drugs to treat the symptoms of mental illness. Although these chemicals do affect mood, perception, and thought, they rarely cause euphoria or trigger high states; as a result, people generally do not take them unless they are psychiatric patients. Psychiatric medications fall into four main categories: antipsychotics, antidepressants, antimanic drugs, and antianxiety agents. We discussed the last of these in Chapter 7.

Antipsychotic Drugs (Major Tranquilizers)

Major tranquilizers revolutionized psychiatry when they were first introduced in the early 1950s. They provided a new and easy way to manage schizophrenia and other severe mental diseases, making patients calm and emotionally quiet. In some cases, the major tranquilizers have enabled psychotic persons to lead rea-

> I firmly believe that if the whole materia medica as now used could be sunk to the bottom of the sea, it would be all the better for mankind and all the worse for the fishes.
>
> — Oliver Wendell Holmes (1809–1894), American physician and author

sonably normal lives and function outside hospitals. More often, tranquilizers make these people more manageable and docile rather than less crazy.

The most widely used drug in this group was chlorpromazine (Thorazine). It belongs to a group of drugs called phenothiazines that also include prochlorperazine (Compazine) and trifluoperazine (Stelazine). In addition to their use in treating mental illness, the phenothiazines can be used to end bad reactions to psychedelic drugs and other states of confusion. Some of them are also used to treat purely physical problems, such as itching, dizziness, nausea, vomiting, and hiccups.

In normal people, small doses of these compounds cause drowsiness, lethargy, and boredom — hardly the kinds of effects that encourage recreational use. In addition, the major tranquilizers regularly produce uncomfortable physical effects, such as dryness of the mouth. In high doses and long-term use, they can also cause more serious toxicity, such as liver and eye damage and permanent disorders of muscle movement and coordination.

Newer types of antipsychotic drugs are now in wide use, such as haloperidol (Haldol), risperidone (Risperdal), and clozapine (Clozaril). They are more effective than phenothiazines for some schizophrenic patients, but all have the potential to cause serious toxicity.

Because the physical and mental effects of antipsychotic drugs are at best uninteresting and at worst very unpleasant, nonmedical use of them is nonexistent.

Antidepressants (Tricyclics and SSRIs)

The word *antidepressant* sounds attractive. It suggests a drug that lifts your mood and makes you feel good, something like a stimulant. The antidepressant drugs used in psychiatry today, however, do not give the good feelings of stimulants. Instead, they often cause sedation and a variety of uncomfortable physical effects.

These drugs date from 1958, when the parent compound, imipramine (Tofranil), was invented. It is still in use today, along with a close relative, amitriptyline (Elavil), and a number of other similar drugs, called tricyclics for their chemical structure. Some depressed patients respond very well to these medications but not until after at least two weeks of regular use. On the other hand, the toxic effects begin right away: sedation, dry mouth, blurred vision, constipation, difficulty in urinating. Normal people are likely to notice only these "side effects" without any positive mood changes.

A newer class of antidepressant drugs is the selective serotonin reuptake inhibitors, or SSRIs; the first to appear was fluoxetine (Prozac). It was followed by sertraline (Zoloft), paroxetine (Paxil), and citalopram (Celexa), all of which have become extremely popular medical drugs. SSRIs can produce different side effects from the tricyclics: anxiety, impotence in men, and suicidal thinking, for example. Some commentators complain that widespread prescription of SSRIs has made many Americans less interesting and less creative.

One anomalous antidepressant drug is bupropion (Wellbutrin), also marketed as an aid to smoking cessation under the brand name Zyban. Unlike the other compounds discussed here, it is a stimulant of the central nervous system, and some users of stimulants may like that effect. Bupropion also commonly causes anxiety and jitteriness and, in high doses, seizures.

Like the major tranquilizers, the antidepressants do not lend themselves to recreational use because few people like their immediate effects. Often, even depressed patients who are helped by them like to cut their dosage to a minimum and do without them altogether when they can. Do not be misled by their name: antidepressants will not make you high.

Drugs for Treating Bipolar Disorder

Manic-depressive psychosis, also known as bipolar disorder, is a serious mental illness in which people swing back and forth between extremes of mood, from intense elation (mania) to intense depression. There is a high risk of suicide in these patients. An older drug used to treat bipolar disorder is lithium carbonate (Ekalith), which evens out the mood swings and is especially good at preventing manic episodes, although it is also used to treat depression. It has many side effects and can produce serious toxicity in the nervous system, heart, and kidneys. A newer drug is divalproex sodium (Depakote), also with a significant potential for toxicity. Neither of these drugs has any effect on the mind that would recommend them for nonmedical use.

Prescription Drugs Not Commonly Thought to Be Psychoactive

Many medical drugs have mental effects that are ignored by doctors who prescribe them. Often, these effects are listed as "side effects" in the fine-print information that manufacturers include with drugs. Sometimes, patients find the side effects more prominent than the main effects.

Antihistamines

Some allergic reactions are mediated by an endogenous substance called histamine that strongly affects nerves, blood vessels, and other tissues. In an effort to suppress allergic symptoms, pharmacologists have invented a number of synthetic drugs to

> Throughout junior high school and high school, I suffered from bad hay fever. My family doctor prescribed antihistamines for me. They definitely worked, but they made me feel so bad. Finally, I came to prefer the hay fever. I was happier sneezing than being so depressed and logy. Once, while in college, I took a twenty-five-milligram tablet of Thorazine and I was amazed at how similar the effect was to the antihistamines. I hate that feeling. I managed to get rid of most of my allergies by changing my diet and lifestyle. I haven't taken an antihistamine in years.
>
> — thirty-eight-year-old man, musician

block the actions of histamine. Many antihistamines are now available; in large-dosage forms, they are dispensed by prescription, but lower-dosage forms are sold over the counter. Some of the ones in widespread use are diphenhydramine (Benadryl), chlorpheniramine (Teldrin, Chlor-Trimeton), brompheniramine (Dimetane), dexchlorpheniramine (Polaramine), tripelennamine (PBZ, Pyribenzamine), tripolidine (Actidil), promethazine (Phenergan), pyrilamine, and doxylamine.

Although antihistamines are strong drugs that affect many systems of the body, they are often not very efficient at doing what they are supposed to do: counteract histamine and suppress allergies. The central nervous system is especially sensitive to antihistamines. Often, these drugs cause profound alterations of mood, not for the better. They make people depressed, grouchy, lethargic, drowsy, and unable to think clearly. Some of them are related chemically to major tranquilizers like Thorazine and produce similar effects on mood. The sedation caused by antihistamines is likely to interfere with driving and other activities requiring concentration, clear thinking, and good reflexes. These effects are intensified by the simultaneous use of alcohol and other depressants. Recently, new antihistamines have appeared that do not enter the brain. The best known of these is terfenadine (Seldane). It does not cause sedation and depression but often causes headaches and other uncomfortable side effects. It is much more expensive than older antihistamines.

Despite their tendency to put people in bad moods, antihistamines are among the most widely consumed of all medical drugs, and neither doctors nor patients think of them as psychoactive. Furthermore, antihistamines are common ingredients of many over-the-counter preparations, such as cold remedies and sleeping aids; they sometimes even arrive in the mail as free samples of these products. Anyone suffering from chronic depression and lethargy should make sure that they are not consuming these chemicals in one form or another. Allergy sufferers should also know that allergic symptoms frequently respond to nondrug treatments, such as changes in diet and mental state, making it possible to avoid antihistamines entirely.

A few drugs in this class are used specifically to prevent motion sickness. Dimenhydrinate (Dramamine) is the best known. Like its relatives, it often makes people drowsy and puts them in unwelcome states of mind.

Oddly enough, one antihistamine is used by some people, mostly junkies, to get high. It is tripelennamine, sold under the brand names PBZ and Pyribenzamine. Because a common form of it is a blue tablet, it is known as "blues" on the street. The combination of morphine and blues is called "blue velvet"; some junkies like to inject it intravenously. A more popular combination is the synthetic opiate pentazocine (Talwin) and PBZ, which is known as "T's and B's" or "T's and blues" and is also taken intravenously. Except for this strange practice, recreational use of antihistamines is rare to nonexistent.

The use of antihistamines in high doses or over long periods seems unwise. These drugs have known toxicity on the physical body, and no one should spend more time than necessary in the mental states that they produce.

Corticosteroids (Cortisone and Relatives)

Besides producing adrenaline, the adrenal glands secrete other hormones that control metabolism and body chemistry. This group of hormones comes from the gland's outer layer, or cortex, so the principal one is called cortisone. Cortisone and its relatives all have a distinctive molecular structure known as the steroid nucleus (which they share with the male and female sex hormones described later in this chapter). Pharmacologists have learned to make many semisynthetic drugs with this same structure, starting with raw materials found in certain plants. As a group, these drugs are all called corticosteroids, or, simply, steroids, both the endogenous ones and the manmade ones.

One of the dramatic effects of corticosteroids is to reduce inflammation and certain allergic reactions, such as skin rashes. Pharmacologists have maximized this action in some of the new steroids that they have created in laboratories. When these drugs are applied topically — that is, when they are put on the skin — they are reasonably safe and sometimes miraculously effective. Doctors also frequently prescribe steroids for systemic use — that is, to be taken internally. There are clear indications for such use, but because steroids seem almost to have magic powers, doctors tend to overprescribe them, sometimes dispensing them for mild cases of poison ivy, diaper rash, back pain, and other conditions not severe enough to warrant their use.

The trouble is that the desirable anti-inflammatory properties of steroids are just one of many actions of these powerful hormones. Even in moderate doses, systemic steroids can drastically upset the chemical balance of the body and cause serious toxicity, including death. They can also shut off the body's production of its own steroids with such consequences as increased susceptibility to stress and infection.

The adverse physical side effects of steroids are well known to doctors, but less attention is paid to their psychoactivity. These drugs can produce extreme euphoria, resembling the manic phase of manic-depressive psychosis. In such cases, judgment can be severely impaired and behavior can become erratic and illogical. With continued use, this initial euphoria may turn into intense depression. Steroids can make some people psychotic or suicidal. Not everyone taking steroids systemically experiences these dramatic reactions, but many probably experience more subtle changes in mood; nervousness, insomnia, depression, and other mental changes are common with long-term use. People with a history of psychiatric problems should be cautious about taking steroids. Everyone should be aware that these compounds are among the strongest drugs known and so should be saved for the treatment of really serious illness.

Anabolic Steroids

Male sex hormones are also called anabolic steroids because they stimulate anabolism, the building-up phase of metabolism. Under their influence, protein synthesis increases in bone, muscle, and skin, leading to increased bone density, muscle mass, and skin tone. These hormones are also androgens — that is, they stimulate the development of male sex characteristics: facial and body hair, male distribution of fat and muscle, deep voice, and so forth. (Female hormones — estrogens and progesterone — are actually derivatives of androgens; both types of hormones are present in both sexes and in delicate balance. Estrogens produce female characteristics but, except for maintaining bone density in women, do not have the general anabolic actions of androgens.)

For some time now, male athletes and body builders have taken anabolic steroids to increase muscle bulk and enhance performance. In fact, the practice has become astonishingly common. Most physicians deplore this use of steroid hormones, but until recently, some wrote prescriptions for them to all comers. In 1991, the Drug Enforcement Administration made anabolic steroids controlled substances, ending legal prescription of them. A black market now supplies both oral and injectable forms of these drugs, but they are of questionable purity. In our experience, people determined to use these drugs cannot be dissuaded by warnings about their harmful effects. The promise of rapid development of big muscles and a powerful body image is totally seductive, especially for teen-agers and young men. Competitive body builders say that they cannot take the chance of not using steroids since everyone else is using them.

Anabolic steroids may be hazardous to both physical and mental health. They weaken resistance by unbalancing the body's hormonal system and predispose those who take them to weakness rather than strength in later life. They commonly increase aggression, possibly encouraging violent behavior (" 'roid rage"). They may also undermine sexual potency and desire. Women athletes who take steroids may become masculinized; for example, they may develop deep voices and facial hair.

Proponents of steroids say that adverse effects are rare and that medical science has failed to document any serious consequences of use. They say that instead of condemning nonmedical use of anabolic steroids, researchers should be trying to invent new compounds that are anabolic without being significantly androgenic.

Cough Suppressants

The oldest and most effective drugs for coughs are the opiates. They directly depress the center in the brain that controls the cough reflex. It is not always a good idea to stop people from coughing; sometimes they need to expel material from the respiratory tract. If an unproductive cough continues, however, it should be stopped.

The most common opiate prescribed for coughs is codeine, a relatively less powerful one that is reasonably active by mouth. Because of the danger of dependence, doctors do not prescribe opiates casually. Pharmacologists have tried to vary the molecules of opiates to come up with new compounds that will suppress coughs but not cause euphoria or dependence. Some of their inventions are available by prescription, such as hydrocodone, a semisynthetic derivative of codeine. Although these narcotic

I've had asthma all my life and am allergic to just about everything . . . As a child I took a lot of codeine for coughs. For the past ten years, I've been on Hycodan, which I understand contains a narcotic [hydrocodone]. Originally, I took one tablet four times a day; now I take two, four times a day. If I try to cut down the dose, I start coughing and get really congested. Also, I get upset and can't sleep.

If I think about it, I guess I know I'm addicted, but I don't like to face that. I've never had anything to do with drugs.

— fifty-two-year-old woman, university guidance counselor

cough suppressants carry warnings about dependence, patients and doctors may not appreciate the reality of the risk until it is too late. Also, these drugs, like other narcotics, are depressants and can interfere with thinking and motor coordination. If they are the only thing that works for a bad cough, they should be taken intermittently or for only a few days in a row so as to avoid habitual use.

Gastrointestinal Drugs

One of the commonest drugs used to treat intestinal cramps and diarrhea is Lomotil, a combination of a synthetic opiate called diphenoxylate and atropine, one of the constituents of nightshade plants. Both of these drugs reduce the movement of the intestines by paralyzing the nerves that control them. Diphenoxylate is a close chemical relative of meperidine (Demerol), one of the strong medical narcotics. Like its relative, diphenoxylate can cause depression of the nervous system that may be intensified by simultaneous use of other depressants. It can also cause euphoria and dependence. Many patients who take Lomotil for intestinal upset experience narcotic effects on mood but have no idea that they are using an opiate.

Atropine by itself has little psychoactivity in low doses; most people find high doses unpleasant. Some combination drugs mix atropine with other nightshade derivatives, including scopolamine, the main psychoactive principle of the nightshade family. Donnatal is an example of such a mixture; it also includes some phenobarbital as a sedative. Doctors frequently maintain patients on these drugs, especially patients with ulcers, gastrointestinal spasms, and urinary disorders. Rarely do doctors or patients consider the potential of these treatments to affect mood and thought, but as noted in the section on deliriants (see pages 157–63), nightshade drugs can influence the mind profoundly. The psychoactive effect most likely to be noticed by people who take these drugs is drowsiness, but over time or in high dosage, they may cause more bizarre changes.

Bronchodilators

Bronchodilators are drugs that open the airways in the respiratory tract. They are widely prescribed as pills and aerosol inhalers to patients with asthma to relieve the wheezing and difficulty in breathing characteristic of that disease. Most of these drugs work by stimulating the sympathetic nervous system, which regulates the muscular walls of the bronchial tubes. As a result, in addition to their desired effect, they commonly cause stimulation, anxiety, jitteriness, and insomnia. Patients often dislike these side effects but have no alternatives to the drugs if they want to breathe.

Another problem with the stimulant bronchodilators is their strong tendency to cause dependence. When the effect of a dose wears off, bronchial constriction increases as a reaction to the drug, making further doses necessary. Asthmatics frequently inhale bronchodilators throughout the day, in addition to taking them regularly by mouth. This frequency of use increases the risks of addiction and mood change.

One of the most widely prescribed of these drugs — theophylline — has recently come under close scrutiny as a possible cause of bizarre and violent behavior. Theophylline is the active principle of tea and is a near relative of caffeine. For many years, most asthmatics have swallowed large daily doses of this stimulant, which was considered a safe and effective drug. Now, with increasing evidence that it can produce serious behavioral changes, its days of use as a medical treatment are numbered.

"Mild" Analgesics

Pharmacologists have been unable to come up with analgesics (pain relievers) of medium strength to fill the gap between aspirin and morphine. They have given us several derivatives of opiates that they claim are more powerful than aspirin but safer and less addicting than morphine. If these drugs are effective at controlling pain, however, they always turn out to be attractive to opiate addicts and are likely to cause dependence.

One such drug is propoxyphene (Darvon), a prescription analgesic widely used in recent years. Sometimes it is combined with aspirin and caffeine to make it more effective. Despite the enthusiastic claims of its manufacturer, most doctors and patients have found Darvon to be not much more effective than aspirin. (Some even feel that when it is combined with aspirin, it is the aspirin that does most of the work.) Besides, the abuse potential of Darvon is of the same sort as that of the strong narcotic analgesics. It took some time for doctors to acknowledge the existence of Darvon abuse, but they are now very familiar with it and much more cautious about dispensing the drug.

In addition to the drugs in these categories, many other prescription drugs may have psychoactive effects, even if doctors, pharmacologists, and manufacturers don't recognize them. Sometimes these effects show up in many patients who take a drug, sometimes in only a few. If you begin a course of prescription drug treatment and experience sleepiness, depression, highs, unusual dreams, or other mental changes that you cannot account for, the drug may be responsible. To prove it, you would have to stop the drug and, after an interval, start it again to see if there is a relationship between it and the symptoms.

Over-the-Counter (OTC) Preparations

Cough Syrups

OTC cough syrups are of varied composition. Some contain no obviously psychoactive drugs. Others contain known depressants, such as alcohol and chloroform; stimulants such as pseudoephedrine; antihistamines; and derivatives of opiates considered to be nonnarcotic. Sometimes, people who are desperate for drugs and who cannot get anything better consume overdoses of these preparations in an effort to get high.

The principal OTC cough suppressant is a drug called dextromethorphan, a relative of codeine that quiets the cough center but is not supposed to produce euphoria, dependence, or the other characteristic effects of narcotics. Some people use it to get high, however. It is in Robitussin cough syrup and Coricidin cold tablets ("red devils," "triple-Cs") and can be found on the street in pure form called DXM. Users take large amounts to produce a zombie-like state called "dexing" or "robotripping." The addictive potential and medical harmfulness of excessive use of dextromethorphan are not known.

Cold Remedies

Capsules and tablets for relieving symptoms of colds account for a large percentage of OTC drug sales. Like the cough syrups, cold remedies are a mixed bag of different formulas and strengths. Common ingredients are antihistamines, aspirin and other pain relievers, nightshade drugs to dry up excess secretion in the nose and throat, and caffeine and pseudoephedrine or synephrine to offset the sedative effects of the other ingredients. Usually, these mixtures are packaged in multicolored tablets and flashy capsules to make them look exotic and powerful. Whether they affect the course of a cold or significantly reduce the symptoms is questionable. (Even when they do suppress symptoms, they may actually prolong colds by making people less aware of their illness and less likely to take good care of themselves.) What is more certain is that OTC cold remedies can affect mood, usually in undesirable ways. Alternate methods of treating colds to avoid these problems include taking hot baths, forcing fluids, eating less, increasing rest, and decreasing stress and stimulation.

Nasal Decongestants

One of the physical effects of stimulants is to constrict blood vessels in the nose and sinuses. This constriction shrinks those tissues, allowing freer passage of air. The effect is temporary and, when the stimulant wears off, is usually followed by an opposite reaction, or "rebound," in which the nasal passages become more blocked than before. This pattern is similar to the one that occurs with the bronchodilator drugs described earlier.

Early nasal inhalers contained strips of paper impregnated with amphetamine. Many users experienced general stimulation from them, some got high, and some became dependent. Some even broke open the containers and extracted the amphetamine in order to put it into their bodies in other ways. Eventually, manufacturers stopped using amphetamine in nasal inhalers, replacing it with other drugs supposed to be less stimulating and less addictive.

Today, the OTC inhalers and sprays sold to unblock stuffy noses are not considered psychoactive. Some of the inhalers contain no drugs but only aromatic substances such as menthol. They may be pleasant to use but are not nearly as effective as chemicals that constrict blood vessels. The sprays and those inhalers that do contain drugs certainly work in the short run, but though the manufacturers claim otherwise, they are still stimulants and frequently cause dependence.

Not everyone experiences general stimulation from these products, but those who do may come to use them habitually. Probably, a greater risk of dependence arises from the temporary nature of the relief that they offer. If people continue to use them to treat the rebound that follows the initial dose, they quickly find themselves unable to breathe without them. Longer-acting preparations may be safer in this respect.

A few oral forms of decongestants are available, for example, pseudoephedrine (Sudafed), a close relative of the natural stimulant ephedrine. Since it goes into the mouth rather than the nose, it is less likely to cause rebound and dependence, but for some people and in high doses, it is definitely a stimulant. Synephrine, a product of the bitter orange tree, is also a stimulant.

Appetite Suppressants

We mentioned these oral forms of stimulants at the end of Chapter 6. Until recently, they contained ephedrine, sometimes combined with caffeine, and are packaged and named to look like amphetamines.

OTC Uppers

Pure caffeine is sold in most drugstores — for much more than it is worth — in clever disguises meant to suggest powerful amphetamines. For example, a product called Caffedrine, in large green-and-white time-release capsules, looks just like pharmaceutical Dexamyl. No doubt, some people who buy it resell it on the black market as Dexamyl to gullible buyers. Older and more straightforward products are Vivarin and No-Doz, in the form of simple white tablets. If these products are more effective than coffee or tea, it is only because people believe in pills.

OTC Downers

A variety of products is available in drugstores to promote sleep at night (Nytol, Sominex, Unisom). They are widely used as nonprescription analogs of the stronger minor tranquilizers and sleeping pills. All of them contain antihistamines, usually diphenhydramine (Benadryl), pyrilamine, or doxylamine. As we have pointed out, these chemicals are not innocuous and tend to affect mental function in unpleasant ways. They will make people drowsy but can produce depression as well and can be habit-forming.

We favor less toxic remedies for insomnia, such as increased exercise during the day, decreased use of stimulants, especially in the evening (remember to read the labels of any pain pills, cold tablets, and other remedies to see if they contain caffeine or other stimulants), relaxation techniques, warm baths, and simple nutritional supplements such as calcium and magnesium tablets, which relax many people when taken at bedtime.

Analgesics

Although nonnarcotic pain relievers do not directly affect the mind, they can change moods dramatically by decreasing discomfort and so can be habit-forming. The common OTC analgesics, such as aspirin and acetaminophen (Tylenol), are effective remedies for occasional use, but when pain persists, people should seek to identify and treat the causes rather than rely on these drugs. Some analgesic compounds contain caffeine solely for its stimulant and mood-elevating effects.

OTC drugs are big business and are not regulated in the same way as prescription drugs. Manufacturers can get them on the market without doing much to prove their effectiveness, can deemphasize their adverse effects, and can make outrageous claims in their advertising. Most people assume that the products heaped on drugstore counters are mild but effective, nontoxic, and nonaddictive. Those are not safe assumptions. Anyone who uses OTC drugs should know what they contain and how they affect the body and mind.

Herbal Remedies

With increasing interest in alternatives to regular medicine, the marketing of herbal remedies and medicinal plants has boomed.

Most health food stores have herb departments, and some of the products they sell are even appearing in drugstores and supermarkets. Many are just pleasant herbal teas, such as peppermint and chamomile, without significant drug effects, but a few are really psychoactive. In Chapter 6, we discussed *guaraná*, maté, yohimbe, and ephedra, all stimulants.

A plant with the opposite effect is valerian; its root is a strong natural sedative that does not depress vital functions or cause the kind of dependence that sleeping pills do. Preparations of valerian root, including tinctures and capsules, are obtainable at health food stores. Valerian has a strange, musty odor that some people find disagreeable, but it is easy to take as a capsule or tincture and does work. For people who need nighttime sedatives, it is probably a better choice than more dangerous synthetic drugs.

Kava, or kava-kava, is another herbal depressant whose effect is of a more general anesthetic nature than a sedative. It is the root of a large tropical plant related to black pepper and cultivated on many islands of the South Pacific. Natives there make drinks from fresh or dried kava root and consume them as ritual and social drugs. Preparations of the fresh root are more powerful, putting users into a pleasant, dreamy state while numbing their bodies. Drinks made from the dried root are more relaxing than intoxicating. Kava ceremonies take place at night and often bring large groups of people together for the main social event of island life. Only dried kava is available outside the South Pacific. Herb stores sell it as a coarse powder or larger chips of root. When chewed, dried kava makes the mouth numb and may be relaxing. Some people brew it into a tea, which they like as a mild downer.

In the 1990s, many extracts of kava appeared on the market in capsule form. In Germany, both prescription and over-the-counter versions were in wide use as natural antianxiety agents. Then reports began to accumulate of cases of severe liver disease in people using kava; as a result, its popularity has dropped off sharply. We do not know the exact cause of these reactions, which mainly occurred in Europe. Perhaps the alcohol extracts of kava in use there contain toxic compounds not present in water extracts. Until the issue is settled, people with a history of liver problems should avoid kava.

One of the most famous of the plant drugs is ginseng, obtained from the roots of several species of woodland plants, one from China and Korea and another from the northeastern United States. People in Asia have used ginseng for centuries, paying high prices for the best quality roots and valuing them as a general tonic. They believe that ginseng increases vitality, resistance to disease, and longevity. It is especially used by men, and those who use it often say it increases sexual power, particularly as they grow older.

Ginseng has only recently become popular in the West, and Western scientists still do not understand it very well. They are convinced that ginseng has effects, but they don't yet know what all of them are. One source of confusion is that commercial products vary tremendously in potency; some have no activity at all. For some people, ginseng is a strong stimulant. It may raise blood pressure and should be used with caution by people with high blood pressure. Other users claim that it tones their muscles and skin and increases their physical endurance. "Siberian ginseng" is not true ginseng but comes from a related plant; it is less of a stimulant.

The effects of ginseng are cumulative, often not becoming apparent unless the drug is used regularly for weeks or months. The chemistry of the root is very complex. Some compounds in it may affect the production of steroid hormones, which could explain the results that users report. In any case, ginseng is a drug, not just a dietary supplement or new-age hoax, even though it now appears in everything from toothpaste to soda. If you want to try ginseng, avoid these senseless preparations and be prepared to spend a lot of money for whole roots, capsules, or extracts of reliable potency.

Smart Drugs

Since many people in our society turn to drugs for solutions to everything from heartburn to boredom, it is not surprising that they would get excited about drugs that are supposed to boost intelligence, memory, and concentration. Students are always looking for ways to increase their brain power. Users of alcohol, pot, and cocaine worry about the adverse effects of those substances on their minds. Some people approaching middle age become obsessed with extending their lives, enhancing their declining sexuality, and fortifying their brains against the ravages of old age. For all of these concerns, there is a new answer: smart drugs.

Smart drugs are a diverse group of compounds. Some are prescription drugs marketed openly in this country. Others are prescription drugs from other countries and are not generally available here but can be obtained by mail order or from Mexico. Still others can be had in health food stores and from other sources selling nutritional supplements.

Two kinds of smart drugs are nootropics and cognitive enhancers. The word *nootropic* (meaning "mind-turning") was coined to describe substances believed to improve learning and memory without affecting the brain in other ways and without causing toxicity, even at high doses. "Cognitive enhancer" is a vaguer term for substances that might improve general mental functioning.

Many of the smart drugs have been around for years, but information on them became widely available only in the 1990s. The media first began paying attention to them at this time, probably because of the appearance of "smart bars" in San Francisco and other cities. Smart bars are clubs that serve nonalcoholic drinks spiked with smart drugs. Who goes to smart bars? Students studying for exams are frequent patrons, but all sorts of people wander in to try the concoctions.

Here is a selection of some of the more popular smart drugs.

Piracetam and Relatives (Oxiracetam, Aniracetam, Pramiracetam, and Pyroglutamate)

These drugs, known collectively as pyrrolidone derivatives, are the most important family of nootropics. Smart-drug enthusiasts say they cause remarkable enhancement of memory. No one knows

> Piracetam keeps me alert when I am driving. It also helps
> me formulate new and different ideas when I am taking
> essay tests in school.
>
> — twenty-one-year-old woman, student

how they work, but they may affect nerve pathways in the brain
that use acetylcholine as a neurotransmitter. Acetylcholine declines
with age and may account for slowed mental function in the el-
derly. Users say piracetam is a central nervous system stimulant that
wakes up the brain. They claim that it has no toxicity or addictive
properties. Piracetam is not sold in the United States but can
be ordered by mail or purchased over the counter at Mexican
pharmacies.

DHEA (Dehydroepiandrosterone)

DHEA is an endogenous steroid hormone made in the adrenal
glands. It is related to male sex hormones and has weak androgenic activity. Smart-drug enthusiasts say that it combats obesity,
aging, and cancer, extends life, and keeps you looking youthful.
They also think that it can protect brain cells from the degenerative changes of old age. Research to back up these claims is lacking. The drug is available from "buying clubs" that supply unapproved drugs to AIDS patients. (DHEA is also supposed to boost
immunity.)

DMAE (Dimethylaminoethanol)

This endogenous substance, present in small amounts in the
brain, also occurs in some fish (anchovies and sardines). It is described as a nutrient that has mild stimulant properties and can
also elevate mood, increase intelligence, and counteract fatigue.
Like piracetam, it may work on acetylcholine pathways in the
brain. Health food stores sell DMAE as a nutritional supplement.

Hydergine

Hydergine is a pharmaceutical drug, derived from ergot, and is available by prescription in the United States as a cognitive enhancer for people suffering from mental impairment as a result of age or brain injury. It has little toxicity, and its mechanism of action is unknown. Although many doctors question its efficacy, the drug has a large following among smart-drug fans, who believe that it improves memory and learning and protects the brain from weakening with age. Hydergine is quite expensive.

Selegiline (Eldepryl, Deprenyl)

A newer prescription drug, recently introduced for the treatment of Parkinson's disease, Eldepryl has gained a strong reputation as another smart drug, one that wakes up the brain, increasing alertness and energy and enhancing all mental functions. Eldepryl is metabolized to amphetamine and methamphetamine in the body, which probably accounts for these effects.

Vasopressin (Diapid)

Vasopressin is an endogenous hormone produced by the pituitary gland. Also known as antidiuretic hormone, or ADH, it causes the body to retain urine. Doctors prescribe it in the form of a nasal spray to treat patients with a rare disease called diabetes insipidus, marked by frequent urination. Smart-drug enthusiasts say that vasopressin spray also affects the mind, improving attention, concentration, and memory. In addition, they say, it instantly counteracts the crash that follows the use of stimulant drugs and the grogginess caused by high doses of marijuana and alcohol. Vasopressin nasal spray can give you a number of uncomfortable side effects, including nasal irritation, runny nose, headache, and abdominal cramps.

It is difficult to assess the benefits and risks of smart drugs, because not enough research exists on them. Although doctors question their safety, especially when used in the combinations that their fans prefer, safety may be less of a concern than efficacy. It is not at all clear that these substances really have the beneficial effects claimed by their promoters, and we do not have enough information to know just what are the effects of long-term use.

SUGGESTED READING

Two useful books on medical drugs are *The Essential Guide to Prescription Drugs* by James W. Long (sixth edition; New York: Harper-Collins, 2002) and *Over Dose: The Case Against the Drug Companies: Prescription Drugs, Side Effects, and Your Health* by Jay S. Cohen (New York: Penguin USA, 2001).

Is There No Place on Earth for Me? by Susan Sheehan (Boston: Houghton Mifflin, 1982) is a vivid case history of a young schizophrenic woman who, during repeated hospitalizations, is treated with ever-increasing doses of virtually all the major tranquilizers then in use.

Prozac Backlash: Overcoming the Dangers of Prozac, Zoloft, Paxil, and Other Antidepressants with Safe, Effective Alternatives by Joseph Glenmullen (New York: Simon & Schuster, 2000) is a provocative look at the treatment of depression. Lauren Slater's *Prozac Diary* (London: Penguin, 1999) is an excellent personal account of Prozac use. So is Elizabeth Wurtzel's *Prozac Nation: Young and Depressed in America: A Memoir* (New York: Riverhead Books, 1997). Finally, see *Listening to Prozac: A Psychiatrist Explores Antidepressant Drugs and the Remaking of the Self* by Peter D. Kramer, M.D. (New York: Viking Penguin, 1993).

Also, see *Pills a Go Go: Fiendish Investigation into Pill Marketing, Art, History, and Consumption* by Jim Hogshire (Venice, Calif.: Feral House, 1999) for an informative account of pharmaceutical drugs.

An excellent all-around guide to herbal medicine is *The New Age Herbalist: How to Use Herbs for Healing, Nutrition, Body Care, and Relaxation* by Richard Mabey and Michael McIntyre (New York: Fireside, 1988). See also the periodical *HerbalGram* from the American Botanical Council (www.herbalgram.org)(last accessed February 2004).

The best references on smart drugs are *Smart Drugs & Nutrients* by

Ward Dean, M.D., and John Morgenthaler (Petaluma, Calif.: Smart Publications, 1991), and *Smart Drugs II: The Next Generation: New Drugs and Nutrients to Improve Your Memory and Increase Your Intelligence* by Ward Dean, M.D., John Morgenthaler, and Steven William Fowkes (Petaluma, Calif.: Smart Publications, 1993).

12. Problems with Drugs

IN THE PRECEDING CHAPTERS we have discussed the risks and problems associated with using specific drugs. Here we will comment on some more general problems that drug users are apt to encounter.

Uncertainty of Dose and Quality

When drugs come from legal sources, they are likely to be pure, of standard dosage, and correctly labeled. Yet even medical drugs can be outdated and mislabeled, and they sometimes contain fillers and colorings that can be harmful to some people. These problems are insignificant compared with those of black-market drugs, which are regularly cut with impurities, are of uncertain dosage, and are often completely misrepresented to the buyer.

Buying pills and powders on the street is a risky business at best. Not only do you have to deal with unsavory characters and participate in illegal transactions, you have no assurance of getting what you pay for. If you are lucky, what you buy will contain some of what it's supposed to contain and be cut with nothing more dangerous than starch or sugar. If you are less lucky, the pills and powders will be inactive, and if you aren't lucky at all, they will contain something actively harmful. Not only are you likely to get ripped off on the black market, you can also wind up in a hospital emergency room. People who inject street drugs are in greatest danger, because putting impurities directly into the bloodstream gives the body no chance to deal with them.

Some help with these uncertainties is offered by private testing labs that will analyze samples of drugs for a reasonable fee while protecting the customer's anonymity. Drug enforcement authorities will not allow these labs to give quantitative results, however, so that although you may find out what is in your material, you still won't know how potent it is. About the only way to be sure that you are getting what you want in the way of nonmedical drugs is to grow your own drug plants or collect them in the wild. Otherwise, you must know your sources; remember that the black market encourages deception and misrepresentation, and be extremely cautious about consuming any substance obtained on the street.

Mixing Drugs

In a few instances, the results of mixing psychoactive drugs are clear. For example, we have noted the additive effects of combining alcohol and downers or tranquilizers. In many more cases, the effects of drug combinations are unpredictable, depending more on the individual and on set and setting than on pharmacology. Mixing drugs can increase the problems associated with individual drugs and may create some new ones.

At the very least, drug combinations take getting used to. Many marijuana smokers use alcohol while smoking, but there is no predictable result of this combination. Some people find themselves more stoned, others less stoned, others sleepy or headachy. Until you know the effects of a given combination on *you*, you should proceed cautiously. People who get into bad relationships with drugs often use many drugs together, and some combinations may promote dependency and abuse. People who ingest alcohol and cocaine together often wind up taking more of both than they would if they used either by itself. Coffee and cigarettes together form a very stubborn habit — it is almost as if one triggers a desire for the other.

These days it is not unusual to see groups of people drinking alcohol, snorting coke, and smoking pot, as well as using tobacco, drinking coffee, and eating chocolate — all at the same time and in large doses. Such polydrug consumption tends to promote immoderation and lack of awareness about the nature of the substances being consumed.

Drug combining is a problem in medicine as well. Medical patients often receive many prescription drugs simultaneously, and doctors are often ignorant about how they interact. Interactions of medical drugs and recreational drugs are also largely unknown. If you are taking medical drugs, keep in mind that they might change your reaction to recreational drugs. If you use recreational drugs, consider that they might combine unfavorably with prescribed medication.

Medical Problems

Acute Problems

Overdosing and allergic reactions are the most important acute medical problems that can arise from taking psychoactive drugs. Mild overdoses of drugs may produce nausea and vomiting, which usually require no treatment but can be very unpleasant. Large overdoses can cause convulsions, coma, and death; they are medical emergencies requiring immediate treatment in a hospital. Anyone who suddenly loses consciousness or stops breathing after taking a drug should be seen immediately by a doctor. If you are around someone who develops an overdose (OD) reaction, put all legal considerations aside and summon medical help. Never administer more drugs — of *any* type — to a person suffering from overdose.

Intravenous users of drugs are in the greatest danger of dramatic overdose reactions, but people who smoke or snort stimulants and depressants can have them, too, as can people who take very large doses by mouth. Remember that ODs can quickly result in death if hospital treatment is not obtained immediately.

Allergic reactions to drugs take many forms, ranging from itching and swelling of parts of the body to death from asphyxiation because of the swelling of tissues in the windpipe. Serious allergic reactions are very unpredictable and may occur because of contaminants in street drugs as well as the drugs themselves. They may also develop suddenly in people with no prior history of allergy. The symptoms of serious allergic shock are itching in the throat and difficulty in breathing. Again, this is a medical emergency requiring prompt treatment. Anyone who develops such a reaction should be taken to a hospital at once.

Chronic Medical Problems

Any drug used in excess over time can produce illness. Different drugs irritate different systems of the body. In some cases, the association between a drug and a disease is very clear, as it is with alcohol and cirrhosis of the liver or tobacco in the form of cigarettes and lung cancer. We have reviewed these specific physical consequences in previous chapters.

People who use any drug intravenously expose themselves to other risks that are consequences of that method of administration. Putting a crude and unsterilized needle into a vein carries the grave danger of introducing serious infection. Viral hepatitis is probably the most common disease transmitted in this way; it can make people sick for months and cause permanent liver damage. Of even greater concern is AIDS, a fatal, incurable viral infection that destroys the immune system. Intravenous drug users are at risk for this devastating disease if they share needles. A needle used by an infected person can easily transmit the virus to the bloodstream of the next user. Another potential calamity is bacterial endocarditis — an infection of the heart valves. In addition, needle users frequently suffer from abscesses and inflamed and damaged veins. Intramuscular and subcutaneous injections are less dangerous but not without risk. They transmit hepatitis and AIDS equally well.

Smoking anything irritates the throat, bronchial tubes, and lungs. In susceptible individuals, regular smoking of any drug, whether it's tobacco, marijuana, or crack cocaine, can result in respiratory infection, decreased breathing capacity, coughing, bronchitis, and, probably, a greater risk of emphysema and lung cancer. It is also important to keep in mind that smoking puts drugs into the bloodstream and brain very directly, even faster than intravenous injection, making the drugs more toxic and more addicting. Snorting drugs is less direct than intravenous injection but not nearly as safe as oral use; snorting can lead to chronic irritation and erosion of the nasal membranes. Even taken by mouth, some drugs in excess are very irritating. Heavy drinking can cause chronic inflammation of the esophagus and stomach, and too much coffee often gives rise to chronic indigestion.

Heavy users of drugs often have an erratic lifestyle that interferes with regular sleep, good nutrition, and healthful habits of hygiene and exercise. In addition, the drugs they take may suppress appetite, rob the body of vitamins, and upset normal metabolism. All of these effects can lead to such chronic problems as malnutrition, anemia, and decreased resistance to infection. For example, dietary deficiencies in the alcoholic greatly increase the liver's susceptibility to the toxicity of alcohol and contribute to the development of cirrhosis.

Drugs and Pregnancy

Women expose their unborn babies to harm by consuming drugs — any drugs — during pregnancy. Many doctors now advise that expectant women take no drugs whatever during the first three months of pregnancy and as few as possible thereafter. Psychoactive drugs are no exception. In the 1960s, thousands of badly deformed babies were born to women who took the sedative thalidomide, prescribed as a "safe" relaxant and promoter of sleep.

Recreational drugs can also be risky to the fetus, but in most cases, the exact dangers are unknown. It is known that pregnant women who smoke cigarettes have more miscarriages and regularly give birth to babies that weigh less than normal, are more susceptible to respiratory infection, and die more frequently in infancy. Drinking alcohol during pregnancy also increases the rate of birth defects; unfortunately, no one can say what a safe intake of alcohol is for a pregnant woman.

Most of the drugs discussed in this book enter the system of the fetus and affect it in some way. For example, pregnant heroin addicts give birth to addicted babies who must be weaned off opiates in the first few days of life. Given these facts, pregnant women should make an effort to discontinue the use of all psychoactive substances until after they deliver. Even then, they should be careful if they breast-feed, because if they take drugs, their milk may contain amounts high enough to affect a baby. Smoking around an infant can also put drugs into its system, and babies are very sensitive to smoke of all sorts.

Psychiatric Problems

The most common acute psychiatric problem is panic. Typically, people will take a drug, feel it begin to work, and become convinced that they are dying or losing their mind. Panic reactions occur most frequently in people with little drug experience, especially in settings that encourage anxiety. A teen-ager who has never smoked marijuana and is pressured into trying it at a party with strangers is a good candidate for a panic reaction. People who are unaware that someone has slipped them a drug, or who wind up taking much larger doses than they are used to, are also likely to panic. Panic can be very dramatic, making people agitated, helpless, incoherent, and a source of great anxiety to others. People in panic often use the anxiety that they produce in others to fuel their own reactions.

Doctors have sometimes misdiagnosed a panic reaction as an episode of psychosis and have prolonged the episode by confirming the patient's fears of going crazy. People who are panicked need to be reassured and calmed down, preferably by someone with experience, such as a worker at a drug crisis center. Panicky people should not be given sedatives, tranquilizers, or other psychoactive drugs. A hospital emergency room may not be the best place to take people in panic, because it can produce more anxiety than reassurance. Most panic reactions will end quickly, provided that they are recognized for what they are and not intensified by improper management.

Paranoia and "bad trips" are similar to panic reactions and are also mostly products of set and setting. They, too, will subside by themselves if left to run their course.

True psychotic reactions are occasionally triggered by a drug experience, but they are not nearly so common as panic reactions. Just as a first sexual experience or going away from home to college or losing a job can trigger psychosis, so can a stressful drug experience. A person who becomes mentally disturbed after taking a drug and who continues to be disturbed after the effects of the drug wear off should be seen by a professional.

Coming down from drugs ("crashing") presents special problems. People who rely on drugs to feel good may become depressed when the drug wears off. Not only can this depression encourage frequent and abusive drug-taking, but it can also become a chronic psychological problem. Psychiatrists these days often see severely depressed patients who are heavy users of cocaine, and similar depression can occur with the regular use of any psychoactive drug. Depression is often a component of dependence on alcohol and downers, as well as dependence on stimulants.

Crusaders against drugs like to cite many other chronic psychological problems that are supposed to be drug connected, but there is little evidence to support most of their claims. There does seem to be a pharmacological basis for the paranoia and hallucinations that occur in people who shoot amphetamines, and alcohol certainly can cause brain damage, producing distinctive losses of mental function. Heavy use of cocaine and speed often causes personality changes in the direction of irritability, paranoia, and hostility. Major psychological problems may also go hand in hand with heavy consumption of other drugs, but whether they are a direct effect of the drugs is seldom clear.

As an example, there has been much talk of "burn-outs" —
young people who are supposed to be casualties of intense use of
marijuana, psychedelics, and other illegal drugs. Certainly, there
are people who wind up as aimless, confused misfits after using a
lot of drugs, but what were these people like before, and what
other factors played a role in the change? Many of them were run-
aways, engaged in unusual sexual experimentation, or joined religious cults in addition to taking drugs. It is easy to blame the
drugs, but evidence for their causative role is lacking.

An even better example of the false linking of a problem with a
drug is amotivational syndrome. As we have said, it makes much
more sense to view heavy marijuana smoking as an expression of
amotivation rather than the cause of it. Many amotivated people
smoke a lot of marijuana, but so do many well-motivated people.
Amotivated people would probably behave in other unproductive
ways if marijuana were to disappear. The tendency to see disliked
drugs as causes of disapproved behavior is understandable, but it
is not valid scientifically and does not help solve the real problems
associated with drugs.

Social and Behavioral Problems

Drug-taking can lead to a variety of problems with other people.
Many drug users feel guilty about their habits, and their guilt is often an obstacle to intimacy. Using illegal drugs automatically puts
people into conflict with social authorities and with parents, teachers, and employers. One of the commonest sources of family tension today is the suspicion or discovery by parents that a child is
using drugs. This issue is so emotional that most people are unable to deal with it openly. Often, it creates a climate of distrust
and misunderstanding that pervades every aspect of the family's
life. Drug use may also isolate children from the mainstream of
their peers, driving them into the company of other drug users
and limiting their possibilities for balanced social interaction. Of
course, children are not the only ones who encounter social prob-

I guess my drug of choice is wine. Two glasses of good wine put me in just the right state after a trying day. John drinks wine, too, but for getting high he prefers marijuana.

In the past few years, our different preferences in drugs have become a problem for us. My not liking marijuana separates me from John's closest friends and weakens our relationship. I don't think married people have to do everything together, but this is something important, and my inability to share John's highs bothers me. Also, I find I resent his smoking friends, since I'm the outsider, the "straight wife," when they are around. Yet I know that if I object, I will just drive him out of the house to get high with them elsewhere.

— thirty-five-year-old woman

lems as a result of drug use. Different preferences in recreational drugs are frequently a source of conflict in couples and can even result in the breakup of a marriage.

People who abuse drugs, whether legal or illegal, usually find themselves in social trouble on all levels. The alcoholic father who can't provide for his family and antagonizes his friends and coworkers is a classic example. The heroin addict who steals from a friend to buy his next fix is another. In fact, it is rare to find a drug abuser who does not provoke some degree of social conflict.

The drug laws in our society compound the social problems of people who choose to use illegal drugs. For one, illegal drugs are very expensive; buying them regularly can significantly drain a person's economic resources. Second, although casual users of illegal drugs generally obtain their supplies from friends, at some point the lines of supply connect to the criminal underworld. Heavy users are apt to be drawn into this sphere, especially if they begin to sell illicit substances to support their own drug habit.

The dangers of associating with professional drug dealers cannot be overstated. Many dealers handle large sums of cash, are heavily armed, and live in a paranoid world of rip-offs, busts, and informers. Those who grow or smuggle drugs on a large scale are also likely to be caught up in raids by police or federal agents. The ugliness of drug dealing is a direct consequence of laws that criminalize the possession and sale of disapproved substances. Narcotics agents who enforce these laws sometimes behave as disreputably as the people they try to catch, violating civil liberties and recklessly employing violence to chase down "drug traffickers."

Unfortunately, major traffickers are seldom touched by the law, because they are usually rich enough, smart enough, and powerful enough to stay in business. Instead, drug-law enforcement falls disproportionately on small-scale dealers and users. In recent years, so much enforcement has been directed at these people that our court and prison systems are now overwhelmed.

Quite another sort of problem arises from associating with people who are intoxicated on drugs, whether legal or illegal. Intoxication increases the likelihood of accidents and trouble of all kinds. If you keep company and go out in public with drugged friends, you may suffer for their blunders.

Drunk drivers are as dangerous to their passengers and other people on the road as they are to themselves. You have a choice whether to accept rides with them, as you do with drivers who are stoned on pot, tripping on psychedelics, or under the influence of any other drug that might compromise their driving skills. It can be very difficult to refuse a ride with friends because you feel that they are intoxicated, but learning to exercise that choice may save you from injury or death. In Sweden, where alcoholism is common and driving-while-intoxicated laws are strictly enforced, social custom dictates that one member of a group attending a party abstain from drinking in order to be the driver for the evening. The "designated driver" is still a new custom in our society, so individuals who associate with drug users must learn to judge when

> Money is the main reason why my friends and I deal drugs.
> Also, there's a lot of status in it. I mean, if you've got
> money and drugs, you've automatically got power and
> prestige. People say you're crazy to take the risk, but at the
> same time they're envious of you, and that's the truth.
>
> **— seventeen-year-old man**

they should go their separate ways. By the way, police now have an effective field test to identify drugged drivers. Called the Horizontal Gaze Nystagmus Test, it uses eye movements to detect intoxication by most psychoactive drugs.

These days, because of the widely accepted practice of urine testing, and the newer method of hair sample analysis, recreational users of illegal drugs run a greater risk of exposure than ever before. Many employers require their workers to submit to random urine testing and also screen job applicants in this way. Positive test results commonly mean that you will be fired.

Developmental Problems

The use of drugs by younger and younger children is very alarming to grown-ups. In the 1960s, college students were the main consumers of marijuana; today, pot is commonplace in high schools and, in some parts of the country, even in grade schools. Significant numbers of adolescents have now tried cocaine, alcohol, tobacco, tranquilizers, solvents, psychedelics, and probably more. Drugs have become prevalent in rural as well as urban schools and seem to cut across all class and ethnic boundaries.

Parents, teachers, doctors, and lawmakers generally assume that drug use by the young is especially dangerous. They fear that it will cause permanent physical and psychological damage as well as create whole generations of addicts, criminals, and zombies. It may well be that young people are more susceptible to the adverse effects of psychoactive drugs, but there is little hard evidence on this point. Among Native American groups who use drugs ritually, children are often introduced to natural psychedelics at a very young age without suffering any apparent harm. However, the social context of psychedelic use among these peoples is different from anything that exists in mainstream society.

Psychologists say that adolescence is, at best, a difficult time. Teen-agers must grapple with a host of problems and pressures, some caused by internal hormonal changes, others by the changing expectations of society as they approach maturity. One concern of psychologists is that the addition of drugs to this already turbulent process will make it significantly harder. Another concern is that young people will use drugs to avoid facing the conflicts that must be resolved if they are to develop into healthy adults. At the moment, there are no studies of adults who began using marijuana and other drugs while they were kids. Perhaps when such studies are done, the results will allay some of the worst fears. However, until then, it is no doubt safer to assume that children and adolescents *are* at greater risk and that, below a certain age, drug-taking may impair normal mental and emotional development. At the very least, using psychoactive drugs in childhood and adolescence to avoid boredom, conflict, and other bad feelings is likely to establish unhealthy patterns of drug-taking that will persist and cause problems in later life.

Legal Problems

Getting arrested for possession of drugs can be devastating. At best, it can absorb a great deal of time and money (including sei-

> I have been a criminal ever since the day I smoked my first joint.
>
> — forty-year-old man, landscape architect

> To think that a man should be allowed a gun and not a drug!
>
> — Alexander Trocchi, from his novel *Cain's Book* (1960)

zure of your house, car, and other assets); at worst, it can subject you to the horrors of prison and leave a permanent blot on your record. Current drug laws are the product of society's fears and prejudices and would certainly strike an unbiased observer as irrational, if not insane. In some states, people convicted for small-scale dealing of drugs such as cocaine and LSD are treated more harshly by the law than rapists, armed robbers, and even murderers. We think that the drug laws have done much more harm than good, but the fact is that they exist and are enforced. The current war on drugs has spawned tougher drug laws, with mandatory minimum sentences and "zero tolerance" of even casual users' possessing small amounts of marijuana. People who share drugs with friends may be considered dealers by the law, subject to heavy penalties if convicted.

If you run afoul of the drug laws, waste no time in getting the advice and help of a lawyer who specializes in this area. If you have no idea where to turn for information and have little or no money, contact a local office of the Legal Aid Society, which is listed in the telephone directory of most cities. Legal Aid can advise you and help you find a lawyer. The National Organization to Reform Marijuana Laws (NORML) is a good source for legal information and assistance. You can contact the group at www.norml .org/index.cfm (last accessed April 2004).

Dependency and Addiction

A chief characteristic of a bad relationship with a drug is difficulty in leaving it alone. Dependence on drugs is common and provokes so much censure and fear that it makes it hard to see that

Nothing is more destructive of respect for the government and the law of the land than passing laws which cannot be enforced.

— Albert Einstein

dependence is a basic human problem not limited to drugs. People can become dependent on many substances and practices; sources of pleasure are obviously the most frequent: food, sex, drugs. People can also become dependent on certain experiences, such as falling in love or having sex, seeking them out compulsively to the exclusion of other activities. It is also easy for people to become dependent on other people. Such personal relationships share many features of drug dependence, including tolerance (diminished pleasure with frequent exposure) and withdrawal (difficulty separating). People become dependent on jogging, gambling, watching television, shopping, working, and talking on the telephone. These observations suggest that dependence has more to do with human beings than with drugs. When people talk about the "addictive potential" of a substance, what they are really talking about is the tendency of human beings to get addicted to it.

The terms *addiction* and *dependence* are used loosely today. Properly speaking, drug addiction is a special kind of dependence, marked by physical changes: tolerance that requires increasing doses of the drug to achieve the same effect and a withdrawal syndrome if the drug is discontinued. People who become dependent on marijuana do not show tolerance and withdrawal as heroin addicts do. This fact has led many experts to talk about "psychological dependence." However, psychological dependence is a fuzzy concept. How does it differ from doing something repeatedly because you like it? Is there anything wrong with doing something you like repeatedly if it does not hurt you?

The real problem with dependence is that it limits personal freedom.

Of course, everyone is dependent on food, water, and other people; no one can ever be completely self-sufficient. Dependencies become a problem when they take up vast amounts of time, money, and energy; create guilt and anxiety; and control one's life. It is easy for people to ignore the extent to which dependencies control their lives; sometimes other people can see the problem more clearly.

Dependence on anything is not easy to break. More often than not, people simply switch dependencies, substituting one for another without achieving greater freedom. Still, it is no doubt better to be dependent on exercising, say, than on watching TV. Perhaps the tendency to become dependent is incurable, but to a certain extent people can choose what they are dependent on. Tobacco addicts who give up smoking by becoming compulsive joggers may not be any freer, but they may live longer, be healthier, and feel better about themselves.

Dependence on drugs may be better than dependence on some things and worse than dependence on others, but such value judgments are difficult to make without reference to particular individuals and situations. Is it better to be dependent on skydiving or snorting coke? On masturbating or eating chocolate? On fighting or shooting heroin?

Good relationships with drugs do not involve dependence. Once you become dependent on a drug, it may be difficult or impossible to get back into a good relationship with it. Most experts on alcoholism say that alcoholics cannot learn to be social drinkers; their only choice is between continued alcoholism and abstinence. Most people who smoke cigarettes nonaddictively never were addicted smokers; they formed a good relationship with cigarettes and maintained it. The surest way to avoid dependence on drugs is never to use them. If you do use drugs and want to avoid becoming dependent, you will have to take steps to create a good relationship with them right from the start.

The treatment of drug addiction has become big business. Private treatment centers charge thousands of dollars a week to get people off cocaine, alcohol, marijuana, narcotics, and tranquilizers. Twelve-step programs modeled on Alcoholics Anonymous have proliferated in all cities, and special programs now exist to treat the relatives of dependent persons — Adult Children of Alcoholics and Codependents Anonymous, for example. Despite the boom in the treatment industry, the rate of addiction has only increased.

We think that addiction is a basic human problem whose roots go very deep. Most of us have at some point been wounded, no matter what kind of family we grew up in or what kind of society we live in. We long for a sense of completeness and wholeness and most often search for satisfaction outside of ourselves. Ironically, whatever satisfaction we gain from drugs, food, sex, money, and other "sources" of pleasure really comes from inside of us. That is, we project our power onto external substances and activities, allowing them to make us feel better temporarily. This is a very strange sort of magic. We give away our power in exchange for a transient sense of wholeness, then suffer because the object of our craving seems to control us. Addiction can be cured only when we consciously experience this process, reclaim our power, and recognize that our wounds must be healed from within.

SUGGESTED READING

The autobiographical books listed in the Suggested Reading sections of preceding chapters give firsthand descriptions of problems with various drugs.

Two books written about teen-agers and drugs are *Smoking, Drinking, and Drug Use in Young Adulthood: The Impact of New Freedoms and New Responsibilities* by Jerald G. Bachman et al. (Mahwah, N.J.: L. Erlbaum Associates, 1997) and *Dirty: A Search for Answers Inside America's Teenage Drug Epidemic* by Meredith Maran (San Francisco: Harper, 2003). For a fictional account of drug dependence among high-school students, see *Go Ask Alice* by Anonymous (New York: Avon, 1972).

The National Center on Addiction and Substance Abuse at Columbia University (CASA) has published the excellent 2003 report "Teen Cigarette Smoking and Marijuana Use." This and other reports may be downloaded for free from www.casacolumbia.org (last accessed February 2004).

The National Institute on Drug Abuse, in conjunction with the University of Michigan's Institute for Social Research, has published a comprehensive two-part report monitoring drug use from 1975 to 2002, *Monitoring the Future* (Rockville, Md.: National Institute on Drug Abuse, National Institutes of Health, 2003). The first volume examines drug use among secondary school students, and the second looks at people aged nineteen to forty. Both may be downloaded at no charge from http://monitoringthefuture.org/pubs/monographs/vol1_2002.pdf and http://monitoringthefuture.org/pubs/monographs/vol2_2002.pdf (last accessed April 22, 2004).

Coming Clean: Overcoming Addiction Without Treatment by Robert Granfield and William Cloud (New York: New York University Press, 1999) is an important account of forty-six individuals who recovered from serious addictions without help. It examines the implications for drug abuse professionals and policymakers of recovery without treatment.

Stanton Peele's *The Meaning of Addiction: An Unconventional View* (reprint; San Francisco: Jossey-Bass, 1998) is one of the most insightful commentaries on addictive behavior. See also Chapter 7 of Andrew Weil's *Natural Health, Natural Medicine: A Complete Guide to Wellness and Self-Care for Optimum Health* (revised edition; Boston: Houghton Mifflin, 2004).

Some insight into the dangers of drug dealing and smuggling is provided by two entertaining books of true-life adventure: Robert Sabbag's *Snowblind: A Brief Career in the Cocaine Trade* (reprint; New York: Grove Press, 1998) and Bruce Porter's *BLOW: How a Small-Town Boy Made $100 Million with the Medellin Cocaine Cartel and Lost It All* (revised edition; New York: Griffin Trade Paperback, 2001). The latter was recently made into a popular movie. Another film, *Midnight Express,* is a horrifying story of the consequences of getting busted for drug smuggling abroad.

A readable history of our drug laws appears in *The American Disease: Origins of Narcotic Control* (third edition; New York: Oxford University Press, 1999) by David F. Musto, M.D. *Drug Control in a Free Society* by James B. Bakalar and Lester Grinspoon, M.D. (Cambridge: Cambridge University Press, 1988) is a balanced analysis of the arguments for and against various types of drug control.

13. Alternatives to Taking Drugs

A S WE MENTIONED at the beginning of this book, the main reason that people take psychoactive drugs is to satisfy a basic human need to vary their normal experience. Even very young children seem to have this need and experiment with techniques for altering their conscious state. Why should changing consciousness be so attractive and what do drugs have to do with it?

People who learn to change their conscious experience in safe and positive ways seem to be the better for it. They are healthier physically and mentally, more creative and productive, contribute more to society, and are more fun to be around. We believe that a desire to explore the various facets of consciousness is normal and good, but we are concerned about how people do it.

Being high does not mean being drugged. Clearly, drugs can sometimes make people feel high — at their best, energized, whole, expansive, creative, and connected. But why is it that many persons achieve high states without ever taking drugs, and why do the people who take the most drugs lose the very effects that they seek? The answer is that *drugs do not contain highs.* Highs exist within the human nervous system; all drugs do is trigger highs or provide an excuse to notice them.

That people cannot feel high whenever they want is one of the curious frustrations of the human condition. It seems necessary to work for highs or to find tools outside ourselves to evoke them. Drugs do this by making people feel temporarily different. They directly affect the nervous system and physical body in obvious

ways. For example, stimulants make people feel wakeful and energized, and psychedelics alter body sensations and perceptions.
Different drugs have different pharmacological effects, which is
why they make people feel different in different ways.

No drug makes a person high automatically. One must learn to
interpret the physical effects of drugs as the occasion for a high. It
is expectations of individuals and society (set and setting) that encourage people to associate inner experiences with the physical
feelings that drugs produce. If this association fails to develop or
breaks down, people can take the largest imaginable doses of
drugs and not get high — just feel drugged. This is precisely the
problem of those who get into bad relationships with drugs by taking them too frequently: as the novelty of the drug's effect diminishes with repetition, it no longer produces the needed signal.
First experiences are powerful because the novelty of the change is
greatest.

It is very easy to confuse the signal with the desired experience,
the drug with the high. Many drug users are convinced that the experiences that they need and like come from outside themselves
in the form of drinks, joints, pills, and powders. It is this confusion that leads people to abuse drugs; they take more drugs more
frequently in pursuit of ever-vanishing highs.

The fact that highs exist within is a cause for optimism.   It means
that the potential for these states is always there and many techniques must exist for eliciting them. There really *are* alternatives
to drugs, because drug highs differ from other highs only in su-
perficial ways. One day, scientists will understand what goes on in
the brain when people feel high. It may be that these states are actually mediated by the brain's own neurochemicals, which can be
stimulated equally by many different influences, including one's
own thoughts. Everyone has had the experience of being rocketed
out of a gloomy state by a word of praise, a demonstration of affec-
tion, or the arrival of a check in the mail. That change in mood
might be exactly the same on the cellular level as the rapid eupho-

ria that follows a snort of cocaine. In fact, it might not be accurate to talk about "natural" highs as opposed to "drug" highs, since both may depend on the body's endogenous drugs.

Is it any better to get high without drugs than with them? The main advantage of drugs compared to other techniques is that they work powerfully and immediately. *Their main disadvantage is that they reinforce the notion that the state that we desire comes from something outside us.* Not only can this idea lead to trouble with drugs, but it can also make people feel inadequate and incomplete. Even those in the best relationships with drugs often feel some degree of guilt about relying on them. Perhaps this feeling is so common because most people doubt their own worth and fear their abilities are not sufficient to meet the demands of life. Needing drugs to feel high confirms such fears. In any case, feeling guilty can't be good.

Of course, nondrug highs can present the same problem. People who are dependent on falling in love are equally at the mercy of outside forces. Many individuals get a rush from making money, and their lives are consumed in its pursuit. One variation on this theme is addiction to gambling. We have seen fanatical joggers who experience severe mental and physical discomfort if circumstances prevent them from running for even a day — a kind of withdrawal syndrome painful to them and those around them. If the only effective way you have of getting high is downhill skiing or hang-gliding, you are going to have to spend as much time and money getting high as any serious drug user and will expose yourself to equal or greater physical risk. There are men who get their greatest highs from killing; some of them find acceptable roles in society as professional soldiers, whereas others become criminals and terrorists.

The goal should be to learn how to get high in ways that do not hurt you or others and that do not necessarily require huge expenditures of time or money for special materials and equipment. Furthermore, you should be able to get high in enough different ways so that you can have the experience wherever you are, even if your external resources are minimal. You should also be willing to experiment with new methods of getting high as you mature and change.

Meditation, chanting, prayer, communing with nature, playing music, and artistic expression of all sorts are especially attractive ways of changing consciousness because they require little outside oneself. This is not to say that you shouldn't play polo if playing polo gets you high, but it would be useful to have some simpler, cheaper method in your repertoire as well.

Ways of changing consciousness without drugs do not work as fast or as powerfully as popping a pill; to master them, you may have to invest some time and effort. Many people may have little motivation to acquire these skills, especially since society neither admits the value of other modes of consciousness nor teaches us practical ways to achieve them. People who use drugs regularly may have to work especially hard to get high in other ways, because they often grow accustomed to the physical sensations of their drugs and consider them necessary components of the experience. People who use dilute forms of drugs infrequently and by mouth will find it easier to appreciate more subtle changes than people who put more concentrated drugs into their body more directly and more often, because they will not have learned to identify highs with intense pharmacological effects.

If getting high by simple methods takes more initial work, it may be worth it in the long run, because the simple methods do not fail with repeated use. In fact, methods requiring no external aid become more effective with practice. People who exercise, meditate, or do yoga to get high usually report that their experiences get better and better over time, which is a great contrast to the reports of heavy users of drugs.

There are so many ways to change consciousness that it is not worth trying to list them. Methods that work for some people may leave others cold. We know people who have learned to get high through Sufi dancing — a grown-up version of the spinning that children love — and others who find that this produces nothing

> Speaking in tongues makes me high. It makes me experience an altered state of consciousness. It lets me glimpse another reality — infinite realities — beyond the scope of my "normal" state of consciousness.
>
> — thirty-year-old woman

more than motion sickness. Contact sports give some people terrific highs but offend the sensibilities of others. Some methods may have more followers or seem more glamorous, but the only issue of any importance is whether they work for you.

As we have noted, people also take drugs for reasons other than getting high, and alternatives exist for these reasons as well. For instance, it isn't necessary to take drugs to treat disease; many drugless systems of therapy exist, such as acupuncture, massage, and regulation of diet. Moods can be altered and performance improved by changing patterns of eating, sleeping, and exercise. Creativity can be stimulated by traveling, reading books, talking to people, and having new experiences. You can explore your mind with the aid of psychotherapy, hypnosis, or writing or singing about your inner experiences. Since the use of drugs has become so habitual in connection with certain activities (a glass of wine with dinner, a joint before a movie), it may be hard for some people to imagine life without them. The fact is, however, that if people are determined enough, they can eliminate drugs from their lives and never miss them.

SUGGESTED READING

For all of the talk about alternatives to drugs, precious little is in print on the subject.

One of the best books is *Natural Highs: Supplements, Nutrition, and Mind-Body Techniques to Help You Feel Good All the Time* by Hyla Cass and Patrick Holford (New York: Avery Penguin Putnam, 2002).

Mind Games: The Guide to Inner Space by Robert Masters and Jean Houston (New York: Quest, 1998) is a manual of exercises in guided fantasy and trance states. The authors have written extensively about psychedelic experiences and are well qualified to discuss altered states of consciousness.

Originally published in 1968, *The Master Game: Pathways to Higher Consciousness* by Robert S. De Ropp and Iven B. Lourie (Nevada City, Calif.: Gateways Books & Tapes, 2003) remains an excellent book and practical guide.

Finally, Andrew Weil's *The Marriage of the Sun and Moon: Dispatches from the Frontiers of Consciousness* (revised edition; Boston: Houghton Mifflin, 2004) gives firsthand accounts of various nondrug highs and points out their relationship to drug experiences.

14. Final Words

SOME PEOPLE MIGHT THINK that giving the information in this book to young people will encourage them to try or to use drugs. We would like to address that question head-on.

The truth about drugs cannot do harm. It may offend some people's sensibilities and disturb those who do not want to hear it, but it cannot hurt people. On the other hand, false information can and does lead people to hurt themselves and others.

Our intention is not to encourage drug use by anyone, nor is it to discourage drug use. As we wrote at the very beginning, young people (and adults, for that matter) must decide for themselves which drugs, if any, to use and which to reject. We strongly recommend adopting alternatives to drugs, and we strongly recommend learning to use drugs wisely rather than falling into habits of excess, dependence, and abuse.

People make decisions on the basis of the information available to them. The more accurate the information, the better their decisions will be. We have worked hard to present balanced information that is as accurate as our best efforts can determine. We have not tried to make any drug attractive in our selection of facts.

If we have played down concerns about some drugs — say, the health hazards of marijuana — we have done so because they are products of bias and not in accord with our experience or compatible with the results of good scientific inquiry. In the end, such exaggeration of the dangers of marijuana leads more people to try the drug and more people to abuse it. We have countered those misconceptions by emphasizing what we see as a real danger of marijuana: the ease of sliding into a dependent relationship with it by smoking it thoughtlessly and excessively.

If we have stressed the ill effects of accepted drugs — say, those of coffee or antihistamines — we have done so because the findings about them are in accord with good scientific evidence and with our experience, and because we worry that ignorance of these hazards results in widespread overuse with attendant consequences on physical and mental health.

In short, we sincerely believe that the information that we have presented in these pages is reliable and will enable people to make intelligent choices about the use of drugs, which should help to prevent drug abuse before it starts.

Permit us to repeat the most important points that we have made:

There are no good or bad drugs, only good and bad uses of drugs. Drug abuse is not any use of a disapproved substance; abuse is the use of any substance in ways that impair physical or mental health or social functioning and productivity. Abuse develops from bad relationships with drugs, and learning to recognize such relationships early is one key to preventing abuse. Bad relationships with drugs begin with ignorance or loss of awareness of the nature of a substance and its effects and overuse of it to the point of losing the initial desired effect. Overuse, in turn, leads to difficulty in leaving the drug alone and to eventual impairment of health and productivity.

People must learn to look at and analyze their own and others' relationships with drugs. Recognizing drug abuse is not a matter of searching a child's room for cigarette papers or looking for dilated eyes or certain styles of dress or types of behavior. It involves the ability to know dependence in oneself and others, to watch how experiences with drugs change over time, to observe changes in health and look for correlations with drug use, to see whether drug usage interferes with work at school or on the job, to see whether it promotes associations with undesirable people. This kind of analysis is a lot harder than searching a room for cigarette papers.

Learning to recognize drug abuse is important, because treatment is not easy, and the earlier a problem comes to light, the better chance there is of correcting it. Prevention of drug abuse is always much easier than treatment. As we have said before, prevention depends on being informed, being aware, and exploring alternatives to drugs. For those who decide to use drugs, prevention depends also on associating with people who use drugs wisely rather than with people who abuse them, and on making intelligent choices about what substances to use and how and when to use them.

Treatment is another matter. Even with the best help possible, the only alternative for many abusers is to give up their drugs forever and admit that they have lost the chance to be in good relationships with those substances. In any case, treatment must begin with an abuser's own recognition that abuse exists and is a problem, and it will depend for its success on the individual's motivation to change. (Alcoholics Anonymous, Overeaters Anonymous, and other such self-help groups take this same position.) A drug abuser who is insufficiently motivated will not be cured by any approach.

Treating addiction often requires outside help: from doctors, counselors, clergy, and other professionals trained to advise people in trouble. Finding help is rarely easy, since some of the people most eager to work with drug abusers are in no way qualified to do the job. Above all, never put yourself or a child, relative, or friend in treatment for a drug problem with anyone you do not trust or consider fully informed and qualified, no matter what degree or certification the person holds.

Drug-abuse treatment centers are often staffed by ex-addicts. Such counselors may not be the best people to go to for help in improving your relationship with drugs, since they failed to form good ones themselves. Many reformed abusers behave like self-righteous fanatics when they appear in public: they inflame discussions about drugs, polarize audiences, and obstruct the drug-education process. It is also worth considering that the drug-abuse treatment profession has a vested interest in seeing drug abuse continue; its members make their living from the problem.

It is uncertain whether going to doctors for help is the best course of action. Medical schools do not teach much about the effects of psychoactive drugs. Unless physicians take the trouble to inform themselves, they are as likely as others to propagate untruths. Doctors have caused a great deal of the drug abuse of the past hundred years by carelessly prescribing opiates, cocaine, amphetamines, and tranquilizers without having clear ideas of the nature of those substances. Also, doctors themselves may be in bad relationships with alcohol, tobacco, coffee, and other depressants and stimulants legally available to them.

In sum, finding reliable help with drug problems is not simple. You have to shop around, ask questions, and use your own judgment. Do not hesitate to ask a prospective counselor to explain to you his or her attitudes toward drugs and recommendations for treatment of abuse. If you agree with the ideas in these pages, you might ask the person to read this book as a basis for your initial discussions.

If all of our warnings and cautions sound discouraging, it is because the treatment of drug abuse is discouraging. For that reason, we stress prevention as the better course and come back to solid, truthful information about drugs as the single best measure.

Suggested Reading lists follow most chapters, and we urge you to use them as a guide if you require more detail on a particular subject. The more you inform yourself on the complicated and ever-present issue of drugs, the more you can protect yourself and those around you from trouble, and the more you will be doing your part to steer society onto a less destructive course.

APPENDIX:

FIRST-PERSON ACCOUNTS

AND COMMENTS

GLOSSARY

INDEX

Appendix: First-Person Accounts and Comments

Drugs in High School A lot of kids in my high school were into drugs. The upperclassmen — myself included — smoked pot regularly and drank (mostly beer) on the weekends. The big status drug was cocaine, only no one could ever afford it. There was one kid who used to steal it from his parents, though, a little every day, and save it up for parties.

The main reason most kids took drugs — in my opinion — was peer pressure. Of course, we didn't admit that to ourselves. We weren't even conscious of it, really. It wasn't too obvious; if it had been obvious, it probably would have been a lot easier to resist. But it was a subtle thing, an attitude. We didn't think about it, but it was there.

— twenty-eight-year-old man, carpenter

The Coffee Cantata Johann Sebastian Bach (1685–1750) wrote the Coffee Cantata around 1732, when the new drink began to leave the male society of coffee houses in Germany and invade private homes, where ladies began to consume it. In the cantata, the father is angry because his daughter is a coffee addict. He threatens not to provide her with a husband unless she promises to stop drinking it. Here are a few excerpts from their dialogue:

FATHER: O wicked child! Ungrateful daughter, why will you not respect my wishes and cease this coffee drinking?

DAUGHTER: Dear Father, be not so unkind; I love my cup of coffee at least three times a day, and if this pleasure you deny me, what else on earth is there to live for?

DAUGHTER [continues in solo aria]: Far beyond all other pleasures, rarer than jewels or treasures, sweeter than grape from the vine. Yes! Yes! Greatest of pleasures! Coffee, coffee, how I love its flavor, and if you would win my favor, yes! Yes! let me have coffee, let me have my coffee strong.

FATHER: Well, pretty daughter, you must choose. If sense of duty you have none, then I must try another way. My patience is well nigh exhausted! Now listen! From your dress allowance I will take one half. Your next birthday should soon be here; no present will you get from me.

DAUGHTER: . . . how cruel! But I will forgive you and consolation find in coffee . . .

FATHER: Now, hearken to my last word. If coffee you must have, then a husband you shall not have.

DAUGHTER: O father! O horror! Not a husband?

FATHER: I swear it, and I mean it too.

DAUGHTER: O harsh decree! O cruel choice, between a husband and my joy. I'll strive no more; my coffee I surrender.

FATHER: At last you have regained your senses. [The daughter sings a melancholy aria of resignation.]

TENOR: And now, behold the happy father as forth he goes in search of a husband, rich and handsome, for his daughter. But the crafty little maiden has quite made up her mind that, ere she gives consent to marriage, her lover must make a solemn promise that she may have her coffee whenever and wherever she pleases.

Coffee Has Never Failed Me   In the morning I drink two cups of coffee. If I don't, I feel irritable. If I drink three cups, I get a little speedy, but with two I feel just about right.

If I drink coffee after about three in the afternoon, I cannot fall asleep when I like to, about eleven-thirty. If I drink coffee after dinner, as little as a half cup, I lie awake long past midnight. If I have something important or risky to do the next day, especially some public performance, coffee late in the day invariably interacts with my nervousness to produce stark insomnia.

This sleeplessness after coffee feels pharmacological. I can reach a dreamy peacefulness and experience some of the floating state that usually precedes sleep for me, but then I just hang on the edge, never quite slipping into unconsciousness. When I get up the next morning (angry at myself for not having slept), I feel relaxed but not rested by my seven hours in bed.

When I know that I have a long drive ahead of me, one that will mean driving late into the night or straight through it, I don't drink coffee for two or three days before. (I settle for lower doses of caffeine in tea or cola.) On the night of the drive I drink coffee twice, first a cup or two when I get drowsy at my usual bedtime, then two cups or more about three hours later. If I have been drinking coffee steadily for the few days before, I seem to get less stimulant effect from drinking it at night. It is almost a matter of "saving up" the coffee I would have consumed on the two or three days preceding and then drinking it on a particular night to keep me awake on the road. Used in this way, coffee has been a great help to me and has never failed me.

— **thirty-nine-year-old man, college administrator**

Coffee Addiction   My wife and I have drunk a lot of coffee for many years. I used to be a cigarette smoker but stopped with great difficulty twelve years ago; she still smokes, and I don't think she will ever be able to stop. I begin the day with two cups of coffee and drink about six more cups until dinnertime. Recently, we started drinking decaffeinated coffee with dinner, because we found the regular kind made it hard for us to fall asleep at bedtime.

A few years ago, I developed a shake in my left hand. The doctors call it a tremor and have no explanation or treatment for it. In the past year, it got worse and made me self-conscious. A number of people told me that caffeine might be causing it or, at least, making it worse, so I thought it would be a good idea to cut it out. Since I never thought that coffee did much for me or was much of a drug, I never thought it would be hard for me to stop.

My wife also thought of coffee as just a pleasant drink that we liked, and she agreed that we should switch to decaffeinated completely. So we did. I didn't notice any difference the first day, but on the second day I got very tired at my office and started to get a bad headache. I decided to come home early. When I arrived, I found my wife lying on the couch groaning. She said she had one of the worst headaches of her life and couldn't even stand up. Since my headache was steadily getting worse, I realized we must be experiencing a reaction to lack of caffeine. I told my wife that, but she refused to believe me. I told her I would prove it. I went to the kitchen and fixed us both cups of strong regular coffee. Within ten minutes of drinking them, we both felt our headaches disappear as if by magic and felt like our old selves. It astonished me to see how addicted we were to caffeine; my wife could scarcely believe it, since she was even less aware than I that coffee can be an addicting drug.

Since then, we have been trying to wean ourselves off caffeine by gradually substituting decaffeinated coffee for regular. We've cut our consumption in half so far but still cannot do without the two cups in the morning, even after a year of trying. We're determined to do it, however, and I know we'll succeed. Seeing the addiction for what it was gave us the motivation we needed.

— **sixty-eight-year-old man, lawyer**

Kicking the Chocolate Habit   Five years ago, hoping to kick a chocolate habit that was significantly affecting my life, I enrolled in a program at the Shick Center for the Control of Smoking, Alcoholism, and Overeating, in Los Angeles. I was then thirty-three. I could not remember the last time I had managed to get through a whole day without eating chocolate in one form or another, usually in quantities most people would regard as excessive, if not appalling.

Though not overweight, I indulged many of my chocolate cravings in secret, often in the middle of the night, when, if I had no chocolate in the house, I would think nothing of getting in my car and driving halfway across L.A. to an all-night supermarket for a fix. Although the Shick people told me they could cure my chocolate addiction in ten sessions, I was skeptical. My behavior was so compulsive and out of control that the best I thought I could hope for was a slight, temporary reduction of the cravings I suffered constantly. Still, I was willing to try anything.

The Shick Center places no importance on willpower, since it believes any form of self-imposed denial is doomed to failure. Instead, it uses a behavior-modification technique so simple as to seem ludicrous. Following instructions, I arrived for my first session with plenty of my favorite food (Hershey bars) and was seated in front of a mirror and handed a paper plate. A gadget was then strapped to my wrist that could give a very low-level electric shock. Far from being painful, this sensation was barely noticeable. I was told it was meant to have a purely subliminal effect. Thus equipped, I spent the next half-hour chewing mouthfuls of chocolate, which, instead of swallowing, I had to spit out onto the paper plate, all the while watching myself in the mirror.

During this first session, my skepticism hardened into utter disbelief. The mild revulsion I felt at the sight of seeing myself spit out the chocolate was more than offset by the pleasure of having it in my mouth. I couldn't see how such an absurd procedure could even scratch the surface of a problem as profound as mine, and were it not for the program's money-back guarantee, I would have dropped out then and there.

The following six sessions were carbon copies of the first. Toward the end of my seventh visit, I remember thinking, "This can't possibly be working; I still love the taste of chocolate as much as ever." Meanwhile, the program made no attempt to restrict what I ate on my own, and my chocolate consumption continued unabated.

It was not until the eighth session that I experienced a trace — it was the merest inkling — of something changing. It wasn't that I liked the taste of chocolate any less, but somehow I did not feel quite so compelled to put it in my mouth. Then, midway through the ninth session, I sensed a subtle but definite change. I didn't experience anything like distaste, but somehow eating the chocolate became automatic and without pleasure. I was still doubtful, especially about lasting effects, but the change was a revelation.

Preposterous as it may sound, I walked out of the tenth session completely cured. Although chocolate does not disgust me, I have no desire to eat it, ever. Flavors I never cared for before — vanilla, for example, or strawberry — appeal much more to me now, and I will choose them over chocolate every time. I don't consciously avoid chocolate out of fear of getting hooked again, either. I suppose I could get hooked again if I worked at it, but even though I test myself occasionally, my indifference to it remains the same.

Frankly, I am mystified by what happened and to this day cannot explain it. Being addicted to chocolate was so much a part of my definition of myself that it constantly amazes me to think that I am free of it. Needless to say, I am very grateful. The only problem is, I am now addicted (though somewhat less severely) to cake.

— **thirty-eight-year-old woman, social worker**

Trouble with Cocaine   I first tried cocaine in the early '70s. I had been using speed to help me with schoolwork and with my art. Cocaine was much more expensive than speed in those days and seemed less powerful, but I began to read a lot of information about the dangers of speed and thought cocaine might not be as harmful.

A few years later, I sold cocaine for a short time, although I still was not very involved with it. When I went to Europe on a vacation, I gave away what I had.

By the mid-70s, cocaine was more common, partly because the drug generation was older and had more money and partly because the dangers of speed were then well known. I found that coke gave me a good boost for getting work done. When I snorted it, I would feel inspired, brilliant, and energized. My art work went much faster with it because I could really focus on it and feel good at the same time. The ideas I got on coke were good ones, and I could get them down on paper. I came to see cocaine as an inducement and reward for getting work done.

Four years later, I began to realize that I could not work easily without cocaine. If I didn't use it, I felt bored, tired, and out of focus, which made me want to have it around all the time. As a result, I spent more and more money on it. I think I also began to get less patient, more critical, and paranoid. I started selling coke to friends to cover my needs, although I found dealing with friends as customers confusing and stressful. I got more and more difficult to be around. I was under a lot of work pressure, too, having to renovate a house I had acquired. I felt the need to rely on coke more and more to squeeze creative energy out of myself.

In 1978, a number of personal problems built up to an emotional crisis. A long-term love relationship broke up, and I ran into a dry spell with my art. I turned even more to coke to sustain me during this period. At first, a gram might last me a week, but soon I was using half a gram to a gram every day, sometimes having the first snort as soon as I got up. I would go for days without sleep. Also, I paid little attention to my diet. At one point, I had to go to the hospital with severe pain that turned out to be a kidney stone. I think it resulted from episodes of bad dehydration, since coke made me urinate more, but I would put off getting something to drink for hours while I buried myself in work.

In order to relax while using cocaine so heavily, I had to drink alcohol or take Valium. Even so, I would often lie in bed for hours with my heart racing, unable to fall asleep. I was really living in the extremes — either groggy and depressed or speeding. Finally, all that coke made me crazy. It gave me false inspiration and a kind of tunnel vision that hurt my creative efforts. Also, I began to suffer severe depressions. I'd play hide-and-seek games with the coke, locking it away and telling myself I wouldn't use it today. But as long as I knew it was there, I couldn't stop thinking about it and finally would give in and use it. Then I'd feel guilty as well.

I finally stopped taking it because the depressions outweighed the highs. After a few months, I tried it again but got the same results: depression and no high. I never again used cocaine, but I missed it for several years and had to relearn how to work without it. I feel strongly that I have to avoid any contact with that drug from now on.

— **forty-eight-year-old man**, artist

Speeding Through European History I was miserable and homesick during my first year at college and, as a result, wasn't a particularly good student. In fact, I spent the better part of my time bad-mouthing the school and sitting around feeling sorry for myself, and very little time studying. Therefore, when midterms came around, I had little hope of distinguishing myself. I decided to try and make up for lost time by staying up all night to study for my European history exam, but by midnight the text was blurring before my eyes. I was studying in the dining room of my dorm with several other girls. Seeing me losing my struggle to stay awake, an upperclassman took pity on me and offered me a green-and-white capsule along with the promise that my drowsiness would be cured by taking it. I took it without a second thought, and within half an hour or so found myself studying like mad. Not only was I completely engrossed in European history, I felt exhilarated; I was actually enjoying myself for the first time in months.

You always hear stories about people taking exams on amphetamines and thinking they've done brilliantly, only to find out later that they wrote page after page of incomprehensible gibberish. I almost wish that had happened in my case. I got an A on my history exam — as I was sure I had — and have been involved, to some extent, with amphetamines ever since.

— **forty-eight-year-old woman, writer**

A College Speed Freak I was a speed freak in college but did not know it, because a doctor got me to take it and never told me I could get hooked. I was about thirty pounds overweight and had never been able to diet for long. A school doctor started me on daily doses of Desoxyn and told me it would suppress my appetite. It did. It also made me feel great, at least at first. He also gave me a diet to follow, and I soon lost most of my excess weight. After several months, however, I began getting irritable and depressed and also didn't sleep well. I ate more when I was in these moods and gained some weight back. I found that taking more Desoxyn made me feel better and eat less.

It never occurred to me that the Desoxyn could affect my mood. I was completely ignorant of what it was; I think I considered it a kind of dietary supplement that took away hunger. My doctor never made me feel I needed to worry about taking it all the time. Soon, I was taking three times the original dose.

Even when speed began to get a bad reputation in the late 1960s, I didn't know I was on it. I was really shocked to learn that Desoxyn was just a brand name for methamphetamine and even more shocked to find that I couldn't stop taking it. If I tried to cut down the dose or stop, I would be groggy, depressed, and unable to concentrate or do my school-work. I would also eat a lot and gain weight. By the way, I also drank a lot of coffee and smoked cigarettes, so I was really a heavy user of stimulants.

When I told the doctor I was worried about being addicted, he made light of my fears, saying Desoxyn was a safe drug. It took many visits over the next year to convince him that I had a drug problem and took me another year beyond that to get off speed entirely. When I did, I was back where I started as far as being overweight. I feel I was a victim of that doctor's ignorance and probably of the drug company's promotion of the stuff for weight loss. Also, I know I was not an unusual case, because I have met other people who had similar experiences. I do not think I will ever take any kind of amphetamine again, because I am afraid that I would easily fall back into the same pattern of addictive use. Maybe those drugs have some good uses but not in the way I took them.

— forty-six-year-old man, lawyer

Speed in College: Another View   As a college student in the 1960s, I used speed to take important exams. Caffeine never helped me stay up; I could drink all the coffee I could stand or take many times the recommended dose of No-Doz and still fall asleep. So I went to the student health services, where a doctor listened to my story of getting sleepy when I had to study. He gave me a prescription for Dexamyl. The first time I took the stuff, I felt so good that I wrote a paper for a course effortlessly. I took another capsule the next day and got about half the effect. That made me realize I should not use it regularly.

The pattern I developed was to save the speed for the day of a big morning exam. I'd stay up studying as late as I could — say, till 3 A.M. — then go to sleep and set the alarm for seven. When I woke up, I'd study a little more and take a Dexamyl capsule when I left my room to walk to the exam. By the time I got the questions, I'd be buzzing with energy and confidence and be eager to start writing.

I did well in all the exams I took that way and never got any complaints that I'd written my name over and over. For me, Dexamyl really increased concentration and mental performance. (Of course, I had to know the material; it didn't put information in my head if I did not study.)

After I had made several visits to the student health service for new prescriptions, the doctor gave me an unlimited one that I used for several years, and [it] enabled me to give Dexamyl to classmates who also needed it at exam time. I never used speed in any other situations, and no one I knew in college had problems with it. I suppose that kind of prescription is not allowed anymore, and I know amphetamines have a bad reputation today, but I think we used them sensibly, and they helped us cope with a system that paralyzed many students with anxiety.

— **forty-nine-year-old man, corporate executive**

What I Think About Crank   Who would've thought my little town on the prairie would become the methamphetamine capital of the state? But it seems to be true. At least, the newspapers are full of stories about meth labs being raided and blowing up all over the county. Things are pretty bad around here. Family farms are going down the tubes, a lot of places on Main Street are boarded up, and most people who could move away have moved away. I know a few people who take crank to drive at night or do housework, but I've never run into any hardcore addicts. Meanwhile, just about every kid is on speed for ADD [attention deficit disorder]. Imagine my surprise when I found out that the most popular prescription drug for kids around here is Adderall, which is — guess what? — methamphetamine. It seems to me something is wrong with this picture.

— **twenty-nine year-old woman, beautician**

A Nonaddicted Smoker   Like Mark Twain, I find it easy to give up smoking; I have done it countless times. In fact, I consider myself a non-addicted smoker, since I have been smoking cigarettes on and off for twenty-five years without ever getting so hooked I couldn't stop just like *that* whenever I chose to. I would see nothing extraordinary about this, were it not for the wonder and admiration it excites in other people. Since it is mostly unheard of to smoke cigarettes only now and then, acquaintances regard me as a woman of superhuman willpower, a notion I hate to disabuse them of.

However, the sad truth is, I have no more willpower than anyone else and probably less than many. What saves me from being a cigarette junkie is that I recognized early how easy it would be for me to get hooked on tobacco, and, knowing that if I did get hooked I'd hate myself, I have always been very careful to keep my smoking under control.

For one thing, I never smoke before five o'clock in the afternoon. That, in itself, might seem adequate insurance against addiction, but, even though I have no desire for a cigarette before that time, I have been known to smoke up to five in a row once I begin — making myself very sick in the process. So I limit myself to one cigarette before dinner and try not to smoke more than five or six in the course of an evening. Also, I monitor my consumption very closely, and whenever I notice a rising trend, I swear off entirely for a few days.

Since my husband is a confirmed and heavy smoker, it requires some effort on my part to refrain entirely for days at a time. On the other hand, having him around helps me in the long run because he provides a living example of the sort of dependency I want so much to avoid.

— thirty-seven-year-old woman

Love versus Cigarettes These days I run into lots of people who have stopped smoking, and they always say, "You could do it, too." I suppose they're right in theory. I mean, in theory I could run the triathalon if I put my mind to it, but in practice I know it isn't so.

I come from a long line of smokers. At seventy, my mother still smokes heavily. Her mother smoked well into her eighties (and lived to be ninety-three). I took up the habit at age thirteen, and for the next twenty years I never once seriously considered denying myself the pleasure [that] smoking afforded me.

Then, several years ago, I fell madly in love with an ex-smoker, a man who, though broad-minded in other respects, was a fanatic on the subject of cigarettes. He forbade smoking anywhere in his vicinity — not only in his own house and car but also in other people's houses and cars, as well as in restaurants and movie theaters, where he would not hesitate to browbeat people into putting out their cigarettes even when they were legally within their rights to smoke.

Very early in our relationship, I realized it would be futile to expect him to compromise on this issue. Not only did he object to cigarette smoke in the air he breathed, he hated the smell of it on my breath, in my hair or clothing. He was also highly sensitive to the odor of cigarettes, and though I bent over backwards to avoid offending him, my efforts were mostly unsuccessful. I grew increasingly defensive and insecure, and soon had to face the fact that we couldn't possibly have a long-term, intimate relationship unless I quit smoking. I therefore resolved to do so, and one day, feeling very virtuous, I tossed out my cigarettes and went cold turkey.

My friend assured me that I would soon begin to feel great as a result of not smoking, but in fact the discomfort I experienced from abstinence was intense and unrelenting, even after five weeks. Smoking had become so woven into the fabric of my life that everything seemed to come unraveled without it. I could not get my mind off cigarettes for more than ten seconds at a time. I craved them not only every minute of every day but also in my dreams at night.

Naturally, my agony put a lot of stress on what was still an untried and untested relationship, and the relationship did not bear up well under it, I'm afraid. No doubt, I wanted much more credit and consideration from my friend than I deserved, but I also deserved, I think, somewhat more than I got. Having gone through the ordeal himself, he was, if anything, less compassionate. He did not want to hear about my suffering and put me down for continuing to make such a fuss. Then, after five weeks of steadily mounting tension, he had to go to Europe on business for a month. I started smoking again as soon as his plane took off.

When my friend returned from Europe, he was most unhappy to find that instead of being out of the woods, I was right back at square one. He was willing to try again, but this time, instead of urging me to quit for reasons of my own health and well-being, he wanted me to do it for him. What meant more to me — him or cigarettes? That was the choice I was faced with. In other words, it was a test.

Well, to make a long story short, I failed the test — not once or twice but repeatedly, almost every day for ten straight months, in fact. Had my lapses been matters merely between me and my conscience, they would have been bad enough. But, as I said, my friend was very sensitive to the odor of tobacco. No matter what precautions I took, he was able, even hours after the fact, to smell the evidence on my breath. So I was constantly humiliated as well, and my failures became the subject of endless arguments, and, toward the end of the affair, the cause of several knockdown, drag-out fights. There were, of course, other differences between us, but the issue of smoking became a sort of lightning rod, attracting more and more of the emotional charge.

I had always thought I'd be able to kick my addiction for someone I loved. That assumption turned out to be wrong. In the end, when forced to choose between love and cigarettes, I chose cigarettes. It was that simple.

I did make one resolution at the time, which I have stuck to ever since. It was that I would never again become involved with a man who does not smoke cigarettes.

— **forty-one-year-old woman, teacher**

I Like Alcohol   I like alcohol. It is a powerful drug and, God knows, for some people a hellish one, but if used carefully it can give great pleasure. After a long, hard day, the splendid warm glow that strong drink provides is one of my favorite feelings; it starts in the pit of my stomach, then spreads to my limbs and brain. I know that alcohol is a depressant, but it acts and feels like a gentle relaxant — of the spirit as well as of the physical body. Just notice the increased vivacity and noise level at a cocktail party after a drink has been served to see how alcohol can put people at ease emotionally.

Aside from the pleasureful intoxication of strong drink, I also enjoy the tastes of lighter forms of alcohol. Few sensations are more delightful than the wet but dry taste of cold beer to a parched throat. The subtle, taste-enhancing, enriching relationship of wine to food is a subject that has inspired many poets and writers far more capable than I of putting words together, but I can tell you that what they say is true. The fascinating, complex flavor of good wine can be profoundly sensual.

— **sixty-two-year-old man, psychoanalyst**

Bad Drinking Habits   I was sixteen when I first got drunk. It was a revelation, more fun than a barrel of monkeys. I screamed and hollered and carried on and did somersaults and hugged my friends (who were also drunk) and just had a blast. Naturally, I kept wanting to repeat the experience.

Pretty soon, a group of my high-school friends and I got into regular weekend parties where we'd get drunk (usually on hard liquor) and lose our inhibitions. Sometimes we'd even bring a bottle to school and sneak out between classes to drink a little. No one knew anything about pot or other drugs in those days. Alcohol was it. It was our main way of getting high and so was very important to us.

When I went away to college, I continued my pattern of using alcohol to get high, mostly at weekend parties. But two things began to happen that bothered me. First, from doing it over and over, the alcohol high lost a little of its fascination for me. Although I still liked it, it didn't measure up to those early experiences in high school. Secondly, I started getting bad hangovers. I mean, I'd really be sick as a dog the next day, and I didn't like that at all. The price seemed much too high to pay for a few hours of fun.

I used to tell myself I'd only drink to the point of getting pleasantly high, but every single time I'd go beyond it. Before I'd know it, I'd be stumbling around, being loud and jovial, insensitive to pain. I'd feel great at the time, and I'd also know what was in store for me. Usually, the sick effects would start when I'd try to go to sleep drunk: terrible nausea with the room spinning. Every serious drinker knows that one. And the next day, I'd be totally out of action, feeling as if I'd been poisoned, which I guess I had. I got really scared one time when I woke up like that and couldn't remember anything of the night before.

Although I kept trying to use alcohol moderately, whenever I'd set out to get high on it, I would always keep on drinking till I got drunk, no matter how many resolutions I made not to.

About that time, pot came along. It took me a little while to learn to get high on it, but when I did, it seemed much better than alcohol for me. There was no problem of taking too much and behaving badly, no getting sick, and no hangover. Becoming a pot smoker got me out of my bad drinking habits. I think if I'd kept them up, I would now be in real trouble.

I've tried various drugs since those days and don't think anything comes close to alcohol in terms of raw strength and potential for trouble. I couldn't learn to control it well, and I see many people around me who have the same problem.

— **thirty-seven-year-old man, college professor**

An Overdose of Downers   The old saying "The cobbler's children go without shoes" applies to the children of physicians, too. Because they deal with sick people all day long, doctors tend to give short shrift to the complaints of family members. As the daughter of a medical doctor, I should know. When I or any of my brothers or sisters came down with anything more serious than a hangnail, my father's standard procedure was to ply us with sleeping pills.

When I was very young, his prescription was for a half-grain or so of phenobarbital, but by the time I was in junior high school, whenever I had a sore throat or stuffy nose, I was sent to bed with two Seconals or Nembutals as a matter of course. The theory behind this treatment was that a good night's sleep would cure just about anything, and though it did not always work out that way, I never doubted the basic principle or questioned the wisdom of using drugs to implement it.

Later, when I was living on my own, my father gave me an assortment of sleeping pills to have on hand just in case. Falling asleep was never one of my problems, so I never resorted to them on my own. Then, one night when I had come down with a severe cold, my father stopped by and advised me to take some sedatives to be sure to get a good night's sleep. I said okay, produced the grab bag of pills, and asked him which to take. He chose two of the biggest gelatin capsules I had ever seen. They were Placidyl, he told me, 250 milligrams each. I protested, sure that one would more than do the job, but he insisted they were very mild, and that 500 milligrams was the standard dose. After I'd taken them, he left.

Meanwhile, I had been waiting for a neighbor to come and walk my dog in the park across the street. After twenty minutes or so, when she still hadn't arrived, I decided I'd take the dog out quickly myself. I was starting to feel groggy and wanted to go to sleep.

I lost consciousness almost as soon as I reached the street. All of a sudden, there was a fantastic explosion of lights, and I remember looking up at the sky, exclaiming "Wow!" before blacking out. That must have been around ten-thirty. When I came to, it was after midnight, and people were shaking me and slapping my face. I was in the park, where some other dog walkers had discovered me on a bench in a stupor. Apparently, the dog had dragged me in a somnambulent state all the way up the block, across a big street, and into the park. The people who found me had been slapping me for several minutes without success. Figuring I had either overdosed on something accidentally or made a suicide attempt, they were on the verge of calling an ambulance. It was obvious to everyone that I was heavily drugged, and, of course, they were all upset. When I realized what had happened, I was beside myself with rage.

Calling my father on the telephone to rant and rave brought no satisfaction. He not only refused to accept any responsibility for what had occurred — sticking to his story about 500 milligrams of Placidyl being a mild dose — he even tried to shift the blame onto me by suggesting that I had some deep, unconscious motive for passing out in the street. I hung up, consciously motivated to strangle him.

As it turned out, my father had given me not 500 milligrams of Placidyl but twice that amount: 1,000 milligrams, or, as the package insert put it, enough to knock out a woman in labor. Nevertheless, he continued to make light of the incident and deny any negligence on his part.

On the whole, the experience was very valuable for me because it taught me something people need to know — namely, that it is good to be skeptical about doctors (whether or not they are relatives) and the casual ways they dispense drugs.

— **thirty-eight-year-old woman, artist**

Experiences with Quaalude Many of my friends and I began using methaqualone, or Quaaludes, in the 1960s. We take them on occasion only and like the way they remove inhibitions and ease social interactions. I know a lot of folks who consider Quaalude their drug of choice, especially for having fun and partying.

I've seen Quaalude produce hilarious situations. One time I went with a group of friends to dinner at a fancy Italian restaurant. Most of us took Quaalude before leaving the house. We ordered dinner in high spirits and, when it came, started eating. Just then, one woman who had taken a double dose passed out and fell face first into her plate of spaghetti. Everyone else stood up and applauded.

I've also seen Quaalude lead to tragic situations. Everyone knows that downers and driving don't mix. I know a woman who was trying to cope with severe depression by taking Quaalude. One night, after exceeding her usual dosage, she went out and almost lost her life in an auto accident. She ran into a parked car.

I've seen other people become violent on Quaalude, then not remember it afterwards — just as with alcohol. One man who saw me professionally told me he once took three Quaaludes and went to bed. The next thing he remembered was being awakened about two hours later by his frightened wife, who told him he had been beating her.

There is no question that Quaalude can be dangerous when used irresponsibly, or that it can be addicting. As a recreational drug, taken on occasion in a responsible manner, it seems to me safe and interesting and gives me an experience different from anything else.

One of the rules I follow is to know my tolerance so that I take the right dose. Black-market Quaaludes are more of a problem, because their quality is uncertain. Usually, they contain less methaqualone than pharmaceutical Quaaludes, but they really vary. I've seen two people with equal tolerance each take one black-market Quaalude and experience different effects. So knowing your drug is important, too.

The other rules that are most important are not to mix Quaalude with alcohol and not to mix Quaalude with driving.

— **forty-six-year-old man, drug counselor**

Down on Valium I hope I never hear of Valium again. A university physician gave it to me as a "muscle relaxant" when I had a pinched nerve in my neck that caused muscle spasms in my right shoulder and weakness in my right hand. He did not tell me anything about the mental effects of Valium, so I was quite unprepared for them. All I remember of the next few days is that I could not concentrate in my office. Then my secretary and wife began acting strange. Only when I stopped taking the drug did I realize how bizarre my behavior had become while I was on it. I would stare blankly into space when people talked to me, not remember anything said to me, and be unable to think or reason. Also, I had no sense that anything was wrong. I think Valium turned me into a kind of zombie for those few days. I can't understand why anyone would want to take it.

— **sixty-two-year-old man, university professor**

Valium as a Tool   I first began taking Valium ten years ago to relieve anxiety and very quickly came to depend on it for writing, or, more exactly, for beginning to write. Once I am at my desk and have actually begun to work, I am fine; the problem for me is to get there in the first place. What I discovered was that very soon after I took a dose of Valium, I felt high, and that during the brief period that the high lasted, getting to my desk was a whole lot easier.

By now, after ten years of experimenting, I have learned that, like any tool, Valium has its limitations. It works best on an empty stomach, for example, and when it comes to dosage, less is definitely more. Two and a half milligrams is the right dose for me; more than that makes me feel groggy. Also, since I become tolerant to its effects if I take it more than two days running, I have to use it intermittently.

Even when I observe all the rules and take Valium under ideal conditions, the period of grace it affords me is extremely brief. Once its effects begin to come on, I have about fifteen minutes in which to capitalize on them. During that critical period, if I happen to be distracted by a phone call or a neighbor dropping by, all is lost. That sounds hard to believe, I know, but it has happened to me many times, and whenever it does, that's it: the day is shot. Besides being too anxious to get to my desk, I will be furious — positively fit to be tied.

— **thirty-nine-year-old woman, writer**

GHB   GHB put me in a state unlike any I'd ever experienced before and would just as soon not experience again. It was given to me by a friend who was visiting for the weekend. We took it at about eleven P.M., after which my guest went off to bed. I continued tidying things up in the kitchen for maybe fifteen more minutes until, all of a sudden, I felt a wave of nausea and started to sweat. I decided to just stop what I was doing and go to bed. Well, I had already come to a stop, so that was no problem. The problem was that I could not go. I wanted to go, but I was not able to move. It felt as if there were a glitch in my automated equipment and I had to reach around and manually operate my brain. It required fierce concentration to advance even in super-slow motion, and concentrating made me sick to my stomach. Whenever I stopped, though, to let the nausea subside, I became paralyzed again, transfixed, until I somehow managed to summon up the will to resume the effort. Ordinarily, I can make the trip between the kitchen and my bedroom in less than thirty seconds. That night it took about a month.

— thirty-three-year-old woman, secretary

An Anesthetic Revelation I once inhaled a pretty full dose of ether, with the determination to put on record, at the earliest moment of regaining consciousness, the thought I should find uppermost in my mind. The mighty music of the triumphal march into nothingness reverberated through my brain, and filled me with a sense of infinite possibilities, which made me an archangel for a moment. The veil of eternity was lifted. The one great truth which underlies all human experience and is the key to all the mysteries that philosophy has sought in vain to solve, flashed upon me in a sudden revelation. Henceforth all was clear: a few words had lifted my intelligence to the level of the knowledge of the cherubim. As my natural condition returned, I remembered my resolution; and, staggering to my desk, I wrote, in ill-shaped, straggling characters, the all-embracing truth still glimmering in my consciousness. The words were these (children may smile; the wise will ponder): "A strong smell of turpentine prevails throughout."

— Oliver Wendell Holmes (1809–1894), American physician
and author, from a lecture given in 1870

The Need for Opiates The first opiate I ever took was codeine. I snorted it. It made me feel right for the first time in my life. I said to myself, "Aha, this is what I've been missing." I never felt right from as far back as I can remember, and I was always trying different ways to change how I felt. I used lots of drugs, including pot, downers, tranquilizers, and alcohol, but none of them ever really did it for me. Codeine was a revelation, and I've been an opiate user ever since.

That first time, I was twenty-three. Before long, I was addicted, although I've always snorted dope, never shot it. Opiates have caused me lots of trouble, but what they do for my head is worth it. Now I'm thirty-four and am on methadone maintenance. I don't think methadone is the best opiate for me; it makes me sweat terribly and has some other effects on my body I don't like, but it's great to be able to get what I need legally, so that I can spend time on things other than scoring. I hope one day more people will realize that some of us have to have opiates just to feel normal.

— **thirty-four-year-old woman, rock singer**

Opiate Addiction I started using heroin in high school, chipped for a long time, then finally became an addict. Presently, I'm on methadone, which works well for me. I use narcotics to keep from feeling sick (withdrawal), to relieve stress, and sometimes for fun. I like to mainline because it's the most economical way to take opiates: heroin is at least three times as active intravenously as orally, although the effects last longer if you take it by mouth.

I've read a lot about opiate users' seeking a "rush" by injecting heroin. To me, the rush has never been that important. It feels like a pleasant warm feeling, especially in the pit of the stomach, accompanied by deep physical and mental relaxation. (Incidentally, smoking many opiates gives a stronger rush than mainlining, but it is wasteful, because some of the drug is destroyed by heat.) In my experience, chippers are more interested in rushes than addicts. They tend to take narcotics on occasion for fun, whereas addicts take them regularly in order to make it through a troubled world. Regular doses of heroin just make many addicts feel normal; they do not give noticeable rushes.

For me, the rush is secondary to the tranquilizing and pain-relieving effects of opiates. I feel I have a metabolic problem due to lack of endogenous opiate-like drugs. By substituting external narcotics for internal ones, I have probably shut off my body's production of the endogenous substances, and now I have to take opiates regularly to make life bearable. Sometimes I'll take a higher than usual dose for pleasure and savor the rush, but that's unusual. Oral methadone does not give a rush, and if rushes were so important to addicts, methadone maintenance would not be accepted by so many of them. As I've said, it works for me.

By the way, my health has been generally good since I've been an opiate addict. I don't get colds when other people do, and when I travel in

Mexico, I don't get dysentery, although my nonusing companions do, and we eat the same food.

— **thirty-year-old man, chemist**

LSD and Psilocybin I have been unable to identify any sign at all of addiction, organic injury, or other in some way unpleasant aftereffects . . . In my opinion, however, LSD and psilocybin cannot and should not become "pleasure drugs" for the general public. Their effects are such that they lead one beyond the customary (and constraining) coordinate system of space and time, and afford insights into the heaven and hell of one's own self — which can be dangerous to one who is not cut out for that, and hence is not prepared.

According to my experience, only several repeated experiments afford a serious appraisal. I also believe that at least one of these experiments should be undertaken in familiar surroundings (under discreet supervision of a trusted person) and with higher doses. *Only* then might the drug show us its, and our, deepest secret.

— **Rudolf Gelpke, a Swiss professor of Islamic studies who took LSD and psilocybin a number of times in 1961**

A DMT Disaster The only time I ever took a psychedelic was a disaster. It was in the early 1960s, and the drug was DMT. I knew nothing about it. Some friends invited me to their place and told me they wanted to share a pleasant experience with me. They said they would inject a small amount of a new drug into my leg. It was safe and would give me a nice feeling for a short time. I agreed to try it.

Within a few minutes of the injection, I was swept into a nightmare world of horrible visions, such as finding myself wading into an ocean where all sorts of monsters attacked me. The real world disappeared so completely I thought I'd never see it again. Even years later, I can still recall the feeling of slimy tentacles grabbing my legs and trying to pull me underwater. When I came back from this frightening place, I was so shaken that I stayed in my room for two days. It took me a very long time to get over being afraid of the ocean afterwards, and to this day I have been unable to try another psychedelic, although I am curious about the good effects people have described to me. I think those friends who gave me DMT were not malicious, just irresponsible. I wonder how many oth-

ers have had similar bad experiences from taking psychedelic drugs with
no preparation?

— **thirty-five-year-old man, movie producer**

Peyote Visions   My first vivid show of mescal colour effects came
quickly. I saw the stars, and then, of a sudden, here and there delicate
floating films of colour — usually delightful neutral purples and pinks.
These came and went — now here, now there. Then an abrupt rush of
countless points of white light swept across the field of view, as if the unseen millions of the Milky Way were to flow a sparkling river before the
eye. In a minute this was over and the field was dark. Then I began to see
zigzag lines of very bright colours . . .

When I opened my eyes all was gone at once. Closing them I began after a long interval to see for the first time definite objects associated with
colours. The stars sparkled and passed away. A white spear of grey stone
grew up to a huge height, and became a tall, richly finished Gothic tower
of very elaborate and definite design, with many rather worn statues
standing in the doorways or on stone brackets. As I gazed, every pro-
jecting angle, cornice, and even the faces of the stones at their joinings
were by degrees covered or hung with clusters of what seemed to be huge
precious stones, but uncut, some being more like masses of transparent
fruit. These were green, purple, red, and orange; never clear yellow and
never blue. All seemed to possess an interior light, and to give the faintest
idea of the perfectly satisfying intensity and purity of these gorgeous col-
our-fruits is quite beyond my power. All the colours I have ever beheld are
dull as compared to these.

— **from an essay by Dr. S. Weir Mitchell (1829–1914), an American**
physician and novelist who drank an extract of peyote in 1896

I Smoked a Toad   In August of 1990 I visited a friend of mine who lived
in the desert near Tucson, Arizona. He is a long-time psychedelic tripper
who mainly likes mushrooms and peyote. I once brought him some
MDMA, but he refused to try it, saying he only took natural psychedelics.
So when I got to his house, he told me he had a new favorite drug: toad
venom. I thought he was kidding me, but he pulled out a vial that held
small, transparent chips of what he said was dried venom he had collected from the big desert toads that come out at night during the summer rains. He showed me some of these guys during my visit; I never
knew toads got so big. He also showed me how to handle them and get

the venom to squirt out of the glands in their heads. Anyway, one night we smoked a chip of this stuff in a small pipe. It had a strong flavor. I took one toke and held it in for maybe fifteen seconds. By the time I exhaled, I felt like I was going up in an elevator to somewhere else. I was lying down in a desert wash, and it was a beautiful night, but I think I was just somewhere else for a while. When I became aware of my surroundings, I couldn't talk for a long time and felt that the sounds of the desert were vibrating in my body. It was very intense and very strange. After a few more minutes, I felt like myself again. Then I started laughing. It just struck me so funny that these big old toads could make you high. I'd like to see the feds try to go after them.

— **thirty-three-year-old man, massage therapist**

The Love Drugs   I first took MDA in 1970. I thought it was the most wonderful experience I ever had. I remember lying in a field with four good friends, just lying in a big hug pile for hours, not wanting anything to be different, totally content, completely in the here and now. I felt like a lion in a pride of lions on an African plain, totally secure in the physical closeness with my brothers and sisters. Over the next few years, I took MDA maybe three or four times a year, always with the same good results, but I did find there was a price to pay: I'd be nonfunctional for a day or two afterward.

When MDMA came along a few years later, I was delighted. It was legal, shorter acting, and the price I had to pay was much, much less, at least at first. I turned a lot of people on to it and saw it do incredible things: save marriages, create lifelong friendships, lead to people falling in love. One of my friends produced a T-shirt that said, "Don't Get Married for at Least Six Weeks After Ecstasy!" I think MDMA could put a lot of psychiatrists and psychologists out of business.

I wish I could still use MDMA once a month, as I used to, but I'm afraid that as I've gotten into middle age, I can't handle the burned-out feeling I get the next day. Even taking lower doses, I can barely drag myself around or focus my mind for the next twenty-four hours. So now I take it maybe once a year. I still think it's one of the best drugs ever invented.

— **fifty-one-year-old man, university professor**

Psychedelic Therapy   As a clinical psychologist who has treated hundreds of patients with psychedelic drugs over the past twenty-five years, I consider LSD, MDMA, magic mushrooms, mescaline, and the rest to be the most valuable therapeutic tools I know to show people how they can change in positive directions.

Because my use of these drugs is not approved under current laws or standards of practice, I cannot publish my findings or engage openly in psychedelic therapy. Still, I have trained many other psychiatrists and psychologists to use this method and have been able to treat many patients successfully. I am very careful in selecting patients for this kind of treatment, very careful in preparing them for a psychedelic session, in conducting the session, and in following it up with the kind of work that enables patients to make practical use of the insights they gain.

Conventional forms of psychotherapy often enable people to understand how their habits of thinking about themselves and others produce frustration and pain, but you can spend years in therapy gaining all this insight and keep on being the same frustrated, neurotic person. One good psychedelic session can make you *feel* what you are doing and show you how to do it differently. In the right hands and settings, these drugs can convince you that the worst problem in your life can be solved by changing your own attitudes and ways of perceiving and can motivate you to make the necessary changes.

It is a shame that more doctors and patients do not take advantage of this potential.

— **seventy-year-old man, psychologist**

The Day the Universe Ended: Salvinorin-A   I consider myself very experienced with psychedelics and was curious to try *Salvia divinorum*. I got a plant of it and was intending to smoke the leaves, but before I got a chance to do it, a friend came by and offered me some pure crystalline salvinorin-A. He put a little bit in a glass pipe, held a flame underneath, and told me to take one deep hit of the vapor. I did, and the next thing I knew, everything ended. I was reduced to a little spark of consciousness, suffocated and trapped by an immense weight. This was it. Eternity. And I kept hearing a malevolent cosmic laugh at my fate as well as a vision of that little pipe. It was as if all my life led up to the moment where I was offered the pipe. I had a choice. And I chose to inhale that vapor. And fall into the trap from which there was no escape. It was eternal imprisonment in a tiny cage with nothing, absolutely nothing, outside of it. I can't begin to convey the psychic discomfort I was in. Of course, at some point, maybe ten or fifteen minutes later, the effect of the drug subsided, and I got some perspective on what had happened. I suppose I took way too much. When I was able to stand up, the first thing I did was throw out the *Salvia divinorum* plant that had been on a window sill. Other people have told me they've had good experiences smoking the leaves, but I have no interest in trying them.

— **fifty-year-old man, computer scientist**

Quitting Pot I smoked marijuana for about seven years, mostly during college and law school. It was great for me at first, a real relaxer and sense-enhancer, and I had a lot of good times with it. Occasionally, I had bad reactions to it — paranoia, shaking, pounding heartbeat, and feeling cold all over. Sometimes I'd have this reaction every time I'd smoke over a period of a week or so, then I wouldn't have it again for many months. I don't know what it came from, maybe being in uncomfortable environments or around people I didn't like.

Eventually, I became a daily pot smoker, sometimes starting in the morning. It was my main way of relating to other people. However, I started getting less and less effect from it that I liked. In fact, it began to make me groggy and sleepy most of the time and also gave me a cough. These unwelcome effects got worse and worse until I realized I would have to stop using pot. So I made a resolution to quit completely.

Well, it surprised me to find that wasn't so easy. It took me three years of trying before I really gave up smoking marijuana, even though I no longer got pleasant effects from it. I never realized how much of a habit I had and how hooked I was on it. I was certainly abusing the stuff. I think I'd better just stay off it for good now. I'm afraid that if I tried to use it once in a while, my smoking would just creep back up to that addictive level, and I'd be in the same spot as before.

I don't have bad feelings about pot. I learned a lot from it and never really got hurt by it. I think it should be legalized. I also think people who use it should be aware that it can have strong effects and can be addicting if you don't watch out.

— **forty-one-year-old man, lawyer**

Marijuana and Driving You want to know about marijuana and driving? When I first tried driving when stoned, it was pretty weird. I would imagine I was cruising along at fifty miles per hour but would only be going twenty. Sometimes I'd feel as if I were very, very tiny behind a gigantic steering wheel. Going through a long tunnel, I thought I was driving vertically down a shaft into the earth. These illusions were both scary and fun. I never had an accident, but I'm a good driver to begin with and was always careful. I can see where pot could be dangerous for someone not used to it.

One time, while I was in college, I was very stoned late at night in Cleveland and had to drive home. I was going through deserted streets in residential neighborhoods. Suddenly, I couldn't remember whether I was in Cleveland or Pittsburgh, where I grew up. I could turn the scene through the window into either city. Then I came to an intersection that was very familiar, only I had to turn left if it was Cleveland and right if it was Pittsburgh. That's the kind of mind tricks pot can play on you at the wheel.

Later, when I had been smoking marijuana for several years, I never had such strong effects anymore, and driving after smoking was pretty routine for me. A number of times I almost had accidents because joints fell apart on me while I was driving or because lighting a pipe behind the wheel took my attention (and hands) off the wheel. Those hazards were more dangerous than direct effects of the drug.

Finally, pot started making me really sleepy and groggy a lot, and that was a problem for driving, especially when I was by myself on a long haul. I'd think, Boy, it would be nice to smoke a joint, this ride is really boring. So I'd light up and feel pleasantly high for ten minutes or so, then spend the next two hours fighting off the nods. It was no different from getting sleepy normally, but that sure is risky on an interstate highway for you and other people, if you don't pull off at a rest stop and either take a nap or somehow wake yourself up.

— **thirty-two-year-old man, lab technician**

Marijuana as Medicine   Twenty years ago, I suddenly developed a paralysis of the right side of my body that baffled the doctors. After ten months, it began to improve, but I also lost my vision and that came back only in part. They finally were able to make a diagnosis of multiple sclerosis.

About three years later, I discovered marijuana. A friend told me it was relaxing. My main problem then, aside from partial blindness, was tenseness and tremors in my muscles. Pot cured it, and I've smoked regularly ever since, about four to five times a week. If I go without it for a week, the muscle tremors come back.

Medical science has nothing to offer me. Most people with MS have repeated attacks and keep losing body function. I'm convinced that pot has kept me in remission all these years. It can't help my vision, because there was permanent nerve damage. Still, I can get around fairly well. It does keep my muscles in great shape. I lift weights regularly and feel pretty strong.

I can't believe that marijuana is not legally available for medical use, that a doctor can't prescribe it for me. I want to see it legalized, and I want the government to supply me with it. I'm a veteran and think I ought to get my pot from the VA hospital.

— **forty-one-year-old man, part-time roofer**

Dr. Mom My son, now eighteen, began getting splitting headaches when he was twelve. A year later, they finally got around to testing him for Lyme disease, he tested positive, and was treated with high doses of antibiotics intravenously. When he was cured, though, his headaches didn't go away. None of the myriad drugs that doctors recommended over the next couple of years did anything but cause all sorts of hideous so-called side effects. He was put on every drug that could conceivably be used to treat migraine headaches — Fiorinal, numerous prescription allergy medications, beta-blockers, calcium-blockers, Imitrex, you name it. Some were worse than others, but they were all bad — bad for your kidneys, your liver, et cetera. Reading the inserts used to drive me nuts. And it wasn't just drugs — we tried acupuncture, cranial manipulation, psychotherapy, biofeedback, homeopathy — and absolutely nothing worked.

I'm not sure when, but at some point, my son started smoking pot and it relieved his headaches. I'm not saying it got rid of them, but it *helped*. So I wasn't going to tell him not to use it. But I still kept taking him to doctors. Eventually, one day when he was in excruciating pain and didn't have any pot, I called a friend and got him some. In other words, I became a criminal. My son was the one who pointed that out and reminded me that in our state, possession of any amount of marijuana is a felony carrying a mandatory minimum three-year prison sentence. Anyway, several months ago I dragged him to the last physician I will ever drag him to, who put him on a drug I'd never heard of called Neurontin. He'd been taking it for several weeks and apparently all it did was make him feel lousy.

Then, one night, he hears this announcement on TV about a class action suit being brought against the makers of a "blockbuster" drug called Neurontin. So I go on the Web and, what do you know — Parke-Davis is being sued because its sales reps allegedly pushed doctors to prescribe Neurontin for eleven different conditions which it wasn't approved for and had no effect on — headaches being one of them. Also, they had allegedly attempted to conceal the fact that there was a very high incidence of nasty side effects: dizziness, nausea, somnambulance, and — especially in adolescents — suicidal depression. Well, that was it for me. I told my son it was over now — I would never make him go to another physician or make him take another prescription medication ever again. The next day, after calling the doctor and giving him hell, I went and bought my son an ounce of lovely, fragrant marijuana.

— **forty-seven-year-old woman, architect**

Inhaling Gasoline   One of the best descriptions of gasoline sniffing as it actually occurs was published in 1955 by the late A. E. ("Tajar") Hamilton of the Hamilton School in Sheffield, Massachusetts, in his classic account of children at work and play, *Psychology and the Great God Fun*. One day, when the other children had gone on an expedition, Tajar Hamilton reports, he found a boy nicknamed Bullet with a can of gasoline and a gasoline-soaked rag. After a few preliminary questions, Tajar (with Bullet's consent) turned on a recorder and preserved the dialogue for posterity.

TAJAR: Bullet, you said you would come up to the attic and tell me about the gasoline and the bicycles. Will you talk your story into the mike, just as you remember it?

BULLET: Well, I was awful mad when they said I couldn't go on the trip. Sure I picked up the axe when Martha told me not to, but I put it back again. Then she said I couldn't go, and Donnie was going, and when they all went I didn't have anything to do to have fun and I began to get madder and madder all the time. It made me feel kind of sick to be so mad, so I went where they keep the gasoline can and I started to smell it.

TAJAR: What made you want to smell gas, Bullet?

BULLET: Well, when you feel bad, you smell it and it makes you feel kind of hot and kind of drowsy, like you was floating through the air. It makes you feel sort of hot inside and different from the way you were before.

TAJAR: And after you smelled the gas and felt better, what did you do?

BULLET: Then I began to feel mad again and had to do something, so I found a nail. It was an old rusty one, and I got a piece of board to push it with so it wouldn't hurt my hand, and I made holes in all the tires except Donnie's.

TAJAR: Why not in Donnie's?

BULLET: Because they're solid and you can't . . .

TAJAR: And after you had punched all those holes what did you do?

BULLET: Mary hollered to come to dinner, so I went and we had hot dogs at the council ring and then we had some games and then I didn't feel so good, so I went and smelled the gas again.

TAJAR: How long have you liked to smell gas, Bullet?

BULLET: Well, here at camp, ever since about two weeks after I came to the farm. I showed Donnie how to smell it. It makes you feel like you was in fairyland or somewhere else than where you are . . .

TAJAR: Bullet, how come so much gas was spilled on the cellar floor?

BULLET: Oh, I just wanted to get more on my rag. If you have a lot it makes you sort of dream. It gets all dark and you see shooting stars in it, and this time I saw big flies flying in it. They were big and green and had white wings.

TAJAR: And you feel better about yourself and about people after you have one of those dreams?

BULLET: Yep, until I begin to feel bad again, or get mad.

TAJAR: Okay, Bullet, that's all for now. Thank you for being so truthful with me.

— quoted in *Licit and Illicit Drugs*, by Edward M. Brecher
and the editors of *Consumer Reports* (1972)

Poppers in the Pool   I was first introduced to amyl nitrite during my senior year in college. The father of one of my friends had a heart condition for which he used the drug. He would amass huge numbers of poppers and give them out to anyone who wanted them. I had read of this drug but had no firsthand experience with it.

My friends and I used to get together on weekends and hang out in a heated pool with a whirlpool bath in the condominium complex where I lived. One cool December evening, after drinking several glasses of wine, we got into the near-scalding, frothing waters of the pool. I was already warm from the alcohol and wondered what it would be like to dilate my arteries all the way. I suggested we try a popper. I broke one and inhaled deeply, filling my lungs with the strong odor.

The effect was immediate. My arms and legs felt like liquid warmth, and at the same time I got a pounding in my head. (We came to call this the "jackhammer effect.") When I exhaled, my vision blurred, with small blue patches filling my field of vision. I then jumped in the nearby unheated swimming pool and got an even brighter visual display. All the effects lasted only a few minutes. I liked them enough to repeat this ritual many times in the course of the evening. In fact, I did it over and over on many evenings.

I never knew about sexual uses of poppers until much later, when a gay friend told me about it. I never got into that. My interest was just in the spectacular rush and sensory fireworks. After a few months of doing poppers in the whirlpool bath, I guess I lost interest in having the same experience over and over. Maybe I just overdid it to the point where it started to get boring. In any case, all that was three years ago, and I haven't used amyl nitrite since.

— **twenty-year-old man, medical student**

In Datura Country   I was on a camping trip with a friend in northern Arizona in remote canyon country. We noticed a lot of datura plants growing around us, some with seed pods. When we ran out of marijuana, I suggested that we try datura. Neither Tom nor I had ever done it.

We each ate about ten seeds and drank a cup of tea made from the leaves. That was just after sunset. We started a small campfire, although it was a warm night, and sat around waiting for something to happen. After about an hour, we both started to feel different. I got restless and walked away from the fire into some big boulders at the base of a cliff.

You have to understand that what I'm going to tell you from this point on is not a clear memory. It's more like trying to put together the pieces of a dream. I have some very vivid pictures in my mind, but they don't all hang together in a logical order, and there are definite holes in my memory.

Anyway, I think I found a comfortable place in the rocks and sort of curled up with my eyes closed. Then I remember seeing bats, a lot of bats and very large ones. They kept flying at me, coming right in close. Their faces were hideous. I thought to myself, "I've never seen bats like that." I wanted to find Tom to see what he made of them, but when I got up, I couldn't tell where I was. It didn't look like Arizona anymore, and Tom was nowhere in sight.

I was in a dark forest or maybe a swamp. It was hot, and the air was thick and hard to breathe. I couldn't tell if it was day or night. I kept getting tangled in these vines and roots and had to fight my way through them to make any progress. Also, there were dark shapes moving in and out of the trees that seemed to follow me, but I couldn't get a good look at them to see what they were. They did not seem friendly. I remember feeling very thirsty, trying to find water, getting more hung up in the undergrowth.

I came to some sort of pool. The water was black and stagnant, and I wasn't sure I should drink it. I scooped some up and put it to my lips. It was warm and thick, not at all refreshing. Then I realized it was blood. That made me think I was going to die. I fell on the ground and started crying. The black shapes got nearer and bigger. I still couldn't see what they were, but I knew they were waiting for me to die so they could devour me. It seemed like an eternity as they closed in.

The next thing I remember is waking up in a burning desert, nothing but sand. I was tied to a stake, left to die of thirst. The sun beat down on me unbearably. I tried to call for help but couldn't make any sound. That also seemed to go on forever.

Then I discovered I was in the rocks just a short distance from our campsite. The sun was up; it must have been ten o'clock. My mouth and throat were completely parched. The light hurt my eyes, and I couldn't focus them. I felt very hung over. Then I remembered eating the datura and was able to sort out some of the weird dreams or whatever they were.

Tom was nowhere in sight. I tried shouting for him, but my throat was so dry I couldn't yell very loud, and drinking water didn't help much. I searched the immediate area and eventually found Tom stumbling around. He had no clothes on and was pretty cut up. He didn't know where he was and couldn't tell me what had happened. I got him cleaned up and made sure he didn't have any serious injuries. He slept off and on for the next few hours, then came to himself, although he was hung over even worse than I was. He had no memory of anything after eating the datura. All he could say was that he thought he'd stick to marijuana from now on.

— **twenty-three-year-old man, ranch hand**

I Ate the Panther Amanita On two occasions I ate the panther mushroom. I was living out in the woods in western Oregon. I once ate *Amanita muscaria* but did not get much effect from it, just a little sick feeling. Word went around that the panther would make you high. Most of my friends were afraid to try the panther. I decided to be the guinea pig. I found a medium-sized specimen, sliced it, and steeped it in hot water and lemon juice. Then I drank the liquid and ate half the mushroom.

About forty minutes later, I was feeling dreamy and relaxed. I lay on my back in the woods and saw images with my eyes closed. There was no sickness and generally no bad effects. The dreamy state lasted about three hours.

That experience encouraged me to experiment further, so a week later I ate twice as much, prepared in the same way. The dreamy state came on faster and was more intense. After an hour, I tried to get up but felt very confused and disoriented. I didn't know whether I was dreaming or awake or what was real. It wasn't scary, just strange.

I crawled out on a big fallen tree over a pond and, while trying to find a good position, fell off. Then I wasn't sure if it had happened or not, so I got back up on the tree and fell off again. I kept having a compulsion to repeat the fall, because I couldn't tell if it had happened or was going to happen. On about the seventh time, I hit my head on some rocks and was bleeding pretty badly. Some people saw me and got scared. I guess I looked bad, although I was unaware of being hurt. They drove me an hour to the nearest emergency hospital. By the time I got there, I thought I had died and gone to heaven. I thought the doctors and nurses were angels and started singing hymns. They did not know what to make of me.

They kept me for a while and made sure I hadn't fractured my skull, then let me go, all patched up. I was coming back to normal when they sent me away, about eight hours after eating the mushroom. My face got all black and blue from the fall, but otherwise I was all right.

I haven't eaten panther *Amanitas* since then. I'm still interested to try again, but I would want to have someone with me to watch out for me, and I think I would take less than that last time.

— **thirty-one-year-old man, unemployed**

Positive Experiences with PCP   I've had very positive experiences with PCP, which, I guess, makes me unusual, since everyone says it's a terrible drug. I used it over a few months about five years ago. It used to come sprayed on dried parsley leaves that were then rolled into very thin joints. From one to three tokes on one of these joints would give me a high lasting four to ten hours. My consciousness would alter within a minute of taking the first toke.

PCP would make me very flexible, allowing me to be active or restful. I could jog farther and longer than normal under its influence, or I could sit still and meditate. I could close my eyes and create inner visions, sometimes seeing colorful, changing, geometric designs, as if I had ingested mushrooms or peyote.

For years, I have suffered lower back pains, supposedly due to the deterioration of cartilage between my lumbar and sacral vertebrae. Whenever I smoked PCP, I felt no pain and, as I've said, could jog comfortably. Even after the drug wore off, I experienced no pain from any athletic activities I performed. A few times, I jogged in six-inch snow, wearing only sneakers and shorts, without getting cold. Even when I got back to the house after such a run, my friends noted that my skin was not at all cold.

My thinking was often imaginative and lucid. And I laughed a lot. I would often laugh so much that people around me, even though they didn't know what I was laughing at (I don't remember now myself) would also start laughing. I remember doubling over and sometimes rolling on the floor in fits of laughter. I loved every second of it.

Finally, there was a strange "psychic" effect of PCP, which I still don't understand. Once in a while, under the influence of the drug, I would feel as though a "ray" or "beam" entered my head through the back; I can't really describe it. When this happened, I would have thoughts or knowledge that I would later find were telepathic or precognitive. I would receive a thought from a friend or realize something would happen in the future. One night, I described to a friend a drug bust that we would be involved in and the aftermath of it in months to follow. It all happened exactly as I predicted.

Maybe these experiences were just cases of heightened intuitive power. My unconscious mind might have had all the information to make these predictions, but it took the drug, or the altered state brought about by the drug, to put the information together and let it come to the surface. I don't know, but that "ray" or "beam" feeling always came first, and when it occurred, I would say to myself or to a friend, kind of nodding my head and rolling my eyes somewhat in jest, "Here we go again." I wondered if I were a psychonaut or just a plain psychic nut. Whatever, it was fun.

My use of angel dust, as I called it, finally got out of hand. I was taking it all the time, and people around me told me I was acting too crazily. So I stopped and haven't used it since. Sometime, I'd like to experiment with it again to explore those physical and mental powers it seems to release in me.

— **thirty-six-year-old man, screenwriter**

Nothing Good About PCP   I've tried most drugs and think most have their place. PCP is one of the few I can see nothing good about. I've taken it in pill form a few times, thinking it was pure THC. One time, I was about to give a lecture to a large group of medical doctors. I was using marijuana a lot then and went outside just before the talk to smoke a joint. Someone I didn't know came along and produced a joint. He lit it and handed it to me. I took a deep drag on it and only noticed the taste of PCP after I had the smoke in my lungs. I couldn't believe that anyone would do that to me, but before I could say anything, I was called in to the auditorium to start my lecture.

On the way to the podium, I started rushing on the PCP. I could hardly control my legs or thoughts and could only get words out of my mouth with great difficulty. If I hadn't been experienced with drugs, I would really have lost it. As it was, I don't think anyone really noticed. It probably seemed that I was just talking pretty slowly for the first five minutes; after that, I got myself together and was able to control the drug. I was furious, however, and when I finished, I found the guy that slipped me that loaded joint and told him what I thought of him. I've never seen him since, and I've never taken any PCP since, either.

— thirty-seven-year-old man, medical doctor

Ketamine Summer   Soon after I began work in a pharmacology lab, I met a coworker who shared my desire to alter ordinary consciousness by means of drugs. One summer day during our lunch break, he handed me the package insert from a box of ketamine. After reading the precautions warning of possible hallucinations, delirium, and dissociative states, we decided to try it that evening.

We wanted to inject a subanesthetic dose, but neither of us knew how to calculate a "recreational" dose or how to give injections. In retrospect, I believe it was this uncertainty that made our first trip on ketamine one of the best. Robert shot first, injecting the drug into the muscle of his leg. Then I took about twice as much, injecting it into my arm muscle.

Within five minutes of the injection, I came on to the drug. At first, all my organs felt like lead, especially my stomach, and I thought I might have to vomit. These physical sensations quickly gave way to an incredible dreamlike state. I lay down and tried to talk, but my words were garbled, and my mouth felt numb. There also seemed to be a delay between speaking and hearing what I said, so that I kept repeating myself in a vain attempt to "catch up" and hear what I just said.

The brick walls of the room began to vibrate. I had to close my eyes to avoid another round of nausea. With my eyes closed, I entered a new dimension, filled with multicolored triangles rotating clockwise. When I tried to get up and walk, the floor heaved up and down, reminiscent of a boat on a stormy sea. I sat down and felt detached from my physical being, lapsing into a state of semiconsciousness. This lasted for what seemed like hours, but by the time I returned to near-normal reality, only forty-five minutes had passed since the injection.

This first experience inspired Robert and me to repeat our explorations with ketamine. We took it every day for the next two months. It was an interesting time. I haven't used the drug since then.

— twenty-five-year-old man, laboratory technician

A Space Odyssey Probably the farthest-out drug-induced experience I've ever had was when a physician friend gave me a shot of ketamine intravenously. Not only did I leave my body, I was rocketed out to somewhere way beyond the solar system. Reduced to a pinpoint of consciousness, I was hurtling through the vast desolation of deep space. Terrifying doesn't begin to describe it, and yet it was very transient. Suddenly, it occurred to me that once upon a time I'd had a body and that I really ought to make an effort to reinhabit it, only I couldn't conceive of how I could accomplish that. Then I realized, much to my relief, that the transformation had, in fact, happened, and I was with my friend back on good old planet Earth again.

— **thirty-five-year-old man, writer**

Addicted to Cough Pills I've had asthma all my life and am allergic to just about everything. Allergic skin rashes and asthma are my biggest problems. I've been in the hospital for the asthma a lot of times, and to control it I have to take a lot of medication, including cortisone and pills for coughing.

As a child, I took a lot of codeine for coughs. For the past ten years, I've been on Hycodan, which I understand contains a narcotic [hydrocodone]. Originally, I took one tablet four times a day; now I take two, four times a day. If I try to cut down the dose, I start coughing and get really congested. Also, I get upset and can't sleep.

If I think about it, I guess I know I'm addicted, but I don't like to face that. I've never had anything to do with drugs, and no one in my family or people I work with would think of me as an addict. Most doctors give me the Hycodan without asking too many questions, but sometimes I've gone to several different ones to get enough prescriptions so that I wouldn't have to worry about running out. I know I should try to stop the Hycodan, but I don't think I can face the day without it. I don't know what I can do.

— **fifty-two-year-old woman, university guidance counselor**

The Wonders of Sudafed I suspect most people take antihistamines just because they have been brainwashed by the pharmaceutical industry. I concluded long ago that I would much rather put up with the symptoms of a cold than endure the depression antihistamines give me.

Two summers ago, I came down with a head cold just as a low pressure system settled over the East Coast. The combination caused one of my ears to close up. After a day or so of constant tugging at my ear, it was becoming sore. I consulted my local pharmacist, who, hearing of my aversion to antihistamines, recommended Sudafed. I had never heard of it.

The Sudafed worked wonders right away, drying up my sinuses and unblocking the congested ear without producing any of the hated side effects of antihistamines. It also really zapped me — better than coffee. In fact, Sudafed is so stimulating that, though I now use it whenever I have a cold, I can't take it too late in the day, or I won't be able to fall asleep that night. I think it's a great drug and am surprised more people don't know about it.

— **forty-year-old woman**

Testimonials to Smart Drugs   My secretary responded so well to piracetam (at doses of only 800 mg) that I decided to give her a small raise so she could afford it. She takes piracetam instead of heading for the coffee machine. Every day she takes it, she is decidedly more alert and intelligent acting, and she smiles more. She is overall a much better employee. She says it wakes up her brain.

I first tried Hydergine six years ago with some fascinating results. During a visit to see my Dad at Christmas, he and I started taking 9 mg per day of Hydergine in the hope it would help to improve our long-term memory. The results were apparent to us both within two days. He was in his forties and could remember events from when he was in his twenties. They were as clear in his mind as if they happened yesterday . . . I was in my early twenties and my memories went back to the childhood years. A unique opportunity had been presented to us to sit down and share in the joys that our life had brought us. What a gift!

During my final year as an undergraduate I decided to change majors from psychology to mathematics. I was also running out of money, and I knew I had to finish in one year and then get a job. I started using a combination of Hydergine, vasopressin, pemoline, and a good vitamin formula with large amounts of choline. This particular combination improved my concentration enormously. I flew through that year, taking a full load of upper-level mathematics courses each semester. Not only did I complete the major in the allotted time, but my grades were better than I was used to. I was getting A's instead of B's. I landed a job in Silicon Valley immediately after graduation. In other words, everything went perfectly according to plan, and I really don't think I could have done it without the smart drugs.

— *Smart Drugs & Nutrients* by Ward Dean, M.D., and John Morgenthaler

Smart Drugs: A Dissenting View I think my mind is just fine, and I've got a great memory. But I'd heard so much about these smart drugs, I thought I'd give them a try. First, I took Hydergine for a month, a high dose: 20 milligrams a day. It cost a fortune, and do you know what the result was? Nothing. Absolutely nothing. I might as well have been swallowing corn starch.

Next I tried Eldepryl. I got a doctor friend to prescribe it for me and was again floored by the price. This one I tried off and on for three weeks. Nothing.

Finally, I went for the vasopressin nasal spray, using it several times a day for two weeks. This time I did get an effect; it made my nose run like a faucet. I mean, nonstop, day and night. As for the promised jumps in intelligence and ability to concentrate and remember, I don't remember any of them occurring. I think I'll save my money in the future.

— **forty-year-old man, dentist**

Cotton Poisoning *Cotton poisoning* is the term used to describe the body's reaction to a particle of fiber, like cotton, or of some other foreign substance that gets injected into the bloodstream. It usually appears in two to four hours after injection and causes muscle cramps, chills, cold sweats, and nausea. After two or three hours of discomfort, it usually passes away, leaving the victim exhausted.

This is my understanding of cotton poisoning after talking to people who have experienced it and after experiencing it myself. My own reaction was different in that it kept recurring. I still don't understand it.

One night, I was with two friends, and we were shooting some drug. I don't remember whether it was Demerol, Dilaudid, or heroin that we were using, but it was something of that nature. We put the drug in a spoon and used steaming hot water to dilute it; then we drew the liquid into a syringe through a piece of cigarette filter. We all used the same needle, and we cleaned it thoroughly between uses with steaming hot water. Everything was done in the normal fashion, and we all got high.

After about two and a half hours, I began to feel cold. I turned off the cooler and put on an extra shirt, and I felt a little better. It didn't take long before I was cold again. I asked my friends if they, too, were cold, but they said they were very warm.

I got colder and colder and broke out in goose bumps. I began to shiver and break out in a sweat. My muscles were very tense from the coldness, and I felt as if I was waiting for a bus in a windy snowstorm without a coat. I was clutching at my chest, shivering, and the muscles in my back and shoulders began to cramp from being so tense. Then I started to sweat very heavily and began vomiting. My head was spinning and throbbing. I didn't know what was going on.

One of my friends said I had cotton poisoning. He said that he had had it before and there was no way of stopping it. It would probably last another hour or two. He went into the bathroom and ran a hot bath for me — that was the only thing that would help, he said. It did help some. I was still cold, but the hot water relieved the backache. I kept sweating and throwing up, though. I don't know how long it took, but I was finally able to get out of the tub and go to bed, completely exhausted.

The next day I was okay, but the day after the whole thing came back, just the same, and I hadn't shot any more drugs, just smoked a lot of pot and drank beer. Over the next few days, I kept having recurrences and they kept getting worse. I thought I was going to die a few times. No one had ever heard of cotton poisoning recurring like that. I finally went to a doctor, but he had never even heard of cotton poisoning, and I had to explain it to him. He was no help at all. Finally, after I got sick every other day for a week, the whole thing went away. I've never had it since.

I've had some bad experiences with drugs. I've had some really bad times with opium in India, including miserable highs and terrible chest pains. I've done hallucinogens that were so strange I once lay down in a bonfire. I've been so wiped out on the combination of morphine and amphetamines that I've lost track of days at a time and regained consciousness in awful situations. Except for my being sent to prison, no drug experience or drug-related experience has been so hard to deal with, so unpleasant, and so painful as my episode of cotton poisoning.

— **twenty-three-year-old man, prisoner**

Panic Reactions   As a doctor interested in drug reactions, I've had occasion to treat many cases of drug panic. I worked in an emergency room in San Francisco during the big, early days of pot and acid, and used to see all kinds of people come in thinking they were going crazy or dying. I soon learned that these reactions were more psychological than pharmacological.

One time, a father and mother came in with their teen-age daughter. The girl was a pot smoker and had been pressuring her mother to try it. Finally, the mother agreed, but, since she didn't know how to smoke, the daughter baked up some pot brownies. The mother ate one. An hour later, she was hysterical, thinking she had been poisoned and was losing her mind. Meanwhile, the daughter had eaten three brownies and just felt very high. Before I had a chance to do anything, a staff psychiatrist came down and got caught up in the family hysteria. (The father, who had come home from work early, was the worst of the three, pleading with us to save his wife.) The psychiatrist gave the mother an injection of Thorazine and admitted her to the psychiatric ward. She stayed agitated and panicked for four days. I could have talked her down in an hour, if I had just been able to get her away from her husband and calm her.

The best method I hit upon for dealing with drug panics in the emergency room was to let the patients know I did not consider their problems [to be] serious. When a couple of teen-agers would come in with a stricken friend, I'd just say, "Okay, have a seat and relax. I'll be with you as soon as I can." Then I'd mostly ignore them. When they demanded attention for the crisis, I'd say, "Look, there are people here who really have things wrong with them that I have to deal with. Your friend is just upset, and all he needs is to calm down. So get him to breathe deeply and regularly, and I'll come back as soon as I take care of the real problems in here."

Usually, by the time I'd come back, the victim would be looking better, and the whole group would just want to make a graceful exit from the hospital. Of course, if it's an older person thinking they are dying of a heart attack or something, you should go through the motions of examining them and telling them firmly that their physical health is fine. I never give tranquilizers or sedatives to panic victims, just reassurance and calming vibes. The worst thing you can do is give the impression that you think something is really wrong.

— **forty-year-old man, general practitioner**

Different Tastes in Drugs My husband and I met in college in the late 1960s. We were both involved in antiwar politics and did some experimenting with group living and using drugs, mostly marijuana and psychedelics. I found the experiences interesting but after a while did not want to repeat them frequently. My husband, on the other hand, thought marijuana was the greatest thing he had ever discovered. Smoking it became an important ritual for him.

Over the years, he's continued to smoke it. Once in a while, I join him, but I've come to find I don't like the effect all that much. I can't concentrate well when I'm stoned and sometimes feel mentally scattered and vulnerable. I guess my drug of choice is wine. Two glasses of good wine put me in just the right state after a trying day. John drinks wine, too, but for getting high he prefers marijuana.

In the past few years, our different preferences in drugs have become a problem for us. My not liking marijuana separates me from John's closest friends and weakens our relationship. I don't think married people have to do everything together, but this is something important, and my inability to share John's highs bothers me. Also, I find I resent his smoking friends, since I'm the outsider, the "straight wife," when they are around. Yet I know that if I object, I will just drive him out of the house to get high with them elsewhere.

We try to talk about our problem but have not come up with an answer. I just don't like marijuana and he does. It may seem like a little matter, but when we are having a hard time with each other, it comes to symbolize all of the differences that keep us from sharing fully with each other, and I can see it harming our marriage. I don't know other couples who have this problem.

— **thirty-five-year-old woman**

Different Tastes in Drugs — From Another Perspective   After two years of living in different places, my significant other and I were finally moving into a joint domicile, when one day he informed me that he had decided not to smoke pot anymore. I was stunned. Why? I asked. His explanation — that he was starting a new business and had to have his wits about him — was rational and indisputable. Arguing with him would have been futile in any case, but, as it was, what could I say? And yet, I've got to admit that from my point of view, it was very bad news. How would we get out of those awful stuck places we were forever falling into? I consider pot to be a really useful tool, vital, in fact. Besides, I like getting high, and if you get high and the person you're with doesn't, well, you often feel they disapprove, and even when you don't, you just can't connect with them the way you would if they were stoned. What I like about pot is that it lets you detach yourself from your point of view, which is, by definition, limited and subjective; it allows you to be a little less egocentric and a little more imaginative in the way you relate to other people.

Now, I don't blame the breakup of our relationship on my friend's not smoking pot, but I think it was a factor. For a while, I tried getting high for the two of us, but the insights I'd have, which might have sparked a dialogue if he'd had a toke or two, he tended to dismiss as mere dope-induced gibberish. It was evident to me that my smoking pot diminished me in his estimation. Not that he loved me less, but he took me less seriously, and I resented it. Years later, when we finally split up, pot smoking was just one of our many irreconcilable differences, but it was a basic one. Pot can't help people resolve their big conflicts, but it can help with the trivial ones, which, in their aggregate, can really take their toll.

— forty-six-year-old woman, teacher

A Mother's Concern Even though my son has a learning disability, which always made things hard for him at school, it never occurred to me while he was growing up that he wouldn't turn out all right in the end. Now, however, I'm not so sure. In the three years since he first became involved with drugs, starting at age fourteen, he has been arrested twice (for bizarre behavior) and hospitalized three times, the last time for a period of more than eight months. Although his severe problems began when he first tried LSD, now even pot can trigger a psychotic episode.

Unlike his friends, and even his younger brother, my son cannot handle drugs. For him, they are simply poisons. He knows this. And yet the social pressure on him to take drugs is often more than he can withstand. Despite his history and my repeated appeals, his friends continue to supply him with drugs, even going so far as to smuggle them into the hospital the last time he was there.

— forty-five-year-old woman

The Ecstasy of Love
Where, like a pillow on a bed,
    A Pregnant banke swel'd up, to rest
The violet's reclining head,
    Sat we two, one anothers best.
Our hands were firmely cimented
    With a fast balme, which thence did spring,
Our eye-beames twisted, and did thred
    Our eyes, upon one double string;
So to'entergraft our hands, as yet
    Was all the meanes to make us one,
And pictures in our eyes to get
    Was all our propagation.

As 'twixt two equal Armies, Fate
  Suspends uncertaine victorie,
Our soules, (which to advance their state,
  Were gone out,) hung 'twixt her, and mee.
And whil'st our soules negotiate there,
  Wee like sepulchrall statues lay;
All day, the same our postures were,
  And wee said nothing all the day.

— from "The Extasie" by John Donne (1572–1631)

Addicted to Running I watched my roommate in college and best friend turn into an addicted runner. Greg took up running in his junior year and quickly got into it big time. I think he didn't have a lot going for him then — no girlfriend, no great interest in school — and running gave him a real sense of purpose and accomplishment. It also got him high. I ran with him a lot at first. To me, running was a lot of effort. I always felt good afterward, but at the time it seemed more like work than fun. But I'd notice that Greg seemed to get into an altered state after about two miles. His whole face would look different, and he'd seem to be flying. He'd tell me he'd get a real buzz on from running, and I'm sure he did. After a while, he started running farther than I cared to: five miles, then seven miles, then ten miles. So I'd turn back early, and he'd keep on.

In his senior year, Greg ran in the Boston Marathon. He trained for it for three months and did really well. He said he just wanted to do it once to see what it would be like. He also said it was the greatest high of his life. So I guess I wasn't surprised when, a few months later, he was training for another marathon. After graduation, he fell into a pattern of running marathons every few months, and it seemed he was always either training for them, running them, or recovering from them. His running seemed compulsive to me and began to drive a wedge between us.

Greg has run fifty- and hundred-mile races since then — impressive achievements, I guess, but he's also injured his knees and back and won't cut down. Sometimes, when we've been on the road together, he's been unable to run because of bad weather or other circumstances, and I find it almost impossible to be with him then. He climbs the walls, just like someone trying to kick a cigarette habit. I think he's become addicted to running as his main high in life and doesn't have a healthy relationship with it. But he has no insight into that and won't listen to me or anyone else who tries to talk to him about it.

— twenty-six-year-old man, photographer

Fireworks Turn Me On I get high from fireworks. I love them and just can't get enough of them. Waiting for the Fourth of July is too hard. I'll drive hundreds of miles to buy fireworks and shoot them off with friends. I guess they're like drugs for me. The good ones are often illegal. They're a little dangerous. And they really deliver.

— **thirty-three-year-old man, engineer**

Speaking in Tongues I speak in tongues. This other language gives me the words my spirit needs to express itself. It happens on two different kinds of occasions. One occurs when I am depressed, anxious, upset, or feel a great sorrow in my heart and don't really know exactly what is wrong. Speaking releases all that bottled-up tension and depression. I also find myself wanting to speak in tongues when I feel really good. I want to express the tremendous love or peace or wonder I feel but can't find words for.

When I speak in tongues, it is as if a voice from within me is talking. Another part of my being — beyond conscious thought — takes over and lets me express what my inner spirit is feeling in a language all its own. I am totally in the here and now when this happens, not worrying about the past or dreaming about the future. The feeling is similar to what some people get from psychedelic drugs. No other reality exists beyond what I am a part of at that moment.

I received "the gift of tongues" (as the Bible calls it) while I was involved with a Christian commune. This group believes tongues is a gift from the Holy Spirit to permit fellowship with the Father. It means believers have direct access to God.

I was once in a remote wilderness area of British Columbia on a canoe trip. In a marshy area around a lake, our group came across big tracks, perhaps of moose or elk. I suddenly felt thrilled to be among wild animals, where man had not destroyed nature. I looked up to see mountains and sky stretch to infinity. I suddenly realized how beautiful the world I live in can be. Then I started to speak in tongues. As I did, I lost my sense of self-consciousness and with it my feelings of loneliness, isolation, and alienation from the rest of the world. I felt connected to all of life.

Speaking in tongues makes me high. It makes me experience an altered state of consciousness. It lets me glimpse another reality — infinite realities — beyond the scope of my "normal" state of consciousness.

Speaking in tongues resembles meditation. One has to come to it with the proper set and setting, to be in tune. I am sure many Christians who speak in tongues feel the release of an emotional burden or, as in Pentecostal churches, a real high; but to have the total here and now experience, one has to come with a desire for it. Tongues is not magic in itself. The magic is in using tongues to open oneself to powers already within each of us.

— thirty-year-old woman

Glossary

Cross-referenced entries are in *italics*.

Abscess: A localized collection of pus surrounded by an inflamed area, often the result of a bacterial infection.

Abstinence: Refraining from using something, such as a drug, by one's own choice. In pharmacology, the term "abstinence syndrome" is equivalent to *withdrawal* syndrome.

Abusers: People who use drugs in ways that threaten their health or impair their social or economic functioning.

Acetic acid: The acid in vinegar.

Acetylcholine: A stimulatory *neurotransmitter* in the *central nervous system*, which also controls muscles and sensory input signals.

Acid: Slang term for LSD (lysergic acid diethylamide).

Acid house: A type of psychedelic music with a strong back beat, often played at nightclubs where people take *ecstasy* and engage in wild dancing. Same as *techno*.

Active principle: The main chemical constituent of a drug plant. Cocaine, for example, is the active principle of coca leaf. Although active principles may be responsible for many of the effects of drug plants, they do not exactly reproduce those effects and in pure form have higher toxicity and potential for abuse.

Acupuncture: An ancient Chinese system of medical treatment that aims to influence energy flow around the body by inserting needles into particular points on the skin.

Acute: Intense and of short duration, as opposed to *chronic*.

ADHD: Attention deficit hyperactivity disorder. Similar to attention deficit disorder, with the addition of excessive activity and disruptive behavior.

Addiction: In reference to drugs, a pattern of consumption marked by compulsive taking of a drug, the need for increasing doses over time to maintain the same effect *(tolerance)*, and the appearance of symptoms when the drug is stopped that disappear when it is reinstated *(withdrawal)*.

Adrenaline: The body's *endogenous* stimulant, a hormone made by the adrenal glands; also known as epinephrine.

Adulteration: The deliberate addition of impurities to a pure substance — for example, the cutting of cocaine with sugars and cheap *local anesthetics* to make it go further on the black market.

Alkali: Any substance that in solution gives a pH of greater than 7.0. Lye (potassium hydroxide or sodium hydroxide), baking soda (sodium bicarbonate), and lime (calcium oxide or calcium hydroxide) are examples of alkalis.

Amnesia: Loss of memory, either partial or total.

Amotivational syndrome: Lack of interest in activities that society considers important, such as school; supposedly associated with heavy marijuana use.

Amys: Slang term for amyl nitrite.

Analgesic: A medication that reduces or eliminates pain.

Androgenic: Having the property of stimulating development of male sex characteristics.

Anemia: A deficiency of red blood cells or hemoglobin, reducing the blood's capacity to carry oxygen.

Angel dust: Slang term for PCP (phencyclidine).

Animal tranquilizer: Slang term for PCP (phencyclidine), because of its use as a veterinary anesthetic.

Antidepressants: Pharmaceutical drugs prescribed for the treatment of persistent and severe *depression*. Fluoxetine (Prozac), sertraline (Zoloft), and paroxetine (Paxil) are examples.

Antihistamines: A large class of *synthetic drugs* used to relieve allergic symptoms.

Antimanics: Drugs used to treat bipolar disorder.

Antipsychotics: Drugs used to treat schizophrenia.

Apathy: Lack of feeling, emotion, or interest in what excites most people.

Asphyxiation: Unconsciousness or death resulting from lack of oxygen.

Asthma: A respiratory disease caused by inflammation and constriction of the bronchial tubes with resultant difficulty in breathing. Wheezing on exhalation is the most characteristic symptom.

Bad trip: An unpleasant experience on a *psychoactive drug*, especially a *hallucinogen*. *Paranoia,* panic, scary *hallucinations,* and *depression* may all occur in a bad trip.

Barbs: Barbiturates, such as secobarbital (Seconal).

Biorhythms: Cyclic changes in biological functions, such as twenty-four-hour cycles of waking and sleeping and secretion of certain hormones, and the monthly menstrual cycle in women.

Black market: The underground distribution system for illegal drugs and other illegal commodities.

Blow: Slang term for cocaine.

Bronchitis: *Inflammation* of the bronchial tubes, producing a painful cough and other breathing difficulties.

Bummer: Slang term for an unpleasant experience on a *psychoactive drug*. Similar to *bad trip*.

Burn-out: A condition of emotional and intellectual impairment supposed to be the result of excessive use of *psychoactive drugs*. Also, a person with this condition.

Bust: An arrest, especially for involvement with illegal drugs. Also used as a verb.

Cacao: *Theobroma cacao*, the source of chocolate, cocoa, and cocoa butter.

Cannabinoid: Any of the chemical compounds that are active principles of marijuana.

Cannabis: Marijuana. Also, the hemp plant, *Cannabis sativa*, and its products.

Cellulose: An indigestible carbohydrate that is the main structural component of all plant tissues and fibers.

Central nervous system: The brain and spinal cord.

Chamomile: A low-growing plant of the daisy family with yellow flowers and a pleasant applelike smell. The dried flowers make a relaxing tea that also alleviates indigestion.

Chemotherapy: The treatment of cancer by giving patients very toxic drugs that kill dividing cells, in the hope that more cancerous cells than normal ones will die.

Chipping: The practice of using *narcotics* such as heroin on an occasional basis without developing true *addiction*.

Chronic: Persisting over time, as opposed to *acute*. As a noun, slang term for marijuana.

Codependence: 1) A relationship in which one person enables or encourages the addictive behavior of another person. 2) An addictive personal relationship.

Coke: Slang term for cocaine. (Others are "blow," "snow," and "powder.")

Coma: Deep and prolonged unconsciousness, usually the result of disease, injury, or poisoning.

Controlled substances: Plants and chemicals listed in the Federal Controlled Substances Act, the law regulating disapproved psychoactive drugs and those approved only for medical use.

Convulsion: An intense episode of muscle contraction, usually caused by abnormal brain function.

Cornea: The transparent outer covering of the eye, overlying the iris, pupil, and lens.

Crack: A smokable, pelletized form of cocaine.

Crank: Methamphetamine.

Crash: To experience *depression, lethargy,* or sleepiness after a drug-induced *high,* especially common after using *stimulants.*

Crude: With reference to drugs, raw or unprocessed.

Crystal, crystal meth: Methamphetamine. In smokable form, also known as *ice* or glass.

Cut: To *adulterate* a drug by adding to it some substance to make it go further. Also, any substance used for this purpose.

Deal: To sell or distribute illegal drugs.

Deliriants: Drugs that cause *delirium.* Datura is an example.

Delirium: A state of mental confusion marked by disorientation and *hallucinations.* Fever and certain drugs are common causes.

Dependence: Inability to separate oneself easily from a substance or activity. See *addiction.*

Depressants: Drugs that reduce the activity of the nervous system. Alcohol, *downers,* and *narcotics* are all depressants.

Depression: Melancholy mood; dejection.

Detoxify: To recover from the action of a toxin on the system. For example, treatment programs exist to help addicts detoxify from opiates — that is, to stop taking the drugs and adjust to being nonusers.

Dilute: Weaker, less concentrated. To make weaker or less concentrated.

Distill: To purify or concentrate a liquid by boiling it and condensing the vapors. The method used to make the strongest forms of alcoholic drinks.

Diuretic: A substance that increases the production and flow of urine.

Dope: 1) Psychoactive drugs in general, especially illegal ones. 2) Specific drugs or types of drugs, usually opiates, *downers,* or marijuana.

Down: 1) No longer under the effect of a *psychoactive drug,* especially a *stimulant* or *hallucinogen,* as in, "If you take *acid* now, you won't be down till after midnight." 2) Depressed, as in, "I'm feeling really down."

Downers: Barbiturates, minor tranquilizers, and related *depressants.*

DTs: Delirium tremens — the most severe form of *withdrawal* from alcohol, marked by agitation, *hallucinations,* and other mental and physical imbalances.

Drug: A substance that in relatively small amounts produces significant changes in the body, mind, or both.

Duster: A PCP-laced *joint* (from *angel dust,* a slang term for PCP).

Ecstasy: Common street name for MDMA.

Ejaculation: In males, the discharge of seminal fluid, usually during orgasm.

Emaciated: Thin and gaunt, as from starvation or illness.

Emphysema: A *chronic* respiratory disease in which lung tissue loses its elasticity and with it the ability to exchange carbon dioxide for oxygen. Patients with emphysema suffer from progressively diminishing breathing capacity and may eventually become bedridden "respiratory cripples."

Endogenous drugs: Drugs produced within the body.

Endorphins: *Endogenous* opiate-like drugs.

Entheogen: Positive term for a psychedelic, meaning "creating God within."

Enzyme: A protein produced by a living organism that catalyzes (speeds up) biochemical reactions. Many digestive enzymes enable the body to process foods, for example.

Estrogen: One of a group of hormones, mostly manufactured by the ovaries in women, responsible for producing female sex characteristics and regulating fertility.

Euphoria: A feeling of great happiness or well-being.

Extract: A preparation of a *crude* substance with water or another solvent to remove and concentrate the active principles.

Fermentation: The process by which yeast converts sugar into alcohol and carbon dioxide.

Fix: Slang term for a dose of a mood-altering drug, especially an intravenous dose of an opiate, as in, "I need a fix." Also used as a verb, as in, "When did you fix last?"

Flashback: A recurrence of symptoms associated with LSD or other *hallucinogens* some time after the actual drug experience.

Freak out: To panic or lose emotional control.

Freebase: A smokable form of cocaine. As a verb, to smoke cocaine in this form.

GABA: Gamma-amino-butyric acid, a simple organic chemical that serves as a *neurotransmitter* in certain brain cells. Its effect is inhibitory and depressing of nervous function.

Gas: Slang term for nitrous oxide.

Gastrointestinal tract: The whole chain of tubular structures from the mouth to the anus concerned with the processing of food.

Gram: A unit of mass and weight in the metric system, defined as one thousandth of a kilogram. (A kilogram is about 2.2 pounds.)

Hallucination: The perception of something that is not there, such as seeing pink elephants or hearing voices that other people cannot hear; also, the failure to perceive objects or events that are perceived by others (negative hallucination). Hallucinations can be symptoms of physical or mental illness, or the result of taking some kinds of *psychoactive* drugs.

Hallucinogens: Drugs that stimulate the nervous system and produce varied changes in perception and mood. Examples are LSD, DMT, mescaline, and *magic mushrooms.* Hallucinogens are also known as psychedelics.

Hash: Slang term for hashish, the concentrated resin of the marijuana plant.

Hash oil: A dark, syrupy liquid obtained by extracting the resin of marijuana with solvents and concentrating it.

Head shops: Stores that sell drug-related products, such as smoking devices, drug literature, and other materials.

Hepatitis: *Inflammation* of the liver, usually because of infection with a virus. Jaundice, weakness, and digestive problems are common symptoms that may last for weeks or months. There is no specific treatment.

High: An altered state of consciousness, marked by *euphoria,* feelings of lightness, self-transcendence, and energy. High states are not necessarily drug related. They may occur spontaneously or in response to various activities that affect mood, perception, and concentration. Also used as an adjective.

Hog: Slang term for PCP (phencyclidine).

Hook up: To obtain a supply of a desired drug. Same as *score.*

Hormone: A chemical substance produced by one organ of the body, such as a gland, and conveyed, usually by the blood, to another organ (or organs), where it exerts a controlling or regulating action. Insulin, a hormone produced by the pancreas, regulates sugar metabolism throughout the body.

Huffing: Slang term for the inhalation of volatile solvents.

Hyperventilation: Abnormally rapid, deep breathing.

Hypothermia: The condition of abnormally low body temperature, usually the result of exposure to cold. Early symptoms are uncontrollable shivering and bizarre changes in consciousness. If not treated, it can progress to coma and death.

Ice: A smokable form of methamphetamine.

Illicit: Illegal.

Immune system: Those organs and tissues of the body concerned with the recognition and destruction of foreign substances, such as invading germs. The immune system includes organs such as the spleen and tonsils, along with the bone marrow and certain white blood cells.

Inert: Without activity.

Inflammation: A characteristic response of the body to irritation, injury, and infection. It consists of swelling, warmth, redness, and pain in the affected part.

Insomnia: Inability to sleep.

Intoxication: The state of being under the influence of a poison or drug, with effects ranging from stimulation and exhilaration to stupefaction and loss of consciousness.

Intramuscular: Within a muscle, such as the injection of a drug into the muscle of an arm or leg.

Intravenous: Within a vein, such as the injection of a drug directly into the bloodstream.

Joint: A marijuana cigarette.

Junk: Slang term for *narcotics*, especially heroin.

Junkie: A heroin addict.

Laughing gas: Slang term for nitrous oxide.

Laxative: A substance that increases activity of the bowels and elimination of wastes.

Lethal dose: The dose of a drug that causes death.

Lethargy: A state of sluggish indifference or unhealthy drowsiness.

Leukemia: A form of cancer marked by uncontrolled multiplication of white blood cells.

Local anesthetic: A substance that blocks transmission of pain by nerves when injected into a part of the body or when applied to mucous membranes. Procaine is a synthetic local anesthetic marketed under the brand name Novocain.

Look-alike drugs: Tablets and capsules made to resemble pharmaceutical *stimulants* and *depressants,* such as amphetamines and Quaalude; sold on the black market or in *head shops.*

Ludes: Tablets of methaqualone (Quaalude).

Magic mushrooms: Mushrooms that contain the natural *hallucinogen* psilocybin.

Mainline: To inject a drug *intravenously.*

Magical thinking: The belief that one can control external events by operations of the mind; an attempt to control sources of fear.

MDMA: Methylene-dioxy-methamphetamine, or *ecstasy.* Also known as E and X.

Messed up: Strongly intoxicated on a drug.

Metabolism: All the physical and chemical processes involved in the maintenance of life.

Methadone: A long-acting, synthetic opiate used to treat heroin addiction.

Mickey Finn: Combination of an alcoholic drink and a *downer*, used to drug unsuspecting victims, usually for purposes of robbery, rape, or kidnapping. Also known as knockout drops.

Microgram: One millionth of a *gram*.

Milligram: One thousandth of a *gram*.

Mood drugs: *Psychoactive drugs* in general, especially *stimulants* and *depressants.*

Multiple sclerosis: An incurable disease of the central nervous system marked by progressive degeneration of the insulating sheaths of nerve cells and consequent losses of body functions. The cause is unknown.

Mystic: One who aims for union with the divine by means of deep meditation. Mystics believe in realities other than the one perceived by the ordinary senses.

Narcotics: A class of *depressant* drugs derived from opium or related chemically to compounds in opium. Regular use of narcotics often leads to *addiction.*

Neurochemical: A chemical substance produced by nerves.

Neurotransmitter: A chemical substance produced by nerves and involved in the transmission of information by nerves.

Nystagmus: Rapid, involuntary, jerking movements of the eyes, usually a sign of *intoxication* or disease of the *central nervous system.*

OD: Overdose, used as both a noun and a verb, as in, "Anyone who *shoots* drugs should know how to avoid an OD," and, "The last time I took a *downer* I OD'd on it."

Opiates: Derivatives of the opium poppy or drugs resembling those derivatives.

Oral: By mouth.

Organic: A term from chemistry referring to compounds of carbon.

OTC: Over the counter, referring to drugs sold legally without prescription.

Paranoia: Delusions of persecution or grandeur; unreasoning belief that one is the target of conspiracies and patterns of events aimed at one's destruction or benefit. In common usage, the term is a synonym for extreme fear, especially of other people and situations.

Paraquat: A chemical herbicide used to kill unwanted plants. Government agencies have sprayed it from the air on marijuana fields, especially in Mexico.

Parkinson's disease: A degenerative disease of the *central nervous system* that produces muscular rigidity and tremor (involuntary shaking movements).

Pharmacology: The science of drugs, their preparation, uses, and effects.

Pharmacopeia: The total collection of drugs used in medicine.

Piece: A small glass pipe used for smoking marijuana.

Pineal gland: A tiny, light-sensitive organ in the center of the brain, also called the pineal eye, or "third eye." In reptiles, it controls changes in skin color. In humans, it is a master gland of the endocrine system, probably regulating many *biorhythms*.

Polydrug use: The consumption of more than one drug at the same time.

Pop: To swallow a drug in pill form.

Poppers: Slang term for amyl nitrite.

Pot: Slang term for marijuana. (Others are "grass," "reefer," "weed," and "chronic.")

Potency: In pharmacology, the measure of relative strength of similar drugs. If a lower dose of drug A produces the same effect as a higher dose of drug B, A is said to be more potent than B.

Powder, powder cocaine: Cocaine hydrochloride, usually snorted.

Prostration: Total exhaustion.

Psychedelics: Synonym for *hallucinogens*.

Psychoactive drugs: Drugs that affect the mind, especially mood, thought, or perception.

Psychosis: Loss of ability to distinguish reality as perceived by others from one's own private mental productions. The most serious category of mental illness, it is often marked by *hallucinations*, delusions, and disturbances of mood.

Rave: A type of loud, synthesized dance music, often played in nightclubs where patrons take *ecstasy*.

Reaction time: In psychology, the time interval between the application of a stimulus and the detection of a response. In a simple reaction time test, a subject is asked to press a button as soon as a light flashes.

Receptors: Specialized protein molecules on cell membranes that combine with drugs.

Refined: Processed in order to concentrate or purify. Opposite of *crude*.

Recreational drugs: Any drugs used nonmedically for enjoyment or entertainment.

Reflex: A simple nervous circuit. For example, a tendon reflex is initiated by striking a tendon; this stimulus travels to the spinal cord along a single nerve and quickly produces a response in another nerve that causes a contraction in the muscle.

Resin: A sticky substance of plant origin that is insoluble in water.

Respiratory tract: The breathing apparatus of the body, including the nose, throat, bronchial tubes, lungs, and associated structures.

Rheumatism: *Chronic* aches and pains in muscles, joints, and bones, leading to discomfort and disability.

Rip off: To rob, cheat, or take advantage of, such as in a transaction involving drugs. The noun "rip-off" refers to both the actions themselves and the person who does them.

Roll: To be high on *ecstasy*. Also used for an ecstasy pill.

Roofies: Rohypnol, a benzodiazipine *depressant*.

Rush: A sudden, dramatic change in consciousness and body sensation resulting from taking certain *psychoactive drugs* by inhalation or injection.

Schizophrenia: The commonest form of *psychosis*, chiefly affecting thought. It is of unknown cause and is generally considered incurable. Antipsychotic drugs are the treatment of choice and may allow some schizophrenics to function better.

Score: To obtain a supply of a desired drug.

Sedation: A state of depressed brain function marked by drowsiness, inactivity, and, eventually, sleep.

Sedative-hypnotics: A class of *depressants* that induces restfulness in low doses and sleep in higher doses. Alcohol, barbiturates, and the minor tranquilizers make up this class of drugs.

Semisynthetic drugs: Drugs created by chemists from materials found in nature.

Sensory isolation tank: An oblong, lightproof, soundproof tank partially filled with a strong salt solution maintained at body temperature. A person floating in the tank experiences little outside stimulation and can explore inner states. Used for relaxation and meditation as well as to investigate altered states of consciousness.

Serotonin: One of the brain's main *neurotransmitters,* involved in the regulation of mood.

Set: Expectation, especially unconscious expectation, as a variable determining people's reactions to drugs.

Setting: Environment — physical, social, and cultural — as a variable determining people's reactions to drugs.

Shaman: Priest of the traditional religion of hunter-gatherer peoples of western Asia and the Americas.

Shoot: To inject a drug *intravenously*.

Skin-popping: The practice of injecting drugs, especially heroin, *subcutaneously* rather than into a muscle or vein.

Sleeping pills: Barbiturates and related *sedative-hypnotics.*

Sniff: To inhale the fumes of volatile solvents to produce changes in consciousness.

Snort: To inhale a powdered drug.

Snuff: 1) Finely powdered tobacco, which may be inhaled or placed in the mouth. 2) Any finely powdered drug intended for nasal inhalation. 3) To take a drug in powdered form by nasal inhalation.

Spacy: Detached or disconnected from ordinary reality as a result of using *psychoactive drugs.* (A related term is "spaced out.")

Special K: Slang term for ketamine.

Speed: *Stimulants,* especially amphetamines. (Other slang terms for amphetamines are "crank," "meth," and "crystal.")

Speedball: A combination of a *stimulant* and a *depressant,* especially cocaine and heroin, intended for *intravenous* use.

Spore: A microscopic reproductive cell of lower plants and mushrooms.

Steroids: A large family of drugs related to the adrenal *hormone* cortisone. They include anabolic steroids and corticosteroids.

Stimulants: Drugs that increase the activity of the nervous system, causing wakefulness. Caffeine, cocaine, and amphetamines are examples.

Stoned: 1) Intoxicated on a *psychoactive drug,* especially marijuana. 2) Having the nature of consciousness influenced by marijuana and other drugs, as in "stoned humor."

Street drugs: *Psychoactive drugs* manufactured and sold illegally.

Stupor: A state of reduced sensibility, often the result of excessive use of *depressants.*

Subcutaneous: Under the skin, such as the injection of a drug just under the skin rather than into a muscle or vein.

Subtoxic: Below the toxic dose of a drug.

Sympathetic nervous system: That branch of the involuntary nervous system that prepares the body for fight or flight by speeding up heartbeat and breathing and, at the same time, shutting down digestive functions. Nerves of this system leave the middle segments of the spinal cord to connect to many organs, blood vessels, and glands.

Synthetic drugs: Drugs created by chemists in laboratories, as opposed to *endogenous drugs* or *semisynthetic drugs.*

Taboo: A prohibition excluding something from use or mention, devised by any group for its own protection.

Techno: Type of music associated with *ecstasy.* See *acid house.*

Teetotaler: A person who abstains totally from drinking alcohol.

Testosterone: The principal male sex hormone, manufactured by the testes and responsible for producing male sex characteristics.

THC: Tetrahydrocannabinol, the principal psychoactive component of marijuana.

Therapeutic: Having healing or curative powers.

Tincture: A solution of a substance, especially a drug or herb, in alcohol.

Toke: An inhalation from a cigarette or pipe. Also used as a verb.

Tolerance: In pharmacology, the need for increasing doses of a drug over time to maintain the same effect. Tolerance is an important characteristic of dependence on drugs and is provoked by some drugs more than others, especially by *stimulants* and *depressants*.

Toxic: Poisonous. Harmful, destructive, or deadly.

Trafficking: In drug law, the distribution, sale, exchange, or giving away of significant amounts of prohibited substances; considered a more serious crime than simple possession.

Trip: An experience on a *psychoactive drug*, especially a *hallucinogen*. Also used as a verb.

Underground chemist: A chemist who manufactures *psychoactive drugs* illegally for sale on the black market.

Uppers: *Stimulants*.

Users: 1) People who use *psychoactive drugs*. 2) People who use psychoactive drugs in nonabusive ways, as opposed to *abusers*.

Vaporizer: A glass pipe with an electrical heating element used to consume marijuana by inhalation without combusting it and producing smoke.

Visions: Mental images produced in the imagination, usually seen with the eyes closed; also, the mystical experience of seeing other realities or the supernatural as if with the eyes.

Volatile: Evaporating rapidly at normal temperatures and pressures.

Weed: Slang term for marijuana.

Withdrawal: 1) The process of stopping the use of a drug that has been taken regularly. 2) Any cluster of symptoms that appears when a drug that has been taken regularly is stopped and that disappears when the drug is reinstituted. Also called a withdrawal syndrome.

X: Slang for *ecstasy*.

Zero tolerance: American government policy of going after all users of illegal drugs, no matter how small the amounts involved.

Index

ABOUT THE AUTHOR

Andrew Weil, M.D., is the best-selling author of ten books, including *Spontaneous Healing, Eating Well for Optimum Health, Eight Weeks to Optimum Health,* and, forthcoming, *Healthy Aging.* Dr. Weil has degrees in biology and medicine from Harvard University. He has experienced and studied healers and healing systems around the world and has earned an international reputation as an expert on alternative medicine, mind-body interactions, and medical botany. He is clinical professor of medicine and director of the Program in Integrative Medicine (www.integrativemedicine.arizona.edu) at the University of Arizona in Tucson. Dr. Weil also writes a monthly newsletter, *Self Healing* (www.drweilselfhealing.com) and has a popular Web site, www.drweil.com.

Winifred Rosen is a freelance writer and the author of numerous books for young people. A native of New York City, she now lives on the east end of Long Island, where she writes and does landscape gardening.

NATURAL HEALTH, NATURAL MEDICINE
The Complete Guide to Wellness and Self-Care for Optimum Health

A comprehensive guide to preventative health maintenance and the foundation for Dr. Andrew Weil's work on maintaining optimum health. *Natural Health, Natural Medicine* is the bible of natural medicine, featuring general diet and nutrition information as well as simple recipes, answers to readers' most pressing questions, a catalog of home remedies, invaluable resources, and hundreds of practical tips.

ISBN 0-618-47903-1

HEALTH AND HEALING
The Philosophy of Integrative Medicine and Optimum Health

Dr. Weil's groundbreaking handbook for people who want to understand the strengths and weaknesses of conventional and alternative medicine, *Health and Healing* presents the full spectrum of alternative healing practices, including holistic medicine, homeopathy, osteopathy, chiropractic, and Chinese medicine, and outlines how they differ from conventional approaches. ISBN 0-618-47908-2

FROM CHOCOLATE TO MORPHINE
WITH WINIFRED ROSEN
Everything You Need to Know About Mind-Altering Drugs

The definitive guide to drugs and drug use, now revised and updated to cover drugs made available in the last decade. This enormously popular book is the best and most authoritative resource for unbiased information about how drugs affect the mind and the body. ISBN 0-618-48379-9

THE MARRIAGE OF THE SUN AND MOON
Dispatches from the Frontiers of Consciousness

A collection of essays about Dr. Weil's travels to South America in the early 1970s in search of information on altered states of consciousness, drug use in other cultures, and other matters having to do with the complementarity of mind and body. These experiences laid the foundation of his mission to restore the connection between medicine and nature. ISBN 0-618-47905-8

THE NATURAL MIND
A Revolutionary Approach to the Drug Problem

Dr. Weil's first book and the philosophical basis for all of his resulting beliefs and tenets on health, healing, and the mind. Now completely revised and updated for the twenty-first century, this is essential reading for anyone interested in Dr. Weil's philosophy of integrative medicine and optimum health. ISBN 0-618-46513-8